MW00855888

Islam, Ethnicity, and Conflict in Ethiopia

Focusing on the role of religion and ethnicity in times of conflict, Terje Østebø investigates the Muslim-dominated insurgency against the Ethiopian state in the 1960s, shedding new light on this understudied case to contribute to a deeper understanding of religion, interreligious relations, ethnicity, and ethno-nationalism in the Horn of Africa. *Islam, Ethnicity, and Conflict in Ethiopia* develops new theoretical perspectives on the interrelations between ethnic and religious identities, by applying the term *peoplehood* as an analytical tool; one that allows for more flexible perspectives. Exploring the interplay of imagination and lived, affective reality, and inspired by the "materiality turn" in cultural and religious studies, Østebø argues for an integrated approach that recognizes and explores embodiment and emplacement as intrinsic to formations of ethnic and religious identities.

TERJE ØSTEBØ is Associate Professor in the Center for African Studies and the Department of Religion at the University of Florida where his research focuses on Islam in Ethiopia and the Horn of Africa and Salafism in Africa. He is the author of *Localising Salafism* (2012) and the coeditor of *Muslim Ethiopia* (2013).

African Studies Series

The African Studies series, founded in 1968, is a prestigious series of monographs, general surveys, and textbooks on Africa covering history, political science, anthropology, economics, and ecological and environmental issues. The series seeks to publish work by senior scholars as well as the best new research.

Editorial Board:
David Anderson, *The University of Warwick*
Catherine Boone, *The London School of Economics and Political Science*
Carolyn Brown, *Rutgers University, New Jersey*
Christopher Clapham, *University of Cambridge*
Michael Gomez, *New York University*
Richard Roberts, *Stanford University, California*
David Robinson, *Michigan State University*
Leonardo A. Villalón, *University of Florida*

Other titles in the series are listed at the back of the book.

Islam, Ethnicity, and Conflict in Ethiopia

The Bale Insurgency, 1963–1970

TERJE ØSTEBØ
University of Florida

CAMBRIDGE
UNIVERSITY PRESS

CAMBRIDGE
UNIVERSITY PRESS

University Printing House, Cambridge CB2 8BS, United Kingdom

One Liberty Plaza, 20th Floor, New York, NY 10006, USA

477 Williamstown Road, Port Melbourne, VIC 3207, Australia

314–321, 3rd Floor, Plot 3, Splendor Forum, Jasola District Centre, New Delhi – 110025, India

79 Anson Road, #06–04/06, Singapore 079906

Cambridge University Press is part of the University of Cambridge.

It furthers the University's mission by disseminating knowledge in the pursuit of education, learning, and research at the highest international levels of excellence.

www.cambridge.org
Information on this title: www.cambridge.org/9781108839686
DOI: 10.1017/9781108884839

© Terje Østebø 2020

This publication is in copyright. Subject to statutory exception and to the provisions of relevant collective licensing agreements, no reproduction of any part may take place without the written permission of Cambridge University Press.

First published 2020

A catalogue record for this publication is available from the British Library.

ISBN 978-1-108-83968-6 Hardback

Cambridge University Press has no responsibility for the persistence or accuracy of URLs for external or third-party internet websites referred to in this publication and does not guarantee that any content on such websites is, or will remain, accurate or appropriate.

To Marit

Contents

Maps

Figures

Tables

Acknowledgments

This study has been years in the making and could not have been completed without the help and assistance of a range of people who need to be acknowledged. To start with, I want to express my gratitude for the generous support from the Norwegian Non-Fiction Writers and Translators Association, enabling me to conduct fieldwork in Ethiopia and to concentrate on writing. I also need to thank the University of Florida for awarding small grants for travel and a full year of sabbatical leave.

The work has been made possible by the valuable help from people in Bale and elsewhere in Ethiopia. First of all, I thus wish to thank all my informants – who are too many to mention by name – in Bale as well as in other parts of Ethiopia for trusting me and for welcoming me into their lives. I am thankful for their willingness to share from their memory, knowledge, and thoughts. The present text belongs, in this manner, to them. I am in particular grateful to Awel Abdullatif, Muhammad Jemal, Nuredin Aman, and Ziad Alieh for being invaluable bridges between my interlocutors and me. I also need to thank Hajji Abadir Hussein and Idris Obsa. I am, moreover, grateful to the late *Qenazmach* Abdulqadir Qadi Ahmed and General Jagama Kello for providing photographs from a bygone era.

My thanks are also due to friends and colleagues within the community of Ethiopianists across the world – for fruitful inputs, reading drafts, and other forms of support: Teferi Adam, Cedric Barnes, Dereje Feyissa, Tobias Hagmann, Mohammed Hassan, James McCann, Hassan Muhammad Kawo, Chuck Schaefer, Kjetil Tronvoll, and Feqadu Tufa. I am similarly grateful for support from colleagues and students at the University of Florida: Yekatit Getachew, Bhakti Mamtora, and in particular my former colleague Manuel Vasquez for detailed reading of earlier drafts.

Cambridge University Press has provided invaluable support getting this book ready. I want to thank Daniel Brown, Maria Marsh, and the editors of the African Studies Series – David Anderson, Catherine Boone, Carolyn Brown, Christopher Clapham, Michael Gomez, Nancy J. Jacobs, Richard Roberts, David Robinson, and Leonardo A. Villalón – for believing in the project. I am also grateful for valuable suggestions from the two anonymous reviewers, and for assistance from the staff at Cambridge University Press.

Lastly, my truly felt gratitude goes to my family. To my daughters, Victoria and Julia, for their patience during their father's periods of absence and for being such sources of inspiration. To my wife, Marit, for all the years together in Bale, for working together in the field, for sharing her findings and ideas from her own research in Bale, for diligent reading of the many drafts of this text, and for her relentless support and encouragement.

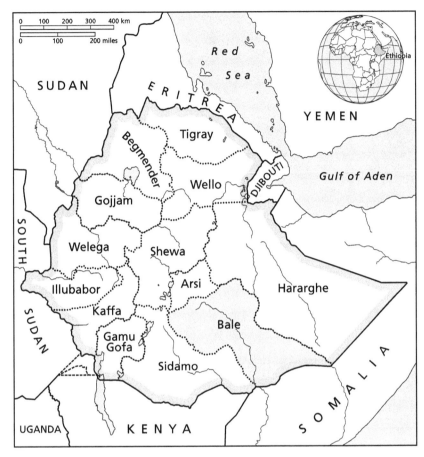

Map 1 Ethiopia – and Bale

1 | Introduction

It is generally agreed that ethnic and religious identities are interrelated. Few attempts, however, have been made to study empirically or to conceptualize how connections between ethnicity and religion actually are materialized. This study seeks to fill that void and offers a new theoretical framework for a better understanding of these relations. Seeking to reign in excessively constructivist perspectives that see religion and ethnicity as disassociated, symbolic, and dislocated, I employ the concept of *peoplehood* as the core one and apply an integrated approach that underscores the concrete nature of local peoplehood and also recognizes how religion and ethnicity are always embodied in individuals and groups, as well as emplaced within socio-material realities.

The question of ethnicity has always occupied students of historical and contemporary Ethiopia. Religion in Ethiopia has, on the other hand, gained lesser attention. One important goal of this study, therefore, is to highlight and explore the often-ignored role of religion in the production of identity, as part of intercommunal dynamics, as well as in conflicts in Ethiopia. It similarly investigates the interplay between religion and ethnicity as integrative aspects of broader dynamics.

The study's case in point for exploring these topics is the locality of Bale in southeastern Ethiopia – where animosity between the people, the ruling elite, and the state culminated in an insurgency that lasted from 1963 to 1970. It is my belief that a thorough investigation of the insurgency, and the factors leading up to it, has the potential to provide a more comprehensive and deeper understanding of the intertwined roles of religion and ethnicity in fomenting identity, demarcating boundaries, and causing conflict. The insurgency was part of a larger context of armed uprisings across the eastern parts of the Horn of Africa during the 1960s, all of which were spearheaded by Muslims. The Bale insurgency was the most famous of these insurgencies and was led by the self-proclaimed general – and iconic – Waqo Gutu. It

1

originated in the eastern and southern lowlands of the Bale province, which soon came under the complete control of the insurgents. The Imperial Government was hard challenged to quell the insurgency and was only able to crush it in 1970, after several major offensives.

Interpreting the Insurgency

Gebru Tareke conducted the most detailed study of the Bale insurgency during the 1970s. Focusing on land tenure, taxation, and social inequality as the key driving factors, the overarching interpretive framework in this seminal contribution is unfortunately trapped in a rather simple Marxist class-struggle perspective. Gebru Tareke understands Ethiopian society as constituted by social classes – primarily the peasantry and the landowning class – and consequently views the insurgency as a *peasant rebellion*. He does recognize ethnicity and religion yet sees them largely as contributing factors and, more significantly, construes them as thwarting the development of class consciousness – in the sense that they "were classes in themselves and not classes for themselves" (Gebru Tareke 1977: 17). This perspective dovetailed clearly with Ethiopian political developments from the early 1970s, when the forces that led to the 1974 revolution heralded the question of class. The academic discourse followed these developments, as noted by Donald Crummey (1986c: 8), with studies on feudalist structures, class, land, land alienation, and the hardships faced by the peasantry (Andargachew Tiruneh 1993; Clapham 1988; Keller 1988; Markakis 1974, 1987; Ottaway and Ottaway 1978; Rønning Balsvik 2005). While this did not render ethnicity completely irrelevant, it was, as expressed by John Markakis (1974: 7), "conditioned by, and usually subordinated to, class considerations."[1] It needs to be added that Gebru Tareke in the published version of his dissertation (Gebru Tareke 1991) has a far more favorable view of ethnicity and religion, recognizing "nonclass forms of social identities" and toning down the Marxist rhetoric. However, he

---

[1] Markakis later came to recognize the relevance of ethnicity, stating, "The widening application of class analysis in the study of African societies during the past decades appears to have inhibited discussion on its own merits of a major element of social conflict in the continent, i.e. the political manifestation of ethnicity" (cited in Tarekegn Adebo 1984: 542). Andargachew Tiruneh is moreover one of the few who denied any connections between the Bale insurgency and class struggle, arguing that it was "based more on ethnic and religious considerations than anything else" (1993: 54).

seems to be struggling with this; although he admits that not every conflict can be reduced to a question of class, economic exploitation and competing classes remain his overarching perspective (Gebru Tareke 1991: 6, 21). This study integrates many of Gebru Tareke's findings; whereas I disagree with him on many occasions, I view my contribution as completing his perspectives.

Subsequent interpretations of the Bale insurgency have shifted the focus to emphasize ethnicity and ethno-nationalism. This is most conspicuous among Oromo scholars, clearly colored by ethno-nationalist sentiments, who interpret the insurgency as an early expression of a pan-Oromo ethno-nationalist movement (Gadaa Melbaa 1988b). Most of these perspectives struggle to relate the ethnic question to that of class, arguing that the fight "against land alienation and unbearable taxation" came to evolve into ethno-nationalist sentiments (Merera Gudina 2007: 89). This underscoring of ethnicity is a clear reflection of political changes from the early 1990s that deliberately brought ethnicity in from the cold and a direct result of the Tigray People's Liberation Front's (TPLF) ideological discourse enacted through Ethiopia's new ethnic-based federalist structure.[2] These developments spurred intense public debates about ethnicity and ethnic boundaries, much of it centered on accusations of past ethnic dominance and subjugation, notions of national unity, and the question of ethnic diversity. Such politicization of ethnicity also entered academia, seen by the production of a new body of literature devoted to the question of Ethiopia's ethnic past and present (Asafa Jalata 2005; Holcomb and Sisai Ibssa 1990; Sorensen 1993). This study questions the – often simplistic – ethno-nationalist interpretations, and I agree with Sara Marzagora that these tend "to serve, sometimes very transparently, sometimes more discreetly, opposite political agendas" and present "power relations in the Horn in a one-dimensional way, positing only two macro-categories of the oppressors and the oppressed" (Marzagora 2015: 242).

Particularly critical is the lack of attention to religion as integrative to the insurgency. Gebru Tareke does point to the relevance of Islam, but he does not explore it in depth and treats religion in a rather instrumentalist manner (Gebru Tareke 1991: 154f.). There

---

[2] This structure divides the country into nine regional states based on ethnicity. The constitution of 1995 grants the states a high degree of autonomy and even bestows each state the right to secede from the federation (Art. 39).

are also those within the ethno-nationalist camp who outright dismisses the religious dimension, seeing the insurgency as an ethnic movement that was deliberately secular (Abbas H. Gnamo 2014: 203f.). There has also been a tendency to view religion as secondary to other dynamics; Markakis, for example, warned against overemphasizing the role of religion during insurgencies in Ethiopia, arguing it "provided the rudiments of ideological construction," before concluding that religion served a political function. As insurgencies were aimed at state power, they were "essentially political in nature" (Markakis 1987: 35). Tim Carmichael has on his part claimed that opposition to the Ethiopian Kingdom in the southeastern areas primarily followed ethno-nationalist lines, and that it merely was "supplemented by a religious stress on Islamic identity" (Carmichael 2001: 192). I argue that this remains too simple and will throughout this study demonstrate how religion remained a highly relevant dimension of the insurgency; rather than being submerged by or derived from other dimensions, it constituted a forceful factor for the demarcation of identity and for collective political action.

The lack of empirical investigations of religion has been a general deficit of Ethiopian studies. A few contributions have paid some attention to religion as part of Ethiopia's past, seen, for example, in Tadesse Tamrat's *Church and State* (1972), but it has mainly been treated as an ancillary aspect of the political center. Recent changes within the religious landscape, with the arrival of religious reformism and the exacerbation of interreligious tensions have fortunately spurred new interest in religion in Ethiopia (Ahmed 1992, 2001, 2006; Boylston 2018; Desplat 2010; Eide 2000; Hannig 2017; Haustein 2011; Hussein Ahmed 2006; Hussein Ahmed 1992; Hussein Ahmed 2001; Østebø 2012; Tibebe Eshete 2009). This development is highly welcome; yet, numerous areas still remain unexplored. We lack detailed knowledge about the importance of religion in the making of diverse cultures and communities, about the role of religion in Ethiopian sociopolitics, about determining power relations and processes of "othering," and how these processes create distinct identities based on religious fault lines.

Imagined Peoplehood, Embodiment, and Emplacement

Given the limitations of the previous approaches to the insurgency, I now turn to the conceptual building blocks of an alternative approach that I argue will yield a richer account. This will frame my analysis of the insurgency's origins, driving forces, actors, and effects.

Rather than talking about religious and ethnic groups, I believe that the concept of *peoplehood*, or *imagined peoplehood*, serves as a better analytical tool to address relations between ethnicity and religion and will in this particular case focus on *Islaama* and Amhara peoplehood. I argue that this concept allows for a greater degree of flexibility in construing the multiplicity of "groupness" and belonging beyond the nation-state. The dictionary definition of *people* is "a group of individuals who perceive and feel themselves as unified and distinct vis-à-vis other group(s)." The suffix "hood," in turn, connotes a set of conditions, qualities, and shared histories and geographies that define a group's specific character and self-awareness qua other groups. Imagined peoplehood is an obvious paraphrasing of Benedict Anderson's term *Imagined Community* (1983) used to highlight, among other things, the central role of culture and language in the forging of the shared sense of belonging that is essential to the formation of modern nations.

Peoplehood has become a common term within Jewish studies, where it was first introduced by Mordechai Kaplan (1934) and applied to differentiate between people and religion in relation to American Jewishness. It gained much traction during the twentieth century[3] and was seen as analytically fruitful by the way it "constructs and gives credibility to a radically new vision of collectivity, by underscoring the historical roots, timeless existence, and essential nature of what ultimately is an innovation" (Pianko 2015: 8).[4] The concept of *peoplehood* has increasingly gained attention in other fields – for example, in political science literature dealing with questions of political identity in a globalized fluid world (Lie 2004; Smith 2003).[5] Another area that has contributed to conceptualize peoplehood is the field of indigenous studies. The antecedents for this was the work of Edward H. Spicer, whose studies of indigenous groups in the American Southwest introduced the notions of "cultural enclaves" and "enduring peoples" to make sense of the durability and dynamic creativity of (ethnic) identities. This was the basis for Robert Thomas's (1990)

---

[3] See Pianko (2015) for an overview of the scholarship.
[4] The utility of the concept has also been contested, where critics argued that internal divisions among American Jewry made the concept ill fitting (Reinharz 2014).
[5] See Croucher (2006) for a review of some of the most important contributions here.

development of peoplehood as a concept that could transcend ethnicity, statehood, gender, nationalism, and religion. He thus suggested a model where peoplehood consisted of four markers: language, sacred history, religion, and land – which he viewed as closely interwoven and mutually dependent. Tom Holm and colleagues (2003) helpfully termed the interaction of these four markers the *Peoplehood Matrix*.

In the literature on ethnicity, the concept of *peoplehood* has been used interchangeably with race, nation, and ethnicity and has also been associated with genetic characteristics (Wallerstein 1987: 380). Joseph Ruane and Jennifer Todd are among the few who have attempted to theorize around the concept, also linking it to religious identity. Ruane argues, for example, that peoplehood has important analytical value because "societies and cultures consist of multiple, interlocking ways of forming community and identity, of which the most important are ethnic, religious, linguistic, territorial and political" and that "[e]ach of these is distinct and none is reducible to any of the others" (Ruane 2010: 122). He and Todd therefore argue that the idea of the ethnic group, or community, is problematic because it creates an inappropriate "sharp demarcation of ethnic from other communities."[6] Instead, they find that peoplehood encompasses in a more inclusive manner such multitudes (Ruane and Todd 2003: 6). Their ideas are less clear when it comes to the relationship between peoplehood and religion. On one occasion, they differentiate between religious and ethnic peoplehood (Ruane and Todd 2003: 6f.), while Ruane, discussing the relations between ethnicity and religion, talks about both peoplehood based on ethnicity and religion and religious peoplehood (Ruane 2010: 122).

My own thinking around the concept of *peoplehood* owes much to the previously outlined scholarship; yet, it moves in a different direction. To begin with, I believe Ruane errs when he differentiates between religion, ethnicity, and peoplehood. Furthermore, I disagree with his separation of ethnic and religious peoplehood. Moreover, I find Thomas's suggestion of peoplehood as consisting of language, sacred history, religion, and land problematic. He provides no justification for why these particular markers are chosen; one is moreover left with the impression of peoplehood as a static container of particular cultural content (cf. Barth 1969).

[6] Goody similarly argues that the term "ethnic" is popular "because it gets around the problem of defining what it is that makes a people – that is, an ethnos – distinctive" and claims moreover that it "covers all as well as covering up" (2001: 8).

I favor a perspective that starts with peoplehood as a more all-encompassing concept – one that enables us to analyze the multiplicity of groupness. *Peoplehood* is a concept that allows for flexibility, that is, similar to the notion of community, clearly of a segmentary nature, ranging "from the family, the lineage, and the clan to the nation or the race" (Brow 1990: 3). For example, Irish or Polish peoplehood is, on the one hand, delimited by nationality and territory, but it also entails being Catholic – something that extends beyond such boundaries to being part of a global community: "[t]o be Polish is to be Catholic" (Demerath 2000: 128). This does not mean, however, that we are talking about two distinct peoplehoods. Rather, it points to the fluid nature of peoplehood in the sense that it generates multifaceted belonging. Another example relevant for this study is how an Oromo could belong to the Arsi branch of Oromo and be part of, let us say, the Raytu clan and the Doyo sub-clan, and who might view himself or herself as part of Ethiopia. If this Oromo was a Muslim, he or she would also belong to the worldwide *umma* (global Muslim community). The concept of "peoplehood" therefore serves, broadly speaking, as a trope that encompasses kinship groups, clans, ethnic groups, religious communities, or nations, being inherently elastic to allow for the intersecting of multiple and simultaneous boundaries and identities. While not everyone is part of a professional group, voluntary association, or political party, everyone is part of a peoplehood. Having said that, peoplehood should not be construed in any essentialist manner as having an a priori existence. Instead, it always needs to be adequately historicized and contextualized.

Crucial for my understanding of peoplehood – which I will elaborate on in the sections to come – is that religion and ethnicity constitute *foundational dimensions* of peoplehood. Barth has characterized ethnic identities as "absolute" and "comprehensive" and claimed that ethnicity is "superordinate to most other statuses" (Barth 1969: 17). Richard Jenkins argued in similar ways that ethnic identity is the "basic or first-order dimension of human experience," a primary identification within which he includes humanness, gender, kinship (2008: 75). My argument falls along the same lines. However, while I recognize that religion and ethnicity are clearly imagined and constructed, I also argue that they are inescapably grounded on visceral experiences.

The point to be made is that peoplehood cannot be fully understood without recognizing humans as embodied and emplaced beings. This

recognition necessitates a perspective that reconsiders some basic epis-
temological assumptions, and I will in the following outline an alternative approach that involves such rethinking. While these ideas are
generated from a particular empirical case that has enabled me to ask
critical questions of my data, I do believe that my suggestions are broad
enough in ways that make them applicable for other contexts.

To begin with, I argue that we need to move away from perspectives
that view social and cultural realities as isolated, self-referential systems
of symbols. We also need to be mindful of excessively detached constructivist perspectives based on a Cartesian epistemology that unduly
dichotomizes mind-body, abstract-concrete, culture-materiality, finite-
infinite, and the cognitive-emotional. Such a detached constructivism
incorrectly understands humans as dislocated and disassociated; moreover, it vitiates our thinking of identity, rendering it overly fluid and
abstract. A relevant example here is Stuart Hall, who, despite important
contributions in cultural studies, disavows any location and construes
identity as a process of becoming rather than being, thus eliminating any
possibility for stability (Hall 1996: 4; cf. Butler 1990).[7] This results in
a disposable, fluid, and empty self – one that deflects any possibility of
continuance, stability, and location.

While acknowledging identity as dynamic and as constructed,
I argue that rather than seeing the individual as constantly "becoming,"
a more appropriate perspective is one that acknowledges how the
individual always self-defines and is defined in relation to
a continuum of cultural and material realities. What we need is an
approach that is grounded in a more integrated understanding of
humanness – as bodies located in the interplay among concrete, material, social, and cultural environments (Vasquez 2011: 83). While the
notion of embodiment has gained increased attention in recent years,
there is a tendency to treat the body as a representation of something
else, or as detached from agency, and construed as a passive physical
shell for the mind.[8] Nonrepresentational theories (Thrift 2007) have

---

[7] Hall invokes Derrida's concept of *differance,* in which meaning infinitely differs
and is deferred, and claims that meaning as related to identity can only be made
through a "temporary break" in the endless semiosis of language (1996: 3).

[8] The body is often viewed as a tool, an agent, and as the locus for symbolic
meaning. This latter aspect is found in Mary Douglas's writings that reduce the
body to a "symbol of society" (1970: 93), as a "text" that can be read. The body
is alternatively understood in relation to certain spheres of human activity, such
as the body and gender, the body and health, etc., while perspective on the

made a point of moving away from seeing the body as a mere representation of some sort of symbolic meaning or as just a metaphor, instead emphasizing the concreteness and materiality of the body and, thus, of the human itself as the primary datum (Csordas 1999). A dilemma with some of these perspectives, however, is that they risk emphasizing the flesh to the extent of underplaying the integral cognitive dimension of the body. I believe Ian Burkitt manages a fruitful balance here, seeing the mind as entailing the body – and humans as "thinking bodies," which moreover extends to the integration of the self's organic and social aspects, enabling an understanding of humans "as embodied social beings" (1994: 8), as "socio-natural entit[ies]" (1987), and of the self as an "ecological self" (Neisser 1988).

Focus on embodiment is a methodological field recognizing "embodiment as an existential condition" (Csordas 1999: 147; cf. Csordas 1994) and is primarily about the realities, experiences, perceptions, and imaginations of being in the world from the standpoint of the body. According to Maurice Merleau-Ponty's phenomenology of perception (1962), being embodied – and emplaced – runs counter to the notion of humans existing on the other side of materiality. He views perception as the primary bodily experience and claims that embodiment is the condition for perception, which in turn is the way objective reality becomes real. Our embodiment opens us up to an existential immediacy and intersubjectivity that is captured in the concept of *being-in-the-world* (*être au monde*). I find this concept particularly useful in framing this study; yet, I will also add the notion of *being-with-others*, reflecting Tim Ingold's perception of the person being situated in "an encompassing field of *relationships*" with other bodies (2000: 144, italics in original). The concepts *being-in-the-world* and *being-with-others* refer to a concrete, embodied form of existential immediacy in the material world, in which humans are part of the world – inhabiting it as active purposive beings. A few studies employ Merleau-Ponty's framework in relation to ethnic identity (Dion et al. 2011; Geurts 2002; Retsikas

"multiple body" divides it into entities as the individual body, the social body, and the political body. Michel Foucault (1979, 1980) perceives the body in relation to discursive processes of domination and as a product of power plays. Richard Jenkins (1996: 60f.) discusses embodiment and identity and relates identity to the embodied self yet ends up focusing on the mind and cognitive processes of identity formation and maintenance, thus reducing the human body to "a basic metaphor for symbolising and imagining collective identities" (1996: 143).

2007), and although I have found them inspirational, my thinking around this is rather different.[9]

According to Merleau-Ponty, the fact that the individual's experiences and perceptions are from an embodied, emplaced, and located point of view means he or she sees the world as boundless, and which "arouses the expectation of more than it contains" (1962: 3). An important aspect of the being-in-the-world and being-with-others is the urge to make sense of this boundlessness, which entails a process of structuring elements as parts of a whole, mapping out and making sense of oneself and one's realities. Such processes of abstraction – or social construction – are never linear but always complex and reciprocal, in the sense of being dialectically related to embodied interactions with other human beings and to the material world (cf. Tweed 2006: 158). This process of relating parts to a whole is, I argue, about *belonging*, about developing an identity in the process of establishing relations with other beings and objects and reciprocally relating oneself to these others. The relational character of belonging is clearly noticeable in the way the term has little or no meaning in itself. It makes no sense to talk about belonging unless we talk about "belonging to," "belonging in," or "belonging with."

The ability of abstraction, or imagination, is a unique faculty among humans, which forms the basis for social construction, symbolic production, and categorization. Important here is that abstraction is never severed from human material existence but that it is the very embodied and emplaced reality that enables human imagination and abstraction. Humans are, I claim, simply incapable of abstraction severed from the material world. Building on Mark Johnson's theory on metaphors, I suggest that abstraction is not about generating internal representations of external reality, as the dualist Cartesian worldview would have it. Rather, it emerges in the dynamic and intimate entwinement of bodily and physical realities (Johnson 1987, 1999; Lakoff and Johnson 1980). Metaphors are vehicles for understanding, playing a critical role for any form of abstraction, and for human ability to exist. It is not about "consciousness of non-real objects but as a projection of a lived body in a lived environment" (Dion et al. 2011: 321), meaning that nothing abstract or imagined can exist

---

[9] Dion et al. apply – as extensions of being-in-the-world – remembering being-in-the-world and being-in-the-world with others (2011: 312).

without being connected to a material reality.[10] The centrality of metaphors in this context lies, moreover, in their capacity to unite reason and imagination in such a way that the latter adds an affective dimension to the former (Lakoff and Johnson 1980). Tweed (2006) has similarly suggested how tropes as analogical language function as modes of transport, and how they with their "cognitive-affective fluidity" can "create associations, stir affect, and prompt action" (2006: 45f., 68, 96).[11]

Embodied and emplaced realities form the basis for imagining peoplehood. Drawing upon Max Weber's ideal types, Alfred Schutz (1967: 176f.) distinguished between face-to-face knowledge of an individual's fellows and abstracted indirect knowledge of his or her contemporaries. While we can distinguish between real and imagined relations, the two are, at the same time, more interconnected than one might think and "always from the domain of the physical . . . onto the social, epistemic, and speech-act realms" (Johnson 1987: 62). The point is that while peoplehood is imagined, it does not cease to be made up of real embodied people. One might say that peoplehood consists of "people" as the real and of "hood" as what constitutes the imagined; those who are imagined as the "we" and demarcated from the "other."

I have found it useful to apply family and home as relevant tropes. These are tropes that refer to primary relations and primary places and that, moreover, have clear affective aspects (cf. Anderson 1983: 143).[12] Affect is a phenomenon that generally has been unacknowledged in Western scholarship. As rightly pointed out by Walter Connor, academia has always had a "discomfort with the nonrational" (1994: 75) – a discomfort that reflects the enduring strength of the Cartesian body-mind dualism.[13] The focus on rationality as associated with the mind

---

[10] It is here important to underscore that the nature of such abstraction and the usage of metaphors are highly contextual depending on the nature of physical realities (Lakoff and Johnson 1980).

[11] Tweed's usage of tropes deals with transportations between different domains of abstract language, experience, and culture, but I believe they also have the capacity of transporting attention from the material to the abstract, being "tools for making and remaking imagined worlds" (2006: 68).

[12] Alonso claims that kinship tropes are imbued with sentiments and morality, pointing in particular to how this provides nations with a religious dimension (1994: 385).

[13] Günther Schlee, for example, who unilaterally emphasizes the cognitive aspect of identity formation, admits "a relative helplessness when dealing with emotions" (2010: 17).

means that feelings and desires have been seen as raw and primitive forces located in the domain of the body, different from and subject to the disciplining power of the cogito. With the "emotional turn" emerging in the 1970s, emotions have, however, gradually been brought back in from the cold (Lemmings and Brooks 2014). I am situated within this emerging scholarship and understand emotions as intrinsic to lived experience, as activating "distinct dispositions, postures and movements which are not only attitudinal but also physical," and which reflect "the experience of embodied sociality" (Lyon and Barbalet 1994: 48). Important here is to recognize the bodily, physical nature of emotions, while not severing connections between emotions and humans' cognitive faculties. We also need to acknowledge that emotions are more than only something "internal," but that they also are inherently relational, social, and public. This goes against the common (Western) perception of the autonomous self-contained individual and recognizes the human interconnectivity and relational nature of affect wherein we find ourselves "in intimate proximity with other feeling bodies" (Schaefer 2015: 65). Emotions are thus not only "socially efficacious," but they also have a "social ontology," in the sense that the "emotion as an experience involving physical and phenomenal aspects has simultaneously a social-relational genesis" (Lyon and Barbalet 1994: 58).

The affective nature of ethnicity and religion is something most scholars have recognized, and so-called ethnic groups are sometimes referred to as "communities of feelings" or "emotional communities" (Berezin 2002; Hochchild 1983). Few have, however, managed to say much about the role of emotions.[14] Anderson, for example, points to how nationhood commands "a profound emotional legitimacy", and contrasting this with other forms of collectivities, he laconically states that no one is willing to die "for the Labour Party, the American Medical Association, or perhaps even Amnesty International" (1983: 4). Both Connor (1994) and Clifford Geertz (1963) emphasize the deep affective bonds produced by notions of common descent and shared blood ties, but neither they nor existing literature offers much theoretical reflection. Geertz, in fact, underscores the affective aspect to that extent of arguing that ethnicity is ineffable. Yael Tamir, writing about nationalism, echoes this, characterizing it as "a force that lies

---

[14] See Schaefer (2015: 8, fn. 26) for an overview of studies on religion and affect.

beyond theoretical analysis" (1999: 70). I believe that the emotional aspect is not as ineffable as it seems. Perceiving emotions as bodily, relational, and social – as well as intertwined with the cognitive – has significant consequences for how we understand belonging in relation to peoplehood.

Ethnicity as a Dimension of Peoplehood

Ethnicity is one of the many categories that have evaded precise definitions. It has been perceived as something that can take different forms, exist on various "levels," and have potentially different meanings across time and space (Brow 1990). Ethnicity has been understood as a creation by colonial powers for the purpose of control (Ranger 1993) and as closely connected to states' need to categorize citizens – which reciprocally have paved the way for collectives to distinguish themselves from others. Ethnicity is, moreover, often instrumentalized by political actors or could be a potent force for social mobilization. It has thus become, according to Marcus Banks, something of which numerous scholars "have written in apparent ignorance of the work of other authors who claim to be writing about the same issues. One occasionally gets the sense that the wheel has been invented several times over" (1996: 2). I will therefore not rehash the old debates about ethnicity (which has become mandatory for every study of the ethnic) related to primordialism vs constructivism (Brubaker 2002, 2004; Van den Berghe 1981) and to content vs boundaries (Barth 1969; Cohen 1985). I am not interested in the many possible appearances of ethnicity, as briefly mentioned earlier, but rather in the fundamental aspects that form it, and in the seemingly salient power of ethnicity. While I obviously understand ethnicity as constructed, I do not believe it is constructed out of "thin air." I similarly argue that applying a too-detached constructivist perspective is unfruitful and problematic and believe we need to apply a very different perspective in order to reach a fuller understanding.

My approach to ethnicity therefore underscores the individual's embodied and emplaced experiences of being-in-the-world and being-with-others as the point of departure. Foundational here is the family as the individual's primary and most intimate relations with his or her significant others: the physical, embodied, and locally

embedded relationship he or she has with parents, primary care-
takers, or kin. While there obviously are huge cultural variations in
the setup, the child's basic relationship with these significant others is
the most foundational one in human life. They are the first ones
catering to the child's physical and emotional needs, as well as
being the most important in processes of socialization. It is
a primary reference point in an individual's awareness – cognitively,
emotionally, and physically – of his or her belonging: "One's parents
give one life. The locality in which one is born and in which one lives
nurtures one; it provides the necessary for one's life. The larger
collectivity in which one is born and in which one lives protects
one's life from the potentially threatening chaos of the external
world" (Grosby 1994: 169).

The ethnic dimension of peoplehood is also deeply connected to the
individual's emplacement in his or her physical environment and, in
particular, to places that are regarded as the "sphere of nurture"
(Ingold 2000: 149). This refers to home as the primary place that signifies
the intimate, protected, and controlled space "that provides for bodily
needs – shelter, sleep, sex, healing, and food – and usually, though not
always, is inhabited by some members of the family" (Tweed 2006: 105).

Home is a complex concept, being "at once both concrete and
abstract" (Benjamin 1995: 2). Home is, however, more than
a concept: it is more than maps in the minds of people. Home is
material in the form of houses built on actual land, be it the family's
homestead, the clan's pastures, or the nation's territory.[15] Places do not
move, and even for those in exile or diaspora, home is something
durable and stable, a primary place that becomes the materialization
of stability and being-with-others from the outset of our lives, as well as
constituting a key reference point during our journeys across space and
time (Tuan 1977: 29). Crucial here is the home as a relational site,
wherein interactions with embodied others make it more than any
random house.[16] Therefore, thinking of home or homeplace requires
that we recognize the materiality of place, imbued with its sights,
sounds, textures, and smells. This relates back to my earlier discussion

---

[15] For discussions on home and house, see Stea (1995) and Rapoport (1995).
[16] Bourdieu has discussed this in relation to the physical house in Kabylia,
particularly the ordering of gendered space (1977: 89f.). For similar
arrangements among the Oromo, see Marit T. Østebø (2007: 47).

of the importance of emotions and affects in the study of ethnicity and religion. One's home is something that produces strong affective sentiments, in the same way that being emplaced incorporates "the memories and dreams of the inhabitants" (Pallasma 1995: 143).[17] Yi-Fu Tuan describes this as *topophilia*, which expresses humans' love of place or the affective ties with the environment (1974: 92). Arguing that emotional experiences cannot be held separate from their objects, Tuan emphasizes the permanent feelings one has "toward a place because it is home, the locus of memories, and the means of gaining a livelihood" (1974: 93; cf. Ingold 2000: 146f.). Emplaced belonging is thus "based in feelings, consisting in skills, sensitivities and orientations that have developed through long experiences of conducting one's life in a particular environment" (Ingold 2000: 25).[18]

Many readers could easily accuse me of essentializing family and home in an unwarranted manner, overlooking the inherent composite and fluid nature of these social phenomena.[19] My response is that cultural theory needs to acknowledge that not everything "melts into the air" and to overcome our fear of building larger ideas. In a poststructuralist, post-essentialist, postmodern, and post-nearly-everything world, we have become so focused on deconstructing to that extent that construction becomes impossible. We have similarly become so attentive to every possible variation and nuance when investigating social and cultural phenomena, paying so much attention to the variations and the exceptions so that they overshadow commonalities, similitude of features, and universal validity. As we emphasize the existence of all kinds of anomalies, the critical point is that we view the anomalies as the general. There is, as already noted, no doubt that there is much variations in what we call family and home, but there is far more that is in common. I therefore argue for an approach that is not dictated by anomalies but that starts from commonality. I believe

---

[17] Tuan points to how such emotions are evoked by particular things, like "the hidden corner, a stool, a gilded mirror" that can be felt and touched (1977: 144).

[18] While the home may constitute a primary site, it is important to note that home as a place always exists in relation to other places, like neighboring homes, being part of a village, or interlinked with other villages. Moreover, all places are embedded in environments, including immediate farmlands and urban landscapes, as well as territories like region and homelands.

[19] See Duncan and Lambert (2004) for an overview of literature on family and home that includes questions of politics, gender, fear, homelessness, and migration.

that an approach that carefully balances between the general and the specific should not too quickly be boxed in as dated forms of "essentalization" or "universalization."

The key point here is that these embodied and emplaced human realities are the point of departure for the construction of the ethnic dimension of imagined peoplehood. This does not mean, however, that peoplehood, in any of its varied forms and with its many levels, is just the linear projection of family and home on a large scale. My point is that in addition to being the point of departure for a person's identity, the same embodied and emplaced realities of family and home continue to be the reference point, as well as constituting the returning point for imagined peoplehood. The construction of the ethnic dimension is then a result of the reciprocal interplay between intimate sensory experiences and abstraction of broader forms of belonging – generated through the person's ongoing sociocultural and ecological trajectory.

The importance of embodied and emplaced realities for the ethnic dimension can be illustrated by how words associated with primary relations and primary place are used as metaphors for peoplehood. Relevant examples are how members of peoplehood become metaphorical brothers and sisters, and how particularly important national figures are labeled as *Pater Patriae* (father of the nation/father of the fatherland) or as founding fathers – made close and appropriated as "everyone's" father.[20] Similarly, we see how home as primary place reflects the way the territoriality of peoplehood, often in the form of the nation-state, is depicted as motherland, the land of the fathers, or the homeland (Alonso 1994: 385f.; Anderson 1983: 143; Duncan and Lambert 2004; Horowitz 1985: 57f.).

The relational character of these tropes, the constant references to primary relations and primary place, and the way they are associated with intimate love are what make the ethnic dimension so potentially powerful – something to defend with one's life. Steven Grosby claims that this is a universal phenomenon, arguing, "human beings have sacrificed their lives and continue to sacrifice their lives for their own family and for their own nation" (1994: 169). Ana Maria Alonso has forwarded more nuanced suggestions, arguing that the power of such tropes is a result of "the fusion of the ideological and the sensory, the

---

[20] *Pater Patriae* stems from the Roman Empire and has later been used for individuals like George Washington, Kwame Nkrumah, and Nelson Mandela.

bodily and the normative, the emotional and the instrumental, the organic and the social" (1994: 386). It is what produces a deeply and viscerally felt sense of attachment, loyalty, a shared identity, and belonging that is an essential ingredient for our sense of self, as both individuals and members of peoplehood.

Common in most of the literature is the notion that ethnicity is, in one form or the other, related to descent. Such a notion can be traced back to Weber (1978) and has more recently been discussed by Connor (1994), Grosby (1994), and Stephen Cornell (1996), who construes ethnicity as "its emphasis on real or assumed bonds of kinship," and as "descent from a common homeland" (1996: 268). Cornell even argues that omitting descent deprives the concept of ethnicity of "analytical utility" (1996: 268).[21] Ronald Cohen, for his part, refers to ethnicity as involving "a set of descent-based cultural identifiers" and an "aura of descent"(1978: 387). While I agree that the salient power of ethnicity is related to notions of (putative) shared descent, the dilemma is that such connections often are just taken for granted without any explanations, or as something that simply cannot be understood. Connor, for example, reduces the notion of shared descent to "an intuitive conviction" that resists explication (1994: 202); although he talks about family and home as important tropes for ethnicity, he ends up concluding they are "metaphors that can magically transform the mundanely tangible into emotion-laden phantasma" (1994: 205; cf. Lakoff and Johnson 1980). National identity is similarly construed as constituted by traditions, institutions, and narratives of a symbolic nature – something clearly evident in Anderson's notion of *Imagined Communities* as well as in Michael Billing's *Banal Nationalism* (1995).

I argue that the emphasis on shared descent, on one hand, and ethnicity as constructed, on the other, is somewhat contradictory, and that this can be solved by an approach that moves beyond the already discussed Cartesian dichotomy and by foregrounding the concept of peoplehood. A key characteristic of peoplehood is its "temporal dimension of pastness" (Wallerstein 1987: 381), and Holm et al. speak about pastness in the form of sacred history as one of the markers of

---

[21] This is also the common perspective among members of peoplehood, which through *everyday primordialism* often view themselves as sharing the same blood and originating from the same ancestor (Fearon and Laitin 2000: 848; cf. Schlee 2010: 100).

peoplehood (2003: 13).[22] Don Handelmann connects ethnicity to "a corporate history in time and space," suggesting that history offers an explanation to members of ethnic groups as to "why they are members, where they originated, and why the existence of the category is substantial and legitimate" (1977: 190). I believe, however, that the term *descent* is too narrow because it fails to capture the complex temporal dimensions of peoplehood. Instead, I prefer the concept of *provenance,* understood as "origin" or "to come from" (Ruane and Todd 2003). Provenance enables us to grasp how the ethnic dimension of peoplehood collapses time in the way of producing history that bridges the past with the present and the future, bringing the past to a kind of present coexistence (Brow 1990: 3; Ingold 2000: 141), thus providing peoplehood with a sense of immortality (Stewart 2009: 21). Belonging is, in other words "nourished by being cultivated in fertile soil of the past" (Brow 1990: 3).

Provenance is captured in the peoplehood's multi-leveled and collective memory of origin formulated and maintained in the form of narratives transmitted across generations. Such narratives are not merely nostalgic artifacts from a bygone past or "stories of the dead," but they are actively enacted in the presence by significant others and realized through primary processes of embodied socialization, nurturing, and disciplining. Nor are narratives dissociated from lived realities, but, as tied to active dwelling, they make it possible to imagine places of origin, thus producing roads to an emplaced past that is made present. As the individual constitutes and defines figures, places, and events in the past as his or her own history that are "etched in the deep recesses of memory and yield intense satisfaction with each recall" (Tuan 1977: 141), it moves the individual beyond his or her immediacy and opens up and produces expectations and awareness of something more, something that transcends time (Merleau-Ponty 1962: 4). In African contexts, we observe how oral narratives frequently make use of spatial references as markers – "critical to maintaining group identity and relationship with others" (Shetler 2007: 21). Memory and identity are, according to Jan Bender Shetler, "inscribed on land" in the sense that human biographies are anchored in a sequence of places (2007: 17,

---

[22] Alfred Doja has argued that what "distinguishes ethnic identity from other . . . is its orientation towards the past" (2000: 432).

20). The role of narratives in attaching people to place is also noted by Tuan, who argues that narratives not only provide the basis for embodied belonging together with other people but that they also, "by weaving in observable features in the landscape (a tree here, a rock there), strengthen a people's bond to place" (Tuan 1991: 686).

Religion as Ultimate Belonging

Religion is, similar to ethnicity, an elusive, yet powerful, category. It is made even more elusive by the tendency to perceive it as ineffable feelings or deep beliefs, as existing merely in the minds of people, or an archetypal category represented through narratives, texts, myths, or a "system of sacred symbols" (Geertz 1973).[23] Such a disembodiment reduces religion to signification and semiotics – to "expressive texts to be enacted and decoded" (Vasquez 2011: 220; cf. Asad 1993: 43f.). Religion is moreover construed as largely an individualistic and personal matter, reduced to "interior, personal, and utterly unique states and dispositions" (McCutcheon 2003: 55) and as a personified relation between the human and the deity, where individual faith as a choice is emphasized. This is clearly a product of a Western Protestant Christian tradition that has come to color much of Western academic thinking about religion (Asad 1993: 43f.; King 1999: 36f.). Talal Asad argues that such a concept of religion is also "a product of the only legitimate space allowed for Christianity by post-Enlightenment society, the right to individual *belief*" (1993: 45, italics in original). Too often, this "private affair" perspective of religion is presented as a universalized model and uncritically extrapolated to religious traditions and contexts other than Protestant Christianity, where religion is more of a collective matter.

Attempts have been made to recognize the collective nature of religion, but the way such forms are viewed as anomalies demonstrates the continued bias toward the private affair perspective. Claire Mitchell, for example, refers to collective religion as "religion once removed" and talks about people who have "no active faith in their day-to-day life" (2010: 54). N. J. Demerath, on his part, notes that "cultural religion" should be understood as "a style of religion that resides in

---

[23] Arguably, the most powerful expressions of this understanding in religious studies are the idea of the holy (Otto 1958) and the sacred (Eliade 1959).

'the culture' without compelling active belief or participation" (2000: 136). Such perspectives give the impression that people who do not have a developed conscious individualized "faith" are not really religious and that practicing "popular Islam" or "folk Christianity" are divergent or inferior forms of religiosity.[24] I would argue that for most of the people across the globe, religion is a matter of collective identity, and that belonging to a religion or being religious is not dependent on conscious faith. As Nancy Ammerman argues, "[i]nstitutionalized rituals, stories, moral prescriptions, and traditions are usually recognized as religious, whether or not the participants themselves think a Sacred Other is involved" (2007: 225). I believe that an alternative post-Cartesian approach offers important adjustments to the private affair perspective, where also the application of peoplehood as a conceptual point of departure facilitates a broader understanding of religion and its importance as a matter of collective identity. Such an approach pays attention to religion as not only having the potential to produce notions of vertical belonging involving the individual and the transcendent but that it also – albeit not necessarily in a Durkheimian manner – creates strong sentiments of belonging that are horizontal in the form of an imagined peoplehood. Seeing religion as a dimension of imagined peoplehood thus means that religious adherence and participation confirm, sustain, and maintain collective religious identities. Important to note is that this is not an either-or matter; religious collective identity does not exclude individual commitment.[25]

Similar to ethnicity, I argue for an approach that starts off by recognizing how religion is located in material realities and is experienced through embodied relations and emplaced existences. I similarly believe that paying attention to the continued importance of family and home as tropes for primary relations and primary places enables a broader understanding of religion. Religion is, to begin with, usually something a person "inherits" from his or her immediate family, and it is this inheritance that in most cases continuously determines whether

---

[24] This is not only true for a non-Western context, where Day (2011) in a study of so-called nominalist, un-churched people in the United Kingdom found that religious identity is not necessarily dependent upon individual commitment or personal "belief."

[25] Cohen and Hill's (2007) dichotomy between individualistic "ascent" religions (Protestant Christianity) and collective "descent" religions (Catholic Christianity, Judaism, Hinduism) poorly represents the multiple levels of variations here.

one is Christian, Muslim, Hindu, or Shinto, and so on.[26] Often introduced at birth through initiation rituals and maintained through socialization, religion remains embodied in relations to family and kin and is
hence closely linked to group membership. The centrality of such
embodied relationships is highlighted by Abby Day's study from the
UK, where her respondents first and foremost related their religious
identity to immediate family members constituting the model and
affective reference point for their religiosity (2011: 156), before referring to a British Christianness (2011: 180). Day underscored that
people "have relationship-centred and relationship-guided beliefs,
informed by experience and the emotions they (re)produce" (2011:
204).

The making and maintenance of religion through primary relations
also has a spatial aspect, where the primary place of the home plays an
initial and crucial role for shaping religious identity. It is where religious socialization takes place, where stories are told, where rituals are
performed, and where artifacts are displayed. It is where the child first
smells, hears, and tastes religion, and where he or she incorporates the
performance of daily routines through the modeling of his or her
parents' embodied religiosity. The home exists in relation to
a broader network of religious sites. There are often well-trodden
paths between the home and these sites, be they the village church,
the mosque, the temple, or the shrine. Also important, in many contexts, are natural sites in the landscape, such as springs, hilltops, or
rivers that emplace the sacred, serving, for instance, as pilgrimage sites
or sites of apparitions or miraculous events:

Particular territories are always mentioned in sacred histories, and quite
often creation and migration stories specify certain landmarks as being
especially holy. Ancestors are buried in particular places. Shrines are erected
and certain parts of the immediate environment – plants, water, earth, animal
parts – are often utilized in religious ceremonies. (Holm et al. 2003: 14)

Similar to ethnicity, religion is also linked to the notion of provenance.
This is shown by how people represent common descent through

---

[26] This does not, however, preclude the possibility of religious conversions. While
conversions entail rejection of previous narratives, traditions, and ritual
practices, they also often alienate the individual physically from his or her family
or kin. Conversion, thus, means dislocation, which only can be mended by
relocation within a new embodied community.

religious narratives about origin and creation (Little 1995). Such narratives may refer to ancestors who are perceived as being imbued with a religious aura. This sacralization then becomes an added aspect to the way in which a particular people imagine its common origin, as part of mythical narratives about primeval beginnings. These narratives then contribute to collapse time, which attaches peoplehood to cosmological beginnings. Reverence for mythical ancestors is about including them in a finite reality, and worship of gods is extensively about the here and now, mediating distance and time by ways of bringing the most distant horizon near (Latour 2005). Religion as spatially located has in a similar manner the potential for collapsing time. While natural sacred sites and shrines are constituted by narratives of origin – linked to an ancestor or a holy man – and houses of worship have their own histories as built at certain points in time, they are, at the same time, places that transgress "real history," thus being representations of an infinite presence. Sacred sites are part of a geography that is both material and imagined, which enables the individual to merge his or her immediate history with a distant past, in terms of origin and, moreover, to localize himself or herself in relation to the future, providing – similar to ethnicity – a sense of immortality (Seul 1999: 560). Bridging the infinite and finite worlds, these venues "mediate devotee's experiences and representations of time" (Tweed 2006: 93; cf. Engelke 2007).

The religious dimension is furthermore "not only locative and translocative, but also supralocative" (Vasquez 2011: 286), having the potential to transcend finite time and space, thus enabling belonging that moves beyond the immanent. Tweed has in fact argued that the quest to traverse the boundaries between the finite and infinite is what "distinguishes religious and nonreligious cultural forms" (2006: 76). This is not a matter of abstract imaginations; rather, it involves a process where the "transcendent experience of continued belonging is brought into being through embodied, physical sensations and emotions" (Day 2011: 196). Earlier scholars of religion, such as Emile Durkheim and Max Weber have raised the same ideas, and F. Max Müller argued for a "mental faculty" among humans, claiming that people's encounter with material nature enabled "man to apprehend the Infinite under different names, and varying disguises" (cited in Tweed 2006: 95). Justin Barrett and Frank Keil later claimed that "[a]s natural creatures, we can only draw upon our natural experiences in our attempts to characterize God" (1996: 220). This is clearly seen, for example, in the way gods are unavoidably given anthropomorphic features.

While Tweed uses the term *ultimate horizon* as denoting religions' capacity and potential by which people can locate themselves in infinite time and space, I prefer the term *ultimate belonging*. This is related to humans' – although not necessarily explicit or conscious – pondering questions about limitless time and endless space. Such pondering argu-ably emerges from specific corporeal experiences – gazing into the starlit sky, being present at the graveside at the death of a family member, or the marveling over a newborn child. These are moments when, to return to Merleau-Ponty, immediate perception generates expectations of something more than the material – producing imagi-nations and narratives of an infinite reality, of gods and other super-natural beings, and, importantly, of humans' relations to these beings. Robert Orsi echoes such ideas, and points to how religion takes the form of a network of relationships between heaven and earth, "invol-ving humans of all ages and many different sacred figures together." He makes the important observation that these relationships "have the same complexities – all the hopes, evasions, love, fear, denial, projec-tions, misunderstandings, and so on – of relationships between humans" (2005: 2).[27]

Understanding religion and ethnicity as foundational dimensions of peoplehood means that there is an intimate relationship between the two – sometimes to the extent that they become nearly indistinguish-able. While scholars often accept such a relationship as a matter of fact, the nature of this relationship remains highly under-theorized (Mitchell 2006). In most of the social anthropological literature, religion is seen as a marker of ethnicity (Demerath 2000; Gans 1994). This view is explicitly expressed by Manning Nash (1988), who claims that ethni-city is made up of three main markers: kinship, commensality, and common cult (cf. Connor 1972; Horowitz 1985: 41). There are also those who say that it is futile and unrealistic to separate religion from ethnic identity, and who simply suggest that ethnicity is merely religion in disguise (Enloe 1980: 355). Religious studies, on the other hand,

---

[27] Graham and Haidt (2010: 144) write in a similar vein about how morality binds people together in groups, to moral "sacred others," and to a reality beyond a finite reality.

have had very little to say about ethnicity, treating it as a side issue with little relevance. The question of religious identity has obviously been an important topic but has largely been segregated to the subfield of psychology of religion.

Placing peoplehood front and center also helps explaining how the ethnic and the religious coincide and overlap, seen, for example, in the "ethnic" nature of the pre-Islamic Oromo religion and in the way being a Somali is synonymous with being a Muslim. The religious dimension, however, is particular in the way it manages to transcend boundaries – different from the ethnic dimension that contributes to a more local demarcation of peoplehood. I have already pointed out how the Catholic dimension of being Irish and Polish transcends nationality; it is similarly obvious that while being Somali is being Muslim, being Muslim is not the same as being Somali. An Oromo would moreover identify himself or herself according to branches, clans, and sub-clans yet would also, as a Christian or a Muslim, have a broader sense of belonging. This relates to the segmentary nature of peoplehood and to belonging as multi-leveled. Similar to how the potential of these different belongings may vary, so also would an emphasis on the religious dimension reduce the potential of the ethnic dimension. While people may continue to have a shared notion of ethnic-based forms of belongings, religion may offer ways to transcend local ethnic boundaries and build more overarching communal belongings. Conversely, stressing ethnicity may fragment the crosscutting solidarities bridged by religion.

Religion and ethnicity relate to each other on a deeper level, seen, for example, by how the religious dimension of peoplehood also makes use of tropes associated with home and family, tropes that contribute to strengthen both horizontal and vertical attachments. This is most obvious in the way people who practice the same religion often refer to one another as brothers and sisters, and references to "shared blood" are commonly used to express religious belonging (Ruane and Todd 2003: 11). The religious dimension, however, moves beyond immanent realities and applies such tropes as expressions for relations between humans and the infinite. For example, in Christianity, God is called upon as "father" and the Virgin Mary is the divine "Mother."[28] In his

---

[28] This is also something discussed by psychologists since Freud, claiming that gods are projections of one's father or as images of a parent (Barrett and Keil 1996: 221).

work on American Catholicism, Orsi argues, "the saints and the Mother of God draw on the intimate histories of relationships within family worlds," in turn, constituting the bonds between "heaven and earth ... at the most intimate levels of experience" (2005: 13). God then becomes the father in a very "real" manner, transfiguring the members of one's religious community into spiritual brothers and sisters, without erasing their corporality. This enables humans to localize themselves in relation to the infinite, in turn producing a deep sense of belonging.

Ethnic and Religious Conflicts

The question of how to understand the relationship between ethnicity and religion becomes particularly difficult when the two become part of conflicts. So-called ethnic and religious conflicts have for decades occupied scholars from different disciplines, where the most common tendency has been to think of ethnicity and religion in relation to conflicts from an either-or perspective, as either ethnic or religious conflicts. This has also given the impression of a steady increase of ethnic conflicts after the Cold War and throughout the 1990s (Gurr 2000). It is generally assumed that these types of conflicts decreased by the end of the decade, and that by the twenty-first century (particularly after 9/11), religious conflicts were supplanting ethnic ones. This is, in fact, Samuel Huntington's (1996) thesis: with the ideological conflict between communism and capitalism resolved (in favor of the latter), religion would be pivotal in future geopolitical "civilizational clashes," wherein conflicts between Islam and the West would allegedly dominate.

There are good reasons to argue that such assumed rise and fall of ethnic conflicts and the current prominence of religious ones are very much dependent on the gaze of the observer, on taken-for-granted neat typologies wherein conflicts can only be either ethnic or religious. Such an either-or perspective becomes problematic in cases where ethnic and religious precursors and discourses intersect – most typically related to conflicts in Northern Ireland and the Balkans. Some have thus distinguished between ethnic and religious conflicts by referring to two types of identities as the bases for mobilization (Stewart 2009: 5), while others have argued for a combination of ethnicity and religion (Ruane and Todd 2009). This has arguably not brought much clarity;

instead, we keep asking questions such as the following: What are the causes for ethnic or religious conflicts? Do ethnicity and religion overlap and coincide? Do the two exist in opposition to each other, and what consequences could this produce? Can we distinguish between ethnicity and religion in conflicts and what would be the criteria for doing so?

I hope my foregoing discussion has shown that while it is useful for analytical purposes to understand ethnicity and religion as each having its own specificities, histories, logics, and actors, they share common elements based on our intertwined embodied and emplaced being-in-the-world and being-with-others experiences. The task, then, is to study the concrete ways in which this interplay takes place in particular conflictual situations. I am less interested in all possible causes for conflicts, in terms of both underlying factors and sparks that ignite them. What I rather seek is to interrogate how and why religion and ethnicity seem to be salient ingredients of conflict and, moreover, to understand the powerful affective dimension they bring to conflicts.

A large body of literature has addressed the topic of ethnic and religious conflicts that cannot be discussed fully here. Briefly summarized, the dominant perspectives on ethnic conflict are usually divided into the essentialist (primordialist), instrumentalist, constructivist, and institutionalist approaches.[29] Additional perspectives include the "ancient hatred" approach, conflictual modernization, and rational choice arguments.[30] The essentialist/primordialist perspective, as one extreme, is based on the notion of ethnicity as ancient and unchanging, which means that conflicts are inevitable. The opposite perspective claims that ethnic conflicts are created by so-called entrepreneurs or mobilizers, who instrumentalize religion and ethnicity for other purposes (Banton 2000; Lake and Rothchild 1998). Paul Williams has along these lines argued that ethnic conflicts in Africa are all about political struggles over power (2016: 141). This consequently means that there are no religious and ethnic conflicts as such but rather that conflicts are always about real things like economic resources and political power. One particular version of this instrumentalism is the rational choice approach that reads religious conflicts as the product of economic deprivation (Iannaccone and Berman 2006) or as a response

---

[29] See Varshney (2009) for a thorough discussion of these perspectives.
[30] See Kaufman (2006) for an overview of relevant contributions.

to political discrimination. Against this view, substantialist perspectives claim that the causes for religious conflicts are related to the very content of different religions, to how religion refers to existential questions of life and death, and to the divisiveness allegedly inherent to religions (Galtung 1997; Goody 2001).

An integrative approach to religion and ethnicity saves us from viewing the religious and ethnic dimensions as less real or as disguises for something else. While it is clear that so-called entrepreneurs or mobilizers may utilize and instrumentalize religion and ethnicity for different reasons, that does not make religion and ethnicity less real or efficacious. The invoked notion of an "us" in conflict with an "other" is based on already existing embodied and emplaced experiences critical for affective sentiments of belonging. It is precisely these sentiments that are intensified in times of conflicts and make people ready to obey the call to arms. Mobilizers and entrepreneurs may be driven by idiosyncratic motives. However, they are not positioned above or in isolation from those whom they try to mobilize and thus are not estranged from the broader shared affective sentiments. In fact, such figures often combine effective organizational skills with a powerful charismatic appeal, being able to explicitly articulate deep-seated sentiments in a public and representative manner.

The outlined perspectives on conflict – both in isolation and in combination – may be valuable for understanding certain aspects of conflicts, but they fail to consider important key features. The most important, and obvious, aspect is that regardless of how we classify them, conflicts are always conflicts between people. They are real conflicts that involve real people who hurt and harm other people, bodies who kill and are killed. Conflicts cause casualties, injuries, material destruction, and displacement. They produce feelings of loss, grief, anger, humiliation, and defeat, as well as pride, exhilaration, and a sense of victory. They create, in other words, deep, strong bodily emotions. Similarly important and obvious is that conflicts are territorial. This means not only that they are about territorial claims but also that they are fought in actual space, in cities, villages, in the bush, and across open fields. Conflicts are thus inscribed on landscapes, leaving such landscapes scarred with cities in ruins, houses destroyed, and meadows scorched.

The embodied and emplaced character of conflicts is therefore the crucial point of departure for understanding so-called ethnic and religious conflicts. This means we need to start with the notion of peoplehood, simultaneously real and imagined. Embodied and emplaced experiences related to family as the primary relations and home as primary place are foundational for the strong and emotional sense of belonging to an imagined peoplehood and means, moreover, that attacks on peoplehood take on a real character by becoming attacks on one's family and home. Fighting for and dying for imagined peoplehood are therefore not merely abstractions but are intimately concrete matters. The figure of the buried Unknown Soldier may serve as a relevant example. While on the surface he appears as a faceless, anonymous fighter, he becomes, through collective rituals and narratives, a representation of our people, imagined as being of our blood, and the one who sacrificed himself for family, home, nation, and motherland (Anderson 1983: 9). As an imagined hero and symbol of patriotism, he is not merely presented in a dislocated abstract form but is made real in the form of bones buried in an actual grave. Moreover, the veneration of the Unknown Soldier is identical to the respect paid to one's deceased loved ones – through laying down flowers and lighting candles – and serves thus to confirm the ties between family and home and peoplehood in an explicit embodied and emplaced manner. This also speaks to how peoplehood and belonging transcend time and space. While we may discuss the ancient hatred perspective, we should not too quickly dismiss the *longue duré* aspect of affective antagonisms. Such hatred is not merely generated passively through "transgenerational transmission" (Volkan 2006: 17) and is more than dislocated psychological or symbolic sentiments (Horowitz 1985). Hatred is a result of embodied and emplaced experiences intertwined with collective memories of a putative provenance of conflict, about who fired the first shots, about who inflicted the first wounds or usurped and defiled the homeland. Time is collapsed in ways that make past histories of injustice, suffering, and enmity real and present.

  Therefore, privileging the concept of *peoplehood* in relation to religion and ethnicity enables us to move beyond either-or perspectives in relation to conflicts, providing us with a tool that allows a far more integrative understanding. The relevance or potential of the religious and ethnic dimension in times of conflict cannot be taken as a priori givens but needs to be thoroughly investigated. Obviously, in cases where the warring parties adhere to the same religion, the religious dimension could potentially have little bearing. In other cases, the two dimensions might be differently accentuated, and such accentuations will depend on the factors discussed earlier. The emphasis of one or the other dimension by one group could also have reciprocal effects, potentially leading to solidifying the religious or the ethnic dimensions.

Studying the Insurgency

I became interested in the Bale insurgency during my years of living in the region (2000–2003, 2005–2007) and through my research on Islamic reformism (Østebø 2012). Sitting down with and talking to both veterans and victims of the struggle, I was immediately captivated by the many suspenseful combat stories and touched when they showed me scars from bullets and torture. My account of the insurgency is based mainly on the stories of these interlocutors.[31] Above all, this book is a historical ethnography of the insurgency. In addition to oral sources, it is based on – however scant – written sources, mainly in the form of official records such as government reports, military documents, and court files. Making use of different methodological approaches as well as applying a range of theoretical perspectives might make it hard to categorize the study according to a single discipline. This reflects my own positionality as a scholar; while being confidently situated within the study of religion, I have always been inspired by fields like social anthropology, history, and political science.

Christopher Clapham has pointed to several important dilemmas in the study of insurgencies, most prominently how violence and fighting inevitably hamper access to sites and actors (1998: 18). The fact that the Bale insurgency took place more than fifty years ago has made this less of an issue, but it does not mean that investigating the struggle was without challenges. The most obvious one has been the temporal dimension. The history of the insurgency and of Bale itself is largely embodied in the seniors of the region – with hardly anything written down – and currently only a few of the main actors are still alive. For the more than ten years that I worked on the project and revisited the field, I repeatedly experienced that informants had passed away. While

---

[31] All informants' names have been changed and so have the names appearing in interrogation reports. Two exceptions are made in cases of the late General Jagama Kello and *Grazmach* Umar Hussein.

there was a culture of transmission of knowledge of the past, socio-political developments during the Derg regime and in the present have interrupted this practice. A few locally produced books have surfaced in recent years (Hussein Indhessa 2016; Muusaa Haaji Aadam Saaddoo 2014; Yaassiin Mohammad Roobaa and Anbassaa 2014), but most of these lack the critical rigor to provide an accurate picture of the historical developments. We are thus faced with the sad situation that crucial knowledge of Bale's history is being lost.

The temporal dimension has also created a different set of challenges, most notably in the way the present is retroactively projected onto the past. From the 1970s, Oromo ethno-nationalism steadily gained ground in Ethiopia, mainly represented and articulated by the Oromo Liberation Front (OLF). Ethno-nationalism and ethnicity as a point of orientation gained significant ground from 1991, as the Ethiopian People's Revolutionary Democratic Front (EPRDF) initiated policies aimed at recognizing the country's multicultural character and imple-mented ethnic federalism as the political arrangement. This paved the way for politicized and polemic discourses about ethnicity (as well as religion) in general, and about Oromo ethno-nationalism in particular. Current discourses on ethnicity and religion have clearly colored how informants viewed and interpreted the events of the 1960s, extrapolat-ing contemporary categories and notions into their past.

My own personal trajectory has played an important role for the ways I have framed this study theoretically, that is, my emphasis on embodiment and emplacement, family, and home. I left home when I was eighteen and never moved back. I have lived more than half of my adult life abroad – in Ethiopia and the United States – and have during these years moved a lot. As I have gradually realized that I might never move back to my country of origin, sentiments about family, home, and belonging have become more prominent. Thinking about home and remembering the past have made it clear how closely these processes are attached to real persons and real places that were important early in my life, thus shaping my ideas of how our identities are produced by visceral experiences.

To be sure, my account of this past history is not in any way an objective truth, nor do I claim to have reached to any historical core. My own embodied and emplaced reality as a scholar and person entails a particular location that precludes a total, value-free interpretation of this complex phenomenon. I also recognize my own biases, wherein my experiences from my time in Bale have produced affective attachments to the people there, and where my interlocutors' stories of injustices and suffering have generated distinct feelings of sympathy for those who fought and suffered during the struggle. That is also why I am bothered by ethno-nationalist writers' and activists' tendency to politicize, and by implication simplify, the history of the Bale insurgency by intersecting it within an essentialist and unnuanced narrative of the Oromo political struggle. Not only does this belittle honest research, but, more importantly, it also fails to take the accounts of the local actors seriously.

It has taken me nearly ten years to complete this book, and it is a result of painstaking field research. My years living in Bale, my knowledge of language, and my relationships with a wide range of informants who all were keen to participate in the project have been invaluable for the final result. These experiences have also been pivotal for maintaining a much-needed critical attitude, and close interactions between my informants and me have made it possible for us to together interrogate rather than simply reproduce well-rehearsed expressions drawn from current debates. Through careful probing, we were able to peel off layers and to deepen the conversations about the past. The present study is the product of these conversations, and not merely my own account.

Outline

The study starts off in Chapter 2 with an introduction of the topographic diversity of Bale and a discussion of the emplaced nature of Arsi Oromo identity – paying attention to the category of *Islaama* as peoplehood and to the intersection of religion and ethnicity. Chapter 3 provides the historical framework for the study and presents novel insights "from below" on Emperor Menelik's conquest of Bale in the early 1890s and on recurrent acts of resistance occurring throughout the twentieth century. An intrinsic aspect of this local viewpoint is to recognize and soberly investigate the local antecedents of the conflictual relationship between the local population and their new rulers.

The next two chapters are devoted to the insurgency itself. Chapter 4 presents new data and analyzes the immediate causes for the inception of the struggle and examines the different front lines in the lowland areas and the trajectory of the insurgency. Chapter 5 continues with an

analysis of the organizational structure of the insurgency, paying attention to how clan allegiance contributed to a rather fragmented movement. It also discusses the role of what I call "highland activists" –
noncombatants actively supporting the insurgency.

Chapter 6 revisits and interrogates the dominant perspectives that
have interpreted the insurgency as a class struggle. Critically examining
existing sources on the emerging land-tenure system, dispossession of
land, and the introduction of new tax regimes, I demonstrate that land
alienation was not as significant as previously assumed and continue
(Chapter 7) with a discussion of land as more than an economic
commodity. Introducing what I call the "land-clan connection,"
I point to how notions of peoplehood and belonging intersected with
sociopolitical and economic realities and to how the Oromo clan
system had a crucial spatial dimension. A key point here is how changes
in land tenure leading to privatization and commodification of land
severely disrupted the existing land-clan connection and eroded
notions of identity and belonging.

I then shift focus toward analyses of the meaning and role of
religion and ethnicity, taking care to employ an integrated approach
that views these as intimately intertwined and crucial to what
unfolded. Chapters 8 and 9 broaden the scope by situating the
locality of Bale within a larger context, both temporally and spatially. Chapter 8 applies a *longue duré* perspective crucial for understanding the development of a religious fault line in Ethiopia,
focusing on Orthodox Christianity, the notion of Amhara peoplehood, and how "Ethiopian exceptionalism" contributed to lasting
conflictual relations with the region's non-Christians. Chapter 9
analyzes how the Ethiopian state's presence in the southeast spurred
several movements of resistance throughout the twentieth century;
by paying attention to the religious dimension of peoplehood transcending local boundaries, it examines how these diverse movements
drew inspiration from each other and to how the Bale insurgency
intersected with broader developments in the Horn.

Chapter 10 circles back to the particular context of Bale; building on
perspectives provided in the earlier chapters, it examines how an
increasingly complex religious and ethnic landscape generated antagonism and exacerbated hostile relations between the local Arsi Oromo
and the Amhara. Chapter 11 continues the discussion on ethnicity and
religion and revisits the question of class. It also presents new empirical

data on how religious affiliation complicated the insurgency's broader connections – relating this to the Shoa Oromo living in Bale and the linkages between the insurgency and the nascent Oromo ethno-nationalist movement emerging during the 1960s. It demonstrates how the ethnic and religious dimensions of peoplehood generated segmentary and dynamic notions of belonging and identity and analyzes the actors' active negotiations of these dimensions in relation to each other.

2 | Islaama *Peoplehood and Landscapes of Bale*

Any attempt to define or demarcate Bale as a locality must contend with established-yet-contested geographies of power and assumed center-periphery relations. The center-periphery perspective has been a dominant one in Ethiopian historiography, where the prevailing "centrist" narrative has taken historical Christian Ethiopia as the point of departure for understanding the broader region. Fascinated by the historical Christian kingdom – seen as a particular African civilization – scholars have subscribed to the idea of its 3,000-year-old history and have come to highlight historical Ethiopia's stratified sociopolitical structures, the existence of a literary tradition, and a monetary economy. The areas beyond, yet adjacent to, the kingdom were the largely anonymous peripheries, seen as home to the "uncivilized other" who were deprived of agency, commodified as slaves, or relevant only when they encountered the Christian kingdom. These others included the region's Muslims, who in addition to being peripheral also were feared as a menace. Edward Ullendorff has argued along these lines that "Islam [in Ethiopia] can be disposed of very quickly, partly ... because ... [of] the long conflict between Christianity and Islam ... partly on account of its merely secondary importance to an understanding of the essential Abyssinia" (1960: 112–113). Even a writer like John Spencer Trimingham, author of the standard work *Islam in Ethiopia*, claimed, "Islam in the region would have no history without Abyssinia" (1952: 143).

A growing body of literature has since the 1990s made serious attempts to avoid taking Christian Ethiopia as the foundational point of departure. By shifting the focus toward the "peripheries," increasing attention has been given to the "others" – highlighting their cultural features, acknowledging their agency, and thus shedding light on a neglected plurality within Ethiopia. Anthropologists have done much of this work, but as the focus is on the contemporary period, there is still a serious lacuna when it comes to the history of the so-called peripheries. The centrist perspective has, at the same time, proven intransigent in Ethiopian historiography, resulting in a polarized debate between the "centrists" and the "decentrists" both within academia and beyond. The decentrist perspective has, furthermore and somewhat ironically, kept the focus on the center intact. While different from the centrists who laud the center's expansions as state building, the decentrists castigate – often in an "intrinsically ideological and emotionally-bound" manner – its illegitimate marches into the south and violent suppression of the peripheries (Triulzi 2002: 280). The peripheries are then inadvertently mirrored with the center, with a tendency to reduce their inhabitants to agentless victims of the center. Problematic in all this is how the past repeatedly is constructed through a rather selective reading of the historical sources.

While more scholarly work is needed to further develop fruitful and nuanced perspectives on center-periphery relations within Ethiopian studies, John Markakis (2011) is one of the few who has recognized the complexity inherent to the center-periphery perspective and who makes us aware of the multifaceted nature of centers and peripheries and the fluidity of center-periphery relations in the Horn of Africa. Centers and peripheries are thus not always easily identifiable. Factors that constitute one or the other may change over time, and center-periphery relations are also characterized by complex negotiations. Moreover, we need to acknowledge that locations are always based on one's own situatedness, where we as embodied individuals cannot occupy more than a particular space at any given time. As noted by Donna Haraway (1991: 191), being located in this manner means that our particular standpoint is always partial. This is true both for the emplaced actors subject to investigations and for the researchers themselves. Any version of the centrist or the decentrist perspective would consequently entail center-periphery relations that are both subjective and incomplete.

In this chapter – as well as in the study itself – I make an effort to apply an approach that pays due attention to the so-called periphery. Reiterating the viewpoint of religion and ethnicity as more than merely abstractions, and recognizing the importance of emplacement, the chapter sets the geographic, historical, cultural, and religious stage for the insurgency, starting with Bale's landscape, which, in a dialectical fashion, shaped and was shaped by its inhabitants. The chapter moreover investigates the actors in this locality and their role in shaping

their own realities, focusing in particular on the introduction of Islam
and the consolidation of *Islaama* peoplehood. Locating Bale in this way
at the "center," I take the experiences of the people of Bale as emplaced
actors as the point of departure for exploring trans-local interactions in
the larger southeast, and how the existence and constant remolding of
multiple centers and peripheries contributed to shape perceptions of
themselves and others. The latter aspect is of particular importance,
and the key point here is that applying this particular and partial
perspective opens a fruitful discussion of identity, belonging, and peoplehood. The chapter is in this manner a continuation of the
Introduction's theoretical suggestions.

Bale: The Landscapes

Bale became a separate *teklay gezat* (province) in 1960 (see Map 2.1),
covering an area of 128,300 sq. km and subdivided into Genale, Fasil,
Wabe, Dello, and El Kere *awrajas* (sub-provinces) (Henze 2000: 238).[1]
Subsequent regimes implemented additional restructuring, and in 1992,
Bale was defined as a separate zone within the Oromia National
Regional State (hereafter, Oromia), with Robe as the zonal capital.
The former El Kere *awraja* was then separated from Bale – and renamed
Afder Zone and incorporated into the Somali National Regional State.
The area of Bale Zone was by then ca. 66,400 sq. km – and with a
population of more than 1.4 million people (2007). Bale underwent a
major reorganization in 2006 with the redrawing of both the zone and
the *worreda* (district) boundaries.[2]

   Having lived in Bale for nearly six years, I have a particular affinity
for the region and a deep attraction to the beauty of its landscapes. This
has been true for visitors throughout history – for example, Arnold
Hodson, traveling through Bale in 1916, used words like "scenery of

---

[1]   An *awraja* was moreover subdivided into *worreda* and *meketel worreda*. The
   area of Bale according to the 1969 Land Tenure Survey was 124,600 sq. km, but
   subsequent studies adjusted this number to 128,300 sq. km (Central Statistical
   Office 1980).
[2]   The study follows the pre-2006 *worredas*: Kokosa, Nansebu, Dodola, Adaba,
   Sinana-Dinshu, Goba, Agarfa, Gasera-Gololcha, Beltu, Sewena, Raytu, Ginir,
   Goro, Guradhamole, Menna-Angetu, Medda Welabu, and Berbere. In 2006,
   Kokosa, Nansebu, Dodola, and Adaba were transferred to the newly established
   West Arsi Zone, and areas transferred from the Somali region formed two new
   worredas, Dawe Kachen and Dawe Serer.

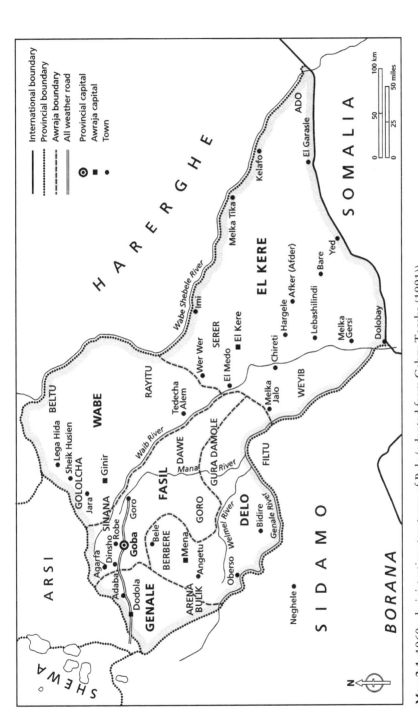

Map 2.1 1960 administrative structures of Bale (adapted from Gebru Tareke (1991))

impressive beauty" and "feeling of awe" (1927: 91). Arthur Donaldson Smith, visiting in 1894, found himself "astonished at the beauty of scenery" (1897: 51) and was particularly struck by beauty of the Sof Umar caves: "[W]ords could not express our astonishment. Our Somali boys, usually absolutely indifferent to beautiful scenery, could curb their enthusiasm no longer, but with one accord broke into prayer, so thoroughly were they convinced that what they beheld was the work of God" (Donaldson Smith 1897: 87).

Bale is marked by a highly varied topography, ranging from arid lowlands to fertile highland plateaus, vast forests, and massive mountain ranges. The region consists of different climatic zones, making it home to a varied flora and fauna with several endemic species. This also means that the landscapes are constantly changing with new colors added according to the seasons and as the sun moves across the spectacular canvas. Bale's northern boundary follows the Wabe Shebelle River, which in some areas has carved out deep canyons, constituting natural barriers for contact with the neighboring northern areas. The canyon reminds one of the Grand Canyon in the United States, with red-brown stone shifting color in the sunlight. The Genale River, part of the southern boundary, separates Bale from the southern Guji and Borana areas. Other major rivers are the Weib, Welmel, and Dumal, where the flow of the Weib has produced a deep and rugged gorge.

The Arsi Oromo have commonly divided Bale into four parts, a division that to a large extent follows the region's topography. Gedeb is Bale's main western highland plateau, with an average altitude of ca. 2,500 meters above sea level (m.a.s.l.). It is located in the northwestern part as a natural extension of Arsi's wide plains yet is marked off by the Wabe Shebelle River as its natural border. Gedeb consists of the northern part of the former Genale *awraja*, today's Dodola and Adaba *worredas*. To the south, the plateau rises into large forested hillsides, which gradually extend into a large mountain massif. The plateau is mainly made up of open fields, producing both wheat and barley. The main road that connects Bale with the rest of Ethiopia (constructed in 1962) crosses Gebeb going east to the town of Goba. The second part, called Alaba, is found in the southern parts of the former Genale *awraja* and covers Kokosa and Nansebu *worredas*. Alaba consists of open plains, hills, and forests. It is the greenest and lushest part of Bale's highlands and ideal for both agriculture and grazing. In fact, it is the only highland area where substantial cattle rearing is still practiced.

Due to influence from the neighboring Sidama, *enset* (false banana) constitutes a major crop. The third part is the area locals refer to as Bale. It is distinctively marked off by a rugged mountain chain in the west, which also is the natural barrier between Bale and Gedeb, and by the deep Wabe Shebelle canyon in the north. It is the region's largest highland plateau, with an elevation of around 2,500 m.a.s.l., and spans Agarfa, Sinana-Dinshu, Goba, as well as parts of Goro, Gasera, Gololcha, and Ginir *worredas* (see Figure 2.1). Robe, the zonal capital, is found in the western part, while Goba, the former provincial capital is located ca. 20 km to the south of Robe. Similar to Gebeb, the plateau consists of wide agricultural fields, and a substantial area of land belongs to three major state-farms established in the 1980s. I have a personal attachment to this area, and the memory of riding between these wheat fields on horseback with the setting sun warming my back and with the soft sound of the wheat rustling in the wind has stuck with me. Two main roads link Robe with the rest of the highlands, as well as with the eastern lowlands, whereas a road going south from Goba across the Sanate plateau connects to the southern lowlands.

Figure 2.1 The central highlands of Bale

While Alaba, Gedeb, and the eastern highlands are the most fertile parts of Bale, cultivated land is only about 15 percent of all land in the area. This might seem insignificant, but it is important to note that the actual size of these areas count for more than 17,000 sq. km (Bale Zone Department of Finance & Economic Development 2004: 27). People in the highlands still keep cattle and goats, but limited spaces for grazing have reduced the size of the flocks. The total amount of grassland is currently listed as no more than 7 percent – or ca. 4,400 sq. km – of all land in Bale (Bale Zone Department of Finance & Economic Development 2004: 27). This corresponds poorly with the fact that 69 percent of the region is lowland areas and reflects a certain agriculturalist bias when defining grasslands.

The distinctive mountain range going north-south and separating Gedeb from the eastern highlands consists of several impressive rugged mountain ridges, with Sebseba Washa as the highest peak (see Figure 2.2). The skyline is marked with additional mountain ranges one behind another, shifting color by the moving sun, and with steep slopes colored bright green by the rainy season. The elevation here ranges

Figure 2.2 Bale Mountains

from ca. 3,000 to 4,000 m.a.s.l., and the cold temperature makes the highest areas barren, with trees. These areas are unsuitable for agriculture, and the few people living there depend on a pastoralist economy. The elevation drops gradually toward the east around Dinshu town, where the landscape is largely covered with alpine forest. Dinshu also hosts the headquarters of the Bale National Park, a popular tourist destination.

The mountain range is part of a huge massif that stretches south and widens out to an even larger area. It circumscribes the eastern highlands to the south, where elevation gradually rises and forms the Sanate plateau, with an altitude of more than 4,000 m.a.s.l. (see Figure 2.3).[3] The increase in elevation corresponds to the decrease in vegetation, and the Giant lobelia is the only type of tree before the plateau becomes completely barren. The plateau itself is rather flat, intersected by occasional roundly formed peaks – with Tulu Dimtu (4,377 m.a.s.l.), Ethiopia's second-highest mountain peak, as the most conspicuous (Bale Zone Department of

Figure 2.3 The Sanate plateau

[3] Mountains cover a total of ca 9 percent of Bale.

Finance & Economic Development 2004). In contrast to the northern edge, the drop in elevation to the south is rather dramatic. There, the plateau opens to magnificent scenery, and the road that crosses the plateau drops and winds itself through the rugged terrain, bringing the traveler down from an altitude of 4,000 m.a.s.l. to 1,500 m.a.s.l. in less than thirty minutes, and into the tropical Harenna Forest.

The last part of Bale is collectively referred to as the *gammojii* – the lowlands – and varies in altitude from ca. 300 m.a.s.l. in the most eastern parts to 1,500 m.a.s.l. (see Figure 2.4). The lowlands can be divided into the eastern and southern lowlands; the eastern lowlands composed of the former Wabe *awraja* and the eastern parts of Fasil *awraja* and includes Beltu, Sawena, Raytu, Goro, and Guradhamole *worredas*. These areas consist of vast arid bushlands, with thorny shrubs, short acacia trees, and a characteristic red-colored soil. Rain is limited and erratic, averaging between 200 mm in the extreme east, to 800 mm closer to the highlands. Most of the trees lose their leaves during the long dry season – making the landscape seem even more inhospitable and desolate. I find, however, a distinct beauty in the lowlands. At the time I lived in Raytu, there was no electricity (and

Figure 2.4 The lowlands of Bale

hardly any water); I remember evenings sitting under a starlit sky in a lowland village, where a mild breeze cooled off the day's dry and dusty heat, where streaks of lights from kerosene lamps emerged from cracks in the doors of the neighboring houses, and where the sound of crickets mixed with the village's muted voices. My informants expressed similar emotional attachments toward what they call home:

I have only spent 5 days in Robe, and I have never been to Addis Ababa. This is the best place. There are no wild animals here at night, and even when it rains, it is never too cold. When it rains, the grass will grow immediately. People from outside say that Raytu is only beautiful three months a year, but we who are from this area, we say it is beautiful all year round.[4]

Moving south, the topography becomes gradually more rugged, and the areas south of Raytu *worreda* are patterned by bluffs and low mountain ridges – creating deep and extensive valleys zigzagging the landscape. Arid bushlands dominate the most southern Medda Welabu *worreda,* which nevertheless remains hillier than the eastern lowlands. Parts of Dello *worreda*, north of Medda Welabu, have slightly higher elevation; as this part receives a higher amount of rain, it is greener and more fertile. The most impressive feature of the southern lowlands, however, is the vast Harenna rainforest, covering around 3,000 sq. km. It begins at the southern slopes of the Sanate plateau, where alpine trees dominate, and stretches into areas with an approximate altitude of 1,500 m.a.s.l. and with a humid climate. Seen from above, the thick canopy covering rolling hills forms a seemingly endless green ocean. Viewed from below, tall and massive trees and dense vegetation make the forest appear largely impenetrable. Roads are few, and only recently constructed, making access only possible by foot or horseback – along numerous narrow paths crisscrossing the forest. A particularly important characteristic of the Harenna Forest is its wild coffee. Reaching a height of ca 2–3 meters, the coffee trees constitute a second layer beneath the main canopy, covering a significant portion of the forest. Coffee has been, and still is, the major source of income for those within and surrounding the forest.

Few places elucidate the contrast between the highlands and the lowlands better than the area of Ginir town, and although I have traveled through the area hundreds of times, I am still struck by the

---

[4] Interview, Adam Yunus, Raytu, June 10, 2017.

dramatic shift in landscape. The town itself is located at the eastern edge of the highlands – which is cut off by a cliff that suddenly drops straight down more than 100 m. Standing on the edge facing east, one has an impressive view of endless lowland plains that stretch into the horizon, eventually reaching the Indian Ocean. The only areas punctuating this vastness are the flat-topped mountains of Sewena *worreda* and the lonely ridge of the Galbi Mountains in the eastern part of Raytu *worreda*.

This marked topographical distinction between highlands and lowlands brings associations to the oft-mentioned Ethiopian highland-lowland dichotomy, which, with its topographical and climatic distinctions, has constituted the basis for marked political, economic, cultural, and religious differences. Topography here coincides with an agriculturalist vs pastoralist economy and Christian vs Muslim populations that also historically determined the extent of state presence. Although the lowlands were considered the periphery, it is important, as noted, to remind ourselves that similar to the multifaceted nature of peripheries, the highland-lowland dichotomy is more complex. Markakis (2011: 12f.) points to the existence of peripheries within the periphery and operates with the terms *highland periphery*, which includes the highland areas of the south, and the *lowland periphery*, composed of the vast arid lowlands that surround the highland areas. While Ethiopia's macro-level highland-lowland dichotomy elucidated and underscored political, economic, ethnic, and religious differences, one needs to consider the different local particularities.

In Bale, the distinct highland-lowland topography has not produced any pronounced dichotomy, but rather a situation characterized by similarity and interaction. First of all, both highlanders and lowlanders share the same identity as Arsi Oromo and Muslims. Moreover, while variances in lifestyles produced by the distinct topographical and climatic zones obviously existed, both highlanders and lowlanders historically shared the same pastoralist economy. This is often overlooked in studies on history of land and land tenure in Bale, where it has been assumed that the highlanders were engaged in agriculture while the lowlanders were pastoralists. This misconception is partly created by the fact that the highland plateaus, in contrast to the arid lowlands, are highly conducive for agriculture. Even if some Oromo adapted agriculture in the course of their migrations during the sixteenth century, pastoralism remained the dominant mode of production until rather

recently. It is true that the Arsi Oromo in the highlands of Bale practiced some agriculture but cultivation was limited to a subsistence level,
concentrated in areas close to the homestead, and carried out mainly by
women.[5] The highland Arsi Oromo could therefore be characterized as
agro-pastoralists. They were sedentary, following a transhumance
form of pastoralism, locally referred to as *godaantuu*, and the abundance of fertile grazing land enabled them to keep their herds in close
vicinity to their homesteads.

Pastoralism dominated the highlands in both Arsi and Bale until the
latter part of the twentieth century, and European travelers recorded its
prevalence. Wilfred Thesiger visiting Arsi in the 1930s narrated that the
"Arussi [Arsi] are in a few cases doing a little cultivating" (2002: 48).
Arnold Hodson, who traveled through Bale in 1916, said that there was
"little cultivation but plenty of [live]stock" in the highlands and except
for some cactuses the highland plains were "bare of trees" (1927: 91f.).
While the transition to agriculture accelerated in the postwar period –
something I will discuss in subsequent chapters – reports as late as 1972
pointed out that "[n]omades and seminomades with cattle are dominant features" and that "[v]ast areas are uncultivated" (Nydal 1972:
1). The arid landscapes of the lowlands and the scarcity of rainfall
meant that migration patterns were more extensive, forcing people to
cross larger distances in search of grazing land. While some livestock
were constantly kept on the move, the lowlanders, similar to the highlanders, maintained permanent dwellings and practiced a transhumance form of pastoralism. The dominant pattern was for the whole
family to move in search of pasture and water during the dry season
and then return to their homes when the rain started. Some changes
toward agriculture did occur in the lowlands, but to a lesser extent and
much later. In the eastern Raytu *worreda*, for example, crop production was uncommon until the last few decades of the twentieth century
(T. Abate et al. 2010: 204).[6] Today ca 35 percent of the population in
Raytu *worreda* is still classified as pastoralist. Droughts, overgrazing,
and encroachment of rangelands over several decades, however, have
seriously impacted the pastoralist lifestyle, causing more and more to
take up cultivation (Teshome Abate et al. 2006).

---

[5] Martial de Salviac claims that each household's area for cultivation was limited
to the "length of a stone or spear throw" (2005 [1901]: 223). The absence of ox-
driven plows further limited the scale of cultivation.
[6] Interview, Adam Yunus, Raytu, June 10, 2017.

The Arsi Oromo

The question about the exact location of the origin of the Oromo has generated much debate, with some arguing that their homeland was in the southern areas of Ethiopia, in present-day Guji (Braukämper 1980b; Lewis 1966a), and other claiming they originated in the Bale highlands (Haberland 1963; Mohammed Hassan 1994).[7] The debate has in recent years taken a new turn with new voices arguing for a much earlier Oromo presence in the central highlands of Ethiopia.[8] This question of an earlier presence in the central highland is intriguing, but far more research is needed before it can be confirmed. In any case, the sixteenth century saw massive population movement – labeled either the Oromo migrations or the Oromo expansions – when the main Oromo branches of the Tulama and the Macca started to move north. While most moved along the eastern escarpment of the Rift Valley, a branch of the Oromo crossed the Genale River entering the southern areas of Bale. After establishing themselves in southern Bale, they subsequently moved further north and overran the Islamic principalities of Bale, Hadiya, Sharka, and Dawaro by the middle of the sixteenth century (Bahrey et al. 1993: 61; Mohammed Hassan 1994: 23).

The Oromo expansion, together with other factors caused major demographic reconfigurations across the southeast areas, but an important development was how the Oromo, as new settlers, entered "into a cultural and racial symbiosis" with the existing population which they gradually assimilated (Braukämper 2002: 85).[9] This process of assimilation was common for the expanding Oromo and is referred to as *mogaasuu* – it was a form of adoption through which others could be fully accepted as Oromo.[10] The Arsi Oromo considered themselves the descendants of Arsee, or Arsi, who had two sons: Mendo and Siko. As the Arsi entered Bale, Mendo settled first on the east side of the Weib River (which is

---

[7] Earlier views claimed that the Oromo inhabited most of the eastern Ethiopian lowlands, including the present-day Somali Region, before being pushed southward by the expanding Somali (Cerulli 1957–64; Huntingford 1975; Paulitschke 1889).

[8] Mohammed Hassan is one of the proponents of such claims; in his thorough study of fourteenth- to eighteenth-century Ethiopian history (2015), he critically examines existing sources and relies heavily on linguistic data. He does, however, treat the data rather randomly, making his arguments unconvincing.

[9] For more details on the demographic shifts, see Merid Wolde Aregay (1974b).

[10] For more details on *mogaasuu*, see Blackhurst (1996).

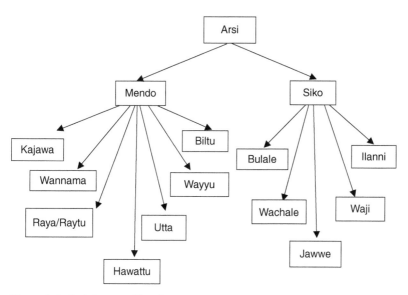

Figure 2.5 Arsi Oromo Clan System

today's Bale), while Siko traveled west and settled in today's Arsi region. Emerging as the two moieties of the Arsi Oromo, Mendo had seven sons, each becoming major clans in Bale, while Siko had five, producing similar main clans (Figure 2.5).

This formed the basis for a complex clan system consisting of numerous clans (*gossa*), in turn divided into sub-clans or lineages (*balbalaa*) with origins that genealogically could be traced back five to seven generations. The smallest kinship unit was the *aanaa*, which comprised several *warra*, or extended families. Belonging to a clan and a sub-clan was, as I will return to, pivotal for Arsi Oromo identity and social structures. The relevance of clans and sub-clans in relation to ethnicity as a category in the Horn has been discussed by, among others, Günther Schlee (1985, 1989) and David Turton (1994). Schlee claims that clans are far older than assumed ethnic groups, and thus more "real"; whereas Turton, in the case of the Mursi, argues that clan identity constitutes the "ethnic," while the overall Mursi category refers to a political identity (1994: 19). While I agree with Schlee that "[e]thnic categories may become straightjackets for our thought ... which blind us to the other categories by which people identify themselves" (1985: 39), I believe it is misleading to think of this as an either-or. Instead, this demonstrates the relevance of how the flexible nature of peoplehood allows us to imagine that categories – ranging from the ethnic to specific lineages – constitute different levels that offer parallel points of orientation for belonging and which, moreover, acknowledge their situational importance. As a whole, the Oromo clan structure provided the basis for a segmentary form of belonging: one was Arsi Oromo, one belonged to one of either moiety, to a clan, to a sub-clan, and to the family within the sub-clan.

In contrast to state formations found among the Oromo in the southwest, political structures among the Arsi Oromo had a decentered, loose, and rather fragmented character. The age-class system known as the *gadaa* provided some overarching structures, but the Arsi Oromo variant of the *gadaa* system was relatively regionalized. Contemporary accounts of the *gadaa* system tend to essentialize and generalize it in ways that fail to consider its adaptability across time and space and often ignore that it became increasingly heterogeneous as the Oromo expanded into new geographical areas. We know very little about the *gadaa* system in Bale prior to the nineteenth century, and this account should not be read as conclusive. It seems clear, however, that the *gadaa* system in Bale had developed some particular local features by the beginning of the seventeenth century. At the outset, it was constituted by five *gadaa* periods over a cyclical period of forty years, and where generation groups organized in age classes (*luba*) succeeded each other every eight years in assuming military, economic, political, and ritual responsibilities.[11] It was, however, organized such that a certain number of clans were clustered in what can be categorized as confederacies, called *dhadacha,* and which had authority over their own defined territories (Haberland 1963: 784; Hassan 2015: 150; Ketema Meskela 2001: 15; Mohammed Hassan 2015: 150).[12] According to Hussein Indhessa, there were eleven confederacies south of the Wabe River in what today is Bale, and nine confederacies in

---

[11] The five periods are the *birmajii, bultuma, waraata, roballee,* and *baharaa.* Such a system is not particular only to the Oromo. Schlee (1989), by summarizing the findings of Jensen (1942), Haberland (1963), and others, has argued that systems similar to the *gadaa* system may have been common to various Cushitic-speaking groups in the southeastern parts (and northern parts of Kenya) of Ethiopia.

[12] A similar decentralized *gadaa* system with four-year intervals was found among the Oromo farther north in Ethiopia. See De Salviac (1901) for more details.

today's Arsi region (2016: 39). Each confederacy was governed by the *abbaa boku* (the father of the scepter), and with the *bahira* as the deputy.[13] In addition, a *gadaa* council (*saddeeta*; the eight) existed within each of these confederations, while a similar council (*shannoo*; the five) existed at the clan level. In the central highlands, the *abbaa boku* belonged to a certain clan within the respective confederation; at one point in time, the office of the *abbaa boku* became a hereditary position belonging to a lineage within that clan.[14] Important sites for the *gadaa* system were the so-called Oda places (*oda*; sycamore trees) where representatives for the different clans met. While there were different Odas in Bale, such as the Oda Welabu in Medda Welabu and Oda Giro in El Kere, the main one was the Oda Roba, in the lowlands east of Ginir.[15] Established in the early seventeenth century,[16] the Arsi Oromo assembled there every fourth year to issue new regulations (*murtii*) for the clans, to solve pending conflicts, and to pass verdicts on major crimes. It is not clear how far the jurisdiction of the Oda Roba meeting reached, but we can assume that it covered the eastern lowlands and parts of the central highlands of Bale.[17]

While the *gadaa* system has been presented as inherently democratic, securing peaceful relations between clans, and while the maintenance of *nagaa* (the Oromo concept of peace) was a crucial aspect of the

---

[13] The *bahira* was in some places referred to as the *hoka* or the *hatti* (Hussein Badhaasoo 2017: 151).

[14] Interviews, Hajji Hussein Awol, Robe, June 8, 2005; Temam Muhammed, Dodola, October 22, 2002; Siraj Muhammed-Amin, Robe, April 2, 2006. One informant gave information about the hereditary rule that could be traced back to the sixteenth century (Sheikh Rashid Hassan, Ginir, December 16, 2002).

[15] Interview, Muhammad Tahir, Raytu, June 10, 2018. By comparison, the Tulama branch made its assembly at Oda Nabi, about 30 km south of Addis Ababa (Ibsa Gutamaa 1997), and the Macha subsequently formed its own assembly in the west, at Oda Bisil. See Knutsson (1967: 179); Mohammed Hassan (1994: 18, 42).

[16] One key figure in the establishment of the Oda Roba site was Ilu Dhabu of the Raytu clan. He lived six generations before Dhadhi Terre (Raytu) who died in the early twentieth century, which means that Ilu Dhabu was born ca. 1600 (interviews, Sheikh Rashid Hassan, Ginir, December 16, 2002; Nuri Muhammed, Raytu, July 13, 2005).

[17] Hussein Indhessa claims that all of the Arsi Oromo confederacies sent representatives to Oda Roba (2016 : 39). See Hylander for a brief description of the rituals (1936: 264).

system, one should be careful not to overstate the Arsi Oromo culture as one of only harmony and unanimity. What is clear is that there existed a distinct warrior culture among the Oromo in general, wherein war was something desirable, and where a man's honor was determined by how many persons or wild animals he had killed (Bartels 1983: 81, 85; Salviac 2005 [1901]: 309). Warfare was insti- tutionalized through the *gadaa* system, which also regulated the use of violence. A man would be considered an apprentice warrior during the third of his *gadaa* age-set, and a full-fledged fighter by the time he reached his fourth age-set. A particularly important occasion for waging war was at the time of the *butta* ceremony – toward the end of an age-set. This usually had the form of large-scale military cam- paigns and was important as a factor for the sixteenth-century Oromo expansions. Gradually, however, the ceremony changed character to cattle raids conducted against both non-Oromo and Oromo enemies (Baxter 1977; Asmaron Legesse 1973: 74).[18] Cattle raids on tradi- tional enemies usually spurred reprisals from the other, escalating into spirals of violence. The main purpose of such raids was not necessarily to loot cattle but rather to kill for honor and collect trophies. Cattle were merely a bonus. Such honor was materialized in severing and displaying the genitals of the victim in a rather maca- bre manner: "the Boran *rabba* used to go on war expeditions which aimed ... primarily at obtaining the severed genitals of slain enemies (of any size from an embryo or baby to an old man) as trophies" (Schlee and Abdullahi A. Shongolo 1995: 10; cf. Hylander 1936: 139); among the Borana, the one with no such trophy "was not welcomed as a son-in-law" (Baxter 1977: 69, 82). The severing of genitals was prohibited, however, during infighting among the Oromo clans and branches, based on the notion that "all the Oromo were of the same blood, so you couldn't cut them."[19] The Guji and the Arsi Oromo, for example, who were traditional enemies, would never mutilate each others' bodies.

The *gadaa* system also served to regulate inter-clan conflicts, which ideally would be ended by the payment of *guma* (blood money). The possibility of refusing such payment, however, always existed, which

---

[18] Constant frictions existed between the Arsi, Guji, and Borana Oromo, and the Arsi Oromo looked at the Guji as their traditional enemies.
[19] Interview, Umar Qassim, Robe, June 14, 2018.

then would mean the continuation of violence.[20] Inter-clan violence often had the form of vendettas – caused by various reasons – which tended to produce continuous fighting among clans. It was therefore said, "when Oromo of different tribes meet each other, their fingers tremble from ancient quarrels, and the spears, which they always carry, treacherously lie in wait or daringly cross each other" (Salviac 2005 [1901]: 333). Warring among the Arsi Oromo followed certain regulations, and the main rule was that inter-clan fighting was prohibited if the involved clans traced their genealogy to the same son of the Mendo or Siko moiety. For example, both the Walashe and the Oborso clans belonged to the Mendo moiety, but because they stemmed from different sons, they frequently fought and looted each other.[21] My own experience of such inter-clan conflict from more recent history may be relevant: as I was drinking tea at a friend's rural pharmacy/clinic in Kokosa *worreda,* a young boy who had been stabbed was brought in. While my friend was attending to his wounds, a man came running in, forcing his way to the patient. He exchanged a few words with the boy, before running out and disappearing. He did not display much interest in the boy's well-being, and the only thing he was after was the name of the perpetrator and his clan. My friend sighed and said: "now he is running back to his clan to mobilize them to take revenge upon the other clan." How far this conflict escalated is unknown.

Islam and the Arsi Oromo as *Islaama*

Islam had already established its foothold along the Somali coast in the eighth century, with the Zeila and Berbera ports as the main bridgeheads; from there, it moved gradually into the hinterlands.[22] Islamization was from the beginning associated with trade and nomadism, as has been noted across Africa (Levtzion 1979), and Islam's expansion was enabled by Muslim control over the trade routes and by the movements of the Afar and the Somali into the interior between

---

[20] Interview, Temam Muhammad, Dodola, October 19, 2002.
[21] Interview, Umar Qassim, Robe, June 14, 2018.
[22] Islam's first contact with the Horn of Africa in AD 615 was an isolated episode when the Prophet Muhammad sent some of first believers to the Christian Kingdom of Axum in search of protection from the persecuting Quraysh clan in Mecca.

the tenth and thirteenth centuries (Braukämper 2002: 37; Taddesse Tamrat 1977: 138; Trimingham 1952: 209). A significant aspect of the history of Islam in the southeast was the formation of several Islamic sultanates, emerging from the ninth century – with the sultanate of Shoa as the first, later succeeded by the Ifat sultanate in 1285 and by Adal as the leading Muslim principality in the latter part of the four-teenth century. Adal later became crucial in the ensuing conflicts with the Christian kingdom in the north and was the point of departure for Ahmed ibn Ibrahim al-Ghazi's (nicknamed Ahmed Gragn) famous sixteenth-century jihad. There were a number of other sultanates, including Dawaro, Arababni, Hadiya, Shirka, Dara, and Bale – all of which belonged to the so-called confederation of Zeila. Very little is known about the Bale Sultanate, which is first mentioned during the Zagwe period. It bordered the sultanates of Dawaro and Shirka in the north, Hadiya in the west, and Adal in the east (Braukämper 2002: 76), and its core areas were assumingly located around the Wabe Shebelle River. Part of it was said to be north of the river, but with the largest proportion located to the south.[23] During medieval times, Bale was known for its production of cotton, while salt, brought from El Kere, was an important trading item (Pankhurst 1997: 71).

Although the Oromo expansion into Bale during the sixteenth cen-tury caused a general decline of Islam, it is likely that a small minority of the early Muslim population remained present. The relationship between these Muslims and the Oromo seems initially to have been rather antagonistic, but the former's continued presence proved deci-sive for the gradual Islamization of the Oromo. This process started in the late eighteenth century and was directly and indirectly linked to developments within the broader Muslim world and to changes taking place within the Horn. The process was also embodied in people who through their movements carved out new Islamized space. I have pre-viously referred to the expansion of Islam as a dialectical process of Islamization of the Oromo and the Oromization of Islam (Østebø 2012: 83), and the key point is that these dialectics discursively merged Islam with a preexisting religious universe.

---

[23] Merid Wolde Aregay (1974a: 617) claims that the Bale Sultanate reached south to the Genale Doria River and westward to the lakes of Abaya and Chamo. Others have been even more specific, situating it in the former Fasil *awraja* and the northeastern part of the Wabe *awraja* (Aman Seifedin 1987: 7).

The Islamization of the Oromo in southeastern Ethiopia started with Muslim Somalis pushing westward on the Harar plateau (Hararge) in the eighteenth and nineteenth centuries. The encounter with the existing Oromo population led to a process of assimilation that produced a bilingual Muslim group known as the *Warra Qallu*, a group that would become instrumental in further expanding Islam in Hararge and beyond. Islamization was also accelerated by *Emir* Abd al-Shakur's (1783–1794) efforts in converting the Oromo surrounding Harar and, later, by the proselytizing campaigns of the Egyptians (occupying Harar from 1875 to 1885). The Hararge region thus became an important bridgehead for the Islamization of Arsi and Bale, with religious teachers going "west of Harar and beyond Wabe Shebelle" (Caulk 1973: 11), and traders who traversed established trade routes brought the new religion into these areas (Waldron 1984: 32; Ahmed Zekaria 1997).

Of particular importance is how these developments contributed to the formation of a distinct peoplehood, expressed in the word *Islaama*. It was the self-referential term used by the Arsi Oromo subsequent to their adoption of Islam, obviously pointing to the religious dimension and to an identity that transcended local boundaries. One should be careful, however, not to overemphasize, or separate, the religious dimension; I believe that Eike Haberland goes too far when he claims that the Arsi Oromo did not "regard themselves as Arussi or Oromo ... but as members of the Muslim world" (Haberland 1963: 783). There was no either-or; it was not about being either Arsi or Muslim, and neither did they objectify Islam as something separate, thinking about it as their "religion" distinct from their Arsiness. Surely, there was an awareness of the Arabic *din,* but this was a term largely restricted to the *ulama,* referring to the tenets of Islam. This speaks to Talal Asad's suggestion that the very notion of "religion," as something autonomous and individual, or that can be contained, is an inherently Western and modern construct (1993: 1f.).

It is true that the Arsi Oromo saw themselves as distinct from other Oromo groups, like the neighboring Guji and Borana – with whom they often had an antagonistic relationship – but there existed, at the same time, an awareness of a sort of commonality with these groups.[24]

---

[24] For more details on the Arsi Oromo's relations to other Oromo groups, see Knutsson (1969).

However, the Arsi Oromo never referred to themselves as Oromo; in fact, when the word *Oromo* entered the official vocabulary during the Derg regime in the 1980s, there were those who refused to be called Oromo.[25] One of my informants narrated this as follows: "Once I asked my wife's father about this during the time of Haile Selassie. He said: we are not Oromo, we are Muslims. I tried to convince him, but I couldn't. He said; Oromo means pagan."[26] The main issue was, in other words, religion. Conscious of their Muslim identity, they understood an Oromo as someone who followed the Oromo religion – a polytheist and a "pagan" commonly referred to as an *awaama*.[27] This term was clearly derogatory, referring to a people outside of Islam who were eating meat slaughtered in a non-Islamic way.

Islaama was the notion of peoplehood and represented belonging and identity and being part of a collective. Being *Islaama* was consequently inheritable, something one was born into. It was embodied in the individual's family, sub-clan, and clan relations and emplaced in the local landscapes. It was the framework where the child, as poetically described by Salviac, is "gradually imbued with the spirit of the family and his tribe. He lives, lulled by the wind that blows from the side of the paternal hearth and from the national forum" (2005 [1901]: 275):

For us Islam is more a culture than something we believe in. My grandfather was Muslim so my father became Muslim. He was a Muslim so I became Muslim, and this I am passing on to my children. So you see, it is something we inherited, something we are born to be and grown up with. ... That is why it is difficult to leave the religion.[28]

Islaama as peoplehood points to the simultaneity of religion and ethnicity and reveals how the ethnic and religious dimensions reinforce each other as foundational for peoplehood. Being a Muslim meant being an Arsi Oromo, which in turn meant being Muslim. The word *Islaama* existed alongside the word Arsi, which constituted the frame for which

---

[25] Interview, Hajji Hussein Awol, Robe, July 2, 2011.
[26] Interview, Obse Ibrahim, Robe, October 9, 2005.
[27] The Muslim Arsi Oromo did not use the word or *Waqeffata*, which is a more recent construct. It is reasonable to argue that the term originates from the Arabic *al-awwam* (sing. *amm*), meaning ignorant or uneducated people.
[28] Interview, Obse Ibrahim, Robe, September 1, 2002.

clan and sub-clan one belonged to, in turn providing the basis notions for provenance.

Born *Islaama* also meant being raised within a collective, wherein socialization took the form of sensory visceral experiences of ideas embedded in practice and experienced through everyday life (Comaroff 1985). While socialization involves the explicit and conscious transmission of ideas, values, and rules, in most cases it "has no need of words" (Bourdieu 1977: 188). Socialization within the Arsi Oromo family was pivotal as laying the ground for being Muslim and Arsi, a collective that was both religious and ethnic: "I make my children pray, I make them study the Qur'an – because I want them to be accepted in their community. I want them to keep their identity as Bale Oromo, as Muslim."[29] My informants often underscored the importance of the family for maintaining one's religious identity, and the reciprocal importance of religion for securing commonality within the family:

[T]he family is important. It is the base. If there is no transfer of Islam in the family, the child may get exposed to other [religions], he may end up a Christian. At school the child learns ABC, at home he learns the Arabic alphabet. My father used to teach me to do *salat*; I was watching him and copying his washing and standing beside him when doing *salat*. When we eat, we learn how to say *bismillah*, and to eat with the right hand.[30]

Socialization also entailed bringing the child to the mosque or, as we will see later, the shrine – places that often (yet not always) mirrored the religious life of home. It also entailed the process of being integrated into a larger religious community, as well as the production of awareness of belongingness to something larger, an imagined peoplehood. Key to this, in other words, was the embodied and emplaced experiences of habitation and movement, serving as the basis for connecting parts to a whole, and thus generating identity and belonging that were both near and that collapsed time and space.

The religious dimension transcended, as I will return to in a later chapter, this immediacy, allowing for inclusive orientations toward other Muslim groups and an imagination that these all shared the same ultimate belonging. *Islaama* as a self-referential term did not mean that the Arsi Oromo viewed themselves as the only Muslims.

29 Interview, Obse Ibrahim, Robe, March 31, 2006.
30 Interview, Abdi Muktar, Robe, August 11, 2005.

There was obviously an awareness of other Muslim groups – yet these, at the same time, were identified by ethnic labels: Harari, Somali, or Gurage.[31] Neither does it mean that the religious dimension was irrelevant in the construction and maintenance of boundaries.

Landscapes of Shrines

Being *Islaama* had, moreover, a spatial dimension being intrinsically tied to active dwelling. Such active dwelling was, moreover, attached to particular landscapes of shrines – in turn related to how Islam spread in Bale. The expansion of Islam in Bale was, as noted, indirectly informed by broader developments in the Muslim world during the eighteenth and nineteenth centuries – usually characterized as a Sufi revival (Martin 1976: 152f.). While this led to the establishment of Sufi *turuq* (Arabic, sg. *tariqa;* Sufi orders) in areas such as Somalia and Eritrea, the impacts of Sufism among the Oromo never resulted in the establishment of any *turuq* or the development of an explicit Sufi identity. Rather, Islam was embodied in so-called saints (Arabic, *awliah,* sg. *wali*) and materialized spatially by shrines dotting the landscape – erected over the tombs of these saints. Such shrines, which in themselves were called *awliah,* were often located at pre-Islamic religious sites and represented thus both continuity and change.

Particularly important for Bale was Sheikh Hussein ibn Ibrahim al-Malkay, or simply Sheikh Hussein, who is said to have arrived in Bale at the end of the twelfth century (Braukämper 2002: 130f.). He played an important role in the spread of Islam, and his burial place was soon made into a shrine still located in the northern part of present-day Bale (see Figure 2.6). Little is known about the role of the shrine in the early Islamic history in Bale, but as the Oromo arrived, the shrine was quickly transformed into a sacred Oromo site, alternatively referred to as Anajina, Karra Milki (the gate of success) or Karra Karayu (the gate of the Karayu (clan)). It was a place for rest and thanksgiving after crossing the treacherous Wabe Shebelle canyon dividing Bale and Hararge, as well as a site for arbitration between feuding Oromo clans.[32] The Zuktum mosque, the shrine's main mosque was moreover

---

[31] Interview, Hajji Hussein Awol, Robe, August 2, 2011.
[32] Umer Nure (2006: 47f.) and Aman Seifedin ((1987: 14) discuss this in detail. See also Nash (1998: 16).

Figure 2.6 The Shrine of Sheikh Hussein

a central site for the performance of Oromo rituals, where milk and butter would be smeared along its walls in conjunction with prayers.[33] The shrine became crucial for the Islamization of the Arsi Oromo, commencing from the late eighteenth century. A key figure here was a certain Sheikh Muhammad Tilma Tilmo from the Wayu clan.[34] He became familiar with the veneration of saints in Harar and returned to renovate the shrine and to propagate Islam in Bale. Sheikh Muhammad Tilma Tilmo established himself as the highest authority and designated imam of Dirre Sheikh Hussein, as the place came to be called (*dirre*; open field), a position that remained within his lineage – referred to as the *warra imaama* (the family of the imam). Authority depended on their possession of *karaama,* which gave the descendants extraordinary power, including the ability to bless (*eebbisuu*), as well as to curse (*abaarsuu*).[35] It is important to underscore that such powers were not viewed as personal qualities in isolation, but as emanating from Sheikh Hussein and the shrine. The *karaama* thus situated the *warra*

---

[33] Interview, Sheikh Muhammed Hajji Abdujalil, Agarfa, May 30, 2006.
[34] There are some disagreements over Sheikh Muhammad Tilma Tilmo's clan, and some claim that the Wayu clan was his mother's clan.
[35] While *karaama* in Arabic signifies miracles performed by those who possess *baraka,* the word is commonly used in Bale as the very ability or power to perform miracles (cf. Ishihara (1996)).

imaama at the interface between a transcendent religious universe and the Bale locality and represents another instance where embodied and emplaced genealogy tied these worlds together.

Mosques were rare in Bale, consequently making Dirre Sheikh Hussein, as well as the numerous other shrines found across the region, the most significant feature of Oromo Muslim identity in Bale, defining the religious component in a demarcated and localized peoplehood, while, at the same time, transcending local boundaries and tying people to a larger collective. As Sheikh Hussein was not considered an Oromo, but of Arab descent, he embodied the bridge through which the local Oromo could imagine themselves as connected to the broader Muslim world. Moreover, as a *wali* he also embodied the link between the people and God, through whom the people could transcend finite boundaries.

With Dirre Sheikh Hussein as its most important shrine, Bale was at the same time home to a number of additional ones. Some of these were attributed to historical figures. The shrine of Nur Amin was for example named after Nur Amin Muhadid (d. 1568), who was Ahmed Gragn's successor, and the shrine of Faqih Siraj was attributed to one of Ahmed Gragn's officers. Particularly important here is that these shrines were associated with, and belonged to, particular clans. The Walashe clan venerated the shrine of Nur Amin Muhadid, while Faqih Siraj was the shrine of the Karmamida clan.[36] Other shrines were directly ascribed to the ancestor of a particular clan, as well as to individuals believed to have brought Islam to that particular clan. Such shrines both maintained and transcended clan boundaries by linking the clans to the broader world of Islam, and the connection to ancestors is a feature rather common in the Horn of Africa. Ioan M. Lewis has for example argued that in a Somali context, "strongly developed indigenous ancestor cults ... offer conditions propitious to the development of a Sufi interpretation of Islam, with emphasis on the development of saints as mediators between man and the Prophet" (1966b: 63).

The connection between clans and shrines was particularly evident in relation to the so-called *hajii torbaan* – the Seven Hajjis (see Table 2.1).[37]

---

[36] Other such figures included Asa Uthman, Faqih Edin, Faqih Abonye, and Sheikh Kimming.

[37] They were said to be the sons of a certain *alim*, Sheikh Dawd, claimed to be a contemporary of Sheikh Hussein. Some claim they were students of Sheikh

Table 2.1 *The seven Hajji, clans, and shrines*

Seven Hajjis	Clan	Location of Shrine
Haji Shabe	Sebro Hanqadin Shire Gurdama Game	Safaage in Dello Sebro (Gasera *worreda*)
Sheikh Ibrahim	Jawwe Shafila	Dhamole (Guradhamole *worreda*)
Haji Ali Bahir	Muhammed Nura	Meceferra (Gololcha *worreda*)
Haji Ali Zeyfaxa	?	In the Wabe Shebelle gorge
Haji Sabir	Sabiro (Arsi)	?
Haji Zadiq	Sadiqa (Arsi)	Sadiqa, near Hindato (Arsi)
Haji Shale	?	Wabe Shebelle gorge (Gasera *worreda*)

The scarcity and the contradictory nature of the sources have made it difficult to establish the historicity of these Seven Hajjis, but local traditions generally regard them as Oromo figures instrumental in the dissemination of Islam among specific clans in Bale, which in turn caused these clans to establish shrines where their "own" hajji was venerated.[38]

Another group was the *Imaama torbaan*, or the Seven Imams, also instrumental in the spreading of Islam in Bale and similarly connected to clan lineages.[39] While the origin and history of the Seven Imams – said to have lived "a long time ago" – remain cloaked in mythical narratives, it is plausible that they stemmed from the original Muslim population of Bale or were early Oromo converts to Islam. The Seven Imams were intrinsically linked to seven specific clans, each said to "have their own imam,"

Hussein, while another tradition argues that they came from Somalia. Braukämper (2002: 158), on the other hand, has suggested that one of them, Hajji Shale, was one of Ahmed Gragn's officers.

[38] Interview, Hajji Hussein Awol, Robe, May 26, 2005. See also Temam Haji (2002: 5).

[39] This group is somewhat similar to the so-called *Qallicha shan* (the five *Qallicha*) found in Arsi, said to have *sharifian* origin (descendants of Prophet Muhammad). Some refer to them as the *Awan shan* (the five *Aw*) (Braukämper 2002: 161) or the *Awa* clans (Temam Haji 2002: 3).

which would be associated with a particular sub-clan and attributed to a specific lineage within this sub-clan.[40] Similar to what has been said earlier, the Seven Hajjis and the Seven Imams dialectically managed to connect the Oromo to the wider world of Islam, while firmly attaching Islam to their own notions of descent and lineages.

The shrines enabled Islam to be inscribed on Bale's physical landscape – as sacred, yet material sites. At Dirre Sheikh Hussein, this was expressed through a requirement to remove one's shoes when entering the main compound (*gamoo*), the touching of the tomb of Sheikh Hussein, the eating and the smearing of the tomb's healing soil (*jawaara*) on one's body, drinking the healing water from the *harroo lukoo* (the shrine's pond), and the prohibition of farming adjacent to the shrine. The divine presence was perceived as carved into the walls and being sites that "incorporate and radiate divine power" (Schielke and Stauth 2008: 7); they were also centers toward which people gravitated – constituting nodes in a network of paths for pilgrimage journeys. Pilgrimage could be a once-in-a-lifetime event, but more often as recurring through life spans. Young children were from an early age brought to Dirre Sheikh Hussein to participate in the different rituals, making the shrine a crucial site for religious socialization. The enactment of these rituals generated embodied experiences, memories, and narratives fundamental for the construction of *Islaama*, a local Oromo Muslim peoplehood.

Rituals at the shrines reflected the early agents of Islamization's deliberate efforts in assimilating traditional cults into a new religious framework, as well as local Muslims' capacity to absorb existing religious elements (Braukämper 2002: 144; Haberland 1963: 470f.). Pilgrimages were thus modified continuations of earlier rituals attached to distinct spatial locations, be it the pilgrimage to the *abbaa muuda* (see below) or the visiting of graves of the forefathers. I would here argue that the latter demonstrates the importance of lineages and clans' founding fathers in enhancing the centrality of shrine pilgrimages. Existing rituals performed at the gravesides also reciprocally took on an Islamic color wherein the deceased ancestors were seen as possessing *karaama*. Rituals referred to as

---

[40] The names of these clans were Gurdama, Kalcama, Qito, Adarsoo, Sheidama, Abrahama, Shafafo. Another account included the names Allasata instead of Kalchama, Dande instead of Adarsho, and Bamo instead of Shaafafoo.
(Interview, Hajji Hussein Awol, Robe, May 25, 2005; Anonymous, interviewed by Jeannie Miller (date unknown)).

sadaqa[41] were regularly performed by the gravesides – often on the tenth night of Ramadan (*Laylat al-Qadr*), on *Id al-Fitr*, or on *mawlid al-Nabi* – which entailed feasting, commemoration of the ancestor, singing of *baaro*,[42] sacrifices, and recitations from the Qur'an. Pilgrimages, shrines, and associated rituals thus served as interconnectors across time, moving beyond Islamic time and representing continuity in change. Even a place like Oda Roba, the place of assembly within the *gadaa* system, was referred to as *awliah* – that is, a Muslim shrine (Hylander 1936: 65).

The dialectics of continuity and change in relation to pilgrimage are particularly relevant through the resemblance between the rituals ascribed to the *abbaa muuda* and those performed at Dirre Sheikh Hussein (Andrzejewski 1974; Braukämper 2002; Haberland 1963; Jeylan W. Hussein 2005; Mohammed Hassan 2005b; Umer Nure 2006).[43] The *abbaa muuda*, or the *qallu*, was a ritual expert located in Dello in southern Bale, at a place called Melka Arba. Labeled as the "final authority" (Knutsson 1967), the *qallu* was the subject for an annual pilgrimage (*jila*), where the adherents brought sacrifices (*wareega*) in return for blessings beneficial for their individual and communal well-being. The *abbaa muuda* was considered to be the pivotal center of the Oromo religion and was venerated far beyond the boundaries of Bale. It embodied a continuing and radiating divine power that reciprocally pulled people back through pilgrimage (Salviac 2005 [1901]: 177f.). The structures of the litanies (*baaro*) sung at Dirre Sheikh Hussein, the material symbols such as the Y-fork-shaped stick (*dhanqe*), the ring (*quube mulki*), and the cloak worn by the leading imam, as well as the physical arrangement of the main shrine as a sanctified space, all indicated how Dirre Sheikh Hussein had absorbed many of the aspects of the cult of the *abbaa muuda*. The same is true for the practice of collecting and offering sacrifices (*wareega*) to Sheikh Hussein, and for the ethical requirements

---

[41] *Sadaqa* is the Islamic term for voluntary giving of alms and has, moreover, been connected to divination with healing purposes, being an important part of the remedy prescribed by the divinatory. See Graw (2005).

[42] *Baaro* are prayer poems dedicated to Sheikh Hussein, and *zekera* is an Oromofication of the Arabic *dhikr,* meaning remembrance, the repetition of formulas in praise of God.

[43] This is confirmed by Haberland's informants saying, "Unsere Pilgerfahrten gehen nach Bali: die Oromo sagen abba muda und die Muslime sagen Sheikh Hussein" (our pilgrimage is to Bale; the Oromo say *abbaa muuda* and the Muslims say Sheikh Hussein) (1963: 413).

for the pilgrimages (Knutsson 1967: 144; Umer Nure 2006: 59f.). Its role as a place for pilgrimage made it particularly relevant for the Oromo of Bale, who by making pilgrimages relatively frequently generated embodied experiences that informed, shaped, and strengthened collective memories about origin and belonging.

The development of Islamic scholarship was an obvious aspect of the Islamization of Bale; however, it was a process that started relatively late.[44] To a large extent, it can be traced back to influences stemming from the northern region of Wollo, where religious policies during the reign of Emperor Yohannes (1872–1889) caused a wave of refugees to the south – including to Bale.[45] Some of these were established religious scholars (*ulama*), making Bale's initial Islamic learning and religious infrastructure embodied by outsiders. The earliest center for a localized Islamic scholarship in Bale was the area of Agarfa, located in the central highlands. The key figure here was Sheikh Abd al-Wahhab Yunus (ca 1839–1942), still revered as one of the greatest *ulama* in Bale. Dirre Sheikh Hussein also gained a reputation as a center for learning, particularly from the 1920s, where Sheikh Abdurahman Isma'il "Adare" from Harar was instrumental in building a *madrasa* (Islamic school) at the shrine. Additional sites for learning gradually emerged in the central highlands around Robe, as well as in the east toward Ginir and Gololcha.[46] Except for Dirre Sheikh Hussein and Agarfa, which functioned as permanent centers, teaching offered at other places could often be rather ephemeral – depending on the particular sheikh offering his service at a particular point in time. The number of students at these centers ranged from fifty to several hundred, who were given accommodation and food by the local community. The *ulama* were similarly dependent on voluntary contributions from the local community and on income from their *wakf* land (endowed land). The vast majority of religious students ended up as Qur'an teachers scattered across the region, teaching children in the

---

[44] The following discussion about the development of Islamic scholarship in Bale is based on Østebø (2012: 74f., 114f.).

[45] At the council of Boru Meda in 1878, the emperor declared that all Muslims of Wollo had to embrace Christianity or leave the kingdom – a decree that was followed by violent campaigns into Wollo (Hussein Ahmed 2001: 167f.).

[46] Important scholars in these areas included Sheikh Ibrahim Tigri, Sheikh Aliyeh Galchota, Sheikh Aliyeh Garado, Sheikh Abdallah Abosera, Sheikh Abdulqadir Qito, Sheikh Muhammed Qatiba, Sheikh Jalil Harawa, Hajji Kadir Hajji Hisu, Sheikh Hassan Sheikh Muhammed Tahi, and later, Sheikh Isma'il Walashe (Sheikh Isma'il Ebu) and Sheikh Juneydin Oborra.

rural villages. Their knowledge was often limited to the basics of Arabic and the Qur'an itself, and teaching was often a trade inherited from the father. The Qur'an teachers also led the main religious ceremonies and were moreover engaged in the production and provision of talismans and in fortune telling based on books on Islamic numerology and astrology.

While pilgrimages to local shrines and Muslim practices evolving in dialogue with an Oromo religious universe were crucial in the formation of and emplaced notion of belonging, the strengthening of Islamic scholarship and teaching expanded the horizon and deepened the imagination of simultaneously belonging to a defined locality and to a wider Muslim world. Such awareness was enhanced and accompanied by the emergence of opportunities for further religious education beyond Bale during the twentieth century. Improved means of communication were an important factor facilitating this, as was the *pax Amharica* emerging after Menelik's conquest of the south, which contributed to ending the constant "fratricidal struggles of the Oromo tribes" (Salviac 2005 [1901]: 334). The centrality of Dirre Sheikh Hussein as a meeting place further strengthened Islamic scholarship in Bale, and the yearly pilgrimages became important occasions for the dissemination of religious texts and for *ulama* from different regions to meet and engage in scholarly discussions.[47]

To complete the story about religion, belonging, and notions of peoplehood in Bale, I end this chapter with a brief discussion of Salafism, which emerged as an important reform movement during the 1960s. As I have provided an extensive analysis of this topic elsewhere (Østebø 2012), I will only summarize the main developments here. *Salafism* is a rather ambiguous term that represents a phenomenon that is both diverse and inherently dynamic. Salafism can briefly be characterized as a religious current devoted to securing doctrinal and ritual purity, guarding the monotheistic principle against *bid'a* (unlawful innovations), particularly pilgrimage to shrines, rituals performed in conjunction with tombs, and more generally practices connected to Sufism.[48] The more "modern" version that has gained much traction is often labeled Wahhabism, stemming from the teaching of Muhammad ibn Abd al-Wahhab and associated with the ideology of Saudi Arabia.

---

[47] Interviews, Hajji Hussein Awol, Robe, May 31, 2006; Sheikh Muhammad Abdullahi, Raytu, June 12, 2006.
[48] For more details on Salafism, see Haykel 2009; Meijer 2009.

The antecedents of Salafi reform were embodied in a small study group established by local merchants in Robe. A tightknit group, they refrained from criticizing their fellow Muslims' religious practice and advocating reform and focused instead on their personal piety by observing each of the mandatory daily prayers, and by avoiding participating in many of the established local religious practices. Developments in Saudi Arabia with the creation of institutions for higher Islamic education would gradually become crucial for the further expansion of Salafism to Bale. Particularly important was the establishment of the Islamic University of Medina in 1961 – generously offering free religious education to foreign students. The first group from Bale taking advantage of such opportunities traveled to Saudi Arabia in 1962. News about prospects for higher religious learning quickly reached Bale; throughout the 1960s, an increasing number of locals crossed the Red Sea. Many of these returned home as convinced Salafis, actively disseminating the new teaching in their respective localities. While the early – and few – reformers initially held a relatively low profile, the famous *khutba* delivered by a certain Sheikh Abubakr Muhammad in Robe's Nur mosque in 1971 constituted a crucial watershed for the Salafi movement in Bale. Boldly raising to his feet and addressing the people in the mosque, he ardently criticized existing religious practices – particularly the pilgrimage to and the offerings at the local shrines. The *khutba* sparked immediate and strong reactions from those present, who were outraged over Sheikh Abubakr Muhammad's words and who staunchly defended the established religious practices. The incident was the start of a deep conflict among the Muslims in Bale and sowed the seeds for lasting divisions within the community.

Although the Salafi movement did not, as I will return to, play a prominent role in the Bale insurgency, it definitely added a complicating layer to the religious landscape of Bale. It did not challenge notions of belonging to the existing religiously and ethnically defined peoplehood, but it certainly complicated the meaning of it. The awareness of and emphasis on Salafi tenets and the critique of established religious symbols and practices that had evolved within the locality of Bale accentuated the religious dimension of *Islaama* peoplehood and contributed to the underscoring of a Muslim identity that opened up for orientations toward a larger *umma*.

Conclusion

The landscapes of Bale ranged from rugged mountains to arid lowlands; with vast fertile highland plains, the region contained a rich variety of topographical and ecological particularities, and different climate zones. These landscapes were, however, more than empty canvases for human activities; they affected and shaped human lives in different ways, in the same way that the people imprinted themselves upon the land. The varied topography also played a role in the historical developments discussed in this study. The Arsi Oromo who arrived in Bale during the sixteenth century settled in a landscape that was the ancient Muslim sultanate of Bali, and among a Muslim population. While their arrival and presence caused the gradual decline of Islam in Bale, both the Arsi Oromo and the land were reshaped through processes of Islamization. As Islam gradually re-penetrated Bale, the Arsi Oromo came to put their own mark on the new religion, carving it into the landscape in the form of shrines and through well-traveled paths leading to these shrines. The Islamic dimension thus became crucial in the formation of *Islaama* peoplehood, which on the one hand was locally emplaced and on the other hand transcended local boundaries. It was moreover embodied in genealogies of the *awliah,* which were fused with narratives of Oromo ancestors, in turn rooted in experiences of embodied kinship relations. *Islaama* peoplehood was thus not exclusively a religious category but came to encompass both ethnicity and religion as fundamental dimensions and denoted community and belonging in a strong affective manner.

Landscape is inevitably about perspective, where one's emplaced location constitutes the center and frames one's peripheries. This means that the Arsi Oromo in Bale, contrary to the conventional perspectives in Ethiopian studies, did not perceive themselves as peripheral. Rather, it was Bale's familiar topography, the memories it invoked, and the people's embodied dwelling on the land that made it the locus for their perception of the world. This means that the Ethiopian state prior to the late nineteenth century was far beyond the circumference of the Arsi Oromo world, being an entity that had little or no relevance for them. The Ethiopian state's expansion through Emperor Menelik's conquest would dramatically change that. In fact, it changed nearly everything, reconfiguring Bale as a provincial periphery and the Arsi Oromo as subaltern and laying the foundation for a lasting antagonistic relationship between the Arsi Oromo and the Amhara rulers.

3 | Conquest and Resistance

Menelik's conquest of the south at the end of the nineteenth century and the establishment of Ethiopia's current borders have stimulated much debate in recent decades – both among ordinary Ethiopians and among academics. The debate has produced increasingly entrenched and polarized positions, where much of the disagreement revolves around whether Menelik was a hero or a villain, whether the conquest was a legitimate reunification of lost Ethiopian territories or a case of oppressive internal colonization. There are those who claim that Menelik "restored and united most of the medieval territories of Ethiopia" (Teferra Haile Selassie 1997: 36), seeing him as "an empire builder of historic proportions" (Messay Kebede 1999: 24). Advocates of this view tend to minimize the violent nature of the conquest and avoid mentioning the atrocities committed by Menelik's forces. Those on the opposing side underscore the southern areas' autonomous and independent status prior to the conquest, thus making the conquest nothing less than an illegal occupation. They also claim that the conquest was overtly brutal, particularly toward the Oromo – sometimes even speaking about an "Oromo genocide" (Falmataa Oromo 2014). As in any heated debate, the general tendency to lose sight of existing shades of gray unfortunately results in a simplified dichotomy between the Amhara as the sole oppressor and the Oromo as the subjugated people. Only a very few individuals have sought to modify this picture, pointing to how the Oromo were among both the oppressors and the oppressed (Merera Gudina 2003: 60).

There is, as this chapter will detail, no doubt that Menelik's campaigns in the south were violent. The cruelty and the lack of empathy of the rulers had even for their own subjects in the north are difficult to comprehend. One account describes how Emperor Tewodros's (1818–1868) soldiers – passing through villages – had their horses and mules crisscross the farmers' fields to destroy the harvest-ready crop, and the source narrates that "I often have seen the owners imploring the intruders, with tears, to remove their animals, but they would neither move [or] pity them" (Crummey 1986a: 140). If this was the condition in the north, one can only imagine the level of violence in the south. Having said this, the degree of violence is always a relative matter, and one should be careful not to be too hasty to pass judgment on one set of actors without considering what others might have been capable of – had the conditions been different. One should not too uncritically apply contemporary human rights standards and rules of war to events occurring in the nineteenth century. In this discussion of the conquest of Bale, I have made an effort to avoid becoming entangled in the current polemic debate about the conquest. By both presenting new empirical data and synthesizing older information, I attempt to understand how it was experienced by the local people of Bale, and thus to construct a view of the conquest "from below." An intrinsic aspect of this is to recognize and soberly investigate how the conquest laid the foundation for a conflictual relationship between the local population and their new rulers, and the manner in which latent animosity repeatedly erupted in recurrent acts of resistance. I believe this will not only add valuable insights to context of Bale but also constitute a lens that can help construe the salience of antagonistic sentiments even today.

While Menelik's expansion into the south was achieved through both diplomatic and violent means, the most important and the most effective of the two was, however, the use of military force. A major reason for Menelik's ability to swiftly and effectively defeat the people in the south and expand the kingdom's borders was his access to firearms. Adding to this was the military force's hierarchical and effective organizational capacity – which was a product of a continued militarization in the Shoa region throughout the nineteenth century (Reid 2011: 39f.). Similarly important was how the political and cultural cohesion that the Christian Kingdom had produced over centuries served as a disciplining force for the Amhara military, while those they encountered were far more fragmented and divided. Such divisions, moreover, provided the Amhara with ample opportunities to exploit local rivalries and form alliances with groups supporting the invaders.

Menelik's forces obviously included groups other than the Amhara, and although I am aware of the complexity and ambiguity inherent in

Amhara as a category, I have deliberately chosen to use it as a major concept. One important reason is that this was the word used by the local Arsi Oromo when making references to Menelik's conquest, to the new rulers, and to Christian settlers arriving in the region. This latter aspect is particularly crucial, because it points to the inherent religious dimension of Amhara. My key argument is that Amhara becomes meaningless unless connected to Christianity. Common for all the northerners invading the south was that they all were Christians and, moreover, that the state's religiously underpinned narrative provided a strong sense of exceptionalism. This notion was crucial in shaping the Amhara's, that is, the Christians', perceptions of superiority and divine destiny.

The Conquest

The occupation of the southeast started in the Arsi area in 1881 but was quickly bogged down by fierce local resistance. It was not until 1886 when Menelik's paternal uncle, *Ras* Darge Sahle Selassie, managed to defeat the Arsi clans in the decisive battle of Azule. The reactions to the local resistance soon proved to be devastating for the Oromo in Arsi. Thousands were taken as slaves, and the confiscation of livestock was on such a scale that it was a deciding factor for turning the Arsi Oromo into agriculturalists (Markakis 2011: 98). After conquering Arsi, Menelik turned his attention to Harar, putting *Dejazmach* Wolde-Gabriel – nicknamed *Abba Sheitan* (father of Satan) – in charge.[1] This campaign was swift and was sealed by the defeat of the outnumbered forces of *Emir* Abdullahi Ali (1884–1887) at the battle of Chalanqo in January 1887. The emirate was subsequently turned into a province and entrusted to *Ras* Mekonnen Wolde-Mikael, the father of Haile Selassie. Initially, the new rulers granted the Harari a certain degree of autonomy, which also included a policy of noninterference in religious affairs (Caulk 1975: 11), yet this gradually changed when *Ras* Mekonnen Wolde-Mikael started to confiscate land, replace the local administration with northerners, switch the working language to Amharic, and construct an Orthodox church in the middle of the town's square.

---

[1] *Abba Sheitan* referred to the name of his horse, and such reference was a common *nom de guerre* used by both the Amhara and the Oromo.

Bale was conquered during 1891–1892 and was thus the last part of the southeast to be incorporated into the new kingdom. Menelik's forces arrived in Bale through Arsi; however, compared with Arsi, the conquest of Bale was achieved largely through diplomatic means. This does not mean, as I will return to later in the chapter, that there was no use of violence. The campaign was led by *Ras* Darge Sahle-Selassie and *Dejazmach* Wolde-Gabriel (Bairu Tafla 1975: 30). With Arsi as the bridgehead, *Ras* Darge Sahle-Selassie sent several secret emissaries into Bale prior to entering the region himself, among whom a certain Sheikh Bushra is the most remembered. According to local traditions, he posed as a religious teacher and allegedly provided clothes infected with poison to his students and polluted the water points for the cattle. This resulted in a devastating epidemic that infected and killed both humans and cattle. The large-scale slaughtering of sick animals is still remembered in local traditions and captured in the word *warrandomsa* (Oromo; a knife that has become dull).[2] It is difficult to verify the historicity of Sheikh Bushra and the nature of the epidemic, but some have suggested that it was smallpox deliberately spread by the Amhara, calling it an early incident of chemical warfare (Abbas H. Gnamo 2014: 161; Gadaa Melbaa 1988a; Temam Haji 2002: 17). There is no real evidence that supports such a notion, and one should keep in mind that the alleged poisoning coincided with the rinderpest epidemic that swept over the Horn of Africa. The epidemic was in turn followed by a widespread famine and other diseases like cholera, smallpox, and typhus and was known in the northern parts of Ethiopia as *Kefu Qen* (Amharic; evil days) (Sanderson 1985: 655).

Ras Darge Sahle-Selassie also met with local leaders while in Arsi, seeking to win them over to his side. The two most famous of these according to local traditions were Kabir Huba of the Siko moiety (Koloba clan) and Watte Debu of the Mendo moiety (Kadu clan). Kabir Huba, who assumingly was familiar with the violent defeat of the Arsi, managed to convince other Siko clans to refrain from resisting Menelik's forces. The promise of submission to *Ras* Darge Sahle-Selassie is still remembered among the Oromo of Bale in this saying:

[2] Interview, Hajji Hassan Faqi, Goba, June 1, 2005. See also Sintayehu Kassaye (1985: 7) and Mindaye Abebe (2005: 45).

Baalee sitti dhufa
Yoo didan, Kooloobaa sitti dhufa
Yoo didan, warri kiyyaa sitti dhufa
Yoo didan, aanaa kiyyaa sitti dhufa.

Bale will come to you
If they refuse, the Koloba [clan] will come to you
If they refuse, my household will come to you
If they refuse, my family will come to you.[3]

Ras Darge Sahle-Selassie entered Bale peacefully in October 1891, crossing the Wabe Shebelle River at a place called Melka Qurulee (later called Melka Amhara) (Bairu Tafla 1975: 30). His forces set up their first camp at Gurranda, in today's Gasera *worreda*, which would become the bridgehead for securing control over the highland areas east and north of the Weib River. Immediately after establishing themselves there, the Amhara constructed St. George Church – the first Christian church in Bale since medieval times.

Watte Debu, however, was less successful in convincing the Mendo clans to submit to the *Ras*. The clans met at Hora Boka, just outside of Robe town, where they discussed whether to fight or surrender. A certain Gogorri Butta was strongly advocating armed resistance and managed to convince the other clans (Hussein Badhaasoo 2017: 346). Resistance proved futile and the Amhara forces easily penetrated deeper into the eastern highlands. *Dejazmach* Asfaw Darge (d. 1906) succeeded his father *Ras* Darge Sahle-Selassie in taking leadership of the forces, and recognizing the strategic value of the hilly areas of the Karmamida clan, he subsequently moved his base from Guranda and established Goba as the region's capital in 1893. Shortly after, he built the town's St. Michael Church.[4] *Dejazmach* Asfaw Darge remained in charge until 1907, when the governorship was transferred to *Ras* Lul Seged who ruled Bale until 1911.[5]

Parallel to conquering the eastern highlands, the Amhara forces also moved southwest into the Gedeb area, today's Adaba, Dodola, and Kokosa *worredas*. The news of the defeat of both Arsi and eastern Bale had by then reached the clans of Gedeb, and they were therefore anxious to negotiate peace with the Amhara. The details of this process

---

[3] Interview, Hajji Hussein Awol, Robe, December 7, 2002.
[4] Interview, Hajji Hussein Awol, Robe, December 7, 2002.
[5] *Ras* Lul Seged was married to Menen Asfaw, who divorced him and became the wife of *Ras* Teferri, Emperor Haile Selassie.

are somewhat unclear, and the history has a rather legendary character. Accordingly, the Gedeb clans chose a certain Bu'i Falama of the Sheidama clan to be sent to the Amhara. He did not have any leadership position among the local clans, and the colorful local tradition recounting his collaboration with the Amhara and his rise to power deserves to be narrated at length:

This [Bu'i Falama] well-known *shifta* [bandit] could slaughter and eat one sheep in one night, even a cow in one night. The same night he would prepare the hide of that cow and wear that the day after. Therefore, the leaders of all the clans sent him; since he was a *shifta*, they didn't consider it much of a loss if he was killed. . . . When he came to the Amhara, *Dejazmach* Asfaw Darge asked: "Who are you?" Bui'i answered: "I am the leader of this area [Gedeb]." *Dejazmach* Asfaw Darge then asked: "Can you make the people surrender, can you bring cattle, butter, honey for my soldiers?" Bui'i answered: "I will do all this." On his way back to Gedeb, and before Bui'i reached the other clans, he took a limestone and rubbed it on his body, in his face – so that it made marks on his skin. His idea was to fool the other clans. When he returned, he said: "Do you see what the Amhara did to me; they beat me and even dragged me on the ground. We have to bring everything they are asking for." When he came back to the Amhara with all the gifts, the Amhara were impressed and happy . . . and put him in charge [of the area].[6]

Having secured the central highlands, the Amhara turned their attention to the eastern lowlands. These campaigns were led by *Dejazmach* Wolde-Gabriel and *Ras* Mekonnen Wolde-Mikael, the already mentioned governor of Harar. Moving in from Hararge in the north, *Ras* Mekonnen's and Wolde-Mikael's main goal was to capture Dirre Sheikh Hussein, before continuing toward the lowlands. The shrine was expected to be "a center of Oromo resistance" and the Amhara were determined to control it (Ketema Meskela 2001: 27). The shrine, however, was easily captured together with the areas of today's Gololcha and Ginir *worredas*. *Dejazmach* Wolde-Gabriel established Ginir as a garrison town in 1894, from where he controlled Bale's eastern areas. The town also served as the point of departure for campaigns further east into El Kere, and upon occupying the southern parts of the Ogaden, *Dejazmach* Wolde-Gabriel turned south toward Borana. *Dejazmach* Asfaw Darge, meanwhile, ventured into the

---

[6] Interview, Daniel Negash, Dodola, October 23, 2002.

southern lowlands of Bale, taking today's districts of Guradhamole, Dello, and Medda Welabu, before he also reached Borana.

The eastern and southern expansions brought Ethiopia into contact with Britain, France, and Italy and made Menelik a participant in the European scramble for the Horn of Africa. He made claims on Ogaden and other Somali areas in 1891, arguing that they lay within the ancient boundaries of Ethiopia. This was not accepted easily by the Europeans; however, through continued campaigns into the eastern lowlands and negotiations with the Western colonizers, Menelik secured lasting control over the eastern regions in 1897. He similarly laid claim over present-day Borana, where his forces quickly pacified the Borana, Garri, and Gabra groups. This brought him into contact with the British in Kenya, and the unsettled border question – which produced an unstable situation with recurrent raids – was not finalized until 1907 with the Anglo-Ethiopian treaty.

The Amhara had little interest in the eastern lowlands, and the Ethiopian state had nearly no presence in those areas. This did not mean that the lowlands could not be exploited. And exploited they were. As the rinderpest in the late nineteenth century had decimated the cattle in the north, the southeastern lowlands enhanced their value as a reservoir for livestock. Harar became the initial bridgehead for expeditions – called *zamacha* – into the eastern Somali-inhabited areas. The early Amhara campaigns from the late nineteenth century, many of which were led by *Ras* Mekonnen Wolde-Mikael, were nothing less than raids that pillaged the people of their resources (Bahru Zewde 1991: 72; Perham 1969: 338). These campaigns increased both in frequency and size from 1891, when a permanent garrison was established in Biyo Kabobo, and important campaigns carried out in 1895 and 1896 and until 1905 penetrated deeper into the southeastern lowlands. The enforced extraction of cattle was in the form of collecting tribute, as well as for punitive reasons. In the latter case, the soldiers usually robbed the pastoralists clean, burned down their villages, and killed the inhabitants. Lack of discipline among the soldiers meant that this also took place when collecting tribute (Garretson 2001). A number of eyewitnesses told stories about excessive brutality, describing the soldiers as a "trail of brown ants ... eating up everything in their path" (quoted in Teshale Tibebu 1995: 36). One observer reported that an

"Abyssinian expedition has returned from the Ogaden bringing with them as booty thousands of camels and cattle and property of all descriptions" (Geshekter 1985: 8). A British army officer witnessing the campaign of 1901, which consisted of between 10,000 and 15,000 soldiers, narrated the following:

> The horrible looting of the friendly villages goes on. Today for some three hours a constant stream of camels, cows, sheep, and goats passed. The Abyssinians [Amhara] estimate the number of camels at 2000 and probably half of the Rer Augaz tribe is now completely destitute. It makes one's blood boil to see such a crime perpetrated by these Abyssinians who set themselves up as being on a par with European nations and fit to treat with them. What will be done with all these camels, goodness only knows, for they are of no use in Abyssinia, the King and Ras already possessing thousands for which they have little use. (Geshekter 1985: 9)

The campaigns obviously had lasting impacts on the local pastoralist population. For example, the number of houses in a village along the Wabe Shebelle River dropped from 500 to 80 because of the Ethiopian campaigns in 1891 (Garretson 2001: 29). One source argued that the soldiers' actions in Ogaden "were brutal to the last degree, – these 'Christians' having devastated the whole country, killing the men and women they did not wish to carry off as slaves" (Donaldson Smith 1897: 119). Others said that the way the Amhara were killing everything that came in their way resembled a "scorched earth" policy (Cavendish 1898: 375). There are not many indications that the situation improved in the beginning of the twentieth century. One eyewitness reported in 1930 that a punitive expedition had completely burned an entire Somali village, killing 111 men, women, and children (Geshekter 1985: 10). As the only experience the pastoralists had with the Ethiopian state was imbued with such violence, they soon became overtly "hostile to state authority in which they had no share" (Markakis 1983: 295).

While similar campaigns clearly occurred in Bale, we have little detailed information about them. The main base for such raids was Ginir town at the eastern edge of the Bale highlands. The town was an established trading center connecting Bale with Somalia and the Indian Ocean (Hylander 1936: 30; Pankhurst 1968: 243, 444). But the constant raids increasingly marginalized the town – as traders, the Arsi Oromo and the Somali lowlanders were too "afraid to venture there"

(Gwynn 1911: 118). Stories collected by Donaldson Smith in 1894 report that the Amhara forces had captured Arsi Oromo children as slaves and stolen all their cattle, leaving them poor and desolate (1897: 43). He further narrates that while traveling through the lowlands of Bale, he passed through a number of deserted villages, saying that "many human bones were lying about the deserted villages, testifying to the raids by the Abyssinians [Amhara]":

They told us the same sad tale we had heard from every Galla [Oromo]. They were fine-looking men, and it was pathetic to the last degree to see them break into tears as they described how the Abyssinians were reducing them to poverty. ... The treatment of the natives by the Abyssinians is everywhere the same, – they are whipped about like dogs, and have always the appearance of whipped dogs when their conquerors are about. (1897: 48, 102)

Early Resistance

The Amhara forces met, as noted, far less resistance in Bale compared with neighboring Arsi. News about the fighting and the Amhara's subsequent retaliatory actions had obviously reached the people in Bale, and it is fair to suggest that this served as a deterrent against taking up arms against the invaders. The few attempts of resistance were largely sporadic and unorganized and carried out by isolated clans and sub-clans without any form of coordination.

Gogorri Butta had, as mentioned earlier, convinced the Mendo clans to fight *Ras* Darge Sahle-Selassie's forces. The first encounter between them and the Amhara took place in the eastern highlands by the river Weib, at a place called Melka Ballo in Gasera *worreda* sometime during the rainy season (July–October) in 1892. Confronting each other at the opposite sides of the river, the high water level in the river prevented any of them to cross, leaving *Ras* Darge Sahle-Selassie's forces halted at the northern side, and the Oromo positioned on the southern side. Armed with spears and shields and unfamiliar with and unaware of the opposing party's possession of firearms, the Arsi Oromo were quite confident. This would, according to local traditions, change dramatically after the first shot was fired. Among the Arsi Oromo was a certain Kusa Obsa, who had the reputation of being a strong fighter and stood out physically as a large man. He was soon marked by Amhara riflemen, who shot him dead with a single bullet. Not seeing any spear or arrow, but simply hearing the gunshot, and then finding Kusa Obsa laying on the ground, the Oromo were shocked and terrified and fled the area immediately (Mindaye Abebe 2005: 53).[7] This incident turned out to be crucial for the Mendo clans' recognition of the Amhara power.

Another incident took place in the areas of the Karmamida clan around Goba while the Amhara forces were still based in Gurranda. As part of the process of establishing cordial relations with the invaders, the Oromo clans of the eastern highlands sent a representative named Arabo Konso of the Karmamida clan to Gurranda with "loads of tribute" pledging surrender (Ketema Meskela 2001: 25). *Ras* Darge Sahle-Selassie accepted Arabo Konso's gifts and promise and subsequently provided him with a small escort to accompany him back to Karmamida. However, as soon as the escort arrived there, they were attacked by the Abarossa and Emari sub-clans of the Karmamida. Only one of the Amhara survived and managed to escape back to Gurranda (Ketema Meskela 2001: 26). Outraged by the killings, *Dejazmach* Asfaw Darge immediately dispatched a large contingent of soldiers to Karmamida, which without restraint burned down the houses, confiscated the cattle, and killed most of the members of the Abarossa and Emari sub-clans (Mindaye Abebe 2005: 55; Østebø 2005: 34).[8] This incident had an immediate and dramatic effect and allowed *Dejazmach* Asfaw Darge to move his forces deeper into Bale without any resistance.

The most significant acts of defiance took place in the eastern lowlands, where the Jawwe, Hawattu, and particularly the Raytu clans were determined to fight, which subsequently earned them the reputation of being fierce fighters. The initial resistance came from a sub-clan of Raytu led by Dima Harre, who sought to block Menelik's forces from entering the lowlands. Overwhelmed by the well-armed Amhara forces, Dima Harre and his men retreated to a place called Felte in Raytu, where he was defeated. Both he and forty of his family members were killed at that place.[9] Dhadhi Terre, the famous *abbaa boku* of the Raytu clan continued the struggle, leading the locals in the battle against *Dejazmach* Wolde-Gabriel by the Chelchel River.[10] Alongside

---

[7] Interview, Hajji Hassan Faqi, Goba, June 10, 2005.
[8] Interview, Hajji Hassan Faqi, Goba, June 10, 2005.
[9] Interview, Hajji Semir Idris, Addis Ababa, June 22, 2017.
[10] Interview, Hajji Semir Idris, Addis Ababa, June 22, 2017; correspondence, Hajji Semir Idris, February 19, 2018.

Dhadhi Terre was the local *qallu,* who had prophesized that the people would be victorious if they waved their *tesbe* (Muslim prayer chain) and shouted the *shahada* (Islamic creed) as they ran toward the enemy.[11] Also this time, the Raytu fighters were easily defeated, and in an effort to co-opt Dhadhi Terre, the Amhara bestowed the feudal title of *Fitawrari* on him and made him their local administrator (*balabat*) of Raytu.[12] Intermittent resistance also occurred in El Kere, eventually quelled by the Ethiopian army in 1895 (Gebru Tareke 1977: 284). A new round of armed struggle erupted in 1916, connected to the conflict around Lij Iyasu (see Chapter 8). Raytu was again one of the main battlefields, and the fighting was led by the same Dhadhi Terre. The authorities dispatched a force led by *Afa Negus* Sileshi, which effectively repressed the rebellion. Dhadhi Terre himself was killed at a decisive battle by the Chalchal River and buried at Arda Terre, close to Ginir.[13] A similar uprising took place in Dello, at Bahr Chaka in the Harenna forest, led by Muhammad Abba Shanko, originally from Wollo. This insurgency lasted until 1920, before being suppressed by *Dejazmach* Haile Selassie Abayneh, an uncle of Emperor Haile Selassie (Abbas H. Gnamo 1992: 253).

Fighting continued into the 1920s, however, in areas such as the eastern lowland Goro *worreda,* where the locals attacked a garrison in Malago. Encounters between the Arsi Oromo and the Amhara forces also took place in the southern lowlands of Dello, where bands of fighters led by Jillo Berisso, Abd al-Jabar Roba, and Adem Bayiu fought for three years before being forced into submission. A more lasting rebellion led by Abba Shaqo occurred in Dello *awraja* from 1928 to 1932. There, the insurgents accessed modern firearms, most notably the gun the locals called *booqqee,* commonly used by Menelik's forces. Another group, led by Chirri Jarra (the father of Aliye Chirri), Kuyye Dibbe, Butta Qumbi, and Dirre Irressa, continued to challenge local authorities in the southern lowlands in the early 1930s. Their field of operation was in the southern Medda Welabu *worreda,* and the insurgency was called the struggle "Malka Amhara" (the ford of the Amhara) because of a victorious battle at the Welmel River (Hussein

---

[11]	Interview, Abdulqadir Muhammed, Raytu, October 7, 2002.
[12]	The meaning of *balabat* was originally – in the north – someone who could claim ownership to land, but during the conquest of the south, the term came to refer to local leaders appointed by the Amhara and responsible to them.
[13]	Interviews, Hajji Semir Idris, Addis Ababa, August 3, 2011, and June 22, 2017.

Indhessa 2016: 79f.). However, all these attempts of resistance remained ineffectual, as the lack of firearms among the Arsi Oromo gave the well-armed Amhara forces a decisive advantage.

The Bale resistance – and the Amhera's experiences of the bloody war in Arsi – not only confirmed their view of the Arsi Oromo as brutal savages but also instilled a strong sense of fear among them. The Arsi Oromo warrior culture certainly added to this. Considering the Arsi Oromo fearless and violent warriors, any Amhara sought to avoid encountering the Arsi Oromo without the needed protection (Hylander 1936: 47). Fear quickly translated into enmity, and acts of resistance were consequently severely punished. European travelers testified to this, and one of the Amhara soldiers accompanying Donaldson Smith openly told him, "the people fought and killed some of us, and we exterminated most of them, and what were left died of hunger" (Donaldson Smith 1897: 69). Punitive actions more-over scarred Arsi Oromo bodies. One case in point is from Raytu, where the soldiers, in response to lowlanders' resistance, gathered the people by the Chalchal River and cut off the right hands of the males and the right breasts of the women (Hussein Indhessa 2016: 76).[14] Amhara retaliations were also imprinted on the landscape; it was not uncommon that the Amhara soldiers would massacre and destroy whole villages, leaving large areas devastated. European visitors all talked about how the violence had sharply reduced the population of Bale, describing the highlands as "bare, uninhabited" (Gwynn 1911: 118). Others used phrases like "the sparseness of the population was again remarkable" (Hodson 1927: 92), and that "not a single perma-nent dweller was to be seen" (Donaldson Smith 1897: 92). They also reported signs of earlier settlements, which were left abandoned, and Donaldson Smith reported seeing "men's skulls lying in all directions" (1897: 69). There is no doubt that this can partly be explained by the previously mentioned rinderpest and subsequent famines, and Donaldson Smith narrates how Dirre Sheikh Hussein was hard hit by cholera, "which had swept away four-fifths of the inhabitants" (1897: 61). But these travelers underscore the punitive actions by the Amhara soldiers (Hodson 1927: 92), and Charles W. Gwynn claimed that the response to resistance "was one of extermination, as these Arussi [Arsi]

---

14 Interviews, Abdulqadir Muhammad, Raytu, October 7, 2002; Nuri Muhammad, Raytu, June 12, 2017.

districts witness" (1911: 118). Acts of resistance had, in other words, come with significant costs for the Arsi Oromo, and they were left with little choice but to succumb to their Amhara lords. It is against this backdrop that their support for the Italian invaders needs to be understood.

The Italian Period and Muslim Resilience

The Italian occupation from 1936 to 1941 constituted a brief interlude in the Amhara's control over Bale. While the period had little lasting political or economic impact on the Arsi Oromo, it proved important in both deepening their religious identity and strengthening their resilience. The Italians were familiar with the situation of the peoples in the south in general, and of the Muslims in particular, and exploited this to their own advantage. Their colonial divide-and-rule policy was thus directly aimed at counterweighting and alienating the ruling Christians, while actively courting the Muslims of Ethiopia with promises of religious equality.

As part of the Southern Front, the Italian forces, led by Rodolfo Graziani,[15] entered Ethiopia in the south from Dolo in southern Somalia. Divided into two contingents, one moved toward Negelle Borana, while the other approached Bale. The Ethiopian defense consisted of *Ras* Desta Damtew's forces in Negelle Borana and those of *Dejazmach* Beyene Merid (1934–1935), the governor of Bale – consisting of 80,000 soldiers altogether.[16] Contrary to the Swedish missionary Fride Hylander's claim that the people in Bale actively fought against the Italians, the bulk of the Arsi Oromo refused the local Amhara administration's call to arm – in turn causing *Dejazmach* Beyene Merid to threaten to brand all males on their forehead with a scorching iron unless they joined his ranks.[17] There is even a report that prominent leaders such as Hajji Adam Saddo and Fitawrari Nuho Dhadhi, the son of the earlier mentioned *Fitawrari* Dhadhi Terre, prepared a letter of invitation that was sent to the Italians in Mogadishu (Muusaa Haaji Aadam Saaddoo 2014: 54). Similarly, another report claims that Fitawrari

---

[15] Graziani would later become the Italian viceroy of Ethiopia.
[16] These two were both sons-in-law of Emperor Haile Selassie. The Italians later killed Dejazmach Beyene Merid (Greenfield 1965: 239).
[17] Interview, Siraj Muhammed-Amin, Robe, June 11, 2006.

Nuho Dhadhi went from Raytu to Somalia, promising Oromo support to the Italians (Hussein Indhessa 2016: 98). Entering the lowlands of Raytu from the east, the Italians soon won the support of the Raytu leader, *Fitawrari* Nuho Dhadhi. He quickly urged his compatriots in the highlands to refrain from taking up arms against the foreigners. Heeding to his and other leaders' calls, and swayed by the Italian propaganda, the people did little to resist the Italians, who easily took control over Bale in May–June 1936.[18] Bale was, together with Hararge, the southern parts of the Afar region, and Arsi subsequently organized as one province under the name of Harar, and Bale itself was divided into two *commissariati* (districts). These were in turn separated into six *residenzi* (sub-districts): Goba, Dodola, Dello, Ginir, Magalo, and Sheikh Hussein. Goba was kept as the seat of administration, and the Italians built a strong garrison in Magalo, close to Sof Umar (Mindaye Abebe 2005: 72). Most of the Amhara fled as the Italians arrived, and those who remained became subject to the Arsi Oromo's vengeful actions, causing the death of some landlords. Some Amhara remained to fight the Italians, labeled as "patriots" and organized as loose guerrilla units. None of the Arsi Oromo joined them, however, and many clans enlisted as irregulars on the side of the Italians – clashing with the Amhara fighters. The most well-known incident took place just outside of Robe, where thirteen Amhara reportedly were killed.[19]

The Italian occupiers formalized the *shari'a* courts, facilitated Arabic as a language of instruction in schools in provinces with a substantial Muslim population, and contributed to the construction of hundreds of mosques all over the country (Sbacchi 1985: 161f.). In fact, the first modern mosques in Bale – in Goba, Ginir, Dello-Mena, and Dodola – were built with support of the Italians.[20] *Shari'a* courts were also established in Bale, and Hajji Muhammed Siraj of Wollo was appointed as the first official *qadi* (judge) of Bale.[21] Another important gesture was the establishment of the Sude

---

[18] The Italians dropped leaflets in Arabic and other languages from airplanes prior to the attacks (interview, Siraj Muhammed-Amin, Robe, June 11, 2006; see also Greenfield (1965: 230)).
[19] Interview, Siraj Muhammed-Amin, Robe, June 11, 2006.
[20] Prior to the Italian occupation, thatch-roofed mosques known as *zawaya* were found in Bale, which were primarily used for private and individual prayers (interviews, Hajji Farid Ahmed, Dodola, March 3, 2006; Hajji Muhammed Aliye, Goba, April 1, 2006). See also Aman Seifedin (1987: 20) and Mindaye Abebe (2005: 73).
[21] Interview, Siraj Muhammed-Amin, Robe, June 11, 2006.

Figure 3.1 Imam Muhammad Sayyid's travel documents (1)

sultanate in Arsi where Hajji Hussein Kimo was renamed Sultan Sude, the
sultanate of Raytu under *Fitawrari* Nuho Dhadhi, and the imamate of
Dirre Sheikh Hussein with Imam Muhammed Sayyid, from the family of
Sheikh Muhammed Tilma Tilmo, as leader.[22] These three individuals were
also among the prominent Muslims sent to Rome and granted audiences
with Mussolini (see Figures 3.1 and 3.2).

The Italian period thus saw the expansion of Islam, and the Italians'
emphasis on expanding infrastructure also enhanced the opportunities
for religious students to travel beyond the confines of Bale in search of
Islamic education. The Italian period thus also proved important to
consolidate a local religious identity alongside the imagination of
belonging to something that transcended locality and linked local
Muslims to the wider world of Islam. Such sentiments were clearly
expressed by one of Temam Haji's informants, who stated, *"bara*

---

[22] Interviews, Siraj Muhammed-Amin, Robe, June 11, 2006; Sheikh Ahmed Hajji
Kadir, Dirre Sheikh Hussein, June 5, 2006; Temam Haji (2002: 40f.).

Figure 3.2 Imam Muhammad Sayyid's travel documents (2)

xaaliyaanii ijaa banaannee" (we opened our eyes during the Italian period) (2002: 47). The period strengthened their identity as Muslims, boosted their confidence, and sharpened their quest for change.

Muhammad Gada Qallu and Continued Resistance

The Italians were defeated in 1941 and replaced by British forces, which also secured the return Emperor Haile Selassie to the throne. The emperor returned from exile to a rather uncertain and fragile situation, and the country was marked with several centrifugal forces. Most prominent was the *Woyane* uprising in Tigray in 1943, which soon was brutally and effectively crushed by the government. In Bale, the restoration of the throne effectively ended any hope that changes achieved during the Italian period would last. Those who had sided with the Italians were branded as traitors, and *Fitawrari* Nuho Dhadhi was taken to Addis Ababa and reportedly killed by injection.[23] The fear of increased

---

[23] Interview, Hajji Semir Idris, Addis Ababa, August 3, 2011.

Amhara domination led to renewed resistance in several places in the southeast. One major yet little known insurgency was the so-called *Jeegir* war that took place in the southern region of Borana from 1942 to 1944.[24] This movement was dominated by Somali clans, mainly the Marehan and the Ogadenis, but also included non-Somali Muslim groups, such as the Arsi Oromo. Many of the fighters had fought with the Italians, which meant that they had access to arms and military skills that enabled them to launch a highly organized insurgency. While the insurgency was concentrated in Borana – on the Ethiopian side of the border – it also extended into British-controlled Kenya and north into Bale.

The *Jeegir* insurgents referred explicitly to their struggle in religious terms. The struggle was presented as a *jihad,* and the Islamic dimension was made unequivocal by the use of green flags with a crescent and Quranic inscriptions. Muslim unity was moreover crucial when mobilizing followers across the ethnic landscape. Little is known about its ideological underpinning, but the movement was focused on fighting Amhara rule and seems to have been influenced by nationalist Somali sentiments. It was also, however, directed toward non-Muslim groups in the region, where the Borana, Gabra, and Sakuye became victims of repeated violent attacks. While the religious dimension played a certain role here too, it is also clear that raiding of livestock as well as long-established interethnic animosity were important factors. The *Jeegir* insurgency created a great deal of unrest across Borana but was eventually defeated by Ethiopian – and British – forces in 1944.

Resistance also surfaced in Bale, where the Gurra, Dhamole, and Hawattu clans fought for six months in the lowlands of Fasil around Goro. The most significant resistance, however, occurred in Dello and was led by Muhammed Gada Qallu, the last *abbaa muuda* of Dello. Muhammad Gada Qallu was born in the early 1890s as the son of the well-known *abbaa muuda,* Abbeyo, and belonged to the Raytu clan. The *abbaa muuda* had to belong to the Doyyo lineage of the Raytu clan, which, as we will see, granted this clan a special status among the Oromo of Bale. Muhammad Gada Qallu had inherited the position of *abbaa muuda* at the time when the institution was declining. The

---

[24] Markakis (1987: 193) and Gebru Tareke (1991: 130) both claim that the *Jeegir* insurgency was connected to the struggle of Muhammad Gada Qallu (see later), and that its leader, Nur Garwein, was an Arsi Oromo from Bale. Gufu Oba (2013: 255f.), who has done a more in-depth study of the insurgency, disproves these claims, which also corresponds with my findings.

pressure from the Amhara was partly the reason for this, but more important was the expansion of Islam. This is clearly seen by the fact that Muhammed Gada Qallu himself converted to Islam in the 1920s or 1930s – changing his name from the original Gada Tesso Chamara (Hussein Indhessa 2016: 83).[25]

The antecedents of the struggle can be traced back to 1933, spurred by a controversy with a certain Gebre Selassie Turuche. He was an important *balabat* in Dello *awraja* who had converted to Christianity and changed his name from Chake Turuche. He made claims on the land of the *abbaa muuda*, and when Muhammad Gada Qallu refused, Gebre Selassie Turuche took the case to the authorities in Goba – who failed to support him. Gebre Selassie Turuche was not willing to give up that easily and retaliated by ambushing and killing Muhammad Gada Qallu's brother, Wayyu Tesso, as he traveled from Goba to Dello. The assassination became a tipping point for Muhammad Gada Qallu, and he decided to take up arms against the local authorities. The initial phase of the insurgency, however, was confined to sporadic ambushes and had little or no consequence. When the Italians arrived in 1935, the insurgents seem to have laid down their weapons (Hussein Indhessa 2016: 84).

When Emperor Haile Selassie returned from exile in 1941, Muhammad Gada Qallu continued his armed resistance. Inspired by the perceived benevolent policy of the Italians and angered by the reestablishment of Amhara rule, his objective was now to chase out the Amhara. In particular, he viewed their arrival and presence as an intrusion into the *abbaa muuda*'s sacred land and reportedly rallied the entire population to rebel against them. In addition to Muhammad Gada Qallu, the so-called three Husseins led the insurgency: Hussein Wayyu Tesso (the son of the assassinated Wayyu Tesso), Hussein Wayyu Morke, and Hussein Wayyu Qallu (Hussein Indhessa 2016: 86; Markakis 1987: 193; Muusaa Haaji Aadam Saaddoo 2014: 76). Although the fighters were few in numbers, the military was unable to secure the area, and the ensuing conflict – locally referred to as the *Biltu* war – continued for eight months, until the authorities invited the insurgents to negotiate. The fighters, however, refused any form of negotiations, causing the government to initiate a military offensive. Led by the governor of Bale, Captain Demisse Amberbir (1944–1948),

[25] Interview, Imro Hussein, Addis Ababa, August 3, 2011.

and supported by Gebre Selassie Turuche, the military entered the Harenna forest, forced out the local people, and drove them to the town of Angetu. There, fifty-six individuals – including the three Husseins – were reportedly massacred (Muusaa Haaji Aadam Saaddoo 2014: 79).[26] The authorities, however, were unable to capture Muhammad Gada Qallu and instead the soldiers killed his livestock, burned his village, and took his family hostage. Now a wanted man, Muhammad Gada Qallu saw no other option than to flee. He decided to travel to Raytu and seek refuge with *Fitawrari* Nuho Dhadhi. Before leaving, he sought the help of a person called Chako Enale, a known *balabat* in Dello, who managed to convince him to surrender. Muhammad Gada Qallu had been promised amnesty if he turned himself in but was immediately arrested and sentenced to twenty years in prison in Goba. He later died there in 1961 (Abbas H. Gnamo 2014: 188f.; Gebru Tareke 1977: 249, 287; Hussein Indhessa 2016: 88f.; Ketema Meskela 2001: 56).[27]

This and other uprisings caused the emperor to embark on the task of consolidating his power and strengthening national unity, and he was in particular concerned about the Italians' concessions to the Muslims (Sbacchi 1985: 135; Teshale Tibebu 1995: 107). The strengthening of national unity had a clear religious dimension, and the emperor was determined to restore and enhance the notion of Ethiopia as a divinely Christian nation. This was accompanied by the notion of the emperor as having both a "secular and religious mandate," which consequently meant that "religious obedience and political obedience are two faces of the same coin" (Marzagora 2015: 125). An important instrument in this regard was *Abuna* Tewoflos, the bishop of Harar, who was sent to different southern regions as sort of a nationalist missionary. He arrived in Bale around 1947, traveling first to the western *worredas* of Dodola and Kokosa, where he arranged a mass baptism of allegedly 20,000 Arsi Oromo, both Muslims and adherents to the Oromo religion (Braukämper 2002: 159).[28] The religious requirements levied on

---

[26] "Koloneel Aliyyii Cirrii," *Oromia Brodcasting Service,* July 10, 2016 (www .youtube.com/watch?v=DfKmGu4KspM; accessed February 27, 2018).
[27] Interviews, Hajji Ibrahim Mustafa, Robe, March 14, 2006; Aliye Jemal, Robe, April 2, 2006; Hajji Abdurazak Hussein, Lais Hafiz, Ahmed Hussein, and Tahir Malik, Dello-Menna, June 15, 2017.
[28] Interviews, Siraj Muhammad-Amin, Robe, June 11, 2006; Daniel Negash, Dodola, October 23, 2002; Hajji Hassan Faqi, Goba, August 15, 2005; Hajji Hussein Awol, Robe, July 2, 2011.

the newly baptized seem to have been rather lax, as they were excused from fasting until they had "learned to make *wott* and *injera*."[29] The conversions did not make lasting impacts, though: "My uncle was *balabat* during the time of Emperor Haile Selassie, and he became Christian, subsequently making his people Christians. That was only in name, though, and they all returned to Islam afterward."[30] The government's religious-nationalist pressure aimed at curbing the space given to Islam did affect the people, though, and the sense of loss is something clearly expressed in this poem:

Mataan amaamaa si baree
Lugtii si kofiyaa si baree
Haile Selassie badee galee
Eessatti baataa ree
Yaa Oromo saree

The head learned to wear *amama*
The head learned to wear *kofiyah*
Haile Selassie went and returned
Where will we go now
Oh, Oromo those dogs.[31]

Another important figure was *Abuna* Basilios, who in 1959 became the Ethiopian Orthodox Church's first Ethiopian Patriarch. He traveled to Goba in 1948, where he assembled the local Arsi Oromo leaders and dignitaries, conveying a direct message from the emperor and calling the people to convert to Christianity. The meeting between the *abuna* and the local people has become almost legendary. As the story has been retold numerous times both by my informants and in written sources, it is difficult to verify its many details.[32] Besides being amusing, the story serves well as an illustration about the nature of the relations between Amhara rulers and the Arsi Oromo of Bale. It points, at the same time to how the emperor viewed himself as the embodied father of

---

[29] *Wott* and *Injera* are common dishes among the Amhara (Interview, Hajji Hassan Faqi, Goba, August 15, 2005).
[30] Interview, Hajji Hassan Faqi, Goba, August 15, 2005.
[31] Interview, Siraj Muhammed-Amin, Robe, June 11, 2006.
[32] This account is based on the biography of Hajji Adam Sado by Muusaa Haaji Aadam Saaddoo (2014: 121), a story in the Amharic newspaper *Seif Nabalbal* (Sword of the Flame) ("Do You Know Hajj Adam Sado," 2005), and oral interviews: Siraj Muhammad-Amin, Robe, August 12, 2005; Ahmed Mustafa, Addis Ababa, June 22, 2017.

the nation and his subjects as his children – being a clear example of the power of the family as a metaphor for peoplehood:

Having gathered the local dignitaries in Goba, and standing in front of them, *Abuna* Basilios read aloud a letter from Haile Selassie, wherein the emperor portrayed himself as the father of all the people, only wishing them well:

– You all know We have great love for the people of Bale, and We know you love Us too. … We also love all the people of Ethiopia, regardless of religion, believing that the people are one.

So far, the letter seemed rather innocent, and had a style and content typical for the emperor. However, what followed made the locals very uncomfortable:

– You also know that We have a great love for Our Christian religion, and when the people accept this religion, Our love for them will be even greater.

The Arsi Oromo leaders did not know what to say. While obviously unwilling to convert to Christianity, they knew, at the same time, that they could not insult the emperor, and they thus had to choose their words carefully. They looked around for someone who could respond to the emperor's invitation, but no one was willing to speak. Finally, a certain Hajji Adam Saddo rose to his feet and said:

– The emperor has great love for his people, and he says to the people of Bale that he loves us. We also have love for him, and we would like to give our opinion on the matter raised in this letter. Because of his love for the people in Bale, the emperor says that the people should follow Christianity, and that he then would have even a greater love for the people. Sure, when a man loves someone, he wants what is best for that person. But Bale's people also have great love for the emperor. Therefore, the people's wish is that the emperor should leave Christianity and turn to Islam. And if he changes his religion, the people of Bale will love him even more. This is our answer to the emperor, please tell him this.

The *abuna* and the local authorities became deeply angered by this response, and immediately ended the meeting.

Conclusion

The focus on Menelik's conquest "from below" and paying attention to how it was played out locally fill in important gaps that enables us to get a more complete picture of the conquest and provides crucial details on how it was received and experienced in the many local contexts. There is, in the case of Bale, no doubt that the conquest and the ensuing new political realities had deep consequences for the Arsi Oromo. The involuntary incorporation into the Ethiopian Kingdom meant that they had to submit to an alien and hegemonic regime focused on extracting as many resources as it could from its new territories, and this gradually impacted their economy, social structures, and established way of life. There is also no doubt that the Arsi Oromo did not view the conquest as an attempt to reclaim lost territories and to reunify the empire. They clearly saw the arrival of Menelik's soldiers as an intrusion and there is no doubt that the new realities entailed subjugation and loss of autonomy.

The Arsi Oromo's acts of resistance were popular responses to the harsh realities brought by conquest, but it is far from clear that the Arsi Oromo at the time viewed the conquest as part of a larger program of internal colonization – as it later has been interpreted. And arguably, detailed micro-studies of the conquest serve to nuance the unproductive dichotomy of viewing it either as national unification or as illegitimate colonialization. The resistance, however, was sporadic, spontaneous, and poorly organized, demonstrating that they did not really understand what they were up against. The fact that armed uprisings would continue after the Ethiopian state had demonstrated its coercive power is notable and points to the deep-seated animosity that existed among the local Arsi Oromo, as well as to their resilience in opposing their new rulers. The Amhara's retaliatory measures intensified this resolve even further. The developments in Bale have arguably broader relevance, constituting a case in point that provides insights into the existing and continuous antagonistic relationship between the local southern population and the Amhara ruling elite. While such hostile sentiments for the most part remained latent and hidden, they were, as noted by Hylander, forcefully simmering under the surface:

The racial hatred towards the oppressors is like the charcoal the Galla [Oromo] hide under the ashes in order to keep the fire alive during the night. The Arsi Galla [Oromo] are still at war with their neighboring tribes, and their honor is determined by how many enemies they kill. "But we don't kill any Amhara," they say. But after one has established a close relationship to them, they add with a wink of the eye: "They [the Amhara] are always found dead in the forest, and there is nobody who has killed them." (Hylander 1936: 122)[33]

The animosity continued to grow but remained hidden in the decades to come. It was not until 1963 that it would rise to the surface and became explicitly manifest in an insurgency that would last for nearly a decade.

---

[33] The author's translation from Swedish.

4 | *Bale at War*

The Bale insurgency erupted in 1963 and would continue until it was crushed by the Ethiopian military in 1970. The fighting took place mainly in the eastern and southern lowlands, spanning across El Kere, Wabe, and Dello *awrajas* – which all were under the complete control of the insurgents for long periods of time. The insurgency's three main fronts were also found in these areas, where the course of the fighting followed rather uneven trajectories and involved a range of different actors. The insurgents were Arsi Oromo and Somali pastoralists from the lowlands, who enjoyed widespread support throughout the region. The locals referred to the insurgency as the *Kuluba*, and sometimes as the *Dhombir* war. *Kuluba* stems from the English word *club*, which, as I will return to in Chapter 9, had its origin in the Somali Youth Club (later becoming the Somali Youth League). People sometimes talked about the *Kuluba* as the struggle, and sometimes as the time of the *Kuluba*, *yeeroo Kuluba*. The word *Dhombir* was, on the other hand, the Somali name for the Italian-made Carcano M19 rifle developed in 1890 – a common weapon used by the insurgents – which on the Ethiopian side was referred to as the *Alben* rifle.[1]

In this chapter, I present new empirical data on the insurgency. I discuss the insurgency's different trajectories along the fronts of Wabe and Dello, the initial triggering points for the insurgency in these localities, the nature of the struggle, and the movement's success in securing territorial control and challenging the Ethiopian state. The chapter also sheds light on the Ethiopian government's reaction to the insurgency, and how this eventually led to the defeat of the insurgents. It is important to underscore that the chapter should in no way be read as a complete narrative about the insurgency; there are several blank spots that need to be filled as well as much uncertainty about many of

---

[1] Interviews, Jawar Aliye, Robe, April 2, 2006; Hajji Abdurazak Hussein, Lais Hafiz, Ahmed Hussein, and Tahir Malik, Delllo-Menna, June 15, 2017.

the details. In addition, the lack of sufficient sources and the fact that many of those participating in the insurgency have passed away have make reconstructions an exceedingly difficult task.

Much has been written about war and insurgency in Africa in general, and in the Horn in particular.[2] Christopher Clapham's (1998) seminal contribution has been particularly important, where he distinguishes between liberation, separatist, reform, and warlord insurgencies. While Clapham's typology has continued relevance, others have pointed out that new forms of insurgencies do not fit easily into these exclusive categories (Bøås and Dunn 2007).[3] The Bale insurgency is one of those. At the outset, it might have been characterized as a separatist insurgency – representing "the aspirations and identities of particular ethnicities or regions within an existing state," and having the goal of "seceding from the state altogether, or else by pressing for some special autonomous status" (Clapham 1998: 6). However, as this and subsequent chapters will show, such a categorization may not be that simple. Explanations of armed conflicts have meanwhile moved away from singular causal theories to recognizing a multitude of intersected factors. Similarly, it has also become more common – and arguably useful – to distinguish between underlying and trigger factors, wherein the former often relate to latent and simmering notions of animosity in a *longue duré* perspective, and the latter refers to the minimum necessary conditions for actors to choose violent struggle (Brown 1996; Sobek 2008; Suganami 1997). Such a perspective can certainly be applied to the Bale insurgency – which followed many parallel tracks, occurred in various localities, and was a product of a series of complex developments.

The Bale insurgency is not well known beyond Ethiopia, and as one of the many insurgencies fought in Ethiopia's remote rural areas, it never attracted much attention from outside observers. The fact that it was, from a military point of view, unsuccessful has pushed it further into oblivion. The defeat also meant that it achieved very little politically, thus making it markedly different from, for example, the Eritrean struggle that eventually led to an independent Eritrea. However, the fact that it took the Ethiopian government nearly seven years to crush

---

[2] For an excellent review of the literature on insurgency, writ large as resistance, see van Walraven and Abbink (2003).
[3] This has later been recognized by Clapham (2007).

the insurgency should in itself be reason enough to brush off the dust of history. In addition, the degree of success should not be the only yard-stick for evaluating insurgency movements, and it is my argument that the Bale insurgency contributes with much-needed insights to broader historical and contemporary dynamics in both Ethiopia and the Horn of Africa, particularly when it comes to the interconnected roles of religion and ethnicity.

The First Shots

The trigger for the Bale insurgency was the new head tax introduced in early 1963, which led to the first shots being fired in March of that year in El Kere *awraja*. Continued unrest followed as the Somalis across the *awraja* refused to pay both the newly introduced tax and unpaid taxes from previous years. Kahin Abdi was a key figure leading the resistance in El Kere. He had a history as an anti-government agitator; when his son was imprisoned in 1963 for failing to pay his taxes, Kahin Abdi attacked the local police station and freed his son by force. Now defined as an outlaw by the authorities, he continued his activism, including the destruction of a salt mine in Afder in September 1963, which enhanced his reputation among the local population. The success of this attack boosted the morale of Kahin Abdi's men and spurred the recruitment of additional fighters – mainly from his Afigam clan (Gebru Tareke 1977: 294). His next step was to attack the town of Hargele on November 21, but that proved far more challenging. During several rounds of intense fighting, twenty-seven of the insurgents were killed and two were wounded, and they lost twelve rifles (Aberra Ketsela 1971: 2). However, the fact that the attack was a complete failure seems not to have discouraged the insurgents. They maintained their pressure una-bated into 1964, launching attacks on El Kere, Hargele, and Imi towns. In February-March 1964, Kahin Abdi was joined by Chamma Ketene and Sheikh Muhammed Abdi Nur, who were relatives of the *balabat* in El Kere town, and by Umar Abar. All of these individuals had their personal grudges against the local administration and had been involved in previous armed attacks (Gebru Tareke 1977: 295). In addition, the insurgents called on the people to boycott the local authorities. This included refraining from visiting any government offices and avoiding contact with the local police. The people were further urged to trade only with other Somalis and not with any

Amhara, and to use only Somali currency. All Amhara were moreover banned from fetching water from the wells (Assefa Addissu 1980: 21).

Realizing that the El Kere *awraja* police force was unable to suppress the insurgency, the government decided to send in the military. This was a rather halfhearted measure, however, as soldiers arriving from Negelle Borana only stayed for eight days before returning to their base. The only result of their actions was to send the insurgents into hiding for eight days, and as soon as the military left, they continued their operations relatively easily, attacking the towns of Lebashilindi and Chireti. During the same period, leadership was transferred to Sheikh Muhammad Abdi Nur, and by late 1965, the insurgents more or less controlled the whole El Kere *awraja*.[4] By then, the unrest had spread to the remaining lowland areas of Bale.

The Wabe Front

While there are no indications of any *direct* coordination between the insurgents in El Kere and the movement that gradually emerged in Wabe *awraja*, it is obvious that news of what was going on further east had reached Wabe (Gebru Tareke 1977: 297). It is possible that the livestock tax was also the spark there, yet this was never mentioned as a cause by any of my informants. The antecedents for the fighting in Wabe *awraja* date back to 1962 and involved an individual Amhara merchant who was driving twelve donkeys loaded with honey from Sewena up to Ginir. On his way, he was ambushed by a certain Sheikh Muhammad Aliye Roba, shot while sitting on his mule, and fell dead to the ground. Sheikh Muhammad Aliye Roba looted the caravan and disappeared. Even if the killed Amhara was an ordinary civilian and not connected to authorities, the local people did not view him as separate from what they considered the structures of oppression:

---

[4] There are some disagreement concerning the time line and the roles of the main actors. Aberra Ketsela (1971: 1f.) claims that the attack on the salt mine was led by Sheikh Muhammad Abdi Nur, who was a former *balabat* of Afigam who allegedly had been mistreated by the salt company. He moreover claims that Sheikh Muhammad Abdi Nur had already died on the battlefield in February 1964. Gebru Tareke, however, argues that Sheikh Muhammad Abdi Nur joined the insurgency in February 1964, and that he died at end of that year (1977: 295, 297).

The Amhara would always come to this area and travel across from marked place to marked place and just demand what they wanted. The people couldn't refuse, they just had to bow and give them whatever they asked for. This particular Amhara that was killed had stolen all this honey from the people, and was taking it to Ginir.[5]

While this could be described as an isolated incident, it was, at the same time, a manifestation of a strong antagonism simmering under the surface. A key person who had started articulating such sentiments was Hussein Bune from the Hawattu clan and a native of Sewena *worreda*. He had already earned a reputation as an anti-government agitator, urging people to revolt against the government in the early 1960s. The murder of the Amhara merchant "was the spark that set off a fire all across this area," and shortly after, Hussein Bune formed a small group of fighters.[6] The nascent group lacked arms and equipment, but after Hussein Bune sold nine of his oxen he was able to purchase three rifles. News about this soon reached the local authorities, who sent the police to his camp at Laga Bosona in Sewena in an attempt to arrest him and his men. Hussein Bune managed to flee, and with additional men joining him, the embryonic insurgency movement set up a new base at Mt. Gona in Sewena (see Figure 4.1) (Yaassiin Mohammad Roobaa and Anbassaa 2014: 39f.).

The most serious problem for the growing movement, however, was the lack of arms. Somalia represented the most obvious source, and in 1963, Hussein Bune sent the first delegation of eight men across the vast Ogaden region to Somalia in search of guns. They were well received in Somalia and managed to obtain eight Carcano M19 (*Dhombir*) rifles and one Thompson machine gun.[7] Later in 1963, Hussein Bune himself and eight of his compatriots made another trip to Somalia, bringing back additional guns, ammunition, and grenades (Yaassiin Mohammad Roobaa and Anbassaa 2014: 44). When he returned, he took the title Colonel Hussein Bune (Gebru Tareke 1977: 299). Soon additional groups of insurgents embarked on the long march to

---

[5] Interview, Jowar Kadir, Sewena, June 13, 2018.
[6] Interview, Jowar Kadir, Sewena, June 13, 2018.
[7] The eight persons were Jowar Elemo Jilo, Abdurazak Badhaso, Muhammad Adam, Abdallah Tubba, Mama Sheikh Ahmed, Abduqadir Hajji Muhammad Balle, Abda Umar Abdurro, and Abdujawad Sheikh Kadir (*The Story of Hussein Bune* 2008: 13).

Figure 4.1 Mt. Gona in Sewena

Somalia, and the movement gradually gained strength both in terms of manpower and military equipment:

We were 50 people who travelled back [from Somalia], arriving in Sewena. We didn't settle in one place but we moved around. The authorities had their spies, and they soon heard about us. They immediately sent the army to catch us. This was by the Dhara river, at a place called Melka Ade. We heard shots, and then we knew they were on to us. We took our positions, and we tried to fight our way out . . . we dispersed and fled in different directions . . . and after that the different groups came together. We identified who were dead, regrouped, and went back and chased the soldiers.[8]

The first major clash between the Wabe insurgents and government forces took place in today's Raytu *worreda* in April 1964, where insurgents attacked a police unit and a local militia. Although it is unclear if the attack resulted in any casualties, it was, for the local authorities in Ginir, the *awraja* capital, an unprecedented provocation that could not remain unchallenged. A police force consisting of sixty-six men and led by *Qenazmach* Negash Worqu and Colonel Berhane Zeleqe was immediately dispatched to Raytu. The force, however, was

---

[8] Interview, Abdo Hajji Mustafa, Raytu, June 12, 2018.

ambushed along the way and easily defeated by the insurgents. A major reason for the defeat was that the commanding officers, and subsequently the rest of the police, speedily fled the scene without putting up much resistance. Both *Qenazmach* Negash Worqu and Colonel Berhane Zeleqe were later found guilty of treason and removed from their positions (Aberra Ketsela 1971: 5).

Defeating the government forces in such a seemingly easy manner boosted the morale of the insurgents and led the locals to believe that this was the start of a total victory – causing many to join the insurgency (Aberra Ketsela 1971: 6; Gebru Tareke 1977: 297f.). The insurgents subsequently launched a second attack on the police station in Dibiso in August 1964, but this turned out to be more challenging than their first operation. As soon as the *awraja* authorities in Ginir received news about the ensuing attack, they swiftly responded by sending in additional police, and the battle ended with Hussein Bune losing eleven of his men (Gebru Tareke 1977: 299). The defeat in Dibiso did not have any lasting impact on the struggle, and with the continuous addition of new fighters, the movement grew stronger. Establishing a base in Sewena, the insurgents started military training of new recruits, and as there were no police stations or any other form of government structures in that area, they were relatively free to move around undisturbed.[9] The insurgents' main base in Sewena remained at Mt. Gona, while the base in Raytu was at El Waq in the Galbi Mountains (Ahmed Abdalla and Hasan 2010: 14).[10] From September 1964, the insurgents had the capacity to launch larger operations and soon turned their attention to Beltu *worreda*. Under the leadership of Hussein Bune, they attacked Legehida, the *worreda* capital, where they burned down the police station and the administration offices. The insurgents did not remain in Legehida but launched a new attack on the town on September 30, 1964. They easily drove out the seven armed officials defending it, and this time they took permanent control over the town. Those who escaped later reported that the insurgents were well armed – carrying Thompson machine guns and rifles. They also said that the insurgents included a certain Captain Makidi, who belonged to the group of Makhtal Tahir, a prominent leader of the

---

[9] Interview, Jowar Kadir, Sewena, June 13, 2018. It is claimed that the number of insurgents in Wabe by then had reached more than 360 men (*Revolutionary Vigor in Somali Abo through History* 1979: 45).

[10] Interview, Adam Yunis, Raytu, June 10, 2018.

insurgency in Ogaden and a person called Isme Abba Washa, who was a lawyer from Ginir and (for unknown reasons) had served time in prison and lost his right to practice law. Joining the insurgency in 1964, he became one of its most important agitators, constantly encouraging people to rise up against the Amhara (*Revolutionary Vigor in Somali Abo through History* 1979: 45f.; Aberra Ketsela 1971: 6f.; Gebru Tareke 1977: 298).

Legehida remained under the control of the insurgents until February 1965, when the Commander of the Bale Police Tesfaye Gebre-Mariam sent forces into Beltu and recaptured the town. The commander did not, however, leave anyone behind to defend it, consequently making it an easy target for continuous attacks by the insurgents (Aberra Ketsela 1971: 22). Simultaneously with the operations in Beltu, the insurgents also attacked Tedecha Alem, the capital of Raytu *worreda*. The Amhara officials in Raytu had by then heard about the operations in Beltu, and when the insurgents struck, most of them had already fled to Ginir (Gebru Tareke 1977: 300). Moreover, in October 1964, a group of insurgents was sent into Gololcha *worreda,* in the northern part of Wabe, seeking to recruit people for the struggle. However, as they approached Jarra, the *worreda* capital, local informants discovered and reported them to the authorities. The administrator of Gololcha, Seyum Getaneh, quickly mobilized the local police and attacked the small group on October 15, 1964. Insurgents continued to operate in Gololcha, and Seyum Getaneh sent additional forces against them, engaging them in a battle at Doyo (ca 15 km north of Jarra) on November 21, 1964. Before retreating back to Jarra, his soldiers reportedly looted the property of the villagers and burnt down more than ninety-five of the houses in Doyo (*Revolutionary Vigor in Somali Abo through History* 1979: 59).

Armed with Somali weapons and continuing to attract followers among the lowlanders, the insurgency movement continued to grow, intensified its activities, and expanded its territorial control across Wabe *awraja*. By the end of 1965, it had taken over Raytu, Beltu, and parts of Gololcha *worredas*, forcing government officials to retreat to the towns of Ginir and Jarra. In fact, the frontline was only 5 km from Jarra (*Revolutionary Vigor in Somali Abo through History* 1979: 69). The insurgents continued to strengthen their position in the year that followed, and throughout 1966, they expanded their control over the lowlands. One important area where the insurgents could move protected and from which they launched many of their attacks was the forested region northeast of Goro town (in Goro *worreda*) toward Ginir. This area was so crowded with insurgents that the military referred to it as "little Mogadishu" (Hussein Indhessa 2016: 114). Although the insurgents were unable to establish lasting control in the highlands, they managed to create a certain degree of instability in the rural areas, forcing local administrators and government representatives to retreat to the towns. The towns were not always safe either, and even Goba was attacked twice by the insurgents (Aberra Ketsela 1971: 22; Gebru Tareke 1977: 310f.). The movement continued its success into 1967, and reports stated that eleven out of eighteen *balabat* areas in Wabe were on the side of the insurgents.[11] While the insurgents were able to launch a major attack on Ginir town in May that year, 1967 would mark the gradual weakening of the movement.

The Dello Front

The insurgency in Dello *awraja* started in early 1964 and was initially spearheaded by a certain Sheikh Abdullahi Ali of the Gurra clan.[12] It had some connections to similar movements in Borana and was assumingly concentrated in the eastern parts of Dello *awraja* (Gebru Tareke 1977: 300). Sheikh Abdullahi Ali's movement seems not to have made a lasting impact, and some informants claim that this was because the Somali government was reluctant to provide weapons to the Gurra, preferring to arm the indigenous Arsi Oromo.[13] Far more important was the insurgency that emerged in the southern *worreda* of Medda Welabu. Led by the iconic Waqo Gutu, this movement soon became the main insurgency in Dello, and the most enduring one. Although the underlying causes for the insurgency in Dello were the same as in the other areas, what sparked it was somewhat particular.

Since the early twentieth century, and particularly since the Italian period, Somali clans had expanded westward into what traditionally

---

[11] Interrogation report, Sayyid Mustafa, Wabe *awraja*, Gololcha *Worreda*. Attachment to: Letter from Colonel Mulat Tamiru, Commander of the 4th Regiment, to Colonel Kebede, Commander of the 7th Regiment, September 2, 1967. No. 2/4/32/1121/140.

[12] The Gurra clan is a bilingual clan considered by most to be Somali.

[13] Interview, Hajji Abdurazak Hussein, Lais Hafiz, Ahmed Hussein, and Tahir Malik, Dello-Menna, June 15, 2017.

was considered Borana territory, inevitably causing frictions with the
Borana.[14] Careful not to further upset the Somali clans, the Ethiopian
government was initially reluctant to deal with the Somali migration;
however, in 1959, it changed its strategy and started to arm the Borana
and the Guji as a bulwark against Somali expansionism (Hussein
Indhessa 2016: 119; Markakis 1987: 195). Encouraged and embol-
dened by such state support, the Borana started to sporadically attack
Somali clans and other non-Borana. In an effort to de-escalate the
situation in Borana, the government decided to resettle any non-
Borana. A majority of these were Somali clans, such as the Hawiya,
Marehan, Degodi, Gerri, and Eder, but there were also a significant
number of Arsi Oromo, including Waqo Gutu and his family. The
administrator of Sidamo *teklay gezat,* Adargacho Mesay, called the
Somali and Arsi Oromo clans to a meeting in Negelle in early 1964 and
ordered them to move to Filtu (about 130 km east of Negelle Borana).
The Arsi Oromo clans refused, saying they did not want to live among
the Somalis. The government gave them seven days to comply with the
order, but in the meantime, the Guji Oromo attacked them.
Overwhelmed by the well-armed Guji, the Arsi Oromo, including
Waqo Gutu and his family, had no other choice than to flee – crossing
the Genale River into Bale, where they settled as refugees around the
town of Bidere in Medda Welabu (Aberra Ketsela 1971: 8).

Having lost land, homes, and much of their livestock, the displaced
Arsi Oromo found their living conditions in Bidere difficult. They were
not much welcomed by the other Arsi Oromo, who viewed them as
aliens. Also, the local authorities treated them with a great deal of
suspicion because of their clashes with the Borana.[15] In the end, the
displaced sent three representatives to the local authorities in Oborso
town, the capital of Medda Welabu *worreda,* to complain about the
situation for the displaced Arsi Oromo. Their grievances were immediately dismissed, and the three individuals were charged with being
outlaws and arrested – before being brought back to Bidere by Captain
Fiseha Muhammad, the head of Dello-Menna police (Aberra Ketsela
1971: 9). The treatment the displaced received from the local authorities contributed to aggravate their resentment and became important
in adding fuel to the insurgency that would ensue. The local authorities'

---

[14] See Gufu Oba (2013: 231f.) for an extensive discussion of this.
[15] Interview, General Jagama Kello, Addis Ababa, October 16, 2006.

rejection of their request for arms – to protect themselves against potential attacks from the Guji and Borana – further fueled their resentment and compelled them to look for ways to obtain weapons.

While in Borana, Waqo Gutu had made contact with Muhammad Salah, an agent for the Somali government, who had told him that Mogadishu was providing weapons to those seeking to rebel against the Ethiopian state. In June–July 1964, shortly after arriving in Bidere, Waqo Gutu collected forty men and left for Somalia. He brought with him a letter from Muhammad Salah, saying that Waqo Gutu was the "*balabat* of Arsi." After spending five months in Somalia, they returned to Dello around November–December 1964 with forty-two rifles and two Thompson machine guns (Hussein Indhessa 2016: 120f.).[16] The purpose of arming themselves was no longer only to protect themselves from the Borana, and the arrival of arms became a crucial incentive for broader anti-government activism. Meanwhile, Aliye Chirri, who had fought with the already mentioned Mohammad Gada Qallu, had formed a small group of insurgents in Medda Welabu *worreda*. Sometimes in 1964, he and his supporters also left for Somalia where they received weapons (Hussein Indhessa 2016: 122). As he returned, he met with Waqo Gutu and his men at a place called Medda, where the foundation for the embryonic movement was laid. That they chose this place is hardly a coincidence, as this was considered the cradle of all Oromo. Waqo Gutu was elected the main leader, while individuals such as Aliye Chirri, Ibrahim Korri, Musa Doya, Dubro Waqo, and Adem Jilo were leading their own bands of insurgents.[17] To what extent the structures at this stage were elaborate enough to coordinate the different groups' activities, however, is doubtful.

The first battle between Waqo Gutu's men and the Ethiopian forces took place at Melka Ana by the Genale River, where a small band of insurgents, armed with twenty rifles clashed with soldiers arriving from Negelle. Although it resulted in the insurgency's first casualties, it also was its first victory, thus contributing to boost morale and to attract followers and supporters among the local population (Aberra Ketsela

---

[16] Interview, Hafiz Hassan, Addis Ababa, June 16, 2011. One source claims that forty-eight men accompanied Waqo Gutu to Somalia (Yaassiin Mohammad Roobaa and Anbassaa 2014: 15).
[17] "Koloneel Aliyyii Cirrii," *Oromia Broadcasting Service*, July 10, 2016 (www .youtube.com/watch?v=DfKmGu4KspM; accessed February 27, 2018).

1971: 11; Hussein Indhessa 2016: 121).[18] The movement was further strengthened when Waqo Lugu, a village judge and a *burqa* from around Dello-Menna town, joined its ranks.[19] He had been engaged in a long-standing quarrel with *Fitawrari* Gelchu Togie, the Medda Welabu *worreda* administrator and, in addition, had been accused of expressing support for the insurgents. News about this soon spread, and the fact that such a prominent person had joined the movement spurred the recruitment of a number of other *burkas* in Dello (Gebru Tareke 1991: 141f.; 1977: 306).

Lacking sufficient arms, the embryonic insurgency movement initially kept a low profile and restricted its activities to the areas between Oborso and Bidere in Medda Welabu. As a result, it became increasingly difficult to travel between the two towns, and a general state of insecurity gradually spread across the rural areas. A significant escalation of the struggle came with the attack of Oborso town on February 8, 1965. Aliye Chirri led the attack, which targeted the *worreda* administration and police station. Defeating the police and the armed civilians, the insurgents looted the government offices and burnt down an orthodox church. A number of people were killed during the fighting, and most of the Amhara fled Oborso for Dello-Menna and Negelle towns. A few days later, on February 11, Waqo Gutu led an attack on Bidere town but faced fierce resistance from a twenty-men strong police force under the leadership of the Captain Fiseha Muhammad and the local militia led by Gelchu Togie. The fighting lasted for three days, and it was not until an army contingent arrived from Negelle that the insurgents withdrew. The military did not stay long in Bidere, however, and as the soldiers returned to Negelle, the insurgents were able to capture the town on June 12, 1965 (Aberra Ketsela 1971: 10; Gebru Tareke 1977: 308f.; Hussein Indhessa 2016: 124; Yaassiin Mohammad Roobaa and Anbassaa 2014: 8). The falls of Oborso and Bidere were key moments for the emerging insurgency in Dello. Having secured these two towns, which were the only places with some sort of government structure, the movement was now able to operate freely across the southern lowlands. Moreover, the victories generated a strong degree of enthusiasm among the local population.

---

[18] Interview, Hafiz Hassan, Addis Ababa, June 16, 2011.
[19] The *burqa* was next-in-rank to the *balabat,* appointed by the Amhara.

Seeing the insurgency as the vehicle that would defeat the government, a growing number of locals joined the movement.

After securing control over Medda Welabu and the southern areas of Dello, the insurgents turned their attention to the north (Gebru Tareke 1977: 309). Beginning in the middle of 1965, they moved through the large Harenna forest, calling upon the locals to join the movement. From there they entered Genale *awraja,* where the *balabat* Umar Kebelo and a large number of people in his area joined the insurgency (Aberra Ketsela 1971: 11; Markakis 1987: 197). In October 1965, the insurgents reached Nansebu and even attacked Adaba, a town not far away from Dodola. The local authorities in Genale *awraja* were forced to respond, and in November 1965, the police and the local militia, under the leadership of Bekele Harargu, the administrator of Adaba, were sent into the forest in an attempt to drive out the insurgents. When the expedition reached the town of Worqa, in Nansebu *worreda,* the insurgents ambushed them. The government force lost a number of men, including Bekele Harargu himself (*Revolutionary Vigor in Somali Abo through History* 1979: 52; Gebru Tareke 1977: 310). The Genale *awraja* authorities responded swiftly and harshly by immediately arresting the local people and confiscating all weapons they could find (Aberra Ketsela 1971: 10f.). These measures only deepened the anti-government sentiments, and local resistance in the southern parts of Genale *awraja* continued unabated. The local authorities subsequently sent in yet another expedition – this one led *Fitawrari* Wolde-Mikael Bu'i, the Genale *awraja* administrator and son of the famous Bu'i Falama (see Chapter 3). Entering the Harenna forest in March 1966, this expedition was also ambushed, and an unknown assassin killed *Fitawrari* Wolde-Mikael Bu'i at a place called Refissa (Aberra Ketsela 1971: 11; Gebru Tareke 1977: 312).

By 1966, the insurgents controlled large parts of the rural areas of Dello, and the movement was constantly attracting new followers. The local authorities had managed to recapture the town of Bidere in late 1965, but without enough forces to defend it, the town again became an easy target for the insurgents who soon restored control over it (Aberra Ketsela 1971: 22). The insurgents also extended their activities into Fasil *awraja,* where a police report lists 152 armed individuals as being part of the insurgency. These were said to be from Fasil, Genale, and Dello *awrajas* and reportedly belonged to various clans. However, the fact that the majority were from the Karmamida and Sheidama clans indicates that the insurgency was also getting a foothold in the highlands.[20] Intrusions into the highlands continued throughout the 1966, with the insurgents clashing with government forces in the highland town of Dinshu.[21] The movement continued to recruit people from the highlands, and a report from as late as 1968 lists eight individuals from Sinana and Goba *worredas* who had traveled to Harenna Buluq to fight.[22]

Overall, the insurgency movement in Bale experienced a great deal of success from 1964 to 1967, establishing control over most of the lowland areas in Wabe and Dello, as well as in parts of Fasil *awrajas*. It has been claimed that by the end of 1966, they controlled almost three-fifths of Bale (Aberra Ketsela 1971: 22). Whether this is accurate is hard to ascertain, but it is important to emphasize that here we do not talk about territorial control similar to that in a conventional war. Rather, the insurgents controlled the main "roads" and strategic points and dismantled all government structures in the insurgency areas. The state's presence had at the outset been restricted to a few officials and police officers found in the *worreda* towns, but they quickly fled to the larger towns in the highlands when faced with the insurgents.

The Empire Strikes Back

The Bale insurgency had initially been a nuisance for the Ethiopian government, and, similar to what Hannah Whittaker has noted about Kenya's *shifta* war (1963–1968), it was "an unwelcome reminder of the weakness of the state at its furthest limit" (2015: 15). The government's initial reaction was thus to adjust some of the existing policies, believing that this would assuage the discontent. In a public statement in 1964, Emperor Haile Selassie announced that people would have the opportunity to reclaim land that earlier had been confiscated, and that tax arrears would – when paid in full – be invested in the region. The emperor moreover promised to give the *balabats* increased land.[23] The idea behind the latter was to co-opt the *balabats* and drive a wedge

---

[20] Letter from Fasil Police Station to Brigadier Worqu Metaferia, September 5, 1966, No. 115/25/4.
[21] Interrogation Report, Aliye Nuredin, November 13, 1966.
[22] Letter from Teferra Abate, Bale Province Administration, to Fasil and Genale *awraja* Administrations, June 25, 1969, No. 2/1560/6.
[23] *Addis Zemen*, March 9, 1964.

between them and the rest of the people. The government's strategy proved unsuccessful, however, and there are no indications that any of these measures eased the situation.

The insurgency gradually became a major concern, and both the central and local authorities were growing frustrated over the prevailing insecurity. By the middle of 1965, the governor in Bale, Worqu Inqu Selassie, had realized that the local police and militia were unable to crush the insurgency. He then wrote to the emperor asking for the army to be deployed to Bale and to be stationed there permanently (Gebru Tareke 1977: 311). The emperor responded by replacing Worqu Inqu Selassie with General Worqu Metaferia in August 1966, and on December 9, 1966, the Military Committee for the Defense of Ogaden put El Kere, Wabe, Genale, and Dello *awrajas* under martial law. General Worqu Metaferia also managed to have two brigades sent to Bale – each with 4,500 men. The Fourth Brigade, led by Colonel Gessesse Retta, operated out of Negelle, while the other, the Seventh Brigade, commanded by Colonel Kebede Yacob, established its base in Goro. It needs to be added that Ethiopia at that time had the largest military force in Africa, with an army of more than 40,000 men. The bulk of its military aid came from the United States, and by 1970, Ethiopia received 60 percent of all US military support given to Africa (Markakis 1987: 92).

In addition to its collaboration with the Bale police, the military actively made use of other and more irregular forces in their pursuit of the insurgents – namely, the *nech lebash*, the territorials, and the volunteers (Gebru Tareke 1977: 313). *Nech lebash* (Amharic) can be translated as "those who wear white" and refers to the *gabi*, a white garb initially worn by people from northern Ethiopia. As a security force, the *nech lebash* emerged in the southern areas shortly after Menelik's conquest and was composed of civilians who were issued a rifle and ammunition and tasked with enforcing official orders. Not anyone could become *nech lebash*, however, and membership was restricted to "trustworthy elements of the local peasantry," which in the south meant "Christian elements of northern origin" (Markakis 1974: 302). The territorials, or the Territorial Army, were similarly an auxiliary military force established in 1959 consisting of civilians between the ages of 18 and 25. In addition to being armed, the territorials also received military training and were supposed to assist the regular military forces in maintaining the peace. The volunteers, the

third category, were another supplementary force made up of individuals from the local population. The word *volunteer* is somewhat
misleading, as they were more or less forced to assist the regular army
during emergencies (Markakis 1974: 302f.). Similar to the *nech lebash*,
the territorials and the volunteers in Bale were largely recruited from
the northern Christian population, pointing to the link between the
Christians and the state.[24] All three groups, however, were poorly
equipped and barely paid, which created a great deal of discontent
and low morale among them – in turn making desertions common
(Aberra Ketsela 1971: 23; Gebru Tareke 1991: 147). It also meant
that pillaging of the local population became an important supplement
to their meager salary. It is, in fact, possible to argue that the *nech
lebash* and the voluntary forces acted as the state's own *shiftas,* who
rather unrestrictedly turned their hunt for insurgencies into "looting
expeditions" (Markakis 1987: 198). While this alone created deep rifts
between them and the Muslim Arsi Oromo, the religious dimension
clearly exacerbated the locals' hatred for them.

Even with the combined efforts of all these forces, the military had
great difficulty quelling the insurgency. The vastness and the rugged
terrain of the region restricted the armed forces' mobility, and the lack
of roads made it impossible to enter areas where the insurgents were
moving. The local police forces stationed in the rural areas similarly
complained that the topography of Bale made it difficult for them to
capture the insurgents, and asked for more soldiers to be dispatched in
the rural areas.[25] Widespread corruption further contributed to the
military's lack of progress, and competition among the officers seriously impeded the coordination of its operations. The insurgents, on
the other hand, greatly benefited from the region's rough terrain, which
was the perfect environment for guerrilla-style fighting, and with the
support of the local population, they could attack and then vanish
quickly without any trace. Moreover, they operated in a terrain they
were intimately familiar with. Rooted in the land through active dwelling, they easily navigated across arid plains, through narrow gorges,
and within vast forested areas. As pastoralists, they knew, as I will
return to in Chapter 9, where to go, where to find water, and wherever

---

[24] This included the Amhara and the Shoa Oromo (interview, Obse Ibrahim, Robe,
April 15, 2005).
[25] Letter from Tesfaye Goji, Fasil *awraja* police station, to General Worqu
Metaferia, September 5, 1966, No. 115/25/4.

the paths crisscrossing the landscape took them, they were never far from home.

The military made no serious efforts to quell the insurgency in El Kere – as it did not pose any serious security challenge – and the state never had any real interest in the remote lowland *awraja*. Moreover, the *awraja*'s large size and scarce and dispersed population made it nearly impossible for the army to establish lasting control. Small bands of mobile insurgents could easily find hiding places, and their guerrilla tactics proved highly effective. Therefore, instead of going after the actual combatants, the government's counterinsurgency in El Kere was marked by a pattern of indiscriminate violence against the civilian population, aimed at punishing those suspected of supporting the insurgents as well as discouraging others of offering future support. Such actions included the burning of villages, arrests of prominent leaders, and depriving livestock of access to drinking water (Barnes and Abdullahi n.d.: 4; Hagmann 2014: 730). The Ethiopian government was, at the same time, constantly concerned with Somali irredentism and worried about the flow of arms and too strong connections between the insurgents and the Somali government. An important strategy for El Kere was hence to contain the insurgency and limit cross-border contacts (Hussein Indhessa 2016: 144).

The government's approach to the insurgency in Wabe and Dello was of a different nature. In Wabe, the fighters were experiencing increased pressure from the military, and as soon as Colonel Kebede Yacob and his Seventh Brigade had established themselves in Goro, they initiated the hunt for the Wabe insurgents. A major offensive was launched on June 9, 1967, with a strategy of encircling the insurgents located in the areas between Sewena and Raytu. The forces moved in from different directions but met significant resistance. Even if the army inflicted considerable losses on the insurgents, the latter usually regrouped and launched counterattacks. The insurgents were even capable of launching larger operations, and on September 9, 1967, they attacked the town of Ginir. This turned out to be devastating for the insurgents, with eight killed and ten wounded. Those surviving were forced to retreat, and with the army in pursuit, they fled toward Sewena. The army attacked the next day, killing twenty-five insurgents and wounding the same number. An unconfirmed report said that Abdulkerim Bune, a brother of Hussein Bune, was among the wounded.[26] Intense fighting between the military and the insurgents continued until April 1968, and although the latter were severely weakened by then, they refused to be beaten. Colonel Kebede Yacob was able to restore some semblance of order in Wabe, but he failed to completely crush the insurgency (*Revolutionary Vigor in Somali Abo through History* 1979: 76; Aberra Ketsela 1971: 23).

Parallel to this offensive, the military started to arm the civilian population in Wabe and to organize them in fighting the insurgents in the first half of 1967.[27] Initially, it was the Christians who received weapons, but from April 1967, reports indicated the military was also arming the Muslim Arsi Oromo. Considering the support the insurgency had among the Muslims in Wabe, this might seem surprising, but serves it as a reminder of how complex landscapes of insurgencies can be. The locals were reportedly eager to receive arms, as this meant that they did not have to travel to Somalia to get guns to defend themselves against the insurgents. While the Christian population was often targeted by the insurgents, mainly because of their collaboration with the authorities and role in the militia, the fact that the Muslim Arsi Oromo believed they needed to protect themselves from attacks from that side illuminates an increased desperation within the movement. Lack of food, clothes, and, weapons clearly affected the morale and discipline of the insurgents, causing some to attack the local Arsi Oromo – of a different clan – stealing food and livestock.[28] The civilians, on their part, were clearly exhausted after years of unrest and the army's punitive actions, and it is safe to assume that the weakening of the insurgency movement made them cautious to support those on the losing side (Revolutionary Vigor in Somali Abo through History 1979: 89). The arming of the local population, and the Muslims in particular, represented a major challenge for the insurgency leaders. They knew that the loss of support would isolate and seriously weaken the movement, and moreover, as the local population was well aware of the activities of the insurgents and had detailed knowledge about the

---

[26] Interrogation Report, Ibrahim Kadir, September, n.d., 1967.
[27] Each individual received one rifle with 150 bullets (Interrogation Report, Umar Isaq, April 5, 1967).
[28] Interview, Ibrahim Hussein, Addis Ababa, July 30, 2011; letter from Colonel Tesfaye Gebre-Mariam, Commander of Bale Police Force to Brigadier General Worqu Metaferia, Governor of Bale *teklay gezat* and Commander of the Army, April 8, 1967. No. 342/3/35.

terrain in which they operated, they would be valuable informants for the government. The insurgents' leadership, and Isme Abba Washa in particular, thus embarked on a propaganda campaign seeking to instill discipline among the fighters, underscoring the movement's objectives, and urging the fighters to reconnect with the people.[29]

Another factor seriously weakening the insurgency, which I will discuss further in the next chapter, was the dwindling of support from the Somali government, particularly from 1968. This had already started in 1967, but reports about the lack of guns and ammunition became particularly noticeable from early 1968, telling stories about how groups of insurgents who had gone to Somalia were coming back empty handed.[30] Desperately in need of arms and pressured by the military, insurgents were along all fronts deprived of their former territorial control and forced to retreat to secluded bases. Many were also constantly on the move, unable to find secure locations in which to settle. But the insurgency was not completely quelled. The military was unable to push much further and, by the end of 1968, the fighting had reached a stalemate. Growing increasingly impatient with the lack of progress, the central government in August 1967 appointed a new governor to Bale, Major-General Wolde-Selassie Bereka (Yaassiin Mohammad Roobaa and Anbassaa 2014: 9). He launched a policy to reinstate morale among the armed forces and cracked down on the widespread corruption found among the army officers and within the civilian administration. This earned him the respect of the local population, and as they saw how his policy produced positive changes, popular support for the insurgency dwindled. At the same time, the newly appointed major-general intensified the military campaign and initiated a new offensive in February 1969. With the use of heavy artillery, the offensive proved devastating for the insurgents. Attacked from different directions and forced to evacuate even their most hidden bases, the insurgents found themselves scattered in isolated groups devoid of any contact with one another. The offensive was particularly effective in Wabe, and during the first part of 1969, the military managed to drive the insurgents out and take control over the *awraja*.

---

[29] Interrogation Report, Aliye Ahmed, January 17, 1967.
[30] Letter from Dello *awraja* police to Dello *awraja* Administration, February 14, 1968. No. 261/39/41/60; Letter from the Dello *awraja* Administration, to Colonel Gessesse Retta, Commander of the 4th Brigade, February 14, 1968, No. 1/113/433/60.

Abdi Hajji Musa, one of the main leaders in Raytu, was at that time surrounded by Colonel Kebede Yacob's forces stationed in the town of Tedecha Alem. Elders were sent to negotiate with the insurgents, and shortly after, Abdi Hajji Musa and a few of his men laid down their arms and surrendered.[31] A major reason for Abdi Hajji Musa's surrender was that the army had taken his men's families hostage and confiscated their livestock. This was part of the government's broader strategy in combating the insurgency: imprisoning a large number of the civilian population and confiscating an even larger number of livestock. Hussein Bune and his men fled to Somalia, where he remained as a refugee (Yaassiin Mohammad Roobaa and Anbassaa 2014: 52f.).

Meanwhile, the armed forces also intensified the pressure along the Dello front, and in February 1967, the army embarked on a larger offensive to free the *awraja* from the insurgents. Coordinating its movements with the police, militia, and local volunteers, the Fourth Brigade set out from four directions, encircling the insurgents' stronghold in Hawo and Buluq in the Harenna forest. The insurgents initially engaged the army through their usual guerrilla tactics but decided, for unknown reasons, to meet the army in an open battle. The result was devastating for the insurgents – according to official reports, more 500 were killed, with sixty wounded.[32] The army on its side had 43 casualties. Hawo base was captured on March 1, 1967, while Buluq was taken on March 27, 1967 (Aberra Ketsela 1971: 23, fn. 9).

The loss of the Hawo and Buluq had lasting impact on the movement. A military interrogation report detailing the different battles leading up to the capture of the bases paints a bleak picture of the insurgents' situation after the offensive. It tells stories about fighters being discouraged and dispersed and how they lacked enough weapons and ammunition and describes how shortage of food and starvation forced them to cook and eat grass. A primary reason for these hardships was that the insurgents had to abandon their cattle as they fled deeper into the Harenna forest. The conditions became so dire that the insurgents held several meetings – on May 24 and May 25, 1967 – discussing surrender. Twelve men were reportedly ready to give up their arms.[33]

---

[31] Interview, Abdi Hajji Musa, Raytu, June 12, 2018.
[32] "Report of the operation from March 1 to April 1, 1967." Ministry of Interior Archives, No. 2401/1395/59.
[33] Interrogation Report, Barisso Ibrahim, June n.d., 1967.

Disagreements between the army, the territorials, and the *nech lebash* on the issue of salaries and the prevailing problem of corruption gave the insurgents in Dello much-needed breathing room. Soon after the main bases in the forest were destroyed, most of the *nech lebash* and volunteers deserted, leaving the army alone to defend its positions. The army gradually withdrew from the area, and by the end of 1967, there were no soldiers left in the forest. Furthermore, the Seventh Brigade suspended any plans of further offensives in the southern lowlands and returned to its main base in Goro. As a consequence, the insurgents were again able to recapture some of their lost territory and remained in control of large parts of the forest. The military maintained a presence in Dello-Menna town. British army engineers helped build a bridge over Genale River, thus strengthening the military's lines of communication with Borana (Aberra Ketsela 1971: 23; Gebru Tareke 1977: 328f.).

Military pressure increased in 1968, yet in spite of this, and while being in dire need of arms and ammunition, the insurgents in Dello were not ready to give up. In fact, they intensified their activities in September 1968, attacking Dello-Menna and other small towns. They even managed to penetrate the highlands, and in June 1968, there were reports of insurgents moving around in Goba and Sinana district, agitating people to join the struggle.[34] The movement was, in the long run, unable to withstand the army, and by 1969, the insurgents had retreated deeper into the Harenna forest, particularly in the areas around Buluq. That was the main base of Waqo Gutu, who at that time still had 1,500 fighters under his control.[35] Moreover, it was estimated that around 2,000 armed men were found in Aleleba, in eastern Dello (Gebru Tareke 1977: 333f.). Yet, by the beginning of 1970, the number of insurgents had dropped dramatically. Waqo Gutu was left with only 200 men, holding out in the lowlands of Medda Welabu (Gebru Tareke 1977: 336). Those who were left found their movements severely restricted. An interesting twist to the developments was that the government started to use former fighters stationed at strategic points to block the movements of the remaining insurgents (Gebru Tareke 1977: 334).

[34] Letter to Fasil and Genale *awraja* Administrations from Teferra Abate, Head of Security, Bale *teklay gezat,* June 25, 1968. No. 2/1560/6.
[35] Letter from Colonel Desta Gemeda, Administrator of Gode *awraja* and military commander to Colonel Tilahun Bishane, Commander of the 9th Brigade, n.d. No. 1/221/5/2/1.

The Human Costs and Material Impacts of the Insurgency

It is impossible for an outsider to fully comprehend the suffering caused by the fighting. However, it is important to remember that conflicts are between real people and to recognize their material character. Only then can we gradually start to understand the salience of conflicts: why people go to war in the first place, why conflicts create intense emotions, and how they leave deep scars on bodies and landscapes. As mentioned in the first chapter, I was always moved by my informants' detailed stories about firefights and battles and was, in particular, touched when interacting with bodies scarred by insurgency. Sometimes the scars would be in plain sight – for example, in the form of a missing limb. In other cases, they were not as obvious, being scars from bullets or grenades covered by clothes. My informants would roll up their pant legs or lift up their shirt to unveil their reminders of the insurgency. Abdi Hajji Musa, the leader of the insurgents in Raytu, for example, once rolled up the sleeves of his shirt for me, showed two parallel scars on his upper arms, and quietly narrated how the Ethiopian army treated him:

I was taken to Ginir, where they tortured me for three months. They tied my arms to my legs and hung me from the ceiling. They did this many times, and they were looking for information, where our arms were. But when they realized I wouldn't give them anything, they let me go.[36]

The insurgency was not only embodied in the combatants but also left similar scars on the civilian population. As part of weakening the insurgency movement, the military simultaneously targeted the general population across the lowlands. Aware of the people's support for the insurgency, the aim was to both punish them and deter them from aiding the fighters. The level of such violence corresponds with Alex de Waal's (1997) concept of "conspicuous atrocity" and included indiscriminate killing of civilians. Muslim leaders were also targeted and killed, while mosques were looted and desecrated (Gebru Tareke 1977: 308). One of the most famous massacres occurred at Argesa Ba'ii – a small village close to Dirre Sheikh Hussein. Surrounding the village at sunrise, the soldiers forced the inhabitants into one crowd and opened fire. Only three persons were left alive. Such actions were "effective" in terrorizing the civilian

[36] Interview, Abdi Hajji Musa, Raytu, June 12, 2018.

population, making them increasingly cautious in providing support for the insurgents: "We were afraid of their [the insurgents'] actions. Not that they would hurt the civilian population, but the government would. When they [the insurgents] attacked somewhere, the government would return and burn down the houses in that area and take the property of the people."[37]

The insurgency also left its scar on the landscapes of Bale – something clearly noticeable when the government decided to bomb the lowlands. In September 1968, the emperor approved the use of planes to bomb assumed insurgent strongholds. The bombs were not only aimed at the insurgents – who to a large extent were able to escape the attacks – but also targeted the civilian population. According to oral testimonies of those who witnessed the bombings, the air campaigns were carried out by six planes, and during the campaign, these planes would fly six missions per day (Hussein Indhessa 2016: 151). Makka Bariso, the widow after Adam Jilo, clearly remembered how the sound of helicopters would warn them about the looming terror:

It was a little before Thuhur [the noon prayer] when we ran to the bushes grabbing only things that were at our sight as helicopters hovered over us to map the area and then jets came to unleash their death dealing weapons. . . . I took my two youngest kids and ran as fast as I could into the bushes. . . . I cuddled up the kids and laid on top of them to hide as the firings rattled the area. Galanni ka Rabbiti, hanga hardhaa ka na jiraachise – Praise be to the Lord who let me live till this day. (Abdullatif Dire 2013)

In August 1969, the government declared another six-month state of emergency in Genale, Dello, and El Kere *awrajas* and intensified its aerial bombing of villages in El Kere and Dello *awrajas*. Villages in El Kere that escaped the bombs were later set on fire by the army. The counterinsurgency continued into 1970, and the severe brutality created a deep sense of terror among the local population in both El Kere and Dello. While such actions have often been the very reasons why people join insurgencies (Peters and Richards 1998; Weinstein 2007), the scale and intensity seem to have the effect desired by the government: people were more reluctant to offer support to the insurgents, in turn forcing an increasing number of them to surrender (Aberra Ketsela 1971: 24; Gebru Tareke 1977: 334).

---

[37] Interview, Obse Ibrahim, Robe, August 25, 2005.

While ordinary bombs obviously put their marks on the landscape, particularly devastating was the use napalm bombs:

I sent people to him [Waqo Gutu] to negotiate, saying that his land and cattle would be returned to him. At the same time, however, we dropped napalm bombs in uninhabited areas and flew over the area with jet airplanes. This was to show our strength for Waqo Gutu while we were negotiating.[38]

Having seen the devastating impacts of "ordinary" wildfires in Bale firsthand, I can barely imagine the scars left by the napalm and other types of bombs. They left the landscape scorched by fire and replaced villages with bomb craters. As homes were shattered, people were driven out of the lowlands and forced to build new homes elsewhere.

Another important, yet often overlooked, aspect of the material impact of the insurgency was the loss of cattle. Not only was livestock the main source of income for the lowlanders but also intrinsic to their identity as pastoralists. I will return to this more in detail in Chapter 7, but suffice it to say that livestock represented capital, insurance, inheritance, and social status for the pastoralist. Having cattle could also be converted into social relationships between the wealthier and those of less wealth within the clan structure, producing mechanisms that reduced inequalities and maintained clan affinities. Large numbers of livestock were killed or confiscated by the military, and as many civilians fled their homes, the cattle became easy prey for the soldiers. The confiscated livestock was either consumed by the soldiers or auctioned away at very low prices. Sometimes the cattle were simply divided among the officers in the army and officials in the local administration (Gebru Tareke 1977: 333). The idea behind this was to starve out the insurgents, but it additionally hit the civilian population hard (Yaassiin Mohammad Roobaa and Anbassaa 2014: 9).[39] During the years 1968–1970, more than 60,000 cattle – 4 percent of the total livestock in Bale – were confiscated (Gebru Tareke 1991: 156). Another source claims that before the insurgency, there were more than 500,000 cattle in the southern lowlands, but afterward only 87,000 were left to be vaccinated (Nydal 1972: 12).

The civilian population also suffered from attacks by the insurgents themselves. Those who were targeted were commonly perceived as

---

[38] Interview, General Jagama Kello, Addis Ababa, October 16, 2006.
[39] Interview, Hafiz Hassan, Addis Ababa, June 16, 2011.

collaborating with the government, and the level of violence was often high. The purpose was obviously to deter others from choosing the "wrong" side, but sometimes the attacks were simple acts of revenge. A certain Hussein Aliye, for example, was attacked by insurgents in Wabe because he had handed his son's gun in to the local authorities. Subsequently, a band of insurgents "looted 40 cattle ... and burned down the six thatched houses including the property inside them."[40] In Dello, alleged pro-government locals were locked in a house that was burned to the ground.[41] Such actions often escalated into a tit-for-tat spiral of violence, and the insurgency also provided opportunities for settling old scores. The most famous incident occurred when pro-government locals in Dello killed a certain *Grazmach* Abera Waqo by tying him up and throwing him alive into a river.[42]

The End of the Insurgency

Parallel to the aerial bombings, the government also initiated negotiations with the insurgents, promising them pardon if they surrendered (Aberra Ketsela 1971: 24). This strategy was in particular applied in Dello, where in early 1970, a delegation of fifteen of the remaining insurgents met with military officials near Bidere town to discuss the terms of surrender. Emperor Haile Selassie was at that time visiting Borana, and the insurgents were allowed to choose three men to meet with the emperor. Their objective was to obtain a written guarantee confirming the amnesty, but as the emperor only was willing to give them a verbal promise, the insurgents hesitated and returned to their bases. Negotiations were by then temporarily discontinued, and the army continued its attacks with increased force. With few options left, Waqo Gutu decided to surrender his four wives, twelve children, and the families of other leaders in the middle of February 1970 (see Figure 4.2). On February 17, his deputy, Waqo Lugu, surrendered, also giving up the movement's arms depot (see Figures 4.3 and 4.4).[43] He was, according to General Jagama Kello, subsequently sent to Emperor

---

[40] Interrogation Report, Ibrahim Kadir, September n.d., 1967.
[41] Interrogation Report, Hassan Galgalo, July 31, 1968, No. 03/7/4043.
[42] Interrogation Report, Musa Kadir, June 10, 1967; letter from General Diresse Dubale, Head of the Public Security Department, Addis Ababa, to Bale Province Administration, August 5, 1967, No. 4436/59.
[43] Interview, General Jagama Kello, Addis Ababa, October 16, 2006.

Figure 4.2 One of Waqo Gutu's wives and sons

Haile Selassie who pardoned him and "a picture of him with Haile
Selassie was taken" – to prove to the rest of the insurgents that the
promise of pardon was real.[44] He was then sent back to Bale and used
by the army to persuade the remaining insurgents to lay down their
arms (Gebru Tareke 1977: 336). Other former insurgents also con-
tacted the last fighters, and this was not without risks. One report
narrates how insurgents caught a group sent by the authorities into
Harenna forest, tied them up, and brought them to a riverbank, where
they summarily were executed.[45]

The key figure in negotiating with the insurgents was General
Jagama Kello, a Christian Oromo from western Ethiopia.
Dispatching a delegation of local elders to Waqo Gutu's base, he
managed to arrange a meeting with Waqo Gutu in Dello-Menna.

[44] Interview, General Jagama Kello, Addis Ababa, October 16, 2006.
[45] Interrogation Report, Muktar Ahmed, June 2, 1968.

Figure 4.3 Waqo Lugu surrenders to General Jagama Kello

There the terms for his capitulation were agreed upon, which included the promise of a pardon and permission for Waqo Gutu to wear his full uniform (provided by the Somalis) and carry his gun upon his surrender. Finally, on March 27, 1970, Waqo Gutu, together with Aliye Chirri and Dubro Waqo, surrendered to General Jagama Kello in Negelle (see Figure 4.5). Shortly after, Waqo Gutu was brought by a helicopter to the towns of Bidere, Dello, Angetu, where he was displayed as a trophy and used to convince those remaining to give up (Hussein Indhessa 2016: 156). General Jagama Kello subsequently brought him to Goba. Arriving at the airport, he was given an honorary reception by the governor and other officials, and paraded through the streets. A few months later, he met with Emperor Haile Selassie, again appearing in full uniform and escorted by twelve of his men, as well as Hajji Adam Saddo and Hajji Ibrahim Bakaro. After Haile Selassie gave a long speech rebuking him for his rebellion, he took Waqo Gutu to the air force base in Debre Zeit to

Figure 4.4 Waqo Lugu's armory

display his military power.[46] Within the palace, there was quite some disagreement about what to do with Waqo Gutu. Prime Minister Aklilu Habte-Wold and the Minister of Defense Aman Andom wanted to throw him in prison, while others, like General Jagama Kello, feared that this would exacerbate the situation and told the emperor that "it is not advisable to imprison him, because there will come others then to replace him and continue the fighting."[47]

Similar to most other popular insurgencies (Scott 1985: 29), the Bale insurgency thus ended with little or nothing achieved. Most of the fighters returned to their normal life, and Waqo Gutu was awarded the feudal title of *Grazmach* and given a piece of land in Medda Welabu (Gebru Tareke 1991: 149, 156).[48] Local politics in Bale continued

---

[46] Interview, General Jagama Kello, Addis Ababa, October 16, 2006.
[47] Interview, General Jagama Kello, Addis Ababa, October 16, 2006.
[48] Interviews, General Jagama Kello, Addis Ababa, October 16, 2006; Hajji Mustafa Ismail, Robe, March 14, 2006; Hajji Idris Boru, Addis Ababa, December 10, 2017.

Figure 4.5 Waqo Gutu surrenders to General Jagama Kello

more or less unchanged, with power remaining concentrated in the hands of Amhara officials. To be sure, General Jagama Kello – an Oromo – served as a governor for a few years, but his appointment was a reward for faithful service to the emperor, rather than an expression of ethnic diversification of authority. Many insurgents never surrendered, and fleeing Bale, they eventually found their way to Somalia. It is not clear how many left for Somalia, but one informant reports that around 2,200 insurgents were living in Koryole refugee camp in the Lower Shebelle Region in the early 1970s.[49]

I suggested in the beginning of this chapter that the Bale insurgency tentatively could be characterized as a separatist movement. However, the goal of self-determination and self-government, which Clapham ambiguously formulated as fighting "for some special autonomous status" (1998: 6), can obviously mean many different things – as well as being concepts that are not easily extrapolated to empirical realities (Higgens 1994: 111f.). There is no doubt that localized understandings of self-rule and autonomy were part and parcel of the struggle, yet without necessarily being articulated in an effective and coherent

---

[49] Interview, Hafiz Hassan, Addis Ababa, June 16, 2011.

manner. Whereas the violent reactions from the Ethiopian state were the main reason for the insurgency's failure, the organizational weakness of the movement also played a role. It was never able to build effective commando structures and coordinated leadership, and it is therefore rather surprising that it lasted as long as it did. The next chapter delves deeper into this, providing new insights to who the insurgents actually were, to the nature of the leadership, and to how the movement was organized.

5 | The Insurgency: Fighters and Fragmentation

Rebellions usually surface rather spontaneously and remain nothing but flares unless effective leadership and an organizational structure sustain them. It is only then we can talk about insurgencies – here defined as non-governmental movements devoted to the use of armed force to achieve their goals. Use of military action, moreover, is not random, but part of a defined political campaign (Woldemariam 2011: 34). Skilled leadership and organizational capacity are crucial for the articulation of objectives, for the communication of these among the rank and file, and for developing mechanisms of discipline – or "hierarchies and the ability to sanction members who seek to disrupt the cooperative equilibrium" (Woldemariam 2011: 51; cf. Clapham 1998: 8). The organizational structures of the Bale insurgency were not very developed, and it has been argued that it did not have "even a degree of coordination" (Markakis 1987: 198). It lacked effective hierarchical structures and consisted of rather independent small groups of fighters who often acted in ways each saw fit. The movement can thus best be characterized as a decentered coalition "of identifiable groups that possess distinct interests," which found themselves "united by the pursuit of a common goal – the violent contestation of state power" (Woldemariam 2011: 49). In spite of this, the insurgency managed to keep the struggle alive for seven years.

This chapter looks more closely at the composition of the Bale insurgency, trying to understand both the nature of its leadership and structures and how the organizational deficit allowed for internal fragmentation that eventually contributed to its failure. An important aspect of the insurgency's makeup, as we will see, was clan affiliation and loyalty – the basic point of orientation among the fighters. This provided, on the one hand, important links with the broader population critical for sustaining the movement; yet, it was, on the other hand, a source of destructive fragmentation. Though the leaders of the Bale insurgency were, like the rest of the movement's rank and file, ordinary pastoralists from the rural lowlands, the insurgency had broad support across the region, and at the end of this chapter I will discuss the role of what I have called the "highland activists." These were individuals who were not directly involved in the military operations but remained crucial in sustaining the movement; through material and moral support. These highland activists were also instrumental in shaping and articulating the ideological underpinning of the insurgency and in linking it with broader ethno-nationalist currents emerging during the 1960s.

Insurgents and *Shiftas*

Insurgents and rebels in Ethiopia – and in the Horn – have often been labeled *shiftas,* the Amharic word for "bandit" or "outlaw." Such labeling was done rather uncritically, without duly considering the complexity of both the concept and armed uprising across the Horn. While the word *shifta* denotes a particular sociocultural phenomenon, it has also been used by the state to label and deny any legitimacy to armed movement challenging its political power. This has been the case for successive Ethiopian regimes, where, for example, both the Imperial Government and the Derg regime denigrated movements like the Eritrean People's Liberation Front (EPLF) and the Oromo Liberation Front (OLF) as *shiftas.*

The Ethiopian *shifta* has been framed according to scholarship on banditry in Africa influenced by Eric Hobsbawm's Marxist-underpinned thesis of the "social bandit" – understood as a type of Robin Hood who articulated social grievances and demands, whose rebellious activities avenged and protected the subaltern, and whose loot was redistributed among the poor (Hobsbawm 1959, 1969).[1] Critics of Hobsbawm's thesis gradually pointed to the limited value it had in African contexts, arguing in particular that a crucial characteristic of the "social bandit" concept was that it emerged in a European context undergoing changes toward agrarian capitalism. It was also said that the alleged social bandits were not as benevolent as assumed – particularly as they would prey on their own constituencies (van

---

[1] Caulk (1984), Crummey (1986a), and Fernybough (2010) have conducted the main studies of *shiftas* in Ethiopia. For studies on "social bandits" in the broader African context, see Crummey (1986b).

Walraven and Abbink 2003: 6f.). There was, as some pointed out, an "absence of the populist distributor type of bandit" (Austen 1986: 93). The *shifta* arguably fits poorly within the social bandit category. The word itself, similar to *shiftanet* (banditry, brigandage), comes from the Amharic verb *meshefet*, which means "to run away or to flee." "To flee" denotes how a *shifta*'s career started when he (in most cases), for various reasons, is forced to escape into the bush or to a remote area – which then becomes the basis for his violent acts.[2] *Shiftanet* is a phenomenon with a long history in Ethiopia's northern parts that over the centuries became an integrated and recognized part of the northern feudal society. The *shifta* was predominantly an individual nobleman aiming at advancing his career, who by seeking to climb socially and access political power would disturb the peace and challenge the authorities through raids and looting. The *shifta* remained an ambiguous character, however, clearly a predator but also depicted in legendary terms and heralded as a heroic figure. Yet nothing indicates that the Ethiopian *shifta* resembles any Robin Hood figure but rather one that plundered for personal economic or political gain (Fernyhough 2010: 249).

Shiftanet has occasionally been associated with rebellions and popular uprisings among peasants and viewed as embodying the social grievances of the wider society. In such cases, the term was usually used in its plural form, as *hizbu shefete* (the people fled, went beyond the law), and the *shiftas* are then the ones who take up arms against exploitive and unjust authorities (Aregawi Berhe 2003: 95). The connection between *shiftanet* and rebellion has, however, been treated rather simplistically, producing an inaccurate picture. In some uprisings, peasants were involved in banditry, acting on behalf of the broader peasant community to address inequality or when feudal oppression became too unbearable. Such occasions, however, were few and such peasant-led rebellions were usually "inarticulate, or merely exploited by the elites, and their 'programme' no more than an obstinate refusal to submit" (Fernyhough 2010: 242). Far more common were rebellions where the peasantry was forcefully recruited into outlawry by the nobility (Crummey 1986a: 133f.). Therefore, even if it is possible to say that the *shifta* was an ambiguous figure in northern

---

[2] A *shifta* is, however, different from a criminal, *wongelegna* in Amharic.

Ethiopia, having a dual character as both predator and protester, the common situation was that banditry – inherently violent in nature – was a significant addition to peasants' already burdensome reality, and that the peasants generally viewed the *shiftas* as nothing less than "parasites" (Fernyhough 2010: 241).

While the *shifta* clearly is a phenomenon restricted to the northern parts of Ethiopia (including Eritrea), it has, at the same time, often and rather uncritically been extrapolated to other parts of the country. This reflects a broader tendency in Ethiopian studies of assuming that certain sociocultural phenomena, usually with roots in the north, are of a pan-Ethiopian nature, or, alternatively, that phenomena in the south may be identified and construed on the basis of concepts, language, or patterns in the northern areas. *Shiftanet*, therefore, originating in the northern highlands of historical Ethiopia, cannot uncritically be applied to mean the same in other contexts, or that criminal and/or violent acts necessarily should be understood within this framework.

This does not mean that *shiftanet* did not exist in the south, but the important point is that it was a post-conquest phenomenon. Timothy Fernyhough, in his discussion of banditry in southern Ethiopia, makes it unequivocally clear that "there exists no evidence nor tradition of banditry prior to Ethiopian incursions at the end of the nineteenth century" in the south (Fernyhough 2010: 260). His survey of the prevalence of banditry across the south – from the Gibe area in the west, to Borana and Ogaden in the east – makes it crystal clear that those engaged in such activities were disaffected officials, deserted soldiers, and fortune seekers – all from the north. While mirroring the north as a means for social mobility, banditry in the south offered new opportunities for economic enrichment for those arriving from the north. These *shiftas* could sometimes be regular outlaws as well as part of the local Amhara ruling elite; yet, they would in any case prey upon and loot the local population in the south in a highly violent manner. This corresponds with the broader pattern wherein, as we have seen, Menelik's conquest was very much about plundering the south (particularly in pastoralist areas). Moreover, it supports the notion of the Ethiopian state as a "predatory state" (Teshale Tibebu 1995) and illuminates the "criminal undercurrents of all form of state power" (Crummey 1986a: 133).

While Fernyhough acknowledges that banditry was a northern phenomenon and recognizes that the southerners who joined bands of northern *shiftas* were "few and far between" (2010: 282), he never-theless refers to insurgency leaders in the south as *shiftas* and claims that "[b]anditry in southern Ethiopia was a form of resistance to class and ethnic oppression" (2010: 286). His failure to make a distinction between banditry and political resistance in the south is even stranger because *shiftanet* during Emperor Haile Selassie's reign gradually lost its political connotation and became connected with criminal activities (Crummey 1986a: 135). Moreover, the fact that *shiftanet* was, as we have seen, about social ascension, political power and personal enrich-ment, and the fact that *shiftas* were involved the looting of the civilian population means that there are important differences between *shifta-net* and politically motivated insurgency.

Fernyhough views the Bale insurgency along similar inaccurate lines, labeling it a form of banditry. Building on Gebru Tareke, who uncriti-cally branded the insurgency leaders as "peasant bandits" (Gebru Tareke 1977: 298, 1991: 141), he moreover claims that figures such as Kahin Abdi, Hussein Bune, Isme Abba Washa, Waqo Gutu, Waqo Lugu, and Hajji Isaq Dhadhi had a history as *shiftas,* before turning into insurgents. His argument that "banditry and insurgency went hand in hand in Bale" (Fernyhough 2010: 285, 287) is rather surprising and corresponds poorly with my findings. Nothing in the available sources – written or oral – points in this direction. While the insurgents surely were not boy scouts, the insurgency was *not* about looting of civilians or brigandage but rather aimed at targeting government infra-structure and attacking police and military forces. This relates to what was said earlier about the problem of uncritically transferring a concept rooted in one sociocultural setting to another. Although Bale was politically integrated into the Ethiopian state, and while a certain degree of acculturation had occurred by the 1960s, the region (as well as other areas of the south) had its own historical distinctiveness, a different social configuration, and particular religious-cultural fea-tures. This makes it meaningless to apply *shiftanet* as a concept for political resistance.

Who Were the Insurgents?

Further discussions of who the insurgents were – their backgrounds, personalities, and so on – serve to elucidate these points. It is obviously impossible to discuss in great detail the rank-and-file insurgents, and it would likewise be beyond the scope of this study to provide an exhaustive picture of all of the insurgency's leaders. Individuals such as Waqo Gutu, Hussein Bune, Hajji Isaq Dhadhi, Waqo Lugo, Adam Jilo, Aliye Chirri, Hassan Roba (see Figure 5.1), Mahmoud Bune, Aliye Dhadhi, and Isme Abba Washa are remembered today in Bale as legendary heroes, and each of their individual stories could fill volumes. I will in the following present the key figures and discuss Waqo Gutu, Hussein Bune, and Hajji Isaq Dhadhi – the main leaders of the insurgency – in more detail. My major point is to give a picture of how they as embodying the struggle provide insight into the insurgency's character, its objectives, as well as its underlying causes.

The key leaders at the Dello front included individuals such as Adam Jilo and Aliye Chirri. The former was born around 1917 in Medda Welabu *worreda* and was at an early stage agitating against what he saw as the repressive policies of the Ethiopian state, encouraging his compatriots to refuse to pay taxes and to revolt against the

Figure 5.1 Hassan Roba

government. Consequently, he was briefly imprisoned in 1962–1963. Aliye Chirri was similarly from Medda Welabu *wor-reda*, born in 1920 at a place called Chirri, belonging to the Karayu clan. His father, Chirri Jarra, was a well-known and wealthy man and had, as mentioned in Chapter 3, fought together with Muhammad Gada Qallu. Aliye Chirri himself also joined the struggle of Muhammad Gada Qallu at the age of 12, and it is safe to assume that this experience, together with seeing his father arrested, had a lasting impact.[3] Aliye Chirri died on November 11, 2017.

The most important leader at the Dello front, however, was the iconic Waqo Gutu (see Figure 5.2). He has sometimes been referred to as the General of Western Somalia, giving the impression that he was the insurgency's supreme leader (Gebru Tareke 1977: 318f.). This is, as I will return to later, inaccurate. Waqo Gutu was born in 1924 at a place called Oda, close to the town Bidere in Meda Welabu *worreda,* as the son of Gutu Usu Camarri and Dhulo Ali Hassan. Little is known about his early life, except that he and his family migrated to Borana, where he grew up (Yaassiin Mohammad Roobaa and Anbassaa 2014: 11). The direct reason for his involvement in the insurgency, as discussed in Chapter 4, was the expulsion from Borana and the difficulties the displaced Arsi Oromo faced in Medda Welabu. Waqo Gutu continued his armed struggle after the revolution in 1947 and became a leading figure in the Somali Abbo Liberation Front (SALF), which fought against the Ethiopian government throughout the 1970s. When SALF, together with the Somali military, was defeated in the Ogaden war (1977–1978), Waqo Gutu returned to Somalia. From there, he continued his political activism and became, for a short period, part of the Ethiopian Transitional Government in 1991. A year later, he left for Kenya where lived until he died on February 3, 2006. He was then, somewhat ironically, given a state funeral and buried in Meda Welabu *worreda* (Anonymous 2006; Yaassiin Mohammad Roobaa and Anbassaa 2014: 30).

The main leaders at the Wabe front included individuals such as Aliye Dhadhi, Abdullahi Bedhaso, and Isme Abba Washa – to mention a few. Isme Abba Washa was born around 1897 in Dello Sebro in Gasera *worreda* and led the struggle in the area around Jarra in

---

[3] "Koloneel Aliyyii Cirrii," *Oromia Brodcasting Service,* July 10, 2016 (www .youtube.com/watch?v=DfKmGu4KspM; accessed February 27, 2018).

Figure 5.2 The leaders of the insurgency. From the left: Aliye Chirri, Dubro Waqo, Waqo Gutu

Gololcha *worreda*. His real name was Isme Hisu, and he was called Abba Washa after his younger brother. The key leader of the Wabe front was, however, Hussein Bune. He was born in 1922 at a place called Jiddo Boru in today's Sewena *worreda*.[4] Hussein Bune is said to have been conscious about the Amhara suppression and harbored anti-government sentiments at an early stage, and those close to him argue

---

[4] Some sources claim that he was born in either 1898 or 1905, which means that he would be in his 60s when the insurgency started (*The Story of Hussein Bune* 2008: 5; Yaassiin Mohammad Roobaa and Anbassaa 2014). The fact that he continued fighting until the end of the 1970s makes this highly unlikely.

that this was something he developed on his own, not mainly as a result of outside influences or generated through contacts with others. In fact, he hardly traveled beyond his locality.[5] He was, like those around him, fully aware of the suffering of the Arsi Oromo in both Arsi and Bale – such as the massacre in Anole.[6] When the local authorities demanded that the people in Sewena should pay tax on their grazing land, Hussein Bune reportedly refused to pay. One informant elaborated: "when he refused to pay taxes it means that we would pay all but hold back one birr. This was done deliberately to provoke the Amhara. It was done to get a reason to fight."[7] This one birr earned him three months in prison in the early part of 1963 (*Revolutionary Vigor in Somali Abo through History* 1979: 34). Shortly after he took up arms against the government and followed by his brothers Mahmoud Bune and Abdulkerim Bune and a few others, he remained the main leader of the insurgency in Wabe.[8] Ending up as refugees in Somalia, he and his men received political and military training. Immediately after the revolution in 1974, he returned to Bale and continued the armed struggle until 1978, when he again was forced to flee to Somalia. He lived there until he died on February 14, 2002.

　　Hajji Isaq Dhadhi of the Raytu clan was a crucial figure for the insurgencies in both Dello and Wabe. He was born in Raytu, probably at the beginning of the twentieth century and was the son of the already mentioned *Fitawrari* Dhadhi Terre and the brother of *Fitawrari* Nuho Dhadhi. Hajji Isaq Dhadhi spent much of his childhood and adolescence studying Islam, attending religious schools in Harar, Djibouti, and Yemen. The details about his early life are rather scant. Some sources claim that he spent most of his adult life in Addis Ababa, where he was on good terms with the political authorities – receiving salaries and properties. It is also said that he served as a security and intelligence officer in Bale and Borana (Aberra Ketsela 1971: 7; Gebru Tareke 1977: 297). Other sources, including members of his own family and others close to him, contest this latter point and tell a different story. Most informants argue that he was put under house

---

[5]　Interview, Hajji Isaq Ismail, Skype, September 29, 2019.
[6]　The massacre in Anole, Arsi, took place during the fighting between Menelik forces and the locals, where the soldiers – as a punitive measure – cut off the breasts of the females and the right hand of the males.
[7]　Interview, Jowar Kadir, Sewena, June 13, 2018.
[8]　Interview, Jowar Kadir, Sewena, June 13, 2018.

arrest in Addis Ababa by the emperor. Some sources say that this was due to his family's involvement in the armed struggle against the government and his own anti-government sentiments, while another source, who interviewed Hajji Isaq Dhadhi, claims that it was because he refused to collaborate with the government in converting the Muslims of Bale to Christianity.[9] This was either in 1948 or in 1952, and while he was free to move around in the city, he had to report to the authorities twice every day.

In 1963, at the time when unrest emerged in the southeast, one of his relatives from Raytu, *Dejazmach* Abdulkerim Sayyid Muhammad,[10] came with the message that Hajji Isaq Dhadhi's wife (in Raytu) was dead – a pretext to get him out of Addis Ababa.[11] Hajji Isaq owned several plots of farmland in Ginir *worreda* that he also needed to attend to; however, as soon as he arrived in Bale, he discovered that an Amhara called Yiglattu was in the process of taking over the land. He then became entangled in a complex legal battle that soon developed into a violent conflict during which Yiglattu was killed. There is some disagreement among the sources about what actually happened, but the most probable version is that a person called Ahmed Tikko killed him. Hajji Isaq Dhadhi was, however, accused of being the perpetrator and became a wanted man.[12] Some claim that this was the very reason why Hajji Isaq became an insurgent (Aberra Ketsela 1971: 7; Gebru Tareke 1977: 298), but those close to him claim that this was only the trigger for his anti-government activism: "the Yiglattu case was like something sent from God."[13] In October 1963, he gathered his family and men – altogether forty individuals – and fled to Somalia.[14] Arriving in Somalia, he made contact with Makhtal Tahir, the leader of the Ogaden insurgency, who, in turn, introduced him to Somali officials. Hajji Isaq Dhadhi remained in Somalia throughout the insurgency, where he functioned as the main contact person between Mogadishu

---

[9] Interview, Hajji Isaq Ismail, Skype, September 30, 2019.
[10] He was the son of Sayyid Muhammad Abdile Hassan – the "Mad Mullah" – discussed in Chapter 8.
[11] Interviews, Hajji Semir Idris, Addis Ababa, August 3, 2011 and December 9, 2017; Abdo Hajji Mustafa, Raytu, June 12, 2018; field log, June 12, 2018.
[12] Interview, Hajji Semir Idris, Addis Ababa, June 22, 2017.
[13] Interview, Abdo Hajji Mustafa, Raytu, June 12, 2018.
[14] Interview, Hajji Semir Idris, Addis Ababa, August 3, 2011.

and the Oromo insurgents. He remained in Somalia for the rest of his life and died in Saudi Arabia in June 1985.[15] All of these individuals had much in common. They were all from the lowland rural areas, had little or no education, and most were assumingly illiterate. This is in contrast to the typical profile of insurgency leaders both in the Horn and in Africa, who generally hailed from social elites, were from the urban areas, and had a certain degree of formal education (Clapham 1998: 9). The leaders in Bale, moreover, had already reached a mature age when they got involved in the struggle: Waqo Gutu and Hussein Bune were both around age 40, while Hajji Isaq Dhadhi was around age 60. This was another contrast to other movements in the Horn engaged in anti-government activism – wherein the leadership was far younger. The youth factor was most explicit in the Somali Youth League (see Chapter 9), where membership was restricted to people up to a certain age.

More importantly, however, was that they all had a particular status in their respective localities – a status that was based upon their clan membership, lineage, and inherited authority. Both Waqo Gutu and Hajji Isaq Dhadhi were from the Raytu clan, while Hussein Bune was from the Hawattu clan. The Raytu clan was mainly concentrated in today's Raytu *worreda*, but it expanded over large areas in the lowlands, reaching as far south as Dello *awraja*. The Hawattu clan was mainly found in the areas of Sewena and Ginir *worredas*. The two clans had a special position within the Mendo moiety, where they as Raya and Hawattu were direct sons of Mendo. Waqo Gutu and Hajji Isaq Dhadhi furthermore belonged to the Doyo sub-clan within the Raytu, the former from the same lineage as the *abbaa muuda* of Dello, while the latter hailed from a prominent lineage connected to the *gadaa* system.[16] Many of the leaders also came from lineages with a history of anti-government activism. Hajji Isaq Dhadhi's father, *Fitawrari* Dhadhi Terre, as we have seen, had been engaged in armed struggle in the early twentieth century, while Waqo Gutu's granduncle was no other than Muhammad Gada Qallu. Waqo Gutu was around age 18 during his struggle, and although he was then living in Borana, it is clear that

---

[15] Interview, Hajji Semir Idris, Addis Ababa, August 3, 2011.
[16] Interviews, Khalid Adam, Raytu, September 26, 2005; Sheikh Hussein Abdallah, Gomorra, July 17, 2001.

the news had reached him and his family. Undoubtedly, the struggle of his granduncle served as an inspiration for his own struggle. An interesting detail is that Waqo Gutu received the *quube meetaa* – a silver ring reserved for the *abbaa muuda* – from his uncle while in prison, indicating the linkage between the two insurgencies (Umer Nure 2006: 44). Another common feature for many of the leaders was that they belonged to families that held positions within the government structure – and therefore were influential and wealthy. *Fitawrari* Dhadhi Terre was the first *balabat* of Raytu, a position that later was inherited by his descendants, his son Nuho Dhadhi and his grandson Muktar Nuho. Members of Waqo Gutu's family were given similar appointments, and Waqo Gutu's younger brother, *Grazmach* Chemerri Gutu, served as a *balabat* while living in Borana. Waqo Gutu himself had also acted as a *balabat* in Borana (Aberra Ketsela 1971: 11). Hussein Bune's father, Bune Darara Godena, was part of the state's administrative structures through his position as a *burqa* – a position that was passed over to Hussein Bune.

Such appointments within the state apparatus were a part of the state's practice of indirect rule and reflected how positions were granted to lineages with traditional authority. It was also how the state attempted to co-opt unruly elements and should not be read as signs of collaboration with the regime. It is moreover clear that the state never effectively succeeded in co-opting the local authorities: in fact, the contacts they had with the state and their exposure to its repressive hierarchical structures often strengthened their antagonistic sentiments. As I will discuss in the following chapters, holding such positions often meant that one was put between a rock and a hard place – acting as the state's representative while protecting one's clan. However, relations between the people and the *balabats* and *burqas* were strengthened in the course of the insurgency, as the former looked to the latter for leadership. The insurgency was also the time when the *balabats* and *burqas* abandoned their Amhara masters, sided with the people, and thus reclaimed lost traditional authority.

Organization, Fragmentation, and Insurgent Clans

It is difficult to determine the actual number of insurgents, and estimates fluctuate significantly. Official figures list more than 21,000 surrendering in the late 1960s, but a substantial number of these were women and children. Gebru Tareke estimates that the core insurgency movement consisted of 4,000 to 5,000 active fighters but argues that it was able to mobilize 10,000 additional ones if needed (1991: 150). There are reasons to believe that the number of active fighters was higher, though. One informant recounts how 6,000 under the command of Waqo Gutu and 4,000 under Hussein Bune arrived in Somalia in 1966 in search of arms: "the fighters were arriving with their camels, and the caravans were entering the camp in the straight line. It took over nine days for them all to arrive and settle in."[17] This is confirmed in reports from the Ethiopian authorities, which claim that up to 10,000 insurgents were found in Somalia receiving military training, and moreover, in 1967 alone, more than 3,000 insurgents traveled to Somalia in search of arms. Waqo Gutu was said to have 1,500 men under his command. In addition, the number of insurgents surrendering in 1970 just at the Dello front was nearly 2,000.[18]

Gebru Tareke has argued that according to official Ethiopian records, the insurgency had a command structure with two generals, sixteen colonels, forty-four majors, and more than one hundred platoon leaders (1991: 150). A closer look at such intelligence records, however, reveals a far more complex and incoherent picture, and the lack of consistency is confirmed by my informants' often contradictory accounts of the movement's organization. Some claimed that the movement was well organized with one central command, while others said there was no such thing.[19] The truth is probably somewhere in between, and the fact that the insurgency emerged rather spontaneously in the different localities clearly impacted its organization. While structures did exist, with hierarchies of officers and fighters, these were highly decentered, fluid, and sometimes ephemeral. Vast operational spaces and lack of communication equipment can partly explain the lack of coordination between the different fronts, and although more elaborate structures were put in place in 1967, the movement's inherently fragmented nature and the increasing pressure from the Ethiopian military undermined much of

---

[17] Interview, Hajji Isaq Ismail, Skype, September 29, 2019.
[18] Memo by Tesfaye Gebre-Mariam, Commander of Bale Police, May 31, 1967. No. 431/19/35; Letter from Colonel Sirak Tesfa, Public Security Department, Addis Ababa, to Bale Province Administration, August 7, 1967. No. 4199/59; Interrogation Report, Ibrahim Kadir, September 12, 1967; "Report of the Operation in Dello Awraja from February 2 to April 7, 1970." Ministry of Interior Archives, n.d. No. 2401/3/MA/4QM/47/673/667.
[19] Interview, Hajji Semir Idris, Addis Ababa, December 12, 2017.

these efforts. The insurgents were thus – in contrast to many other African insurgencies – also incapable of developing any form of governing structures in the areas they controlled. Even if government infrastructures and the *balabat* institution were dissolved, no alternative structures were put in place: "we didn't get the chance to develop a government; we were too busy fighting."[20]

There is, however, no doubt that Waqo Gutu and Hussein Bune were the top commanding leaders of the Dello and Wabe fronts, respectively. Waqo Gutu had a defined second-in-command, the previously mentioned Waqo Lugu, while important leaders with military ranks included Colonel Aliye Chirri and Colonel Adam Jilo in Dello, Colonel Kahin Abdi in El Kere, and Colonel Umar Kebelo in Genale. It is unclear how they received these military titles, and there are those who say they were appointed by the Somali government, while others claim they were appointed by Waqo Gutu (Gebru Tareke 1977: 320).[21] Waqo Gutu himself, in an interview with Aberra Ketsela, argued that "we appoint each other" – meaning that titles and ranks were decided locally by the insurgents (1971: 12). This latter point is underscored by a centrally placed informant, who claimed that the fighters allocated military titles to those trusted with leadership roles.[22]

The movement's basic units were a number of smaller and larger groups similar to platoons, with the number of members ranging from thirteen to sixty. Some of these were hierarchically related, but such relations were not consistent. Military ranks or titles did not necessarily mean that a leader of one group could claim command over other groups or that some groups were subordinate to others. The fact that titles were given rather randomly makes it fair to assume that the different groups operated relatively independent of one another. They consisted, in general, of individuals from the same locality who often belonged to the same clan or sub-clan, and whose allegiance was similarly determined by clan connections. The sources list a number of names of leaders of these groups, but it is unclear if both the units

---

[20] Interview, Jowar Kadir, Sewena, June 13, 2018. This is also in stark contrast to the Eritrean People's Liberation Front (EPLF) and the Tigray People's Liberation Front (TPLF); both created effective governing structures in their respective areas.

[21] One informant claimed that the Somalis appointed officers with the ranks of colonel and captain (interview, Hajji Isaq Ismail, Skype, September 29, 2019).

[22] Interview, Hajji Semir Idris, Addis Ababa, June 22, 2017.

and the leaders remained stable throughout the period of the insurgency. Most likely there was a great deal of pragmatism in terms of their composition and leadership. Each group's area of operation was rather limited, as they operated out of a particular locality and were responsible for controlling a defined territory. The insurgents within these different units knew the area well and had good connections with the local population, giving them important advantages.

The different groups of insurgents were moreover locally confined to particular areas. Waqo Gutu, Waqo Lugu, and Aliye Chirri, for example, operated out of Meda Welabu *worreda*,[23] while Kadir Waqo was in charge of the area between Angetu and Buluq in the Harenna forest. He reportedly had 2,500 fighters under his command. This force was organized into smaller units led by individuals who had the rank of captain or sergeant, and who controlled different territories within this area.[24] The Wabe front had a similar decentralized organizational structure with individuals controlling defined territories. While Hussein Bune was the main leader in Wabe, his authority was, at the same time, limited. Together with his brothers Mahmoud, Muhammad, and Abdulkerim Bune, he was in charge of the eastern part of Ginir *worreda* toward Sewena. One informant claimed the leadership at the Wabe front consisted of four colonels, all accountable to Hussein Bune – and who each had four officers with the rank of captain under them.[25] Colonel Abdullahi Bedhaso was the commander in Ginir *worreda*'s northern parts, Colonel Hajji Ousman Imama was the main leader at Dirre Sheikh Hussein,[26] Colonel Isme Abba Washa in Sebro (Gasera *worreda*), and Colonel Tilmo Ali in Beltu *worreda*. Other key figures in Beltu

---

[23] Letter to Dello *Awraja* Administration, June 15, 1967. No.1/3/3/5000/9; letter from *Fitawrari* Meharene Minda, Deputy Governor of Bale to Bale *teklay gezat* Administration, March 17, 1967. No. 2/1296/6.

[24] Colonel Dube Bati was said to control the area around Bekure, also in the Harenna forest, while Captein Shita Ware was in charge of the areas toward Nensebo *worreda*, and Captain Qasim Wado controlled areas close to Angetu. The main leaders in the area around Menna town were Hassan Ture Jilo and Tore Boru. Galchu Gobena, furthermore, led operations in the area toward Berbere *worreda* (Interrogation Report, Barisso Ibrahim, June n.d., 1967; Interrogation Report, Hussein Hassan, June 29, 1968; letter from Tesfaye Goji, Fasil *awraja* Police Station, to General Worqu Metaferia, September 5, 1966. No. 115/25/4; see also Hussein Indhessa (2016: 129).

[25] Interview, Hajji Isaq Ismail, Skype, September 29, 2019.

[26] He was the brother of the famous Qadi Ahmed Imama, who I will return to later in this chapter.

were Ali and Mame Harqa and Abdullahi Sani, while Abdi Hajji Musa Dhadhi (the nephew of Hajji Isaq Dhadhi), Hassan Dhadhi, and Tahir Abdullahi had the command in Raytu _worreda_.[27] Each of these individuals led units that operated rather independently.[28] Hussein Bune even claimed, on one occasion, that he had no authority over the units in Gololcha, Raytu, and Beltu.[29]

The insurgents were ordinary pastoralists who took to arms, operating in vast stretches of lowlands intimately familiar to them. The inaccessibility of these areas also made it possible for many of them to continue with their daily activities around their homes – instead of retreating to secluded bases. This meant that it was sometimes hard to distinguish the insurgents from the ordinary pastoralist population, and being an insurgent was for many a "part-time" activity. The insurgency was also, in many ways, an extension of their pastoralist lifestyle, and a particular aspect was that in addition to male fighters, the movement often consisted of the fighters' wives, children, other relatives, as well as their livestock. The scale of this is documented in official documents reporting, for example, that more than 2,200 women and 3,200 children were among those who surrendered in Dello in 1970.[30]

A particularly important aspect of the insurgency was how it was intimately intersected with the clan system. The structures of the clan system paralleled the military hierarchy, and the movement's geographical organization very much dovetailed with the clan distribution. The clan system, moreover, was the primary point of orientation for the

[27] Other leaders included Ahmed Hussein, Aliye Hajji Jarso, Sheikh Muhammed Aliye, Jowar Elemo, Jowar Qassim, and Bedhaso Elemo in Ginir; Hassan Sal'uu, Aliye Dhadhi, Sheikh Abdisamad, and Hussein Arru in Sewena; and Hajji Aliye Geno, and Siraj Sheikh Hassan in Gololcha (interviews, Hajji Semir Idris, Addis Ababa, December 9, 2017; Abdo Hajji Mustafa, Raytu, June 12, 2018; Hajji Isaq Ismail, Skype, September 29, 2019).
[28] Isme Abba Washa had thirty men in his unit, Muhammad Bune had forty men, and Aliye Hajji Jarso had fifty men. Hussein Bune himself is listed with twenty men in his unit (interview, Hajji Semir Idris, Addis Ababa, December 12, 2017; Interrogation Report, Sayyid Mustafa, September 2, 1967; Interrogation Report, Ibrahim Kadir, September n.d., 1967; letter from Colonel Haile Belaineh, Deputy Governor of Bale Province, to Colonel Gessesse Retta, commander of the 4th Brigade, June 17, 1967. No. 2/3573/59).
[29] Interrogation Report, Umar Isaq, April 5, 1967.
[30] "Report of the Operation in Dello Awraja from February 2 to April 7, 1970." Ministry of Interior Archives, n.d. No. 2401/3/MA/4QM/47/673/667.

fighters, in the sense that while the movement had its leaders at various levels as well as fighting units of different sizes, both the leaders and their units were of the same clan and/or sub-clan. The different clan groups' activities were also limited to the area of their clans. The size and standing of the clans meant that some had higher sociocultural prestige than others, which in turn became an important factor determining rank in the movement. I have already pointed out that the prominent position of both the Hawattu and Raytu clans within the insurgency was related to their status within the clan system. Belonging to a clan was also a determining factor for joining the movement, and it is safe to say that clan leaders exerted pressure on their kinsmen. Official positions such as *balabat* and *burqa* – which largely dovetailed with traditional forms of authority – were crucial in securing recruitment, and often everyone within a *balabat*'s or a *burqa*'s area was expected to join the movement. In addition, the clan structure was crucial in connecting the insurgents to the broader population, which was indispensable in providing them with material support, protection, and shelter, as well as gathering information about enemy movements.

Clan affiliation, on the other hand, constituted a major obstacle in generating an effective organization. First of all, the notion of "pastoralist egalitarianism" (Schneider 1979) impeded the establishment of an operative commando structure – in sharp contrast to insurgencies in northern Ethiopia, which emerged out of "hierarchical societies with long traditions of statehood" (Clapham 1998: 11). Second, the clan system proved to be a divisive factor for the struggle. This seems to contradict rather established notions that ethnically homogenous movements are less likely to fragment (Gates 2002). Such notions are, I would argue, based on a too narrow understanding of ethnicity and point to the value of peoplehood as an analytical tool. Peoplehood allows us to recognize the inherently elastic aspect and segmentary nature of belonging and helps us understand how the ethnic dimension potentially can refer to clans, sub-clans, and lineages – which represent different levels of belonging. It is not uncommon that clans or sub-clans constitute more forceful points of orientation than the so-called ethnic group (Schlee 1985, 1989; Turton 1994). While there clearly existed a sense of communality and shared determination within the movement, as I have discussed in Chapter 2, legacies of inter- and intra-clan feuds remained a lingering divisive factor. Such fragmentation according to clan and subsequent disunity seem to have been an inherent problem for the Oromo. This was noted by Salviac in the late nineteenth century, who describes this in rather poetic terms:

When an enemy, powerfully organized into hierarchy, tramples as conqueror on the soil of the fatherland, the untimely rivalries preventing the concentration of the Oromo forces, will paralyze the brilliant efforts of their valiant warriors, and will lead these incoherent bands operating by fits and starts and by disjointed jerks to the slaughter. The guns of Menelik could not have beaten the number and valor of Oromo spears, if the internal struggles had not scraped the iron (of the spear) and vanquished in advance the heroic arms that maneuvered them. (2005 [1901]: 226)

He accordingly argued that the clans in many areas were so divided during Menelik's conquest "that one tribe never helped the [attacked] neighbor but was happy in its weakening" – and moreover that the indifference among the clans meant that they "reciprocally abandoned each other to the hecatomb of the conquest" (2005 [1901]: 350). While it obviously would be incorrect to essentialize such disunity as an inherent aspect of the Oromo, internal divisions were a major problem for the Bale insurgency. Separate clan-affiliated units would commonly carry out military operations, and these were seldom coordinated with other clan-affiliated units. In fact, if fighters from one unit came under attack, they could not always count on support from others – unless they belonged to the same clan or sub-clan. Undoubtedly, this weakened the movement significantly:

There was a weak leadership.... There was no one leader, they were all divided. Moreover, they didn't listen to each other. The groups were organized according to clans, and there was a competition among the different clans. Each one wanted to be number one in the fighting, and if one group was engaged in a battle, the others didn't come and help them.[31]

This aspect of the Bale insurgency has received little attention. As "factional infighting and internal wrangling are usually perceived as catastrophic for rebel organizations" (Woldemariam 2011: 39), this has – unsurprisingly – deliberately been omitted from the narrative. My informants were very reluctant to talk about this, and ethno-nationalist–colored accounts of the Bale insurgency make no mention of it. It was only after I had gained a high level of trust among my

---

[31] Interview, Hajji Semir Idris, Addis Ababa, December 12, 2017.

informants that they were willing to talk about this. This was clearly an important factor for the failure of the movement – yet not the only one. Another crucial reason was the end of the crucial arms supply from Somalia.

The Somali Factor

I made many references in the previous chapter to the Somali connection – to the role of the Somali government in providing arms for the insurgents and to how important Somalia was as a place of refuge from the Ethiopian forces. I will similarly in Chapter 9 further elaborate on the role of Somalia in the production of ideological orientations for the insurgency movements in Bale and in the broader southeast. In this section, I provide details on the practical aspect of the Somali connection and what it meant for the Bale insurgency.

Links between the Somali government and the insurgency have led some to think of the insurgency as a tool of the Somali government's irredentist policy (Tibebe Eshete 1991). Such claims have been made with reference to the insurgency leaders' military titles, and the Ethiopian government saw them as proof that the insurgency was remotely controlled by Somalia. The fact that Waqo Gutu had his own seal with the title General of Western Somalia surely demonstrates the Somali government's involvement. While there is no doubt that the Somali government sought to actively organize the insurgency, there are some confusion about the different organizations established. Gebru Tareke claims that the first one was named the United Liberation Front for Western Somalia (ULFWS), said to have been established by Ethiopian Somali and Oromo refugees in Mogadishu on June 5, 1960, and linked to and funded by the Somali government (Gebru Tareke 1977: 293, 322). There is also the claim that the ULFWS was based in Baghdad, and that it was a purely Somali organization with the objective of "liberating" the Ogaden and the Northern Frontier District in Kenya (Makinda 1985: 23). This is contested by some informants, who argue that the only organization in the early 1960s was the Liberation Front of Ogaden (LFO), established by the Somali government in 1963 (Henze 1985: 30).[32] In 1968, the Somali government established the Western Somalia Liberation Front (WSLF)

---

[32] Interview, Hajji Isaq Ismail, Skype, September 30, 2019.

with Muhammad Umar as the president, Sheikh Hussein Sura as the general secretary, and with figures such as Jarra Abba Gadaa (Abdulkarim Ibrahim Hamid) and Abdullahi Muhammad "Lungo" involved in the leadership.[33] Sheikh Hussein Sura, who I will return to in Chapter 9, was from Ginir in Bale and became the key spokesperson for the insurgents in dealing with the Somali authorities and had since 1966 been asking them for permission to establish a separate organization. Both he and the insurgency leadership knew that the WSLF was an attempt to co-opt the struggle, and that they were being used by the Somalis. However, lacking resources and completely dependent on the Somalis for arms – there was little they could do than accept being represented by the WSLF. It is here important not to reduce the Bale insurgency and other similar movements across the southeast as instruments for Somali interests. This is, at best, a simplification that serves to inaccurately deprive non-Somali actors of independent agency.

The new organization enabled the insurgents to connect with the broader Middle East. Our knowledge about this, however, is rather limited, and this brief account should not be considered as conclusive. After the establishment of WSLF, the Somali government facilitated contacts with several Middle Eastern countries, and soon the governments of Iraq, Kuwait, Syria, and Yemen expressed interest in supporting the struggle and issued invitations to the leadership. The Somali government demanded, however, that the delegation had to include an equal number of Somalis. The insurgency leaders strongly opposed this and decided instead to secretly send Sheikh Hussein Sura, who under the pretext of going for *umra* (the lesser pilgrimage to Mecca), traveled to Saudi Arabia and then to Egypt. There he met with two Ethiopian students, and together they continued to Bagdad. Sheikh Hussein Sura was well received by the Iraqis who promised both military and financial support, and soon he was sending money back to Somalia. The funds were wired directly to the previously mentioned Abdullahi Muhammad "Lungo," but the high amount transferred quickly caught the attention of the Somali government, which immediately arrested him.

---

[33] Jarra Abba Gadaa became the founder and leader of the Islamic Front for the Liberation of Oromia in 1985.

The Iraqi arms meanwhile were sent to Aden in Yemen, where Elemo Qilitu (Hassan Ibrahim) handled them.[34] Elemo Qilitu was originally from Hararge but had moved to Aden in 1956, where he had established himself as a successful businessman. He had been active in seeking support for the emerging Oromo ethno-nationalist movement in the Middle East and became instrumental in smuggling the weapons into Somalia. This was made possible through small groups of insurgents crossing the Red Sea and taking the weapons with them back – until also this was stopped in October 1969 (Mohammed Hassan 2005a).[35] Sheikh Hussein Sura remained in the Middle East where he opened offices in Iraq, Kuwait, Syria, and Yemen – before establishing the Ethiopian National Liberation Front (ENLF).[36]

The most crucial support from the Somali government was, obviously, arms, and the flow of guns and ammunition was decisive in sustaining the Bale insurgency and similar movements elsewhere in the southeast. The most common gun was the already mentioned Italian-made Carcano M19 rifle. Other weapons included the Sola Leger and Thompson machine guns.[37] Increasing support from the Soviet Union secured the Somali government's access to more modern military equipment, and this also meant that the armory provided to the insurgents became increasingly sophisticated – including landmines, anti-vehicle grenades, and hand grenades (Markakis 1987: 88). Kahin Abdi, the leader of the struggle in El Kere *awraja*, was important in connecting the Arsi Oromo insurgents with the Somalis, but the main figure was the already mentioned Hajji Isaq Dhadhi, appointed as the key liaison officer between Mogadishu and the Arsi Oromo insurgents. The fact that he wore a Somali uniform and traveled around in a Somali police car illustrates his close connections with the Somali authorities.[38] Anyone arriving from Ethiopia in search of arms had to go through him.

---

[34] Elemo Qilitu was instrumental in the establishment of the OLF and was killed in battle in 1974.
[35] Hajji Isaq Ismail, Skype, September 30, 2019.
[36] The ENLF was one of the forerunners of the OLF.
[37] Interrogation Report, Ibrahim Kadir, September n.d., 1967. The Italians left behind both the Carcano M19 and the Albini-Braendlin rifles, and the latter were also used by the early Eritrean insurgent Hamid Awate (Michael Woldeghiorghis Tedla 2014).
[38] Interrogation Report, Kadir Yunus, September 17, 1967.

The only access to Somalia was by foot and crossing the vast Ogaden region was both arduous and hazardous. Access to water was crucial in the arid lowlands, and constantly risking being intercepted by the Ethiopian forces, travel could only happen at night. The insurgents in Dello would follow Welmel or another of the smaller rivers east until they encountered the Genale River, which would take them to Dolo town at the Somali border. Those from Wabe *awraja* had their own different route:

> I went five times to Somalia to get guns. The trip took twenty-one days. We would go from here to Imi, and we would follow Wabe Shebelle River [and then] to Dolo at the border, and from there enter Somalia. The people from Dello *awraja* stayed in Luq, while we from Wabe *awraja* would go to El Berd. Hajji Isaq Dhadhi was operating in both places.[39]

After being received, the weapons would be loaded on camels and brought back to Bale along the same route. Obtaining arms, however, was often a cumbersome process that could take several months – and even up to one year. This was partly because of the inefficient distribution system but also because there simply were not enough weapons.

The Somali government also provided training for the insurgents. This was primarily in the form of guerrilla-style military training, while some claim that it also entailed political education. The training was mostly carried out in Luq and in a place called Gerewey. As noted in Chapter 4, thousands of insurgents received such short-term military instruction. In addition, between 1964 and 1966, between 500 and 900 insurgents received a one-year advanced training in handling heavy weaponry (Assefa Addissu 1980: 28; Gebru Tareke 1991: 153). One report from the Ethiopian intelligence claimed that in the beginning of 1966, more than 2,000 insurgents were found in Somalia, and that these insurgents gradually were returning to Ethiopia in groups of several hundreds.[40] More than a year later, in May 1967, Commander of the Bale Police Tesfaye Gebre-Mariam reported that around 8,000 Arsi Oromo were receiving training at Luq, while another report a few months later put this number at 10,000.[41] The

---

[39] Interview, Adam Yunus, Raytu, June 11, 2017.
[40] Interrogation Report, Ahmed Mahmoud, Muhammad Yunus, Olana Waqo, Oda Gutama, Hassan Jobir, February 11, 1966.
[41] Memo by Tesfaye Gebre-Mariam, Commander of Bale Police, May 31, 1967. No. 431/19/35; letter from Colonel Sirak Tesfa, Public Security Department,

Somali training, however, was of a far more random and of a different type than, for example, the training offered by the Eritrean insurgency movements and the Tigray People's Liberation Front (TPLF). These movements placed much emphasis on ideological and organizational instruction, which was crucial in motivating and disciplining the rank and file.

The Somalis' support for the insurgencies – which also included offering them a safe haven in Somalia – represented a thorn in the side for the Ethiopian government, which made repeated appeals to Mogadishu to end the support. When the Somali government simply ignored the Ethiopian requests, Emperor Haile Selassie eventually lost his patience. With the support from the United States, he moved an army division into Ogaden in early 1963 and initiated a counterinsurgency operation that eventually advanced toward the Somali border. In January 1964, the Ethiopian army launched several attacks on Somali border posts, from Tug Wajale in the north to Dolo in the south, while the air force conducted bombing raids on towns like Hargeisa (Markakis 1987: 180; Reid 2011: 164). Negotiations facilitated by the UN and the Organization of African Unity (OAU) prevented further escalation of the conflict, resulting in a ceasefire agreement signed on March 6, 1964. The agreement called for the withdrawal of Ethiopian forces and for Somalia to end arming the insurgents (Issa-Salwe 2000: 68).

Mogadishu only partially complied with the demands, however, cutting off support for the insurgents in the Ogaden. Although this effectively ended the nascent Ogadeni movement, the Somali government established, at the same time, a military training camp for former and future Ethiopian Somali insurgents, bringing in ca 1,200 men from Ogaden (Markakis 1987: 181). It continued in the meantime to support the insurgency in northern Kenya and in Bale with arms. For example, there was a report that ten camels loaded with guns and accompanied by 100 insurgents had arrived in Wabe *awraja* as late as January 14, 1967.[42] Moreover, in May the same year, reports told about more 1,500 insurgents who were intercepted in the Ogaden on

---

Addis Ababa, to Bale Province Administration, August 7, 1967. No. 4199/59; Interrogation Report, Ibrahim Kadir, September 12, 1967; "Report of the Operation in Dello Awraja from February 2 to April 7, 1970." Ministry of Interior Archives, n.d. No. 2401/3/MA/4QM/47/673/667.

[42] Interrogation Report, Ahmed Assaba, January 17, 1967.

the way to Somalia.[43] Provisions of arms seem to have continued in the first half of 1967, and reports talked about hundreds of guns flowing into both Wabe and Dello.[44] One source claims that the support of arms was sanctioned by top officials, such as Somalia's President Aden Abdullah Ousman and Prime Minister Abdirashid Ali Shermarke.[45] However, signs of a changed Somali policy surfaced, indicating that Somalia was seeking to improve its relations with Ethiopia. When Ibrahim Egal took over as prime minister in July 1967, he shifted focus to more domestic issues, and trying not to provoke Addis Ababa, he sought to limit the flow of guns to the insurgents and suspended Radio Mogadishu's anti-Ethiopian broadcasting (Gebru Tareke 1977: 332; Markakis 1987: 181). By 1968, the flow of arms from Somalia was effectively ended.

Highland Activists

Although the insurgents were from the lowland areas, the movement had, as briefly mentioned in the introduction to this chapter, broad support among the people of Bale – including in the highlands. Particularly important in sustaining the insurgency was what I call the "highland activists," who, as also noted, were not directly involved in the fighting but provided important support for the movement. Such support included the provision of money, food, clothes, and other necessities for the fighters. They were also instrumental in gathering moral support and in advocating for the movement. Many of the highland activists came from lineages vested with traditional authority, while others held official positions within the regional administration in Bale. It is again impossible to mention all these individuals and to do justice to their stories, but the following list some of the most important ones.[46]

---

[43] Memo by Tesfaye Gebre-Mariam, Commander of Bale Police, May 31, 1967. No. 431/19/35.

[44] Letter from El Kere *awraja* Administration to Bale *teklay gezat* Administration, June 14, 1967. No. 1113/34/2/56; Interrogation Report, Kedir Meliye, June 8, 1967.

[45] Memo by Tesfaye Gebre-Mariam, Commander of Bale Police, May 31, 1967. No. 431/19/35.

[46] Compiled from interviews, Hajji Ibrahim Mustafa, Robe, August 5, 2005; Siraj Muhammad Amin, Robe, August 12, 2015; Interrogation Report, Nasrallah, November 13, 1966; Muusaa Haaji Aadam Saaddoo (2014: 125).

Hajji Adam Saddo	Hajji Muhammad Sheikh Waliye,
Qadi Ahmed Imama	Shaza Hajji Hussein Sheikh Sheku
Grazmach Umar Hussein,	Hajji Mahmoud Lami
Hajji Abubakr Darga	Masqala Gunbicho
Aliye Qadi Ahmed Imama	Gari Watare
Fitawrari Hussein Mame	Kebede Tullu
Hajji Muhammad Qanqu Mame	Hajji Orera Jima
Kabir Junda Sheikh Adam	Sheikh Khadir Ture
Abda Garado	Kadir Bushra
Qassim Hussein Abba Boqa	Adam Bushra
Hassan Jima	Hajji Muhammad Sheka,
Hajji Hussein Sheikh Muhammad	Hajji Nure Hajji Abubakr
Hussein Alo Abba Turke	Gira Sani Mame
Hajji Umar Hajji Adam Zikri	Hajji Ibrahim Bakaro

One important figure among these was Qadi Ahmed Imama. He was a native of Dirre Sheikh Hussein and belonged to the *warra imaama* – the lineage of Sheikh Muhammad Tilma Tilmo. His uncle was Imam Mahmoud, the main leader at the shrine during the 1960s. Qadi Ahmed Imama was born in 1910 and lived most of his adult life at a place called Wolenzo in Gololcha *worreda,* not far from Dirre Sheikh Hussein (Birch-Iensen 1960: 119). He served as a *qadi* in Bale, among others in Ginir *worreda,* and held different public offices. He was an *awraja* judge in Wabe and the administrator of Gololcha *worreda* before he assumed the position as the vice-administrator of Fasil *awraja* in the 1960s.

Another important person was *Grazmach* Umar Hussein. He was born in 1930 in Goro *worreda* and, similar to Qadi Ahmed Imama, held various positions in the local administration in Bale, serving as a secretary in Guradhamole *worreda* and as a judge in Goro *worreda* from the late 1940s into the 1950s, before being transferred to the municipality of Dodola in June 1961. Both of these individuals harbored strong negative feelings about the Amhara domination and what they saw as "foreign" rule of Bale and became active supporters of the insurgency.

The leading figure among the highland activists, however, was Hajji Adam Saddo – a person who today has become an iconic figure, in both Bale and beyond (see Figure 5.3). Born in 1884 in Magida in the vicinity

Figure 5.3 Hajji Adam Sado

of Goba town, Hajji Adam Saddo was of the Darara clan and belonged to a family referred to as the *Saddo Sheekaa*, or the Saddo sheikhs. He was moreover from an *abbaa boku* lineage, the son of a *burqa*, and a man who enjoyed deep respect among the Oromo in Bale (Muusaa Haaji Aadam Saaddoo 2014: 4). He is described as an impressive figure, tall, handsome, and with a charismatic nature that invited confidence. He was always dressed in white, grey, and black, and with an *amama* (the Muslim headdress) in the same colors (Muusaa Haaji Aadam Saaddoo 2014: 10). Hajji Adam Saddo devoted much of his childhood to Islamic education, studying the Qur'an in his mother's home area, Harsadi, before continuing with *fiqh* (Islamic jurisprudence) under, among others, Sheikh Isma'il Walashe. He later studied *tafsir* (Quranic exegesis) under Sheikh Ibrahim Gurdubaj and was throughout his life a devoted pilgrim to Sheikh Hussein. During the 1950s and 1960s, he served as a *qadi* in Goba, Dodola, and Dello-Mena and was moreover a *worreda* administrator in Menna-Angetu, Ginir, and Gasera during the 1960s.[47]

Hajji Adam Saddo voiced his opposition to the government's policies in Bale from an early stage. According to local sources, he staunchly opposed the introduction of tax reforms and land classifications in the 1940s and was constantly advocating for the Arsi Oromo's land rights.[48] He was, as I will return to in more detail, mainly concerned

---

[47] Interviews, Adam Hajji Muhammad, Addis Ababa, September 2006; Hajji Muhammad Aliye, Goba, April 1, 2006; Sheikh Azhar Waliye, Robe, October 13, 2005; Obse Ibrahim, Robe, April 15, 2005.
[48] Interview, Siraj Muhammad Amin, Robe, August 12, 2005.

with religious rights and was very conscious of his Muslim identity. One informant told the story about how he refused to remove his *kufiyah* when the Ethiopian flag was raised, an act that earned him time in prison.[49] At the time when the insurgency started, Hajji Adam Saddo had already established quite a reputation among the local authorities, and in an attempt to paint an image of him as a collaborator with the government, he was in 1964 appointed as administrator of Menna-Angetu *worreda*. The plan backfired, however, and the appointment created opportunities for Hajji Adam Saddo to garnish contacts with Waqo Gutu and other leaders of the Dello front, as well as to establish links between them and the emerging embryonic Oromo ethno-nationalist movement (Muusaa Haaji Aadam Saaddoo 2014: 111). The local authorities then transferred him to Gasera *worreda*, hoping that this would isolate him from the struggle. Yet, he also established contacts with the insurgents there and actively passed information to them.[50]

A number of oral stories tell about the highland activists' involvement in the developments leading up to the insurgency. Some of the stories appear to be accurate, but there are several instances of exaggeration, as well as accounts of events that cannot be sufficiently confirmed by other sources. In 1958, for example, several prominent figures from the highlands are said to have met at Hajji Adam Saddo's home to make plans for an armed insurgency in Bale. They allegedly decided to select young men to be sent abroad to be educated and to Somalia for military training. Consultations were then held with Fitawrari Nuho Dhadhi in Raytu and with Waqo Lugu in Dello about getting the young men out of Ethiopia. In 1960, another meeting was reportedly held in Hajji Adam Saddo's house and at Dirre Sheikh Hussein later that year, where it was decided to send a delegation to the newly formed government in Somalia. Shortly after, a group of fifty men were allegedly sent to Somalia for military training.[51] While it is clearly possible that there were consultations among the highland leaders, it is hard to ascertain many of the details in the accounts. For example, Fitawrari Nuho Dhadhi had by that time already passed

---

[49] Interview, Sheikh Muhammad Sheikh Kadir, Adama, June 3, 2011.
[50] Interviews, Siraj Muhammad Amin, Robe, August 12, 2005; Obse Ibrahim, Robe, April 15, 2005.
[51] Interviews, Hajji Ibrahim Mustafa, Robe, August 5, 2005; Siraj Muhammad Amin, Robe, August 12, 2005.

away, and Waqo Lugu was yet to join the insurgency. There is a report that claims that Hajji Adam Saddo's son was sent to Saudi Arabia, and that twenty other youths were sent to Egypt, but it is doubtful whether anyone actually was sent to Somalia or elsewhere for military training.[52]

There are also claims that as the insurgency gained strength, the main highland activists organized themselves into a committee, consisting of, among others, Hajji Adam Saddo, Qadi Ahmed Imama, and Hajji Abubakr Darga (Muusaa Haaji Aadam Saaddoo 2014: 125). If existing, the committee must have been of a highly informal nature, and it would be wrong to think of it as representing any organizational structure. Contacts between the highlanders continued, though, and it is also clear that the insurgents were moving around in the highlands, obtaining provisions at the rural markets in Sinana-Dinshu and Gasera *worredas*.[53]

Pilgrims and Politics at Dirre Sheikh Hussein

The connections between the highland activists and the insurgency were in particular emplaced at Dirre Sheikh Hussein. By the middle of the twentieth century, the shrine was the major site for Muslim life in Bale. Located in the northern part of the region, close to Arsi and Hararge, it attracted tens of thousands of pilgrims every year and was moreover an important place for learning and Islamic scholarship. In addition to "professional" pilgrims like the *fuqras* and *geribas*,[54] the vast majority were ordinary people from all walks of life who traveled to the shrine during the designated times of pilgrimage. The number of pilgrims is estimated to have been between 100,000 and 120,000 in the late 1960s, and while many of them came from other parts of Ethiopia, there is no doubt that the vast majority were from Bale (Braukämper 2002: 141; Hylander 1972: 4). If the estimation of 98,000 households in Bale is correct, it means that "everyone" participated in the pilgrimage.

---

[52] Bale Province's High Court: Verdict against Hajji Adam Sado, Goba, May 31, 1959.
[53] Letter to General Worqu Metaferia, Governor of Bale, June 13, 1967. No. 118.
[54] The word *geriba* which in Arabic means "something peculiar" or "something strange" is the term used for individual devotees of Sheikh Hussein covering wide distances in their pilgrimage.

The guardians of the shrine, the so-called *darga* community lived in a village adjacent to the shrine. This community consisted of peoples from various clans and lineages, commonly referred to as the *sakina*, who had settled there from the late nineteenth century. The main leadership was, as already noted, held by the *warra imaama* (the family of the imam). The village of Dirre Sheikh Hussein was said to consist of 740 houses in 1959, but many of them would only be used during the pilgrimages (Birch-Iensen 1960: 108). If we estimate that three-fourths of the houses belonged to the permanent residents, we end up with a population of ca 2,000. That corresponds with Hylander's observations that the number of residents had increased from a few hundred in the 1930s to 2,000 in 1971 (Hylander 1972: 4).

The shrine was an ideal hub for exchanging information and, consequently, a crucial site for clandestine anti-government activities throughout the twentieth century. It was a natural site for contacts among the insurgents across the southeast, where they could meet and exchange information about the struggle and the military's movement (Lewis 1980; Umer Nure 2006: 77). At the same time, the opportunities for such contacts were restricted. The fact that the local authorities were fully aware of the role the shrine played for anti-government activism meant that soldiers were always present there during the pilgrimage seasons.

The pilgrimage in September 1966 was a particularly important occasion highlighting the shrine's political importance and would, moreover, have dire consequences for the highland activists. As the whole area was under insurgency control, no soldiers were present at the shrine that year, and this created opportunities for free and open exchanges between the insurgents and the highland activists. A company of 300 armed insurgents from the Wabe front, led by Isme Abba Washa, Hussein Bune, Abdullahi Bedhaso, Aliye Hajji Jarso, and Sheikh Abdushikur Elemo, arrived at the shrine and openly interacted with the highland activists and the pilgrim population. They stayed there for several days, and after having collected support for the movement, they disappeared. Information about this incident soon reached the local authorities, however, who immediately arrested the key highland activists. They were accused of being involved in unlawful anti-government activities, of advocating for the insurgency, as well as of providing material support for the fighters (Ketema Meskela 2001: 88; Muusaa Haaji Aadam Saaddoo 2014: 130).

The arrests were the start of a long and cumbersome legal process that commenced on January 16, 1967, and eventually reached Ethiopia's Supreme Court. Hajji Adam Saddo, Qadi Ahmed Imama, and *Grazmach* Umar Hussein were suspected of being the main figures, but others were also arrested and charged – bringing the total number of defendants to thirteen individuals. Together they were renowned figures in the Bale highlands, much respected in their localities, and known for their anti-government attitudes.[55] I have been able to obtain the court files of Hajji Adam Saddo, Qadi Ahmed Imama, and *Grazmach* Umar Hussein, as well as the files for their (and others') appeal case. These documents provide important details concerning the legal process and contain, at the same time, unique insights into both the activists' ideas and undertakings and the state's perceptions of ongoing anti-government activism. Similarly important is the way they offer valuable information about the existing antagonistic relations between the local population and the Amhara. The court files present, at the same time, some serious methodological challenges, as they obviously cannot be treated as neutral accounts. They reveal obvious and inborn prejudices and biases on the state's side, and this makes it clear that the defendants were not offered a fair trial. Also problematic is that the defendants denied all charges against them. In hindsight, we know that some of these charges were false, while others were correct. In some instances, however, it is hard to determine what is true. This has forced me to read the files very carefully and with a great deal of criticism. Being able to triangulate much of the information with other sources and working closely with informants, I believe I have able to reconstruct a rather clear picture of what took place.

Hajji Adam Saddo and Qadi Ahmed Imama were accused of being the main culprits conspiring with and abetting the insurgents during the pilgrimage. They were charged with having introduced the insurgents to the pilgrims and with collecting money, food, and clothes for them. They were also charged with encouraging the local people to travel to Mogadishu to obtain arms and fight the Ethiopian government, as well

---

[55] The others included *Qenazmach* Abubakr Darga, Aliye Qadi Ahmed Imama, Qassim Hussein, Hussein Alo, Abba Turke, Hajji Umar Hajji Adam Zikri, Hajji Muhammad Sheikh Waliye, Shaza Hajji Hussein Sheikh Sheku, Hajji Mahmoud Lami, Hassan Jima, and Hajji Hussein Sheikh Muhammad (interviews, Siraj Muhammad-Amin, Robe, August 12, 2005; Sheikh Ahmed Hajji Kadir, Dirre Sheikh Hussein, June 5, 2006).

as to "plunder the cattle of the Amhara and the Christians" – thus being accused of creating divisions based on ethnicity and religion. Qadi Ahmed Imama was in addition charged with hosting "a party at his house and slaughtering camels and livestock for them," and where he also had encouraged them to fight for the establishment of an independent government. Qadi Ahmed Imama was depicted as an individual actively conspiring with the insurgents in committing acts of violence, inciting the local people across the lowlands (of Wabe *awraja*) to join the movement, and that he, in lieu of his position as a public servant, acted as an infiltrator providing sensitive information to the insurgents.[56]

Hajji Ahmed Saddo was similarly accused of having "rebelled against the government, influenced by Somali propaganda." He had allegedly provided the insurgents with arms – such as *Alben* and *Dhombir* rifles, explosives, and machine guns – and was said to have promised to give them further financial and material support. He had urged the insurgents to continue the fight to overthrow the "Amhara government" and was in addition said to have tried to send youths to "Arab countries" to study and to have spread hatred for the Haile Selassie's government. Both Hajji Adam Sado and Qadi Ahmed Imama had reportedly underscored that they (the highland activists) and the insurgents all were the *Sowra* and part of the same revolutionary struggle (Muusaa Haaji Aadam Saaddoo 2014: 131f.).[57]

While the previously listed thirteen individuals were charged with additional criminal acts, they were all tried as one case.[58] The trial lasted until June 13, 1967, when the court gave its decision – in a closed

[56] The Supreme Court of Ethiopia: Verdict of Appeal Case, Addis Ababa, January 1, 1969.

[57] Charges against *Grazmach* Adam Saddo – from Seyoum Haile-Michael, Prosecutor to the General Prosecutor, Bale Province's High Court, Goba, January 16, 1967. No. 84/59; Charges against *Fitawrari* Ahmed Imama – from Seyoum Haile-Michael, Prosecutor to the General Prosecutor, Bale Province's High Court, Goba, October 4, 1966. No. 45/59; letter from Hajji Adam Saddo to the Ethiopian Imperial Government's High Court, Goba, January 24, 1967; letter to the Ethiopian Imperial Government's High Court, Goba, May 19, 1967.

[58] *Grazmach* Umar Hussein's case was not even linked to the incident at Dirre Sheikh Hussein in 1966; he was accused of collecting money for "a foreign political party" at Dirre Sheikh Hussein in 1961 and for agitating against the government on other occasions. He was also said to have had links with anti-government elements in the lowlands and to have passed sensitive government information to them (Bale Province's High Court: Verdict against *Grazmach* Umar Hussein, Goba, June 13, 1967).

session. Hajji Adam Saddo, Qadi Ahmed Imama, and *Grazmach* Umar Hussein were, as the three main defendants, found guilty of all charges and all received the following sentencing:

> We have judged unanimously against the defendant[s] to the effect that, a) all his property shall be confiscated and transferred to the government; b) he shall receive 40 lashes and be sentenced to 25 years in prison from the day he was arrested, January 16, 1967; c) he shall complete his prison sentence in another region to be chosen by the Ministry of the Interior of the Emperor's Kingdom.[59]

Hajji Adam Saddo, Qadi Ahmed Imama, and *Grazmach* Umar Hussein appealed their cases to the Supreme Court of Imperial Ethiopia the day after the verdict. While the appeal cases worked their way through the system, the defendants remained imprisoned in Goba for more than a year. While in prison, they also started to encourage other prisoners to also appeal their cases, and soon the list of appellants also included *Qenazmach* Abubakr Darga, Hassan Jima, Qassim Hussein, Aliyeh Qadi Ahmed Imama, and Hussein Alo Abba Turki.[60] The basis for their appeals was largely procedural, and they argued that they had not received a fair trial by the court in Bale. First, they claimed that the judge of the Bale Province's High Court, Sirak Werkeneh, harbored biases against them and had ruled against them in a prejudiced manner. Secondly, they argued that the prosecution's witnesses had been forced and bribed to testify against them, while the defendants' witnesses had been imprisoned and intimidated and thus barred from testifying. Thirdly, they claimed that the court based its verdict on "evidence" that was unrelated to their cases.

The Supreme Court gave its verdict on January 1, 1969, and ruled in favor of all the defendants' claims. The verdict unequivocally reprimanded Bale's High Court for its undue partiality, for "judging them [the defendants] in advance," and for demonstrating a lack of professionalism that would not be expected of a court. The Supreme Court

---

[59] Bale Province's High Court: Verdict against Hajji Adam Saddo, Goba, June 13, 1967; Bale Province's High Court: Verdict against *Fitawrari* Ahmed Imama, Goba, June 13, 1967; Bale Province's High Court: Verdict against *Grazmach* Umar Hussein, Goba, June 13, 1967.

[60] Appeal letter from Hajji Adam Saddo to Bale Province's High Court, Goba, June 14, 1967. No. 24/59; letter from Wolde Gebre-Yohannes, Judge of Bale Province's High Court, Goba, to the Ministry of Justice, Addis Ababa, July 23, 1967. No. E3/W/59.

did not, however, decide whether or not the defendants were guilty but ordered the defendants' cases to be retried at a higher court in Addis Ababa. It set the bail for Qadi Ahmed Imama and Hajji Adam Saddo at 10,000 Birr and at 5,000 Birr (USD 4,000 and USD 2,000) for the remaining five.[61]

As the court failed to set any date for the retrial, months passed by. Unable to pay the bail, the defendants remained in prison. Several people tried to intervene with the authorities, seeking to solve the case.[62] All this was to no avail, and in the end, the wives of the prisoners decided to act. During the spring of 1969, the wives of Hajji Adam Saddo, Qadi Ahmed Imama, *Grazmach* Umar Hussein, *Qenazmach* Abubakr Darga, and Hussein Alo Abba Turki traveled the long way from Bale to Addis Ababa – to appeal the case in front of Emperor Haile Selassie:

We were standing by the wayside with our children when Emperor Haile Selassie came driving from Arat Kilo [in central parts of Addis Ababa]. I had an Ethiopian flag in my hand, and when the emperor saw the flag, he had to pay respect to the flag and ordered the car to stop. When he came out, we cried to him, and he asked what we wanted. I explained our case, and he asked us to come to the palace at nine in the morning the next day.[63]

During the night, the women, with the help of two individuals, Sheikh Muhammad Burka and Muhammad Hussein Kabir Faqih, worked to prepare a written petition. When they arrived at the palace the next morning, they were rebuffed by the guards and told to come again at a different time. After being denied access three times, the women received news that the emperor had traveled to Debre Zeit, ca 70 km south of Addis Ababa, and they decided to approach him there:

We arrived there Saturday evening, and on Sunday morning when Emperor Haile Selassie was driving home from church, we all laid down on the road in front of his car. The car stopped, the emperor came out, and asked again what we wanted. We gave him the petition, and he told us to come to his palace in Debre Zeit. When we got there, he received us, giving us the

[61] The Supreme Court of Ethiopia: Verdict of Appeal Case, Addis Ababa, January 1, 1969.

[62] Interview, Hajji Idris Boru, Addis Ababa, December 10, 2017.

[63] Interview, Amina Hajji Yusuf, Robe, July 2, 2011.

opportunity to explain our case. It was because of our petition that the sentence was changed and the prisoners pardoned.[64]

On August 18, 1969, General Wolde-Selassie Bereka, the governor of Bale, sent out a letter to all *awraja* offices in Bale, saying that the defendants were no longer liable for any crimes – being "pardoned by the great kindness of his Majesty [Emperor Haile Selassie]."[65] Later that year, the released prisoners were back at Dirre Sheikh Hussein, thanking God for what they viewed as divine intervention:

> Before they were released, Hajji Adam Saddo, Qadi Ahmed Imama and *Grazmach* Umar Hussein had promised Sheikh Hussein that if he would help them, they would crawl on their knees from Sheikh Hussein's tomb to the Ayagegn caves. When they were released they did this. Both they and the people wept when they crawled on their knees.[66]

There is strong evidence that the defendants committed the offenses with which they were charged – advocating for and actively collecting support for the insurgency. It is therefore striking that they all denied the state's accusations. Hajji Adam Saddo, for example, did not try to defend his action as part of any legitimate struggle but outright refuted all the charges against him, claiming that he never spoke in favor of the insurgency, that he did not conspire with any of the fighters, and that he did not collect any material support for the struggle. He admitted having made contact with the insurgents, yet he claimed that this was for the purpose of urging them to surrender to the authorities.[67] Expecting that he and the other defendants proudly would defend their actions as legitimate easily rests on an assumption that political activists are fearless heroes always willing to sacrifice everything for their struggle. Such individuals do exist, but more common is that bodily emotions of fear override and outweigh cognitive convictions. This seems to have been the case for Hajji Adam Saddo, and here we have to duly consider the real impact that a guilty plea would have. While I was

[64] Interview, Amina Hajji Yusuf, Robe, July 2, 2011.
[65] Letter from General Wolde-Selassie Bereka to the *awraja* offices of Fasil, Genale, Wabe and Dello, August 18, 1969. No. M/A16/1/173.
[66] Interview, Sheikh Ahmed Hajji Kadir, Dirre Sheikh Hussein, June 5, 2006.
[67] Letter from Hajji Adam Saddo to Bale Province's High Court, Goba, January 24, 1967.

reading the court's verdict together with my Ethiopian friends, it was the flogging, imprisonment for twenty-five years, and deportation that caught my attention. My Ethiopian friends, however, while recognizing these measures were serious enough, shook their heads in disbelief over the confiscation of all the defendants' property. Familiar with a reality where poverty never was far away, they knew that this would have been catastrophic for their entire families.

Conclusion

The Bale insurgency was led by key charismatic individual whose authority was based upon lineage, clan affiliation, and traditional structures. This authority was strengthened in the course of the struggle – through their individual charisma and performance in the fighting. As insurgents, it is incorrect to label them as *shiftas* – common bandits – as some have suggested, and, along the same lines, it is highly inaccurate to uncritically transpose *shiftanet* as a phenomenon to a completely different context. Labeling them bandits further neglects the political aspect of the insurgency, its ideological underpinnings, and distracts attention from its causes and objectives.

The leaders, however, were unable to build any coherent organization and to implement effective commando structures. The movement remained inherently decentered and fragmented, which, to a certain degree, can be explained by the spatial dimension of the insurgency and how the landscapes wherein the fighters operated played a role in its effectiveness. While the lowlands – familiar to the pastoralists – were conducive for guerrilla warfare, the vastness of these areas, the lack of communication equipment, and the distance between the various fronts made coordination of activities highly complicated. The clan system played an important role for the insurgents, and clan affiliation was the main organizational principle for the movement. While this secured close links with the population at large, it was, as we have seen, also an inhibiting factor in developing effective structures and contributed much to continuous fragmentation of the movement.

I have earlier pointed to the difficulty of categorizing the nature of the Bale insurgency. Seeking to investigate relevant and more underlying causes, motivations, and ideas, I will in the following chapters dig deeper into the available material and forward suggestions on how to understand the movement. I will, moreover – and this is of equal importance – show that the insurgency represents something larger and that it constitutes a symptom for the antagonistic and conflictual relations existing in southeastern Ethiopia. These relations were centered on embodied and emplaced peoplehood, and on changes that affected identity and belonging.

6 | *Peasant Insurgency without Peasants*

The Bale insurgency has, as noted, been understood as a peasant rebellion. Gebru Tareke, comparing it with the uprisings in Tigray (1940s) and Gojam (late 1960s), claimed that it was primarily caused by land alienation and heavy tax burdens. While he gives some weight to the "ethnic or national question," his key argument is that "land became the source of national [ethnic] and class antagonism" (1977: 76, 156). This perspective reflects Marxist-inspired scholarship on African resistance and insurgency – typical for the 1970s – emphasizing economic modes of production and class conflict – and presupposes the idea of a shared class consciousness, wherein social groups collectively and unvaryingly act according to their material interest (van Walraven and Abbink 2003: 4). Such perceptions have often resulted in a "class teleology," wherein any rebellion is seen as an act of class conflict (Glassman 1995: 14f.). While the question of class as a social category and as a source for collective action in Ethiopia and the role of the peasantry deserves continued attention, I strongly believe that this needs to be investigated in relation to notions of ethnic and religious belonging. I will return to this topic in Chapter 10.

This chapter critically discusses the interpretation of the Bale insurgency as a peasant rebellion. It provides an evaluation of available empirical data, revisits earlier arguments, and forwards new suggestions on the questions of land alienation, taxation, and socioeconomic changes in Bale in the period from Emperor Menelik's conquest of Bale until the outbreak of the insurgency in the 1960s. The main point is to determine how relevant these issues are for an accurate understanding of the insurgency – as well as for the prevailing antagonism felt by the different peoples in the south toward the Amhara and the state. Was land alienation so widespread as commonly assumed? Was the burden of taxation so heavy that it led to further and significant loss of land? What impact did the low population density have on the availability of land? Is the

155

question of class and economic conflict the appropriate one for understanding the insurgency? In other words, was it a peasant rebellion?

Bale Conquered: New Political and Economic Realities

While the Ethiopian state by 1897 had established control over Bale, effective governance did not necessarily mean a heavy Amhara presence. The Amhara were largely represented by soldiers and were spatially organized in a few garrison towns, such as Gurranda, Goba, Ginir, and Lajjo – places that served as bases for monitoring the population. This spatial arrangement was the precursor for later developments of towns and for the Amhara as largely urbanites. It also distanced them from the rural Arsi Oromo population and contributed to the Amhara's self-understanding of being alien and the need for protection from the potential threat the natives represented. It was in addition an expression of superiority – expressed through territorial distance.

Ras Nadew Haile Selassie succeeded *Ras* Lul Seged as governor in 1911 and divided the region into the five areas of Goba, Dodola, Dello, Ginir, and El Kere, each governed by an appointed member of the Amhara military nobility.[1] The low number of Amhara forces stationed in Bale made indirect rule even more important, where local administration was – similar to other areas in the south – delegated to the *balabat* as the state representative. Hussein Badhaasoo (2017), in his list of *balabats* in both Arsi and Bale, has documented that there were eighty-six *balabats* in Bale. A particularly important aspect of this continuity in change was that the *balabats'* areas of jurisdiction to a large extent followed the spatial organization of the clans in Bale (see Table 6.1). Moreover, with the exception of *Fitawrari* Bu'i Falama from Dodola and Chako Enale, the *balabat* in Dello, all the *balabats* were from traditional *abbaa boku* lineages (Østebø 2012: 105f.). Similar to the *abbaa boku*, the office of the *balabat* became hereditary.

A common claim is that Menelik's conquest led to the immediate and widespread loss of land among the peoples in the south. This was, however, not always the case, and the consequences of the conquest varied greatly in the different regions (Pankhurst 1966: 106). While the

---

[1] Interview, Siraj Muhammad-Amin, Robe, August 10, 2005.

Table 6.1 *Main Balabats, clan affiliation, and geographical locations*[a]

Name	Clan	Abbaa Boku[b]	Area/*worreda*
Fitawrari Sheikh Immo	Walashe	✓	Sinana
Fedo Shunka	Sinana	✓	Sinana
Amu Raya	Dawa Dina	✓	Sinana
Mame Magido	Oborra	✓	Sinana
Bonsho Enage	Garora	✓	Sinana
Abba Galata	Amida	✓	Sinana
Kadu Adamu	Kabira	✓	Sinana
Abba Salia	Sambitu	✓	Sinana
Abba Gurmu	Alusha/Fasila	✓	Goba
Grazmach Feto Deboba	Karmamida	✓	Goba
Fitawrari Darga Macha	Manna		Goba
Darge Dula	Sheidama	✓	Goba
Qenazmach Ebo Subi	Wacho	✓	Goba
Bilo Lole	Se'ii Manna	✓	Goba
Grazmach Hamu	Ilasa	✓	Goba
Sani Mame	Ambentu	✓	Agarfa
Kabir Kabe	Koloba	✓	Gasera
Aliye Tulu	Yebsana		Gasera
Turte Abdulla'i	Yebsana		Gasera
Asaba Ali	Sebro	✓	Ginir
Abdulrahmin Argo	De'e		Jarra
Ali Burunga	Bulale		Jarra
Yubee Umba	Daba'e		Goro

[a] While these acted as *balabats* in the postwar period, the exact period in unclear (interviews, Siraj Muhammad-Amin, Robe, November 19, 2005; Hajji Hussein Awol, Robe, December 7, 2002).
[b] This refers to the clans that had *abbaa boku*.

new political reality brought significant socioeconomic changes for Bale, the region did not experience any extensive land alienation in the years following the conquest. Areas defined as government property were mainly, as I will return to, mountains, forests, and stretches of lowlands. In other words, they were not cultivated or cultivatable land. Land in Bale, different from many other areas in the south, was never organized according to the system called *siso*, wherein the state took two-thirds – of which one-third was given to the church – and where the rest (one-third) was allocated to the *balabats* (i.e., the local population). Neither were the *balabats* or the *burqas*, in this initial period, allocated any additional land (*balabat mehret*). Instead, and as I will elaborate on later, land remained communal and distributed among clans and sub-clans according to lineages and thus continued to be in the possession of the Arsi Oromo (Ketema Meskela 2001: 31). Such land arrangement did not completely exclude land alienation, and there were a few cases where local *balabats* bequeathed land to the Amhara. Such a process, called *awwarrasuu* (from the Amharic *mawras*, to bequeath), usually had the form of land being forcefully transferred to high-ranking Amhara officials. The situation in Bale was very different from the situation in neighboring Arsi, however, where large areas of land were bequeathed, and certainly from Chercher, an area of Hararge, where nearly the whole population was turned into landless tenants (Assefa Dula 1969).[2]

The main – and generally overlooked – reason why Bale experienced such a limited degree of land alienation was simply because relatively few Amhara landlords settled in Bale. The most important reason for this was that Bale was considered a remote region and difficult to access. While the western highland plateau of Gedeb was relatively easy to reach as an extension of the Arsi region's plains – which also saw a higher number of Amhara – the distance from Addis Ababa, the rugged mountain ranges, and the Wabe Shebelle canyon made the region's eastern highland plateau much harder to reach. This was exacerbated by the lack of roads and other forms of infrastructure. It was not until 1969, when an all-weather road passing through Genale *awraja* to the capital of Goba was built, that the region was finally connected to the rest of the country. The eastern and southern lowlands were considered even more remote and represented in many ways the periphery of the periphery. Also important to remember is that the Arsi Oromo, including in the highlands, were pastoralists, and since the land was not cleared, it was not attractive to the Amhara. The result was that Bale was a very neglected region.[3]

---

[2] It needs to be emphasized, however, that such bequeathing of land was far from common in all of Arsi and was rather limited to certain areas (Hussein Jemma 2010; Ketebo Abdiyo 2010: 20f.).

[3] Until the early 1970s, Bale was the region with the lowest number of hospitals (1), doctors (1), and health centers (2) (Gebru Tareke 1977: 118).

Scarcity of Amhara did not mean that the new sociopolitical and economic realities did not have any negative impact on the local Arsi Oromo. Most significant was the introduction of the *gabbar* system.[4] The word *gabbar* can be a little confusing and has often been translated to mean a landless tenant. The root of the word in Amharic is *gibr,* meaning tribute, and the accurate translation of *gabbar* would then be "one who pays tribute and/or tax." The *gabbar* system was thus a tributary mode of production, wherein the *gabbar* could both be a tenant as well as a tribute-paying landowner (Shiferaw Bekele 1995: 75). The tribute was paid to local Amhara administrators and officers/soldiers – referred to as *melkenyas* – who had received land, often labeled as *madeira* in lieu of salary. The *melkenyas* were allocated a certain number of *gabbars* living on the land they were given, who were forced to pay tribute to them in kind and through services. The *melkenyas* main asset was thus not land in itself but the number of *gabbars,* or *quter gabbars* (literal meaning: number of *gabbars*) assigned to each of them. As the *gabbars* in highland Bale were agro-pastoralists, animal products and honey were important parts of the tribute in kind. Tribute as service meant that they were required to work on the landlords' own fields and to serve in their houses. The Muslim *gabbars* were also required to bring the landlords extra gifts during the Christian holidays. Failure to meet these obligations would result in fines or corporal punishments, such as flogging and, eventually, loss of land (Gebru Tareke 1977: 243f.; Ketema Meskela 2001: 32f.).[5] The Amhara administrators and their soldiers were often stationed in Bale for a short period, and this paved the way for a great deal of corruption, whereby both the lords and the soldiers sought to "extract as much surplus from the their *gabbar* as they possibly could" (Ketema Meskela 2001: 39).

Land was also allocated to the Ethiopian Orthodox Church. The church was a major landowner in Ethiopia, and churches in Bale, similar to those in other areas, were constructed with government subsidies, provided with land grants (*semon* land), and exempt from tax. They also had their own *gabbars,* some of whom were Muslims

---

[4] The *melkenya* was more accurately the representative of the landlord, collecting the tribute and administering his property.
[5] Interviews, Obse Ibrahim, Robe, October 23, 2000; Hajji Hussein Awol, Robe, December 7, 2002. See Gebre-Wold Ingida Worq for a detailed list of types of tributes to be paid (1962: 306f.).

who were forced to provide labor and tribute to the church. One should, however, not exaggerate the position of the Orthodox Church in Bale. At the eve of the Italian period, only twenty-six churches in Bale collected tribute on ca 13,200 hectares, which counted for 0.1 percent of the total land. In 1969, less than 2 percent of all measured land was classified as church land (Ketema Meskela 2001: 53; Ministry of Land Reform and Administration 1969). Bale was also the region where the church collected the least of its income (Gilkes 1975: 56).[6] This is in stark contrast to neighboring Arsi, where it is reported that 24 percent of all measured land was held by the church (Stahl 1974: 87).

There were, however, very few *gabbars* available to be allocated to each *melkenya*, which is also why the *siso* system was never implemented. The main reason for this was simply that very few people were living in Bale at that time. The total size of Bale was 128,300 sq. km, which translates into 12,830,000 hectares. Although no numbers on population size in Bale in the early twentieth century are available, estimates based on later figures make it possible to assume it had a population of about 154,000 by the turn of the century. This gives a population density of 1.2 person per sq. km.[7] Such a low population density was, as noted, confirmed by European travelers. Fride Hylander, the Swedish missionary, traveling through Bale in the early 1930s reports, for example, that on his way from the Arsi region to Dirre Sheikh Hussein, he did not see any village or house for four full days (1936: 55). Low density meant few tribute-paying subjects (see later), which also contributed to making the region less attractive to the Amhara.

The important point to be made is that low population density meant abundance of land, which in turn meant that allocation of land to a relatively few Amhara landlords had limited direct impact on the local people. No figures are available on exactly how much land was controlled by the *melkenya* in the early twentieth century, but it is safe to assume that their landholdings were relatively small. A case in point

---

[6] The total church income from Bale in 1961–1962 was around 26,000 Ethiopian *birr*, compared with ca 636,000 and 394,000 *birr* from Shoa and Tigre, respectively (Gilkes 1975: 56).

[7] These figures are based on Mesfin Wolde Mariam's (1961) estimates from 1960, when Bale's population accounted for 1.4 percent of the total national population. See also Richard Pankhurst (1961).

is that *madeira* land in Goba *worreda* in the early twentieth century was limited to only 320 hectares – as opposed to the district's 277,800 hectares defined as private land (Ketema Meskela 2001: 6). Such a limited amount of *madeira* land is significant in light of Goba being the capital of the region, which hence would have a high concentration of Amhara officials. Low population density and abundance of land meant that the Arsi Oromo pastoralists were to large extent able to continue their way of life by keeping large amounts of livestock.[8]

The 1919 decision to grant land to soldier-settlers – or *neftenyas* – brought an increasing number of mainly Amhara settlers to Arsi and Bale. They settled among the local Arsi Oromo population and paved the way for additional settlers to arrive throughout the first half of the twentieth century. While the *neftenyas* were given *gabbars,* the low population density meant that there were too few available to be allocated (Abbas H. Gnamo 2014: 237; Ketema Meskela 2001: 33). Part of the state's reason for settling the *neftenyas* in the south was to expand the basis for revenue. Tribute in the form of cash became increasingly common during the 1920s, and a stronger emphasis on taxation to be extracted from land came in 1932, when Governor *Dejazmach* Nasibu Zamanuel (1932–1935) introduced the first major tax reform to Bale. The taxes were supposed to move up the chain to the Imperial Government; however, as most of it remained in the pockets of the local administrators, the government also introduced the *asrat* tax (one-tenth) to Bale and underscored the need for more accurate measurements of land.[9] The tax reform was also the start of a transformation toward more formalized state structures and a monetary economy – as well as part of an extensive reform of the feudal structure. The latter proved to be a slow process, and although forced labor was banned in 1918, the practice continued through the first half of the twentieth century. Moreover, both the new system of land measurement and the extraction of tax in cash did not reduce corruption. Quite the opposite: it enabled landowners and government officials to continue to fleece the locals as much as they could.

---

[8] A similar situation was found in many other areas in the south, where population density and availability of land secured the local people's continued access to land (Markakis 1987: 40).

[9] The *asrat* was formally introduced in 1878, but it seems that its actual implementation occurred much later in many areas (Markakis 1974: 114).

While tribute and tax so far had been based upon the size of people's herds and an often-rudimentary assessment of their assets, land measurement and the efforts to increase the extraction of taxes became the first steps that would reconfigure the pastoralist economy among the highland Arsi Oromo. The state tax depended on the size and the type of land (see later), and the overall aim of the government's new policy was to increase the control over the *gabbars* by tying them to their land – in turn furthering the extraction of tax based on the produce from the land. Accompanied by the introduction of ox-driven plows, sometime in the beginning of the twentieth century, the Arsi Oromo were forced to abandon their traditional way of life and cultivate increasingly larger plots of land to meet the state's demands. There is not much detailed information on how rapid or extensive these changes were, but as developments in Bale lagged behind other areas, it is clear that pastoralism continued to dominate in the highlands throughout the prewar period. Both the scale and pace of changes would, however, increase in the postwar period.

Postwar Developments

The ousting of the Italians in 1941 and the re-installment of Emperor Haile Selassie secured Ethiopia's continued independence and marked the beginning of a process toward an increasingly centralized and a more active state. Acting as regent under Queen Zawditu, Menelik's daughter, the emperor had in the prewar period met much resistance for his modernization efforts from the conservative feudal lords. As the Italians had literally eradicated these lords, the reforms could be implemented more easily. Most important here was the expansion of government institutions and bureaucracy, the appointment of salaried provincial officials dependent on the monarch, and the creation of a professional army. These reforms contributed to formalizing provincial rule and curbed much of the feudal class's influence and limited the role of the *balabats*. The new officials were largely Amhara from the Shoa region and came to form a new elite attached to the royal palace. The indigenous population was to a limited extent included in the political administration. In contrast to the Ogaden, where the emperor – in an attempt to counter Somali nationalist sentiments – appointed Somalis as salaried district leaders, only a tiny number of Muslim Oromo in Bale were allowed into the government structure – at a lower level (Gebru Tareke 1977: 273; Markakis 2011: 144).[10] Some Muslim Arsi Oromo were appointed to the parliament, particularly in the late 1950s and during the 1960s, but the fact that the parliament had very limited political influence meant that such representation was rather meaningless (Aberra Ketsela 1971: 13).[11]

Before analyzing the questions about land and land tenure in the postwar period, it is important to revisit the question of population size and density in Bale. While more data are available for this period compared with the early twentieth century, it is still difficult to reach any definite conclusions. This has consequently produced widely different estimates – for example, Patrick Gilkes has claimed the figure to be 1.2 million around 1973 (1975: 223). Gebru Tareke (1977: 231), on his part, estimated Bale's population to be between 708,000 and 1.5 million. The yearly *Statistical Abstract* reports for Ethiopia during the 1960s list the population of Bale to be 145,000 in 1964 and 194,000 in 1970. In 1971, however, the number had changed to 693,000 – due to "fresh information" and with no further explanations (Central Statistical Office 1971: 26). Later censuses, meanwhile, report the population to be ca 1 million in 1984, 1.2 million in 1994, and 1.4 million in 2007, thus making the *Statistical Abstract* estimates from the early 1960s too low and the estimates of 693,000 from 1971 too high (Central Statistical Office 1985, 1994). Mesfin Wolde Mariam (1961) assessed that Bale had a population of ca 354,000 in 1960 – out of a total of ca 24.6 million nationally – a number that seems too low. Another source provides more reasonable estimates, suggesting the total population to be 540,000 in 1968 (Yitbarek Muluneh 1970: 17). When applying a growth rate of 2.5 percent, it becomes possible to say – with some degree of certainty – that the population of Bale was ca 440,000 in 1960 and ca 500,000 in 1965. Moreover, converting the population into households gives us an estimated number of ca 80,000 and

---

10 This was the case across southern Ethiopia. Clapham has documented that in 1967, all provincial governors were Amhara from Shoa and that all but two sub-provincial governors were from the north. In the neighboring Arsi region, only four of twenty-two district leaders were Arsi Oromo, and in one district all but thirty public servants were Amhara (Clapham 1975: 76).

11 Interview, Obse Ibrahim, Robe, April 15, 2005. The situation in Bale corresponded to that at the national level, where people from the southern regions were excluded from holding political positions (Clapham 1969: 78).

Table 6.2 *Estimated population size, density, and number of households according to* awraja *in 1968*

Awraja	Population	Area in sq. km	Density	No. households
Dello	75,000	22,300	3.4	13,600
Fasil	250,000	13,900	18	45,000
Genale	40,000	8,100	5	7,000
Wabe	150,000	27,000	5.5	27,300
El Kere	25,000	57,000	0.4	4,500
Total	540,000	128,300	4.2	98,000

Note: Compiled from Yitbarek Muluneh (1970) and Aynalem Adugna (1984).

98,000 households in 1960 and 1968, respectively (see Table 6.2).[12] With a total areal of 128,300 sq. km, the population density then becomes 3.5 persons per sq. km in 1960 and 4.2 persons per sq. km in 1970 – making Bale the least-populated region in Ethiopia.

I have already argued that the conquest of Bale did not lead to any initial *widespread* loss of land and will here, along the same lines, demonstrate that the claim that Amhara rule during the postwar period caused increased land alienation in terms of confiscations needs to be modified. I believe that such claims are often based on ideological preferences and will show that a careful reading of the available data reveals a far more complex picture. It needs to be added, however, that the lack of reliable sources, and their contradictory nature, poses some significant challenges. Categories and classifications are applied rather inconsistently, making it difficult to draw final conclusions. The most important source we have is the 1969 Land Tenure Survey of Bale – one of the many regional surveys done in the late 1960s. The survey's methodological shortcomings, its sample size, and the tendency to both over- and under-report need to be critically considered.[13] One major issue is that the amount of land actually measured in Bale was limited to only 16 percent (Table 6.3), slightly higher than the 10 percent of land measured nationally (Stahl 1974: 69f.). Moreover, the fact that the survey was carried out during the height of the insurgency (July 1968) obviously had an impact on its findings and

---

[12] This is based upon an estimated average of 5.5 persons per household.
[13] See Pausewang (1973) and Mesfin Wolde Mariam (1991) for a critique of these surveys.

Table 6.3 *Distribution of actual land and measured land in hectares according to* awraja

Awraja	Total Area	Measured Land	Percentage of Measured Land
Dello	2,230,000	500,000	22
Fasil	1,390,000	520,000	37
Genale	810,000	430,000	53
Wabe	2,770,000	650,000	23
El Kere[a]	5,630,000	–	–
Total	12,830,000	2,100,000	16

[a] Land in El Kere *awraja* was never measured during the Imperial period and is not included in the survey.
Source: Ministry of Land Reform and Administration 1969.

conclusions. However, if one reads these sources carefully and triangulates the data with other written sources and with informants' accounts, it is possible to identify the main developments with a certain degree of accuracy.

While all land in Ethiopia formally belonged to the emperor, the overwhelming amount of land was in reality in the hands of the local population during the postwar period. Such land was called *gabbar* land, the second meaning of the term, and while *gabbar* land had been the basis for tributes paid to landlords in the past, it became, according to the official definition, land acquired through purchase, inheritance, or grant, on which the owner/holder "pays tax to the government as prescribed by law" (Ministry of Land Reform and Administration 1969: 4).[14] In 1965, more than 98 percent of all measured land in Bale was categorized as private (Ketema Meskela 2001: 63), whereas the 1969 Land Tenure Survey lists this as close to 48 percent of all measured land. It is unclear how much of this land was actually held by local Arsi Oromo, but the fact that only a sampled 19,200 hectares of *madeira* were converted to freehold indicates that a rather small

[14] The notion of land as private was different from that in many of the northern areas of Ethiopia where the common land tenure was known as *rist,* and which usually is understood as an individual's right to a piece of land based upon kinship and descent (Cohen and Weintraub 1975: 31). See Shiferaw Bekele (1995) for a broader discussion of the *rist* system.

amount of land was owned by Amhara landlords/officials. The survey moreover reports that an estimated 14 percent of landowners were absentee owners, with a total holding of 12 percent of all measured land – further indicating that most land was in the hands of the Arsi Oromo.[15]

Gebru Tareke has claimed that a total of 81 percent of all land was under government control by 1967 (1977: 260). It is unclear what the source for this number is, and my argument is that the amount of government land (*mengist* land) was much lower. In fact, the government itself estimated it to be just under 23 percent of all measured land by the end of the 1960s (Ministry of Land Reform and Administration 1969).[16] Important to note here is that measured government land did not necessarily include the vast lowland areas, mountains, and forests – which points to a crucial, yet often overlooked, dimension of land and land tenure in Bale. While the western and central highlands contained wide plains suitable for agriculture, most parts of Bale consisted of rugged mountains, large forests, and vast stretches of arid lowland areas. One source reveals that only 13 percent of all land in Bale was being cultivated, and that 43 percent was used as grazing land. The remaining 44 percent was described as unused scrub and forestland (Ministry of Land Reform and Administration 1971).[17]

The topographical variations of Bale need to be carefully considered in relation to the government's emerging system for classification of land. New land categories were first introduced in 1942/1944, dividing land into "fertile" (*lem*), "semi-fertile" (*lem-lem*), and "poor" (*taf*) land. The 1969 Land Tenure Survey estimated that only ca 9 percent of measured land could be classified as fertile, whereas more than 79 percent was defined as poor (Ministry of Land Reform and Administration 1969: 9). Such classification was obviously based on whether the land was suitable for agricultural production, and the high percentage of poor land in Dello and Wabe *awrajas*, as seen from Table 6.4, reflects the fact that these were almost exclusively lowland areas,

---

[15] This is the lowest percentage of measured land nationally, and only Gamu Gofa had a lower percentage of absentee landowners (Cohen et al. 1976: 55; Ministry of Land Reform and Administration 1969: 13, 23).

[16] The survey uses *gasha* as the unit – which when converted equals 40 hectares.

[17] This correspond roughly to the current situation, where 15 percent of all land in Bale is considered suitable for agriculture (Bale Zone Department of Finance & Economic Development 2004: 27).

Table 6.4 *Distribution of type of measured land according to* awraja

Awraja	Total Percentage	Fertile Percentage	Semi-fertile Percentage	Poor Percentage	In Hectares
Dello	22	1	2	97	500,000
Fasil	37	21	18	61	520,000
Genale	53	15	23	62	430,000
Wabe	23	3	7	90	650,000
Total	16	9	12	79	2,100,000

Source: Ministry of Land Reform and Administration 1969.

Table 6.5 *Distribution of government land according to land classification and* awraja

Awraja	Measured Land Percentage	Fertile Percentage	Semi-fertile Percentage	Poor Percentage	In Hectares
Dello	37	0.1	0.4	99	180,000
Fasil	27	1	4	95	140,000
Genale	20	0.3	4	96	85,000
Wabe	11	1	7	92	71,000
Total	23	0.6	3	97	476,000

Source: Ministry of Land Reform and Administration 1969.

with the vast Harenna forest located in the former. The eastern parts of Fasil *awraja* were similarly composed of lowlands, while Genale *awraja* was home to extensive mountain terrains, also stretching into the southwestern parts of Fasil *awraja*.

There are direct correlations between Bale's topography, categories of land, and land defined as government land. Analyzing this in relation to the different *awrajas*, we see from Table 6.5 that most government land was found in Dello *awraja* (ca 37 percent) and in Fasil *awraja* (ca 27 percent). However, when examining the available data more closely, it becomes clear that an overwhelming amount of government land was classified as poor land: ca 97 percent of all measured land. In contrast, only 0.6 percent and 3 percent of fertile and semi-fertile land, respectively, were classified as government land. Again, we need to remind ourselves that most of the land in the lowland areas remained unmeasured, which in turn means that land categorized as government land counted for a much higher percentage.

The crucial question to be asked is whether the postwar period saw a significant degree of land alienation in the form of land confiscated by the state – as has commonly been argued. The lack of sources represents a problem; yet, a careful interrogation of what is available brings about a more multifaceted picture. The Land Tenure Survey reports that around 210,000 hectares of measured land had been confiscated in the period of 1949–1961, which counts for only ca 10 percent (Ministry of Land Reform and Administration 1969: 24). The total amount of land confiscated by the state (*gebretel* land) in 1963 is reported to be ca 900,000 hectares (Ketema Meskela 2001: 68). Gebru Tareke erroneously claims that that this accounted for 14 percent of the total land, when it actually only amounted to 7 percent. In 1969, however, we see that an estimated 27 percent of all measured land was confiscated. This is not an insignificant number and forces us to ask why there was such a surge in land confiscations during the 1960s.

The reported number of land confiscations appears at first glance to contradict common practice in Ethiopia, where – for whatever reason – confiscations of farmland remained relatively uncommon (Dessalegn Rahmato 1985: 25; Markakis 1974: 343). However, when examining more closely the type and location of land being confiscated, a more nuanced picture emerges. Most striking is that close to 100 percent of all land confiscated was poor land, and moreover, almost all of this was found in the lowland *awrajas* of Dello and Wabe. Only in Fasil *awraja* do we find a high percentage (32 percent) of fertile land confiscated, but the actual number of hectares confiscated in this *awraja* was very low (Table 6.6). It thus becomes simply incorrect to say that the land confiscated was "by far the largest and most fertile parts" (Gebru Tareke 1977: 254).

Confiscation of land has usually been explained by people's failure to meet their tax demands – which are said to have become increasingly difficult due to evolving tax regimes. The streamlining of tax-collecting procedures and the extraction of land tax in cash were a direct reflection of the state's need to increase its revenues, resulting in new tax regulations issued in 1941, 1942, and 1944 – at the time when

Table 6.6 *Distribution of measured confiscated land according to land classification and* awraja

Awraja	Measured Land Percentage	Fertile Percentage	Semi-fertile Percentage	Poor Percentage	In Hectares
Dello	37	0	0	100	180,000
Fasil	0.6	32	26	42	3,000
Genale	0	0	0	0	0
Wabe	58	0	0	100	380,000
Total	27	0.2	0.1	99	560,000

Source: Ministry of Land Reform and Administration 1969.

Dejazmach Mekuria Banteyirgu (1941–1943) and *Dejazmach* Leitubelu Gebre (1944–1947) were governors of Bale. The implementation of the land tax varied, however; in areas around the Harenna forest, it was not introduced until the 1950s (Dereje Tadesse Wakjira 2013: 38). Several rounds of land measurements accompanied these reforms, with the first one conducted in 1944. The taxes subsequently levied on land did not necessarily correspond to the size or quality of land, and the measurements carried out through visual assessment were often highly inaccurate (Ketema Meskela 2001: 57f.).

Land measurement according to the *qalad* system was not introduced to Bale before 1951.[18] *Qalad* literally means rope, which was used to calculate the size of the land. The authorities must have realized that the 1951 measurement lacked accuracy and carried out a new round in 1963 to provide more detailed knowledge on landholdings and a more precise basis for taxation of land. The new measurement showed significant discrepancies compared to the former one, revealing that the taxable holdings were more than twice as large when compared with those of 1951 – subsequently resulting in demands for back taxes to be paid for this so-called excess land. The important point here is that while ordinary taxes were not necessarily high, these back taxes meant that the people suddenly had accumulated significant amounts of unpaid taxes for the period of 1953–1963, and enforcement of these

[18] The *qalad* system had been common in other regions of Ethiopia from the early twentieth century.

arrears in 1963 further exacerbated their conditions (Gebru Tareke 1977: 251f.). Yet, in spite of this, only 7 percent of all land was confiscated in 1963.

The high level of corruption among local officials could be another crucial factor contributing to the acceleration of land confiscations. The *qalad* and other techniques for land measurements were used rather randomly, and in many cases the size of holdings was determined through bribes paid to the officials. One of my informants provided the following account:

> The *balabat* was with us when we were measuring the land. I was holding the rope, and the *balabat* was walking and measuring. Suddenly he fell to the ground, groaning. "What is the matter?" my father said. "I am sick," the man replied. But my father understood at once that he wasn't sick, but that he wanted something from him. He then went to him, bent down and smuggled some money under his *gabi* [blanket]. "Look, what have you got here?" he asked, touching the *gabi*. The man looked and saw the money. And suddenly he was all right and continued working as before.[19]

The local population's lack of knowledge about the details of tax regulations further enabled corrupt government officials to extract additional tax from the illiterate rural population:

> When you came to a public office to pay tax or rent for the land, the administrators, who were all Amhara, would accidentally drop some of the money paid in their lap, and accuse you for not having enough money. The only thing you could do was to pay the "missing" money. There was no way to argue about it. My father . . . placed me in a school at an Orthodox church, where a *qes* [priest] was teaching the *fidels* [Amharic letters]. At that time, all the official papers were in Amharic, and he needed someone to translate them.[20]

The fact that most of the confiscated land was categorized as poor could possibly mean that people were more likely to default on their taxes on such land. We do not have many details about the nature of measured poor land, but it is likely that a large amount of it was grazing land. In line with the government's emphasis on agriculture, it is also reasonable to believe that such land would be confiscated. This relates

---

[19]   Interview, Obse Ibrahim, Robe, October 23, 2000.
[20]   Interview, Obse Ibrahim, Robe, October 23, 2000.

to the state's practice of handing out land as grants, something that often has been underscored as a crucial factor for increased land alienation and tenancy in southern Ethiopia. An important incentive for the issuing of land grants during the postwar period was to increase crop production and subsequently the state's revenues. Land was thus given to those willing and able to clear new areas for cultivation. A case in point relates to northerners being resettled in Nansebu *worreda* around 1966. They were all given forestland and, in an attempt to increase agricultural output, were told to clear the forest and start cultivation (Flintan et al. 2008: 44).

While land grants, in the form of *madeira,* commonly were given as rewards or as pensions to retired officials, the postwar period saw a gradual transformation of *madeira* land into private holdings. Another major characteristic of the government's land policy in the early postwar period was the 1942 declaration of granting land to patriots (those who had fought against the Italians), wounded patriots, exiles (those who were forced to flee during the occupation), and people with no land (Cohen and Weintraub 1975: 60). Around 30 percent of all such land grants were found in Bale, and as the 1942 declaration stated that land would be taken from those who supported (deserters) the Italians, one could assume that this was the reason for the high percentage. According to Ketema Meskela, however, there is no direct correlation between such grants and dispossession of land from the local population. As he convincingly demonstrates, grants were rarely in the form of land confiscated from the local people but rather government land that had not been cultivated. One should moreover not overestimate the amount of land given as grants, and during the postwar period, the actual size of land distributed was only around 310,000 hectares – representing about 2 percent of the total area of Bale (Ketema Meskela 2001: 6).

The crucial point to be made is that land confiscation was not as widespread as assumed and, moreover, that it did not produce a large landless class. Even if the demands for taxes could be excessive, failure to pay would not result in confiscation of all land but rather fractions of it. Such land would then be put out for sale and was usually purchased by other – Arsi Oromo – landowners.[21] This situation needs to be read alongside the already discussed question of population size and density

---

[21] Interview, Obse Ibrahim, Robe, June 16, 2018.

in the postwar period. I have already demonstrated that the population density in Bale was merely at 3.5 persons per sq. km in 1960, which in turn meant that land was abundant. It would, in other words, take a great deal to make a person landless, and it seems clear that confiscations would not automatically lead directly to poverty. The 1969 Land Tenure Survey reports that the average size of landholdings by the end of the 1960s was 80 hectares, and that the largest landholding amounted to 4,640 hectares (Ministry of Land Reform and Administration 1969: 12).[22] These figures seem unreasonably high. As an individual at that time could not efficiently farm more than five to six hectares, it clearly points to a dominating pastoralist economy (Dessalegn Rahmato 1985: 28). This is something generally overlooked, and my informants all talked about the postwar period when land was abundant and in the hands of the Arsi Oromo. In fact, anyone who owned more than 20 hectares was characterized as a *landlord* (Stahl 1974: 88). And landlords increasingly needed tenants.

Tenancy

Tenancy in Bale was reportedly not "a major phenomenon or a difficult condition" until the 1960s. Changes during that decade seem dramatic, however, and Ketema Meskela has claimed that tenants counted for 38 percent of the population in Dodola, Robe, and Adaba *worredas* in 1972 (Ketema Meskela 2001: 96, 98). It would be easy to interpret this high number as a reflection of significant land alienation, the creation of a large landless population, and a situation where the local population was tilling the land of Amhara landlords. The conditions in the southern areas have commonly been described in this way, where Markakis even goes so far as to say that the land reforms in the 1960s made the people in the south "unambiguously dispossessed" (1987: 98). This is a gross oversimplification, and a closer examination of the sources reveals significant local variances.

Bale continued to have relatively few Amhara landlords throughout the postwar period, and it is simply impossible that these could have accommodated such a high number of tenants. It is thus clear that the tenants also must have tilled the land of Arsi Oromo landlords. What is

---

[22] This is in stark contrast to today's average landholding of three hectares per person (Sultan Usman and Adamu Zeleke 2017).

important here is that the development of land as private holdings led
to the emergence of "wealthy Muslim Arsi Oromo landlords, many
who had feudal titles such as *Grazmach, Qenazmach,* and
Fitawrari."[23] Another informant confirmed that tenancy was not
a phenomenon linked only to Amhara: "The [Arsi Oromo] *balabats*
and the *burqas* could all have tenants, and so would also the common
people. My father had tenants. These were poor people, who were
working on his land. While working on his land, they would get some
land of their own to cultivate."[24]

Who were these tenants? There were, no doubt, a few Arsi Oromo
tenants, who due to the accumulation of tax arrears had lost their land.
However, my informants generally agree that tenancy among the Arsi
Oromo remained largely nonexistent: "They were very few. Most of
the Arsi owned land."[25] One informant claimed that around Dodola,
in the western part of Genale *awraja,* there were no Arsi Oromo
tenants; they were all landowners.[26] I will return to the question of
Arsi Oromo tenants in the next chapter, and in the meantime point out
that it is inaccurate to claim that "the [Arsi Oromo] gebbars were
slowly turned into landless tenants" (Gebru Tareke 1977: 262).

An important – and overlooked – aspect of tenancy in Bale was that the
tenants were largely outsiders from other parts of Ethiopia. The region
saw an increase of settlers arriving from the late 1940s. These settlers were
different from those arriving early in the twentieth century, being landless
farmers in search of land. While some of them were Amhara, they were in
no way any a privileged group easily accessing land. Some of them were,
as noted, given undeveloped land by the government, and the influx of
these new settlers led to increased demands for land.

The most important migrant group that overwhelmingly ended up as
tenants under the Arsi Oromo were the Shoa Oromo. Informants in
fact claimed that nearly 100 percent of all tenants were from this
group.[27] As the name indicates, the Shoa Oromo originated from the
region of Shoa, surrounding Addis Ababa. The name is an etic one, and

[23] Interview, Mekonnen Abebe, Robe, December 16, 2000.
[24] Interview, Obse Ibrahim, Robe, October 23, 2000.
[25] Interview, Obse Ibrahim, Robe, April 15, 2005.
[26] Interview, Daniel Negash, Dodola, October 23, 2002.
[27] Field Log, June 16, 2018. Hector Blackhurst's (1974) detailed study about the
       Shoa Oromo in Adaba (western highlands of Bale) dovetails very much with my
       own findings further east. See also Blackhurst (1980).

the Shoa Oromo referred to themselves according to their clan affiliation, such as Meta, Abichu, Jarso, or Salale – which also were spatial
terms signifying their dwelling areas in Shoa. It seems that most of the
Shoa Oromo arriving in Bale belonged to the Salale clan, evidenced by
the fact that the Arsi Oromo referred to all Shoa Oromo collectively as
Salale.

A combination of lack of land and the harsh treatment by the
local nobility in Shoa were the main reasons for their migrations to
the more fertile areas of the south. These migrations started in the
first decades of the twentieth century, and many arrived in the Arsi
region during the 1920s.[28] Landless and accustomed to an agriculturalist economy, they came in search of land. The increase of Shoa
Oromo settlers into Arsi in the early postwar period forced many of
them to continue their migration into Bale – a pattern that continued during the 1950s and 1960s. This story from one of my informants illustrates this trajectory:

I was born in Goha Tsion, around the Abbay [Blue Nile] gorge in 1933.
I came to Bale with my mother and her father, my grandfather ... .
They came here to search for land. My mother had an uncle here, on the
other side of the Wabe Shebelle River, on the way to Asasa town. My
grandfather, though, had enough land. He was a soldier of Menelik and
had gotten land from him. But he also wanted more. We came here
in 1935, the same time the Italians came, and we settled on the land of
my uncle.[29]

The landowning Arsi Oromo were, however, not interested in selling
land to the arriving Shoa Oromo. In fact, sale of land was a totally alien
concept among the Arsi Oromo – particularly to someone outside their
clans. The Arsi Oromo's reluctance to sell land meant that the Shoa
Oromo remained a landless group serving as tenants under the Arsi
Oromo – creating a hierarchical structure with the former dependent
on the latter. Arsi Oromo landowners, on their side, viewed the
Shoa Oromo tenants as a valuable asset. Tilling the land, they produced
crops that could be converted into cash used by the Arsi Oromo to pay

---

[28] The Gulale clan started arriving in the late nineteenth century, pushed out
because of the construction of Addis Ababa (Haberland 1963: 525), and Salale
Oromo government soldiers were garrisoned in Arsi at that time (Shiferaw
Bekele 1995: 104).

[29] Interview, Daniel Negash, Dodola, October 21, 2002.

their taxes.[30] While the vast majority of the Shoa Oromo remained tenants until the land reform in 1975, some were able to purchase land from the Arsi Oromo. Such land transactions were directly linked to the need for cash to pay taxes and to the increased commercial value of land caused by population growth. In some cases, the Shoa Oromo would lend money to an Arsi Oromo landowner, and if the latter was unable to settle his debt, he would transfer a piece of land instead.[31]

Changes in the Lowlands

As developments in the lowland areas differed from the highlands, it makes sense to discuss separately how the political and socioeconomic realities affected the pastoralists. It has been claimed that the "feudal oppression was naturally more intense in the highland areas," and that lowland pastoralists only to "a lesser degree" were affected by the new developments (Gebru Tareke 1977: 233, 263). While it is true that the Ethiopian state had a lower presence in the pastoralist lowland areas, I would nevertheless argue that the presence was clearly felt and that both the short-term and long-term effects of Menelik's conquest were serious enough. They were, however, different from those in the highlands.[32]

State control over the vast eastern lowlands remained initially rather nominal, and in the Somali lowlands, for example, the presence of the Ethiopian state largely consisted of the military.[33] The highlanders shunned these areas, which meant that the lowlands experienced hardly any settlement of Amhara landlords. No highlander sought to invest in any form of livestock enterprises, like for example, ranching (Helland 2006: 10). Hardly anything was invested in the form of infrastructure, and Bale had until the late 1960s only one dry-weather road linking Ginir, the capital of Wabe *awraja*, with the rest

---

[30] Interview, Daniel Negash, Dodola, October 23, 2002. Ketebe Abdiyo, in his study of rural Arsi, has forwarded similar arguments (2010: 146).

[31] Interview, Obse Ibrahim, Robe, April 15, 2005.

[32] The fact that hardly any studies have been done on the history of Ethiopian pastoralists makes the analysis of the lowland situation difficult. Important studies are by Ayalew Gebre (2001) on the Karayu in the Awash Valley and the recent book by Getnet Bekele (2017) focusing on the central Rift Valley.

[33] According to Cedric Barnes, in the late 1920s, not more than fifty to sixty soldiers were stationed in Ogaden (2000: 120).

of the country. There were no roads to Dello-Menna, the capital of Dello *awraja* (Ministry of Land Reform and Administration 1969: 3).

The most immediate effect of the conquest, similar to the rest of the country, was that all pastoralist land was classified as government land – being defined as unsettled. While the 1944 tax reform stated that a landowner could claim private ownership to land as long as he or she had a title to the land, this never became the practice in the lowlands where "pastoral land continued to be owned by the state," and which moreover meant that the pastoralists, "by this definition, were not landowners" (Ayalew Gebre 2001: 88). The state's ownership over pastoralist land was made explicit in the 1955 Revised Constitution of Ethiopia, where Art. 130 defined state domain as "[a]ll property not held and possessed in the name of any person natural or juridical, including all . . . grazing lands." Grazing land was in some cases actively appropriated to serve the state, for example, in neighboring Arsi where some lowland areas were categorized as *warra gannu*: areas for live-stock rearing with the purpose of producing meat and dairy products for the royal palace (Ketebo Abdiyo 2010: 139). There was no such land in the Bale lowlands, and neither was pastoralist land in the lowlands allocated as private grants – as seen in many more centrally located lowlands.[34] The lowlands' peripheral location and Bale's topo-graphy were important reasons for this. Being geographically con-nected to the vast Somali plains and separated from the rest of the country by the Bale mountains, the remote and inaccessible lowlands were part of what the state imagined as the extreme periphery.

As the Amhara viewed the Bale lowlands as unsuitable for agricul-ture and thus refrained from settling there, they also viewed it futile to implement the *gabbar* system. Instead, they focused on the extraction of tributes to be paid in kind primarily as livestock but also in the form of honey and butter. One informant in Raytu *worreda* listed the tri-butes as one ox, one goat, 15 kg of honey, one sack of *besso* (barley mixed with butter), and 20 kg of butter – collected every month. This created a dire situation described as "we even had to give what we

---

[34] The Rift Valley areas south of Addis Ababa are a relevant comparison, where land was measured and put out for sale. The state anticipated that the pastoralists using this land would be potential buyers, but as individual land ownership was at odds with the land-use system, they showed little interest (Getnet Bekele 2017: 36). For another comparison, see Ayalew Gebre's (2001) discussion of state policies toward pastoralists in the Awash Valley.

didn't have."[35] In addition to the tribute, the people were also forced to labor for the Amhara, and failure to meet these obligations had severe consequences:

If a person was ordered to bring something the Amhara demanded, and he failed – he would be beaten to death by a horsewhip. He was not given additional time to search for what he failed to deliver. If an Amhara came and demanded an ox, the person forced to give the ox also had to carry all the belongings of the Amhara and to drive the cattle to his home.[36]

The introduction of various tax reforms in the postwar period also had implications for the lowland areas. Together with the development of a monetary economy, these changes gradually changed the earlier tributary system, supplanting it with taxes to be paid to the state. The first tax reform in the lowlands – dubbed *zelan* (nomad) tax – was first introduced in 1950. It was based on the size of the pastoralists' livestock, and in order to collect the taxes, the government set up police stations in the sparsely populated areas. More important in collecting taxes, however, were the *balabats* and the *burqas*. The *balabat* in Raytu, Abdulkadir Nuho, for example, had ten armed *burqa* responsible for collecting the tax. Most informants agree that the tax was not particularly demanding: "a camel was taxed one birr, a cow 50 cent, and a goat 25 cent . . . . The price of a goat was three birr, the price of a cow six birr, and the price of a camel around 100 birr."[37] The tax was not paid in cash, however, but in livestock:

We estimated [the tax] in the number of livestock and we paid in goats or cattle according to this estimation. It was the *balabat* who took the cattle, and he paid the Amhara in cash, and kept the livestock. That is why the *balabat* was very rich. The *balabat* had no option than to obey the Amhara. But since then I have never liked anyone who works for the government.[38]

The pastoralists in Bale, similar to those in other places, were vehemently resistant to taxation, and in addition to having difficulty determining the size of the people's livestock, the locals' resistance to the tax and their constant movements to evade the collectors meant that the

---

[35] Interview, Abdulqadir Muhammad, Raytu, October 7, 2002.
[36] Interview, Abdulqadir Muhammad, Raytu, October 7, 2002.
[37] Interviews, Adam Yunus, Raytu, June 10, 2017; Muhammad Tahir, Raytu, June 11, 2018.
[38] Interview, Adam Yunus, Raytu, June 10, 2017.

zelan tax was largely ineffective (Markakis 2011: 135). The government consequently imposed a head tax in 1963 – which, as discussed in Chapter 4, was important in sparking the insurgency (Markakis 2011: 135, 145). Local *balabats* remained responsible for collecting the tax and were given an amount they had to collect according to the number of people in his area (Markakis 1983: 299). Increased bureaucratization of the state, more elaborate systems of tax collection, and a higher presence of government officials in the lowland areas from the late 1950s made it increasingly difficult for the pastoralists to escape taxation. For example, if a person tried to avoid paying tax to the local *balabat* by moving to another area, he would be obliged to pay taxes to the *balabat* in that area.[39]

Agriculture remained undeveloped in the lowlands all through the postwar period. The only exception was the higher elevated areas of the southern lowlands around Dello, where corn could be grown. There are reports of Shoa Oromo starting to cultivate land around Oborso in Medda Wellabu *worreda* in the early 1970s, but there is no indication of any Arsi Oromo taking part in this. Cultivation of land was far less common in the eastern lowlands of Wabe *awraja*. One report claims that there were a few fields around the capital of Raytu *worreda* in the early 1970s, but informants from that area contest this, claiming that nobody was engaged in crop cultivation at that time (Currens and Nydal 1974: 15).[40]

Peasant Rebellion?

There is no doubt that the tax pressure became increasingly onerous in the early 1960s, and that it did result – to a certain degree – in confiscation of land in the highlands. As this hardship coincided with the start of the insurgency, it would be logical to assume that taxation and land alienation caused the so-called peasants to rebel. As I have demonstrated, however, there is little evidence supporting Gebru Tareke's claim that confiscation of land caused widespread land alienation, subsequently transforming the peasants into landless tenants. Most of the land that was confiscated, moreover, was categorized as

---

[39] Interviews, Hajji Abdurazak Hussein, Lais Hafiz, Ahmed Hussein, and Tahir Malik, Dello-Menna, June 15, 2017.
[40] Interview, Adam Yunus, Raytu, June 10, 2017.

"poor" land. Another crucial factor that has remained neglected is the demographical situation in Bale. Low population density created a deficit of tenants, which made the region unattractive for the Amhara and provided a relative abundance of land. This means, in other words, that there is no direct correlation between land alienation and the insurgency. Aberra Ketsela also underscores this, arguing that "[t]he landholding system could not have been a cause of rebellion. The majority of the rebels were pastoralist nomads and had little interest in individual land holding" (Aberra Ketsela 1971: 17).

This latter point is particularly important and is an aspect that those claiming that the insurgency was a peasant rebellion overlook: it is hard to categorize the people in Bale as peasants. The fact of the matter is that we are talking about a context where a pastoralist economy continued to be relevant for most of the postwar period. Moreover, those who Gebru Tareke claims were peasants – in the highlands – did not rebel. Rather than being highlanders, the insurgents were overwhelmingly pastoralist lowlanders, and the theater of fighting was concentrated in the eastern and southern lowlands of Bale. This is not to say, however, that the highlanders were completely oblivious to the insurgency or that they did not support the fighting. The insurgency was, as noted, very much a *Bale* insurgency, having broad support from the whole Muslim Arsi Oromo population – in both the lowlands and the highlands.

It could be possible to argue that the major reason why the insurgency took place in the lowlands was the classification of the lowlands as government property. While it must undoubtedly have been a peculiar situation for the Arsi Oromo pastoralists to suddenly have their ancestral clan land defined as government land, it is, however, important to consider the particularities of the pastoralist lifestyle and culture in the lowlands, and how the pastoralists negotiated the new realities. First of all, the classification of land as government land had little direct impact on the daily lives of the pastoralists. There were no measures taken to keep them off the land, and there were few restrictions on their seasonal movements. Second, such movements also enabled them to evade the taxes demanded of them, at least for some time. There are, however, no reports of pastoralists who failed to meet the tax demands, or that accumulation of tax arrears led to the confiscation of pastoralist land. That would not made sense in any case – the land was already the property of the state.

In other words, the Bale insurgency was *not a peasant rebellion.* Significant socioeconomic changes, particularly related to land tenure had clear impacts on people's livelihood, but these remain insufficient in explaining the insurgency. Having said that, there are certain aspects of land that deserve more attention. The next chapter's continued discussion aims to forward a more holistic materialist perspective that understands people's relations to land in more than purely economic or productive terms. It will pay attention to the materiality of affective and emplaced belonging in ways that deepen our perception of both the meaning of land and how central land was for notions of peoplehood and identity.

7 | Land Tenure and the Land-Clan Connection

Land is more than an economic commodity to be sold and bought. This chapter continues the discussion about land – and expands it as a category. In line with the study's overall theoretical argument, it aims to avoid a perspective that isolates socioeconomic material realities from cultural ones – or that perceives the former as more "real" than the latter and subsequently reduces the latter to mere reflections of the dynamics of modes of production. I argue that the ideational is more intimately intertwined with the material – through the embodied and emplaced character of human realities, and through the inherently material underpinning of so-called meaning.

The chapter investigates the question of land and land tenure to better understand how belonging has an intimate spatial and material dimension – essential for the construction of peoplehood. It demonstrates in particular that the introduction of a new land-tenure system in Bale had lasting consequences for what I call the "land-clan connection," affecting people's experiences in their landscapes, their notions of home, as well as overall social structures. In the chapter's first part, I discuss the Arsi Oromo notions of land and their arrangement of land rights and use in preconquest Bale. Special attention is given to land as communal property, to how the land-clan connection secured access to land, and to its significance for emplaced belonging. The second part of the chapter details the impacts changes in the land-tenure system had on these "traditional" perceptions and arrangements – paying attention to processes of privatization and commodification of land. My argument is that the ensuing changes led to increased individualism, to a more stratified society, inevitably affecting the land-clan connection. Such developments, I argue, can be construed through a careful and critical reading of Georg Lukács's (1968 [1923]) concept of "reification" – as fused with Weber's notions of formal rationalization and disenchantment.[1] Reification is also commonly related to Marx's idea of alienation in the course of the development of a capitalist economy, while I here emphasize how privatization and commodification resulted in a process of disenchantment, estrangement, rupture, and loss of community – affecting being-in-the-world and being-with-others. It needs to be underscored, however, that these suggestions need to duly recognize the particular empirical context.

   In discussing these changes, it is important not to fall into the trap of essentializing and romanticizing the preconquest period as static and characterized by harmony and serene cohesion. It is similarly important to avoid dichotomizing this period with a view of the post-conquest realities as exclusively destructive and oppressive. Neither should we reduce the local population to passive victims of change. While the new realities were products of hegemonic forces, there was – obviously – also a degree of continuity in change, and it is clear that the local actors displayed a great deal of agency in negotiating the new realities. What is thus needed is a sober and fine-tuned analysis that pays due attention to the complexities at hand.

Land "Ownership"

The Arsi Oromo's pastoral lifestyle affected their notion of land and land usage and how they organized access to land. Access to grazing was – as for any pastoralist society – crucial for the Arsi Oromo, and livestock herding demanded wide tracts of land. In contrast to agricultural land, which needs to be clearly demarcated, land-tenure systems tend to be more flexible among pastoralists (Barth 1973). Land was perceived as communal property – called *otubaa* – of the various clans, and clan membership secured access to land. As I elaborated in Chapter 2, clans were further divided into *balbalaa* (sub-clans), which in turn were composed of several *warra* (households). The *warra* was also the basis for the *ganda,* the village, which commonly consisted of ten to twenty households from the same extended family. Each household could claim right over land for their homesteads (*arda*), small adjacent fields used for cultivation

---

[1] Reification refers to the transformation of human properties, relations, processes, actions, concepts, etc. into things. The concept has been elaborated and expanded upon within critical theory, most notably by Alex Honneth (2008) and Jürgen Habermas (1984).

and grazing land for calves and heifers.[2] As access to land at any level was determined by clan membership, it meant that virtually everybody had land. While the *balbalaa* and *warra* had their own spatial locations within the territory of the clan, access to land was not seen as exclusive, and there were no restrictions on accessing other *balbalaas'* grazing land.

The clans' land, however, was clearly demarcated, and boundaries were marked by natural phenomena such as rivers, trees, hills, and so on. Both the highlanders and the lowlanders had their own mechanisms for organizing access to grazing and to water points, which in the more sparsely populated lowlands were less elaborate. These regulations stemmed from the *gadaa* system, and the general rule was that members of a clan could access another clan's land after getting permission from that clan. In cases of unlawful trespassing, the clan would mobilize to block the intruder, and the situation would then be solved through negotiations of the involved clans' elders.[3] The main boundary for those in the eastern lowlands was to the east, where trespassing into the Somali-inhabited areas was avoided. The pastoralist in the south would, in addition to avoiding the Somali areas, not cross the Genale River into Guji land.[4]

The important point is that there was no notion of any individual private ownership of land among the Arsi Oromo, and no one could claim exclusive rights to particular areas. The only form of land right that comes closest to private ownership was the area of the homestead and the plots used for cultivation. This was also the land that would be inherited, and being a patrilineal society, sons inherited land rights from the father.[5] Land ownership, however, was never formalized in any modern sense of the word, something that made transfer of land through sales impossible. In fact, as land was considered ancestral land, sales were considered immoral, indicating "disorder" within the family that sold its land (Mamo Hebo 2007: 354).

Livestock, on the other hand, were considered individually owned, and the number of animals was what defined wealth. During the

---

[2] Interview, Umar Qassim, Robe, June 14, 2018.
[3] Interviews, Muhammad Tahir, Raytu, June 11, 2018; Umar Qassim, Robe, June 14, 2018.
[4] Interviews, Adam Yunus, Raytu, June 10, 2017; Hajji Abdurazak Hussein, Lais Hafiz, Ahmed Hussein, and Tahir Malik, Dello-Menna, June 15, 2017.
[5] Focus group discussion, conducted by Daniel Deressa, Dodola, March 2003, and I am grateful to him for providing me with his recordings of the interviews.

Imperial period, a wealthy person could have a herd of more than 500 cattle, while the herd of a poor person would count to 50 cattle (Flintan et al. 2008: 30). Livestock were, moreover, divided in two: the *buel fora*, or satellite herds, that would be taken to more distant pastures, and the *elemolwarra* that consisted of milking cows kept close to the homestead (Ayele Gebre Mariam 1976; Schlee 2012: 31).[6] In the highlands, it was common to divide the animals into flocks of 100 cattle.[7] Livestock were important as insurance in times of drought or other calamities, and Baxter has, moreover, pointed to how they were converted into social relationships: owners acquired affinities, clients, or associates for managing the herds (Baxter 1975: 213). Such relationships would exist between the wealthier and those of less wealth and constituted a mechanism that reduced inequalities. Particularly important was that such relations were intertwined with clan structures – in turn maintaining clan affinities at the expense of social class.

The communal nature of the land-tenure system among Arsi Oromo points in the direction of a society characterized by "pastoral egalitarianism" (Schneider 1979). One should not push this too far, however, as inequalities, for example, based on gender, did exist. It is, at the same time, clear that the role of clans as an organizing principle prevented "the crystallization of class difference" (Azarya 1996: 26; cf. Dahl 1979: 274f.). The centrality of the clans meant that certain clans – and lineages within different clans – had more prestige than others because of size and seniority. Those clans that were the direct descendants of the two moieties Mendo and Siko had the status as *angafa* (the eldest).[8] The Walashe and Sebro clans have been mentioned as particularly strong clans, both having *abbaa bokus* (Ketema Meskela 2001: 22). While feuding between the clans was common, it was rare that stronger clans "colonized" weaker ones, although it did happen that larger clans could expand their territories, or penetrate into new areas. One example here is how the Sheidama clan moved from the eastern parts of Bale to the western highlands around Dodola in the late nineteenth century, expropriating the land of the clans in that area.[9]

---

[6] Interview, Umar Qassim, Robe, June 14, 2018.
[7] Interview, Ahmed Awol, Robe, October 10, 2005.
[8] Interviews, Khalid Adam, Raytu, September 26, 2005; Sheikh Hussein Abdallah, Gomorra, July 17, 2001.
[9] Interview, Daniel Negash, Dodola, October 23, 2002.

The Land-Clan Connection

The spatial dimension of the clans, or the way clans were intrinsically connected to territorial space, can be captured in the land-clan connection. This relates to clans' and sub-clans' attachment to land, in the form of dwelling and grazing areas, and to how clans and sub-clans occupied defined areas of land.[10] The land-clan connection functioned on different levels; from the already noted spatial distribution of the two moieties, Mendo and Siko, to how clans and sub-clans were located spatially in particular territories, and to how a person's place of origin or residence revealed his or her clan affiliation. Each clans' territory also constituted an administrative unit, wherein the *abbaa boku* (later the *balabat*) and the elders (*hayyus*) were responsible for maintaining peace and for protecting the well-being of the clan.[11] Such concrete links to land are demonstrated by the way clan names were congruent with geographical areas, seen, for example, by the way clan names like Walashe, Karmamida, Sinana, and Raytu dovetail with defined areas of land (see Map 7.1) (Abbas H. Gnamo 2014: 63; Haberland 1963: 446f.). Another example was the demarcation of the boundaries of the Raytu clan: "[the boundary] was at the Jawwe [clan] towards Ginir ... another boundary was towards Hawattu [clan] ... another was towards Ilanni [clan] ... and another boundary was towards Kajawa [clan]."[12]

Land in its concrete material form created bonds that tied people to both lineage and place, generating an emplaced and embodied belonging, and situating them in time that collapsed the past and the present. The basis for this was the notion that each clan originated from a putative ancestor who had settled in a particular place – thus making this the land of the clan. This was even more explicit at the sub-clan (*balbalaa*) level, where the ancestor was not that distant and which formed the basis for inherited land rights according to paternal lineages mutually recognized by the members of the larger clan. The history of the *balbala*'s ancestor, his movements, and how he came to occupy the original land were kept alive among the people (Ketema Meskela 2001: 18f.).

---

[10]   This was not something particular for the Arsi Oromo, but common for all other Oromo branches. See, for example, Bartels (1983: 79).
[11]   Interview, Muhammad Tahir, Raytu, June 11, 2018.
[12]   Interview, Muhammad Tahir, Raytu, June 12, 2017.

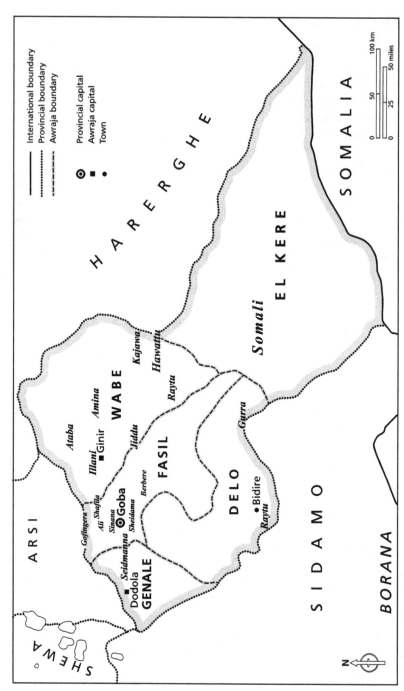

Map 7.1 Clans' geographical distribution in Bale

The land-clan connection was clearly expressed in the term *abbaa lafa;* "the father of the land," as discussed by Jan Hultin (1994). Not only did this signify the original settler and ancestor of a lineage, but it also referred to the descendants of that lineage dwelling upon and claiming right to a particular area of land. Both the historical and the present figures were the *abbaa lafa,* and the latter could lay claim to land because of his descent from the original "father." Yet, it was more than only genealogical connections; just as much as the ancestor was the father of the lineage, the "lineage land is a representation of and, indeed, a chronicle of lineage history" (Hultin 1994: 70). The lineage also continued into the future through a man's sons, and a man who has sons was a man who could not die (Bartels 1983: 307). This aspect of immortality was also carried over to the transfer of property through inheritance – both land and livestock – which constituted "a share of a larger lineage estate" that had been handed down for many genera-tions, thus connecting the future with past (Hultin 1994: 70).

The occupation and settling of the original land were traditionally sealed through the sacrifice of a white goat. Mamo Hebo provides an interesting discussion of this and notes that the sacrifice was accom-panied with the statement *daya re'ee booraa* ("we won or gained the territory through the scarification of the white goat"). *Daya* can also mean "giving birth," which in this context means that lineage had given birth to the land. It thus signifies how the bonds between humans and land were similar to those of parents and offspring (2004: 41). This resembles to a certain degree the Somali couplet of *u dhashay – ku dhashay,* which roughly translates into being "born to (a clan/family)" and being "born in (a place)."[13] Ioan Lewis has argued that the terri-torial aspect of Somali lineages depended on the degree of nomadism, that is, the more mobile the pastoralists were, the less territorial attach-ment (1961: 56f.). The fact that the Arsi Oromo pastoralists had a more limited pattern of migration confirms the relevance of the land-clan connection in Bale.

Not only was territory an important marker for the distribution of clans, but the spatial dimension was also intrinsic to the *gadaa* system – the already discussed Oromo's governing age-class system (see Chapter 2). The main *gadaa* confederacies were organized according to clan, thus having jurisdiction over defined territories. The main confederacy

---

[13] See Cedric Barnes (2006) for a discussion of the term.

in the eastern central highlands was the Saden Jiddo Arso and consisted of the Walashe, Wannama, Karmamida, Agarfa, Raytu Sebro, Sheidama, Kajawa, and Wayyu clans.[14] The name of the confederacy in the Gedeb was the Samu. The lowlands were divided along the main rivers, producing separate confederacies between the Wabe Shebelle and Weib Rivers, between Weib and Welmel, and between Welmel and Genale.[15] The spatial aspect of the *gadaa* system as intersected with the land-clan connection was moreover made explicit in the Arsi Oromo's places of assemblies – the *yaa'a* – where the clans would meet every fourth year, and where legislation (*murtii*) binding for the clans was passed.[16] The main *yaa'a* was, as already mentioned, Oda Roba, which was under the leadership of the Raytu clan. Other sources, while acknowledging the role of Oda Roba, also mention Hora Boka, outside of Robe town, as a major assembly site.[17]

The close connections between land, clans, rituals, and administrative structures meant that land was not disconnected from sociocultural realities. It was, in other words, more than a canvas for human life. Ingold talks about nature as more than a stage upon which lives are enacted, but as something in which humans are embedded and actively inhabit.[18] He introduces the term *taskscape* to refer to active dwelling, to the interrelations between humans and their environment that reciprocally form the environment and human emplaced belonging. It is here important not to think of this as the production of "culture" in the sense of meaning being given to the environment but rather as processes of incorporation, embodied human life lived within material realities (Ingold 2000: 194f.).[19] Land constituted an important and very physical marker of Oromo identity and was a signifier for belonging,

---

[14] Interviews, Hajji Hussein Awol, Robe, December 7, 2002 and June 8, 2005; Siraj Muhammed-Amin, Robe, November 19, 2005.

[15] Interviews, Abdulqadir Muhammad, Raytu, October 7, 2002; Mustafa Tahir, Raytu, June 12, 2017. Some informants claim that the boundary was not the Welmel River, but Dumale (interviews, Hajji Abdurazak Hussein, Lais Hafiz, Ahmed Hussein, and Tahir Malik, Dello-Menna, June 15, 2017).

[16] The various oral and written sources do not always agree on the details around this, and the accounts presented here should be treated with care.

[17] Interview, Hajji Hassan Faqi, Goba, June 1, 2005.

[18] This relates to Thomas Tweed's concept of *dwelling* in his discussion of emplacement, describing it as involving "three overlapping processes: mapping, building, and inhabiting" (2006: 82).

[19] Grosby indicates that "nature has the power to make plentiful the barren of the area in which one lives" (1994: 169), while Geschiere uses the term

wherein membership in a clan, dwelling area, access to common land, and land administration mutually reinforced one another and tied the individual both to his or her clan and to a particular territory. As the lineage system was the defining criterion for being part of a clan – by way of embodying ethnicity – the way the lineage system was spatially emplaced made the matter of identity highly concrete.

Land as *Wayyuu*

The land-clan connection also had a distinct religious dimension, intrinsic to the pre-Islamic religious universe of the Arsi Oromo. It is nearly impossible to reconstruct the details of the Oromo religion as it was practiced centuries ago, and any attempt to do so has to recognize that traditional religions and rituals of the past were dynamic and constantly affected by influxes of change.[20] Key to the Oromo religion was the veneration of *Waaqa,* sometimes referred to as *Waaqa Gurachaa*: the high-god – the creator and sustainer of the universe (Bartels 1983: 89f.). *Waaqa* can also mean sky, and *Waaqa Gurachaa* relates to the "black sky" of the night – which "resembles the elevation and inaccessibility of the sky above the earth" and points to *Waaqa*'s dwelling in infinite space (Knutsson 1967: 52f.). Numerous spirits, the *ayaanaa* or *jaarii,* also inhabited the Oromo religious universe.[21] Although conceptually distinguishable from *Waaqa,* they also emanated from him, in the sense that they in essence constituted the same. While *Waaqa* could be called upon by humans, the spirits were "closer" in the sense that they were emplaced in specific sacred places and embodied in human spirit mediums – enabling people to encounter them through specific rituals.[22]

Land, as part of the material world, was seen as the creation of *Waaqa* and was thus considered sacred and something to be respected.

---

autochthony, which he defines as "sons of the soil" or "to be born from the soil" (2009).

[20] African religious universes were, according to Terence Ranger, "complex, multi-layered, dynamic, with a history of contradiction, contestation, and innovation" and characterized by "creative and resilient pluralism" as well as "remarkable adaptability" (1987: 151).

[21] de Salviac (2005 [1901]: 155) curiously argued that the Oromo referred to spirits as *awliah,* which is the plural form of the Arabic word *wali,* meaning the "loved one" and which often is translated as "saint."

[22] See Østebø (2013b) for more details on the Oromo spirit pantheon.

There were ethical rules for how to treat land, seen, for example, by the way a person should avoid "strik[ing] the ground unnecessarily with one's staff." The only exception to this was when something important was uttered – "then one's speech can be followed by striking the ground with the staff" (Knutsson 1967: 56). Such rules must obviously be seen in relation to how land – in the form of pastures, places of dwelling, water sources – served as the foundation for survival and that which nurtured humans. Reciprocally, land also defined the human, meaning that a person without land was viewed as incomplete. As expressed in this *mamaksa* (proverb) from Bale: *namni lafa hin qabne, nafa lafee hin qabne* ("the one without land is like a body without bones"). What is particularly interesting is that land – as part of creation – seems not only to have existed in a lifeless form but was also perceived to have agency. As described by one of Hultin's informants, it was said to have anthropomorphic qualities potentially affecting people's lives:

You people don't believe us when we tell you these things, but the land has got eyes and ears. However, we humans can't see it. If a man is forced to move, he can say to his land: "Because of this person, so and so, and because of this or that reason, I must leave you now." The man who then comes and takes over that land will not live long. (1994: 76)

The Oromo's reverence of land is part of their broader notions of sacredness and ethics expressed through the highly complex concept of *wayyuu*.[23] The concept could very simplistically be translated as "respect," but this does not capture the depth of it. Derived from the notion of *Waaqa* as the most sacred, *wayyuu* signified the distance and respect that one should have for all things created (Gemechu Megersa 1998); at the same time, there would be certain objects, persons, and spaces particularly set apart as *wayyuu*. One important aspect of *wayyuu* was that it generated a certain ethics that required a particular attitude and behavior. Regulating practice and relationships, it defined a person's relations to what and who that were considered *wayyuu* – determining what could be uttered and what could not, and what could be touched. *Wayyuu* was therefore what constituted avoidance relations, wherein status, age, marital situation, kinship, or gender of the person created

---

[23] Scholars have identified similar concepts among other African groups (Heald 1990; Hodgson 1999; Talle 1995). It is often said that *wayyuu* is equivalent to *saffuu* used by the Macha Oromo in Western Ethiopia, but the way this term is described by Bartels (1983: 330f.) reveals some important differences.

relations that made certain persons *wayyuu* to others (Østebø 2018). Another crucial aspect – and particularly relevant in this context – was how *wayyuu* was inseparably material. It was present in figures, places, and material objects, setting these apart as sacred, yet not dislocating their materiality:

> God *(Waaqa)* is *wayyuu.*
> The earth/land *(lafa)* is *wayyuu*
> The father *(Abbaa)* is *wayyuu*[24]
> A male in-law *(Sodda)* is *wayyuu*
> The mother *(Haati deete)* is *wayyuu*
> A female in-law *(Soddaatii)* is *wayyuu*
> The married woman *(Hadha mana)* is *wayyuu*
> The unmarried girl (the virgin) *(Durbi)* is *wayyuu*
> The pregnant woman *(Dubartii ulfaa)* is wayyuu
> *Gaadii* (leather string that is used to tie the back legs of the cow while milking) is *wayyuu*
> *Gebo, tunxoo* and *cico* (different types of milk containers) are *wayyuu*
> Butter *(dhadha)* is *wayyuu*

The way milk, butter, and the milk-giving cow were associated with *wayyuu* relates to the importance of fertility in a pastoralist society, to procreation, and to continuation of life.[25] Relevant for this discussion, and seen from the list, is how land was imbued with a religious dimension and thus considered *wayyuu*. This meant that "one could not cut down a tree, pick any plants without permission … . One couldn't plow where the cattle were grazing … and one couldn't destroy the area where there was shade."[26] Land was thus, in sum, fundamental for human life:

The reason land was *wayyuu* was because every human was created from land, every human lived off the land, and every human was buried in the land. The land carried both the living and the dead. That is why land was *wayyuu*. *Waaqa* – the sky was also *wayyuu*. That was because God lived there. And because rain came from the sky.[27]

---

[24] This also includes the father-in-law and classificatory kinship brothers of the father.
[25] This is based upon the findings of Marit Tolo Østebø (2018). My own informants gave similar, yet less elaborate, lists; interview, Temam Muhammad, Dodola, October 19, 2002.
[26] Interviews, Hajji Abdurazak Hussein, Lais Hafiz, Ahmed Hussein, and Tahir Malik, Dello-Menna, June 15, 2017.
[27] Interviews, Hajji Abdurazak Hussein, Lais Hafiz, Ahmed Hussein, and Tahir Malik, Dello-Menna, June 15, 2017.

The notion of both land (*lafa*) and father (*abbaa*) as *wayyuu* points directly to how land as *wayyuu* was intersected with ancestors and lineages. The *abbaa* as *wayyuu* relates in turn to the concept of *ayaanaa abbaa* – "the spirit of the father," denoting "a kind of guardian divinity of the family" (Knutsson 1967: 53, 139).[28] Similar to what was said earlier about *abbaa lafa,* both the individual head of a household and the ancestor of the clan and sub-clan would have an *ayaanaa abbaa,* constituting a guardian spirit that protected and secured the prosperity of the ancestor's descendants. The importance of lineage is also demonstrated by the fact that it was only senior members of the lineage who carried out the ritual of sacrificing a bull to the *abbaa ayaanaa* – a ritual that was performed at the gravesides of one's immediate and distant forefathers (Bartels 1983: 114f.). While the emphasis on the lineage signifies how the "pure and straight genealogical line can function as a channel between the living and the dead" (Knutsson 1967: 60), such links and the coupling of *abbaa lafa* and *ayaanaa abbaa* were thus not merely conceptual.[29] The lineage represented the embodied and emplaced aspect of the land-clan connection that simultaneously tied the person to place in a concrete material sense, while also, through the clan lineage, anchoring him or her to a place that transcended time. It inserted a certain quality on places of dwelling and ranges of movement, which meant that these were not random sites, but locations that provided concrete spatial belongings and that, at the same time, were products of collective memories, narratives, and embodied experiences (cf. Basso 1996).

Nothing expresses this more explicitly than the perception of and the practices related to the *handhurraa*, the human umbilical cord.[30] Both the umbilical cord and the placenta were defined as *wayyuu* and needed to be treated in certain ways. The common practice among the Oromo – still practiced in many localities – was that the mother of the newborn child took care of the umbilical cord and buried it either in the *goolaa,* the bedroom, which also is considered *wayyuu,* or sometimes in the

---

[28] There is also the concept of *ayaanaa haadha* – "the spirit of the mother" – being associated with female fertility and, among Oromo in Western Ethiopia, connected to the ritual of *ateetee* (Knutsson 1967: 55).

[29] Karl Eric Knutsson describes rituals among the Macha Oromo (West Ethiopia), but they are to a large degree similar to those earlier performed among the Arsi Oromo.

[30] Similar perceptions and practices are found among a number of groups in Ethiopia, as well as in other parts of Africa.

compound behind the house. Lambert Bartels reports that the Macha Oromo in western Ethiopia added wet cow dung on top of the cord as it was buried. He does not elaborate on this, except that it was connected to notions of fertility (1969: 410). The Macha Oromo also called the first calf a boy would inherit from his father *handhurraa*, signifying the bond that tied "the boy to his father, to the animals in his father's cattle pen, and to his patrilineage" (Hultin 1994: 70). The practice of burying the umbilical cord is a powerful expression of the land-clan connection in a highly concrete manner. The way the umbilical cord physically attached the child to the mother shows how the individual was located in an embodied continuum that also transcended time and linked him or her to a particular genealogy, to a lineage, and to a clan. At the same time, the burial of the cord firmly connected the individual and his or her lineage with land in the material sense and explicitly emplaced this lineage spatially to one's dwelling and home. When a child was born during the pastoralists' seasonal movements, the umbilical cord would be buried in the *desse,* the temporary house used during these movements or in the shade of a tree. Particularly interesting is that a person later could claim the land where his or her umbilical cord was buried.[31] The fact that the umbilical cord among the pastoralists could be buried at places beyond one's dwelling area demonstrates how the pastoralists' mobility forged a perspective whereby emplaced belonging and home were found within broader landscapes and along well-trodden paths, making land, home, dwelling, and movement inseparable. As expressed by one informant: "land is the same as man, it is who he is. It is God who has given us our land, and we spend one night here and one night there. Land is freedom to move."[32]

Another crucial dimension of the importance of land for the Arsi Oromo relates to death. Land was more than empty space, but where a part of themselves was buried. This idea is clearly articulated in the *mamaksa* (proverb): *jaalati lafee nami, irrati lafee looni* ("the human bones lie underground, while the cattle's bones lie on the ground") and is also a reflection of how that land provides the human with "two homes." Mamo Hebo has provided valuable insights into this, and this statement by one of his informants is worth quoting at length:

---

[31] Interview, Hajji Abdurazak Hussein, Lais Hafiz, Ahmed Hussein, and Tahir Malik, Dello-Menna, June 15, 2017.
[32] Interview, Adam Yunus, Raytu, June 10, 2017.

Land is where our two homes are located. Do you understand when I say two homes? I mean that when we are alive we build our houses and live on this land. You cannot build a house wherever you like to build it. You build it on the land that belongs to you, the land that belongs to your father, to your clan and your ancestors. The second home is the grave in which we will be buried when we are dead. This is our permanent home. People may die anywhere, sometimes even far away from their *qe'e* [abode, village]. But their bodies have to be brought to their homeland and buried on their land ... . Even after death, you need to have some place to be buried on. (Mamo Hebo 2004: 46)

Gravesites were therefore important for rituals commemorating one's forefathers and the lineage's ancestor. The dead would either be placed directly in the grave itself or in a separate grotto excavated connected to the main grave. The deceased's sons would place erected flat stones called *soddu* around the grave, and the sons would pour the blood of a sacrificed animal into the holes of the main *soddus* at the grave's four corners (Østebø 2012: 101). The word *soddu* is derived from *soda* ("fear") and besides having the meaning of remembering the dead, the ritual was also meant to placate his or her *ayaanaa* (Leus and Salvadori 2006: 597).[33] The ritual of pouring blood was of great importance, and neglecting it was seen as denying kinship to the dead. Hylander, pointing to the fact that the Arsi Oromo did not construct houses of worship, argues that the grave was the main site for the Arsi Oromo rituals and underscores that the "only trace of human rituals in the sanctuary of nature is butter and milk" (Hylander 1936: 273). Many of these practices lived on after the Arsi Oromo accepted Islam, but this change inevitably gave the rituals a more explicit Islamic flavor – seen, for example, in celebration of *mawlid al-Nabi* (Prophet Muhammad's birthday) at the gravesides – as discussed in Chapter 2. The same is true for how pilgrimages to Muslim shrines – as physical sites – became an elaboration of the practice of visiting the graves of the forefathers (Østebø 2012: 98, 101f.).

Also important was how particular places with distinct physical features were set apart as sacred, such as hilltops, river fords (*melka*), and the shade of the sycamore (*oda*) tree. These were places that constituted locations for ritual performances. River fords were, for example, sites for the performance of *ateetee* in Bale. This was a

---

[33] Further east in Bale, where Islam had a stronger foothold, such stones were replaced by a tall headstone, a smaller one at the foot of the grave, and sometimes one additional stone at each side of the grave (Birch-Iensen 1960: 98).

ritual exclusively for women, and while it was practiced differently among the Oromo groups, it was among the Arsi Oromo always performed at river fords (Bartels 1983: 124f.; Baxter 1979; Cerulli 1922; Knutsson 1967).[34]

In sum, active dwelling and the land-clan connection's spatial arrangement were crucial for the Arsi Oromo's notion of emplaced belonging. Land was more than an economic commodity; it constituted the material underpinning that anchored them in the environment, tied them to their families and kin, and sustained their notion of peoplehood. This also deepened their perception of land as "sacred" – not only symbolically but also in its real material manner. All this would, however, be deeply affected by the socioeconomic developments of the twentieth century.

Privatization

While Menelik's conquest and the subsequent political developments did not, as demonstrated in the previous chapter, cause widespread loss of land for the Arsi Oromo, changes in the land-tenure system, however, would have other and significant impacts on the broader population. The most dramatic one was the transition of land as being communal property to becoming privately owned. Such changes, I argue, had dramatic consequences for existing relations between families, kin, and lineages – and contributed to the gradual erosion of the land-clan connection. The privatization of land was one of the most important changes in the conquered southern areas and had markedly different outcomes compared with those in the north where the *rist* system continued to dominate through the twentieth century (Shiferaw Bekele 1995: 76).

The common trajectory in the south was the redefining of land as government holdings, which then were given out as grants – first as temporarily held land in the form of *madeira* – but then increasingly as private land (Shiferaw Bekele 1995: 101). Government land was also gradually put out for sale, where the intention was to provide land to the landless. The proclamations of 1942/1944 were important in this regard; yet, more significant was the government's edict in 1959, which

---

[34] For some details on *ateetee* among Ethiopian Christians, see Maskal H. Fisseha (1959).

permitted the sale of land grants (Getnet Bekele 2017: 95). However, as the poor lacked the resources to purchase land, the result was the accumulation of land among the wealthier and increased inequality. The move toward privatizing land also took place in Bale, but the process was somewhat different from other regions. There, only a limited amount of land given out as grants, and more important was the increasing pressure upon the landholding Arsi Oromo to reconfigure communal land into private holdings.

Land remained largely communally owned in the beginning of the postwar period. Land measurements introduced in 1942/1944 had little immediate effect, and land continued to be formally considered as holdings of the *balabats,* which enabled the clans to have access to common grazing land and secured the maintenance of a pastoralist economy (Ketema Meskela 2001: 54f.). Registration of land as privately owned started in the immediate postwar years, but land continued to be used by the different clans for grazing purposes, and the main difference was that cattle were grazed on each owner's (formally) private land. During times of drought, there was also the possibility of entering – with the owner's permission – more fertile private land. In other words, as long as land was abundant and as long as there was no restriction on anyone's access to the land, few saw it as problematic that individuals were registered as owners over large areas of land.

Demand for taxes, population growth, and increased competition over land were the main reasons for a real redefinition of land ownership, and land measurement, with its categorization according to type and quality, became key for the transformation of land as individual, private property. These changes triggered the early resistance to the *qalad* system (land measurement) in 1951, as people feared that the individualization of land ownership would impinge on their access to grazing land. Interesting to note is how the *balabat* and the religious leaders at Dirre Sheikh Hussein argued that the introduction of the *qalad* system would lead to appropriation of land by the Christians and, consequently, that anyone who supported the *qalad* system would be deemed enemies of the people (Ketema Meskela 2001: 61). What was emerging was undoubtedly in stark contrast to the Arsi Oromo's traditional perceptions of the meaning of land and their notions of land rights.

These predictions became true as the land measurements in 1951, and later in 1963, were accompanied by new registration regulations and additional requirements for documentation of landownership. The basis for individual ownership was having a title to land, and while one person formally had to be registered as the titleholder (Amharic: *alaqa*), the regulations allowed for "co-owners" (Amharic: *menzer*) – yet without any formal ownership (Ketema Meskela 2001: 64). The common practice among the Arsi Oromo thus became to assign a particular person to be registered as titleholder of what was communal land, with the others from the same sub-clan or lineage assuming the role as informal claimants to that land: "For example, my father was the oldest of his brothers, so he was given the responsibility of our land. He was like a group leader, *alaqa* it was called. The other brothers could use it, but he had the responsibility for managing it and paying tax to the government."[35]

In the previous chapter, I demonstrated that tenancy among the Arsi Oromo was not particularly common, and one aspect of tenancy among them was that it was an integrated aspect of kinship relations, in the sense that those who had less land could enter into a relationship with their relatives that resembled tenancy, accessing the land of their kin. The availability of land and clan solidarity produced a situation where this form of tenancy was a way of caring for the less fortunate and was not necessarily viewed as burdensome (Abbas H. Gnamo 2014: 282, 287f.). This corresponds with Paul Baxter's observations from the Arsi region: he notes that the Arsi Oromo landlords acted more or less like traditional elders who "did not collect rent for pasture in cash or kind" (1991: 213). Such harmonious relations would gradually change.

The relationship between the titleholder and the co-owners resembled in many ways the former practice of communal land ownership and meant that land, for practical purposes, remained common property – securing the continued access for the members of the sub-clan or lineage. The dilemma, however, was that these co-owners had no proper written proof of their claims, and this opened the possibility for the formal titleholder to contest the so-called co-owners' claims. Some saw this as an opportunity for personal enrichment, and as long as the title owners' kinfolk could not produce formal proof of their rights, the co-owners were unable to contest their claims and secure the land for themselves:

---

[35] Interview, Obse Ibrahim, Robe, August 7, 2005.

Land was divided between the people, and this division was based on relationships with the *balabats*. The *balabats* would give land to individuals – calling them *abbaa lafa*. The land was measured with *qalad*. Most of the people didn't understand the significance of this division. But those who understood it, got much land. The people who were living on that land were defined as *chisegna*,[36] and they had to pay rent to the *abbaa lafa*, who then used that to pay the tax.[37]

The titleholder could in theory do with the land as he wished, either keep it or sell it. Traditional Arsi Oromo inheritance laws managed, to some degree, to block this, but contestations over inheritance and co-ownership came to produce entrenched conflictual relations. This is clearly reflected in the high number of land disputes in the court system throughout the 1950s and 1960s. While Gebru Tareke (1977: 257) sees this as proof of increasing land expropriation by the state, he overlooks the effects of the transition from communal to privately owned land. In fact, more than 85 percent of all court cases were related to disagreements over the inheritance of land (Ministry of Land Reform and Administration 1969: 26). Ketebo Abdiyo's findings from Arsi confirm this, and he amply demonstrates that most cases in the postwar period were about boundary transgression, inheritance of land, legal ownership, distribution of land – cases that are all related to privatization and individualization of land. Litigations involved a number of actors and pitted "[relatives] against each other, peasants against peasants, officials against officials, officials against peasants, the church against peasants" (2010: 181). In other words, changes toward privately owned land, requiring each individual to hold a land title, erased the security each clan member had, in turn demonstrating how the new political and socioeconomic realities weakened established mechanisms for land usage and paved the way for internal competition among individuals (Ketema Meskela 2001: 75).[38]

Another pivotal consequence of the developments toward privatization was the commodification of land. When land became an economic resource controlled by the individual, and not an asset shared by the broader clan society, it turned into something that had a value that

---

[36] The word *chisegna* means a landless tenant. It is derived from the Amharic word *chis*; those whose rights were like smoke.

[37] Interviews, Hajji Abdurazak Hussein, Lais Hafiz, Ahmed Hussein, and Tahir Malik, Dello-Menna, June 15, 2017.

[38] Cf. Jan Hultin (1994: 71).

could be measured in cash and could be sold or rented out (Shiferaw Bekele 1995: 114). Land transactions which, as noted, were uncommon among the Arsi Oromo, increased from the 1950s and could be of both an involuntarily and voluntarily nature. The former could mean that the Arsi Oromo landowner was forced to sell land at a very low price to corrupt government officials under the – often false – pretense that the landowner had outstanding taxes and risked losing the land. These officials would, in other words, not only fleece the illiterate farmers by levying additional illegal taxes on them but also claim their plots of land. While a few Arsi Oromo landowners were attracted by the prospect of cash, most of them, as discussed in the previous chapter, remained reluctant to voluntarily relinquish their land. Tax demands, especially from the early 1960s, caused some to sell plots of land, and such land transactions took place mainly between the Arsi Oromo. Only in a few cases was land sold to the landless Shoa Oromo. The Arsi Oromo were also consciously avoiding sale of land to the Amhara, thus actively blocking their access to land: "There were some rich Amhara around Shaya, and they could buy land. But people hated the Amhara so they didn't want to sell to them."[39] However, when examining voluntary land transactions, we need to recognize the asymmetric power relations between the local Oromo and the Amhara. Land would consequently be given as "gifts" – without compensation – to the Amhara, to ease the pressure from them or to gain favors. Land could alternatively be leased to Amhara settlers who gradually claimed this as their private property (Ketema Meskela 2001: 40f.).

Privatization and commodification of land had inevitable effects on the Arsi Oromo's pastoralist lifestyle and led to the gradual, yet slow, transformation to an agricultural economy – in the highlands – toward the end of the 1960s. The literature on changes from a pastoralist to an agriculturalist economy, or the sedentarization of pastoralist societies, argues that this usually is caused by developments toward either excessive wealth or poverty. In the case of the former, pastoralists often have their rangeland cultivated by hired hands, whereas in the case of the latter, loss of livestock leaves them no option but to engage in crop cultivation (Barth 1973: 103f.; Baxter 1975; Salzman 1980: 12f.). Victor Azaria (1996: 33f.) has argued that political factors, particularly in relation to policies of state, need to be added to the picture.

---

[39] Interview, Obse Ibrahim, Robe, June 16, 2018.

These suggestions fail to capture the rather different developments in Bale. As the Arsi Oromo already were semi-sedentary, sedentarization was not a major issue, and the main change was the transformation toward crop production. However, this was not caused by newfound wealth or by poverty, but rather a result of the pressure from the Ethiopian state – emphasizing agricultural production as the means to satisfy its continuous need for revenues. When taxes had to be paid in cash, the only choice was to shift from a pastoralist economy to marketable agricultural production. The leasing of land and the cultivation of rangeland – often by outsiders – further contributed to this process. The contraction of grazing land obviously curtailed the possibility of large livestock herds, contributing to a gradual development of an agriculturalist way of life among the highland Arsi Oromo. Important to note, however, is that this was a slow process. Visitors to the region in the late 1950s noted that large portions of the Arsi Oromo highlanders continued their traditional pastoralist way of life (Birch-Iensen 1960: 44f.), and informants clam that pastoralism continued to dominate until the 1970s.[40] The gradual shift toward an agricultural economy, however, had a spiraling effect; larger areas for agriculture meant less area for grazing, and less grazing land meant reduced livestock. Cultivation of land in Bale was largely carried out by hired hands, thus reflecting, as noted earlier, a trend common among many pastoralist societies undergoing such transformations. These hired hands were mainly outside settlers, and predominantly the Shoa Oromo. Unable to buy land, their only option was, as discussed in the previous chapter, to till the land of the Arsi Oromo landowners, who then could meet their tax demands. This created a reciprocal dependency relationship between the two groups, and it was not until the land reform in 1975 that the landless Shoa Oromo received access to land – land taken away from the Arsi Oromo.

These developments were restricted to the highlands, and the situation in the lowlands was different. The lowlands were never subject to land measurements, and neither did these areas see any developments toward privatization. The notion of private ownership is still largely an alien one in the lowlands. In Raytu *worreda*, for example, people are still free to clear and claim plots of land without having a formal title.[41]

---

[40]	Interview, Obse Ibrahim, Robe, June 16, 2018.
[41]	Interview, Suleyman Adam, Raytu, June 10, 2017.

It would, at this stage, be possible to argue that the developments I have outlined are little different from a mechanic, simplistic class analysis – the perspective I set out to challenge. Privatization and commodification of land seem to point in the direction of significant change in the mode of production, the move toward a capitalist economy, and the enhanced relevance of class. Increased stratification, as I will elaborate in the next section, was an outcome of these developments, but my argument is that the socioeconomic impact of these changes was only part of the picture. More important was how these developments contributed to what have been considered processes of reification and disenchantment: how privatization and commodification of land ushered in increased alienation and detachment that had deep effects on questions of belonging and identity. I also argue that the seemingly abstract effects of this can be measured through a holistic materialistic view of land that moves beyond conventional Marxist perspectives.

Stratification

The already mentioned notion of "pastoralist egalitarianism" has led to the understanding that pastoralist societies are largely devoid of social inequalities. As livestock are the source of wealth, these societies have mechanisms that mitigate social disparities, such as giving animals as loans, gifts, and payment for labor (Schlee 2012: 20). However, processes of privatization and commodification of land – accompanied by increased individualization – have clearly exacerbated economic inequalities among pastoralist communities. What have emerged are more stratified societies and economic inequality.

In southern Ethiopia, the emergence of the office of the *balabat* (and *burqa*) was the most visible sign of the stratification of the local societies. The *balabats* were the ones managing the *siso* land and were in many areas allocated extra land in addition (*balabat mehret*). What used to be clan land was, in other words, categorized as *balabat* land. This formed the basis for the extraction of tribute and tax, collected from every sub-clan within that area. The situation in Bale was, as I have demonstrated earlier, different from many other regions in the south – seen by the fact that the *siso* system was never introduced, and by the way the *balabats* did not receive any additional land. There is no doubt, however, that there were benefits associated with being a *balabat*. As they were responsible for collecting tribute from the *gab-bars*, they were exempt from paying tribute themselves, and were moreover allowed to keep a certain amount of the tribute: "when they [the authorities] demanded ten oxen, the *balabat* and the *burqa* had to collect thirty oxen. Of these, fifteen would go to the *balabat*, five to the *burqa*, and ten to the government."[42] The gradual privatization of land placed the *balabats* at an advantage, and it was not uncommon to use the office as a means for personal enrichment – which in turn led to increased social inequality. This was particularly evident by the way they managed to secure land as private property, and by the fact that the *balabats* started to keep *gabbars*. The number of *gabbars* varied according to the size of the area administered by the *balabat*, and in some cases he could be allocated up to twenty *gabbars* (Ketema Meskela 2001: 36). Moreover, tasked with collecting tax among the people paved the way for increased corruption among the *balabats*. Being a *balabat* was thus attractive, and in the case of the Arsi region, Ketebo Abdiyo has found that there was a great deal of competition for this position (2010: 172).

There is no doubt that the introduction of the *balabat* institution and alien hierarchies imposed upon Arsi Oromo social structures gradually led to a significant reconfiguration of traditional authority. The fact that the *balabat*'s power was delegated from the state does not mean that traditionally based authority became completely irrelevant. Discussing the role of *balabats* in Arsi, Baxter argues that it was not necessarily the formal position or wealth that determined their author-ity. Rather, it was their "social tact or knowledge with words" that relates to the Oromo's traditional respect for "wisdom," management skills, and ability to arbitrate in conflicts (Baxter 1991: 204). My informants confirmed this, adding that the connections to the state complicated the relations between the people and the *balabats*. While the people resented the *balabats* because of their role as government agents, they acknowledged, at the same time, that the *balabats* found themselves in a difficult situation: "they had no option than to obey."[43] Informants also claimed that if the *balabats* refused to carry out the orders of the Amhara, "they would have been beaten or put in prison ...

---

[42] Interview, Ahmed Mahmoud, Raytu, October 7, 2002.
[43] Interviews, Hajji Hussein Awol, Robe, December 7, 2002; Adam Yunus, Raytu, June 10, 2017.

[and] the houses and the cattle would have been taken away from them."[44] Yet, in spite of feelings of resentment, an affinity still existed between the *balabats* and the people that mitigated this: "The people may have hated them, but this was not shown openly. The *balabat* would never touch them [the people]; they were their own flesh and blood. If somebody tried to touch the *balabat*, they would be protected by the clan."[45]

The quote demonstrates how the *balabats* remained integrated with their clans, in turn pointing to the importance of the clan system relative to social class – and arguably the lack of class consciousness. Shiferaw Bekele, in his discussion of class in feudal northern Ethiopia, has argued that the lack of real social difference between nobility and the peasants was the main deterrent to the development of a distinct class consciousness among the latter (Shiferaw Bekele 1995: 85). This could also be true for the southern areas, and for Bale as well, yet more important were how social class was mediated by the clan system and how the latter superseded class as a "class-for-itself" category. Gebru Tareke's statement that "kinship ties were undermined and social differences proportionally increased" (1977: 244) as a result of the political and economic developments thus becomes too simple. My argument is that while the conquest and subsequent political and economic developments clearly led to increased social inequalities and, thus, in (Marxist) theory, to the establishment of new social classes, class remained, as I will return to in Chapter 10, secondary to ethnic and religious affiliation as a force for political mobilization.

The Land-Clan Connection Revisited

Processes of privatization and commodification of land also had deep consequences for the land-clan connection – the practical meaning of clans' spatial distribution, land tenure based on the land-clan connection, and the way land constituted a framework for notions of belonging and for interactions with others. Although we obviously do not talk about a full-fledged capitalist economy, it is clear that these processes contributed to destroying "those bonds that had bound individuals to a

---

[44] Interview, Ahmed Mahmoud, Raytu, October 7, 2002.
[45] Interview, Ahmed Mahmoud, Raytu, October 7, 2002.

community in the days when production was still 'organic'" (Lukács 1968 [1923]: 90).

In contrast to a reality where clan membership was tied to geographical location, thus being decisive for emplaced belonging, division of land into individually and privately owned plots of land meant that such belonging was now to a much lesser degree determined by clan membership. It cut through earlier arrangements and notions of ancestral land as belonging to clans and sub-clans. "Home" and emplaced belonging thus gained a new meaning. Opportunities for land transactions exacerbated this situation, and the arrival of outside settlers – Shoa Oromo and Amhara – further disrupted patterns of clan distribution spatially. Their presence on traditional and ancestral Arsi Oromo clan land was something completely alien, affecting notions of land-based belonging. While the outside settlers would use Arsi Oromo clan-derived names, such as Abba Karra, Sinana, or Karmamida, when referring to their areas of residence, these names did not mean the same for them as for the native Arsi Oromo.

While the land-clan connection served to generate an emplaced and embodied belonging, a particularly important aspect of the new situation was that land became the means that tied people to a new entity – the state. The state's use of land to create ties between itself and its subjects has been a common theme in Ethiopian history, and Shiferaw Bekele noted that "land was the medium through which the state functioned as a state," relating this to the state's granting of land in return for public (civil and military) service. As the state was unable to collect sufficient revenues to function, it meant that "the state was run by land rather than money" (1995: 77, 78). While Shiferaw Bekele discusses the traditional northern Ethiopian Kingdom, it is possible to extend this to the situation in the southern regions and link it to processes of taxation and privatization of land. The implementation of new tax regimes enabled the state to increase its control over the people, tying them to land in a new manner. This was intensified through land measurements that bound people to particular privately owned plots of land. The state determined each individual's holdings, the tax he or she had to pay, and which reciprocally made each subject accountable to the state. Each landowner had, furthermore, to document his or her ownership through a title, and as this was granted by the state, it was no longer the clan that secured each individual's access to land, but the state. On the one hand, it is possible to suggest that this gave people security with regard to land ownership. Yet, on the other hand, such rights were always insecure, as the hegemonic state or its corrupt agents had the power to dispossess the owner. The state thus not only reduced the people to tax-paying subjects responsible to an impersonal state but also made them depend on their plots of land as their only taxable resource. The state was in this way able to exert absolute power over its subjects, and Shiferaw Bekele has pointedly called the process of privatization "absolutization," referring to how private ownership had an *absolute* character (1995: 110). In other words, rather than being attached to land as clan-based communal land, people were tied to land as their individual, private, taxable property.

As for any process of sociocultural change, the transformation of the land-clan connection was gradual. Despite increased privatization and commodification of land, the land-clan connection continued to have some relevance – illustrated by the fact that people who had lost their property and were searching for new land did not want to take land that was at a distance from their kin and clan (Ketema Meskela 2001: 106). Baxter's findings from Arsi in the late 1960s are also telling. He observed that even if land had become privately owned, the common trend was to conceive of land as clan land: "all territory was still spoken of as 'belonging' to particular specified lineages." He also notes that even if grazing land had become scarce, and people to a large extent lived off crop cultivation, they had kept their self-image as pastoralists, constantly expressed through prayers, songs, greetings, and blessings (Baxter 1991: 197; cf. Azarya 1996: 33). Ayalew Gebre has forwarded a similar view in his study about the Karrayu in the Awash valley, arguing that their prevailing view was that land – even if appropriated by the state – belonged to them (2001: 88).

The situation in the lowlands was different, and the developments there did not tie the pastoralists to the state in the same way. This might seem surprising, as it would be easy to assume that this would be the consequence of the transformation of pastoral land into government property. However, the categorization of land as government land was not the critical issue, and the main reason why the pastoralists' ties to the state were looser was that they, in contrast to the highlanders, did not pay land tax.[46] The situation for the pastoralists in Bale was similar

---

[46] See Ayalew Gebre for comparative insights to this issue (2001: 89f.).

to that of those in other areas, where it has been noted that even if pastoral land is defined as state property, pastoralists "usually retain rather vaguely defined rights of access and use" (Helland 2006: 6). Limited ties to the state, as compared with those in the highlands, also meant that the land-clan connection was affected in a different manner: the people largely maintained their affinities and loyalties to the clans and upheld a segmentary lineage structure.

This does not mean, however, that the pastoralists' relations to land remained unaffected. To grasp these impacts, we need to move beyond immediate socioeconomic changes and recognize the more fundamental impact the reconfiguration of land had for notions of belonging. One critical dimension is that the reclassification of their ancestral land as government property impacted their emplaced dwelling across space and their affective attachment to the land. While the state's appropriation of the land did not necessarily affect their access to it, in the sense that the authorities explicitly blocked the pastoralists' movements, the division of land under the jurisdiction of *balabats* who claimed taxes on their main assets – livestock – meant that movements came at a cost. It is here important to acknowledge how pastoralists' paths across landscapes constitute connections between permanent and semipermanent sites of living, being lines between nodes that as a whole mark space for emplaced living. Paths move across time – connecting land to memory, and in this way anchoring present dwelling to historical belonging (Shetler 2007: 16). Their affective ties to land were impacted by the state's imagination of pastoralist land as "unused" and "vacant," in turn contributing to confirm and emphasize the inferior status of the pastoralists. Such processes of reification and disenchantment meant that land not only had become the property of a foreign power, suddenly transforming the traditional owners to trespassers, but also that the pastoralists had largely become invisible, appearing only as subjects for extraction and exploited for tribute and tax. These factors are crucial to understand the level of antagonism the pastoralist lowlanders felt toward the Amhara and why the insurgency surfaced precisely in these areas.

Conclusion

This chapter has demonstrated that an approach that moves beyond a conception of land only in relation to economic production and allows for the integration of the economic with the cultural opens up for a more thorough understanding of land. Land in its concrete material form effected bonds that tied people to both lineage and place, generating an emplaced and embodied belonging. Paul Rodaway talks about haptic geography and haptic habitation and underscores how the body's movements through environments enable human experiences of spatial belonging (1994: 51f.). For the Oromo, land was an integrated part of one's identity: as intersected with clan membership, land and clan mutually reinforced each other as pivotal for the individual's embodied relations and emplaced living.

Such an approach also enables us to more fully comprehend the consequences of the new land-tenure system. Processes of privatization and commodification of land surely had socioeconomic impacts on Arsi Oromo society, but far more important was the way it deeply affected the land-clan connection and the way land constituted a framework for notions of belonging and for interactions with others. As I have demonstrated, the ensuing changes led to increased individualism and to a more stratified society. People became more tied to land in the form of individual, private, and taxable property, which in turn impacted interdependent relations among clan members. This is important for the way it modifies a mechanistic and one-dimensional class perspective and allows for a more nuanced analysis of the gradual disenchantment or de-traditionalization of land and its tight connection with clan organization, identity, and religiously inflected worldview. This moreover demonstrates the relevance of ethnicity and religion as integral parts of a robust materialist interpretation of land.

It is thus clear that the Bale insurgency cannot only be interpreted through a simplistic and reductive class analysis but that we also need to consider how ensuing changes produced a profound sense of loss that became translated into antagonism and enmity. However, the fact that the impacts were more deeply felt in the highlands than in the lowlands – where the fighting occurred – might seem like a contradiction. As the lowlanders were affected by the state's invasive policies to a lesser degree, they did not experience changes in the land-clan connection as disruptive as those experienced by the highlanders. The logical conclusion of this would be that armed struggle should have emerged in the highlands rather than in the lowlands. However, there is no doubt that the impacts on the land-clan connection were felt across the population in Bale, creating similar notions of loss and animosity across the region. The fact that the insurgency was concentrated in the lowlands needs, as I will return to, to be seen in relation to how the lowlanders' loose relations to the state enabled a mobile lifestyle that was crucial for guerrilla warfare.

It is, at the same time, clear that a holistic and materialist under-standing of land alone cannot explain the rise of the insurgency. Rather, we need to recognize and include other factors. The subsequent chapters will widen the scope and investigate other relevant dynamics. Particularly relevant here are the role of religion and ethnicity as intrinsic to broader currents traveling across the Horn, how these influenced the local context of Bale, and how the religious and ethnic dimensions contributed to particular local processes of increased antagonism. Similarly important was how such antagonism – both local and trans-local – was a product of the Ethiopian state's presence and policies, wherein the role of Christianity in the Ethiopian national narrative and in the formation of Amhara peoplehood was crucial for processes of "othering" and policies of subjugation. This is the focus for the next chapter.

8 | Christianity, Nation, and Amhara Peoplehood

A distinct hierarchy marked the historical Ethiopian state, in which the emperor and upper echelon of the nobility held absolute power, thus being, in the Gramscian sense, hegemonic in nature. While Gramsci initially thought of hegemony as based on modes of economic production and class divisions, he later expanded the concept beyond the notion of class and economy to include cultural, moral, and intellectual domains. Hegemony came to be understood as inherently multidimensional and as channeled through different structures of power that were all mutually reinforcing. The links between hegemony and the state are both obvious and intimate, but hegemony's multidimensional character necessitates the inclusion of, and cooperation with, institutions and structures of authority. This means that hegemony is not only maintained by a ruling elite but by "a historic block" (Gramsci 1971: 137, 168). Hegemony can never be merely coercive, however, but involves the establishment of certain degrees of popular consent in the form of securing moral and social authority. Consent in a neo-Gramscian sense also has an ideological dimension, wherein the persuasiveness of ideas hinges on the nature and strength of the system of alliances enabling socialization for the production of popular consent – reciprocally securing loyalty to and identification with the nation, state, and territory (Alonso 1994: 390).[1]

The state in Ethiopia – in spite of endemic regional factionalism and a lack of bureaucratic organization – has always been a pivotal actor. As a highly centralized polity and, to a large extent, personified through the emperor, it has managed through history to augment its circumscribed power through elaborate interconnected

---

[1] Laclau and Mouffe (1985) have provided important correctives to Gramsci's perception of hegemony, criticizing the unwarranted yet continued privileging of class and the economy as ontological categories. Moving away from such essentialized positions, they opened the space for a deeper understanding of hegemony, recognizing a broader range of positions.

structures of political dominance and economic extraction. This was particularly manifest in a feudal land-tenure arrangement wherein the people were tied to the nobles, the nobles were tied to the state, and the church tied them all together. The church represented a particularly important institution in the multidimensional exercise of hegemony. The state and the church were intimately related and mutually dependent and constituted reinforcing elements in exercising hegemony. While the church was a significant economic force, it was more crucial in securing popular consent. Embodied in its clergy and manifest through numerous local churches and monasteries, it provided the tools for "propagation" of social and moral authority. This was not merely restricted to a "religious" sphere but also extended to safeguarding an important Christian national narrative that gave other institutions of domination divine character and legitimacy. The same national narrative also tied people to these institutions, and subscription to the narrative and submission to the institutions of authority were crucial for the production of belonging and peoplehood.

This religiously underpinned national narrative has been instrumental in imagining the creation, historical developments, and destiny of Ethiopia, and the particular nationalistic attributes of Ethiopian Christianity are similarly integral dimensions of Amhara peoplehood. I recognize the multifaceted nature and plasticity of Amhara as a category (Clapham 1988: 24) but would argue that Amhara becomes meaningless unless connected to Christianity. While the religious dimension was crucial for the demarcation of boundaries of exclusion and inclusion, the very content of the national narrative invoked a strong sense of exceptionalism – a notion that is fundamental for understanding the Amhara's perceptions of "self" and "other." Paying attention to content, this narrative serves to remind us to not over-emphasize boundaries vs "cultural stuff" (Barth 1969), and to the need for a more balanced perspective that recognizes the role of cultural content as important for collective identities (Ashmore et al. 2004; Jenkins 2008: 79, 111f.). Such a perspective must, of course, be qualified by the caveat that paying attention to the content of particular ethnic and religious identities should not become an attempt to construe religion and ethnicity in any essentialist or substantialist manner. The point to be made is that "cultural stuff" cannot be severed from boundaries and that paying attention to and unpacking the nature of such content remain crucial for understanding conflicts.[2] In this chapter, I apply a *longue duré* perspective, discussing the important role of Christianity in the Ethiopian national narrative and in state policies, and how this underpinned the developments of antagonistic relations in the south. The Ethiopian national narrative as embodied in a semidivine imperial genealogy and tied to a territorial state was inherently imperialistic and expansionist in nature, and by investigating these policies throughout history, I seek to demonstrate the importance of the religious dimension of the Amhara's encounters with different ethnic and non-Christian groups. A crucial point is that the state's expansionist endeavors were accompanied by the Amhara notion of exceptionalism that paved the way for civilizational policies and a settler mentality (cf. Akenson 1992), in turn leading to the demarcation of rigid boundaries and asymmetric relationships. Expansionism necessitated, at the same time, the building of a nation, and nation building in a heterogenous landscape required assimilation – which, as we will see, also had a religious dimension.

The Christian Kingdom and Religious Nationalism

Christianity was introduced to Axum in the fourth century and spread gradually across the highlands of northern Ethiopia, finding followers among both Semitic- and Cushitic-speaking groups. While neighboring Christian kingdoms along the Nile Valley disappeared mainly due to the expansion of Islam, the Christian Orthodox Kingdom of Ethiopia remained intact. Adhering to the non-Chalcedonian creed and attached to the School of Alexandria, the Orthodox Church was from the very beginning of a particular character. This distinctiveness became further pronounced by the way the process of localization led to the integration of a number of indigenous as well as Judaic elements, seen, for example, through the celebration of the Shabbat and the avoidance of pork. As the kingdom's center of gravity shifted to the hinterland during the Zagwe period (1150–1270), the church became increasingly isolated from the rest of the Christian world. This spurred much speculations

---

[2] Todd has forwarded similar arguments related to the Northern Ireland conflict and points to how the nature of Protestantism and Catholicism was important in that context; the former seeing the latter as backward and primitive (Todd n.s.: 6).

from the side of its European coreligionists, who referred to it as Prester John, a mysterious Christian kingdom hidden somewhere in Africa (cf. Beckingham and Hamilton 1996). Attempts by the Europeans to bring it into the Catholic fold were met with great resistance by the Ethiopian kings and the clergy, producing xenophobic attitudes toward other forms of Christianity and exacerbating the kingdom's isolation in the northern highlands.

The main source for the creation and formulation of a religiously underpinned nationalism was the book *Kebre Negast* (Glory of the Kings). Originating from the thirteenth century, the book has commonly been viewed as the instrument in legitimizing the so-called restoration of the Solomonic dynasty succeeding the Zagwe period.[3] It was, moreover, foundational in providing the underpinning for Ethiopia's "chosenness," setting the nation apart from other nations. Crucial here is that it rendered Ethiopia as a divinely ordained nation, facilitating a "deification of nationality, or nationalization of the deity" (Markakis 1974: 30). As a result, the *Kebre Negast* was "not merely a literary work, but – as the Old Testament to the Hebrew or the Koran to the Arabs – it is the repository of Ethiopian national and religious feelings, perhaps the truest and most genuine expression of Abyssinian Christianity" (Ullendorff 1960: 144).

The book contains the famous story about the meeting between the (alleged) Ethiopian Queen of Sheba and King Solomon in Jerusalem – the former seeking the latter's wisdom, and the latter struck by the queen's beauty. She is lured to spend the night with the king, and the story then details the result of this encounter: the birth of Menelik I. The child is born in Ethiopia, where he also spends his childhood, but coming of age, the young man returns to Jerusalem, where his father, King Solomon, confirms his status as the rightful heir to the Kingdom of Israel. While in Jerusalem, Menelik I accepts the monotheistic faith of Israel and then embarks on his journey back to Ethiopia – accompanied by a number of first-born Israelites and a cohort of priests. Reluctant to leave Jerusalem, these priests sneak into the temple in Jerusalem, steal the Ark of the Covenant or the Tabernacle of Zion as it is called in the *Kebre Negast,* and smuggle it

---

[3] The so-called Solomonic dynasty was established by Yekunno Amlak (1270–1285) and would govern Ethiopia until Emperor Haile Selassie was deposed in 1974.

to Ethiopia. According to the teaching of the Ethiopian Orthodox Church, the Ark of the Covenant is still found in a sanctuary close to the Church of Our Lady Mary of Zion in Axum.[4]

My argument is that the *Kebre Negast* contains three important dimensions fundamental for the construction of Ethiopian nationalism: *genealogical, spatial,* and *confessional* dimensions. The crucial point is that these dimensions connected Ethiopian peoplehood to a broader biblical universe and served to transcend the country's embeddedness by integrating it with the destined history of the Israelites – God's chosen people. The genealogical dimension, as embodied in Menelik I, connected the royal lineage of Ethiopia to the Israelite monarchy, and laid the foundation for the Solomonic dynasty. The *Kebre Negast* clearly states, "no one except the male seed of David, the son of Solomon the king, shall ever reign over Ethiopia" (Brooks 1996: 121). According to biblical tradition, the Israelite kings were bestowed with a particular divine anointment that was accompanied by a blessing that was a sign that the king was sanctioned by God and imbued with spiritual power (1 Samuel 16:12–13). With Menelik I recognized as the son of King Solomon and the heir to the throne, this quality and divine power were extended to an Ethiopian lineage. The designation of "Lion of Judah," which was used by the Solomonic dynasty as its royal emblem, confirms this connection, referring, at the same time, to Christ (Revelation 5:5), whereas the title as the "Elect of God" signifies how the Ethiopian royal lineage was set apart as willed by God. An added aspect different from the Israelite kings was the confessional requirement, as expressed in the *Fetha Negast,*[5] which states that "if he [the king] becomes a heretic, from that moment he is no longer a King but a rebel" (cited in. Markakis 1974: 35).

Notions about the nation are never abstract but rather indivisibly linked to territory through which the "fusion of a piece of land with the symbolic and mythicized history of the nation is what gives nationalism such symbolic power" (Agnew 2004: 227). This is clearly the case for Ethiopia, wherein the spatial dimension of the *Kebre Negast* relates to the juxtaposition of the territory of Ethiopia with Israel and Jerusalem, and the transfer of God's grace from the "original" promised land to Ethiopia. Similar to how God promised the Israelites a particular

---

[4] The Ark of the Covenant was, according to the biblical narrative, the material expression containing the Ten Commandments, signifying the pact between God and Israel.
[5] Meaning "Law of the Kings," a compendium of authoritative traditional laws.

territorial space that was designated as their homeland – a land "flowing with milk and honey" (Exodus 3:8) – God was with Menelik
I giving the same promise and blessings to Ethiopia. The *Kebre
Negast* goes further, however, and narrates that Ethiopia replaces
Israel as the blessed land. This is made clear in the story of King
Solomon, who in a dream saw "a brilliant sun, and it came down
from heaven and shed exceedingly great splendor over Israel ... and
it flew away to the country of Ethiopia, and it shone there with exceedingly great brightness forever" (Brooks 1996: 32). The reason for this
was Menelik's acquisition of the Ark of the Covenant – and its presence
in Ethiopia.

   This latter point relates directly to the third dimension: the confessional
one, which positioned the Ethiopian nation as superior to both the Jews
and other Christians. The former are effectively condemned because of
their crucifixion of Christ and as consequently having lost their status as
God's chosen people. Because of Ethiopia's acceptance of Christ, it
bypasses Israel and becomes the real chosen people, while the Jews –
depicted as wicked, iniquitous, and polluted – become the cursed people.
Even more so, by adhering to the *right* faith: Ethiopian Orthodox
Christianity and the non-Chalcedonian creed, it is deemed superior to
any other denominations and emerges as the only true form of
Christianity. With reference to the early Christological debates, the
Kebra Negast condemns the "Roman" Christians and any other church
and claims that "they [people of Rome] corrupted the Faith of Christ, and
they introduced heresies in the Church of God by the mouth of Nestorius
and Arius" (Brooks 1996: 125). Ethiopia thus emerges "as the sole
authentic bearers of Christianity, the *only* people in the world now
favored by the God of Solomon" (Levine 1974: 107, italics in original).

   Ethiopia is, in other words, effectively linked to the biblical narrative, both the Old to the New Testaments, and these three dimensions
reflect the transference of the divinely ordained qualities of the
Israelites – to become firmly embodied in local lineages and emplaced
in the land of the Ethiopian Kingdom. And by adopting the Israelite
monotheism, and later Christianity, its chosen people are elevated from
the status of being primeval polytheists to righteous believers.[6] The

---

[6] This corresponds with Smith's (1999) suggestions on the affinity between
    a religious myth and ethnic selection that reverses the status of inferiority and
    generates a distinct sense of superiority.

lasting legacy of the *Kebre Negast* and the Solomonic narrative is reflected in the 1955 Ethiopian Constitution, which underscored Emperor Haile Selassie's authority as being "a descendant of King Sahle Selassie, whose line descends without interruption from the dynasty of Menelik I, son of the Queen of Ethiopia, the Queen of Sheba, and King Solomon of Jerusalem" (Art. 2).

Amhara Peoplehood

Before continuing the story, I need to clarify the meaning of Amhara and why I have chosen to apply it as a central term throughout the study. The term *Amhara* is frequently used in a highly imprecise manner, with a tendency to inaccurately essentialize the Amhara as a homogenous ethnic group (Levine 1965). Now, I do acknowledge that my usage of Amhara could conceal inherent complexities, and I agree that it is important to historicize the term and recognize the "changing contours of Amhara-ness" (Heran 1994). In relation to Menelik's conquest, for example, there is no doubt that his forces also included other groups besides the Amhara. While recognizing the term's ambiguity and dynamic character, that it may have different meanings simultaneously, and that it has undergone important changes as it traversed time and space, I also argue that Amhara constitutes a particular peoplehood. As a peoplehood, it was, similar to *Islaama*, tied to localized kin and place, and of a segmentary nature. It was, however, also constituted by an important religious dimension. In the same way that *Islaama* cannot be fully understood without its ethnic dimension, Amhara becomes meaningless without its religious connotation.

It is common to view the Amhara as one of the two main groups in the northern highlands of Ethiopia – the other being the Tigray. However, throughout history "Amhara" was never applied to denote a separate ethnic group, and neither did the people in the Amhara region use the word as a term for self-designation. Before the nineteenth century, it only appeared as a toponym, referring to the central northern highlands of Wollo, Begemedir, Lasta, Gondar, Gojam, and gradually including Shoa (Chernetsov 1996: 20; Mackonen Michael 2008: 396). People (up to today) rather identified themselves in relation to geographical areas, such as Wollo, Gondar, or Gojam. The term gained increased political relevance with the so-called restoration of the Solomonic dynasty in the thirteenth century, linked to kings ruling what was considered Amhara territory, that is, the kings of Amhara. Such close links between Amhara and political power meant that Amhara gradually came to be seen as constituting the ruling people of historical Ethiopia (Perham 1969: 16). Amhara became in this sense *"a metaphor for power"* (Teshale Tibebu 1995: 45, italics in original).

Amhara was moreover, according to Sevir Chernetsov (1996) closely related to militarism and a culture of warfare. Key to his arguments are the terms *chawa* (the emperor's soldiers) and *y'chawa lijjoch* (the emperor's soldiers' children). The *chawa* were the core royal regiments – guarding the emperor's camp, following him on his campaigns, deployed to quell possible regional uprisings, and to settle along insecure frontiers. In return, they were allowed to collect loot from their victims and granted hereditary land, which together created a lifestyle where they "lived on booty in wartime, and their agricultural product in peacetime" (Chernetsov 1996: 23).[7] Intimately connected and loyal to the throne, these soldiers developed a culture that was militaristic in essence and which was passed on to their descendants – the *y'chawa lijjoch* – who became an integrated part of the Amhara peasantry. While there obviously were people across the Amhara region who were not part of such warrior groups, the culture of militarism nevertheless extended to the broader population. Many peasants were also soldiers, and a significant part of the peasantry served as retainers to the army. Marjory Perham describes this as follows: "the humblest villager once he was armed and mounted his sorry nag, with even one ragged squire trotting at his side, had become a real man on the road to fortune and adventure" (1969: 164). The land-tenure system and a tributary mode of production revolved very much around the military, and a large portion of tribute from land supported officers and soldiers. Shiferaw Bekele has documented that two-thirds of the land in many northern areas was allocated as military land (1995: 86f.), and James McCann (1985: 621) notes that in certain areas "one-third of rural males had military obligations."

Militarization also paved the way for a distinctly hierarchal Amhara society, where positions were clearly defined. Such structures were evident at the individual household level, among broader societal groups, and within the political sphere. The maintenance of such structures remained a pivotal moral principle, underscoring "obedience to authorities – parents, Emperor and God" (Marzagora 2015: 128). The father was the

---

[7] The contemporary meaning of *chawa* is "noble" or "proper."

master of the household, feudal lords ruled over the peasantry, and the king was elevated above all his subjects.[8] The extent of hierarchies can be illustrated by the British Consular Arnold Hodson's account of his visit to a small army outpost located in a remote rural part of Borana. Showing the Amhara officers a letter permitting him entry into Ethiopia, signed by, among others, the powerful Minister of War *Fitawrari* Habte-Giorgis, "the whole assembly rose and bowed and remained standing while the content of the passport was read" (1927: 8).

Although Amhara existed as a category, and whereas Amharic was used as the common language, it was, as noted, never used as an emic term for belonging related to notions of an Amhara shared ancestry. What existed, though, was the notion of a putative *wanna abbat* ("chief father") as the apical ancestor for the *beteseb* – the kinship group. The kinship group did not have the form of larger collectives, such as clans, but appeared as small units, or in the form of an extended family, where the *beteseb* would trace its ancestor back ten to twelve generations. Interestingly, this ancestor was commonly remembered as the one who "planted the ark in the church," meaning the one who established the first church in the parish (Hoben 1963: 27f.). The *beteseb* was also the name for the household, usually led by a male *abbat* – father. Spatially, these households were scattered across the rural areas and organized in hamlets, where a cluster of hamlets constituted the parish. Kinship seemed not to determine this pattern of dwelling, as the hamlets consistently included "male heads unrelated to another" (Shack 1974: 28). This is not to say that kinship relations did not matter, and they certainly mattered in relation to distribution of and right to land. Such right, called *rist*, was hereditary and was based on a real or putative ancestor, and access to land was also "the mark of membership in the basic unit of social organization" (Markakis 1974: 77), producing a situation where genealogies and lineages had no meaning without land. Different from the Oromo, however, the Amhara's land rights were premised on private ownership, and meaningful belonging did not extend beyond the *beteseb*. This points to a "rugged individualism" (Gebru Tareke 1991: 14), and in a situation where kinship ties were less constricted, Amhara individualism created opportunities for people to negotiate their positions. It also created possibilities for social

---

[8] Malara and Boylston (2016) have elaborated on such structures, while also underscoring the issue of affection existing within rigid hierarchies.

mobility and produced prospects for an Amhara individual to look beyond the confinement of the *beteseb* and the locality of the homestead.[9]

While the Amhara were a composite of groups and social strata, and whereas the individual households and decentered regional affiliation made the Amhara's notions of belonging and peoplehood relatively circumscribed, there were also ties that bound them together. This was signified through the monarchy as a national, supra-regional institution. Even if the power of the centralized monarchy waxed and waned throughout history, it did represent the imagined ideal. Each individual peasant was a subject of the crown and was required to submit to its authority. Similarly important was the feudal system and tributary arrangements that tied them both to the land and to hierarchical structures.

There was another pivotal dimension of the Amhara notion of peoplehood, namely the religious one. Orthodox Christianity was not only an inescapable part of people's daily life but also the "dominant element of an incipient national identity" (Markakis 1974: 28f.; cf. Donham 1986: 12). Founded upon a collectively shared belief in the Solomonic myth, in the divinely anointed king, and in themselves as a blessed nation, the religious dimension forged a strong consciousness of being members of a larger peoplehood. Such a Christian underpinning of the nation consequently means that Amhara peoplehood, in addition to being attached to kinship and regional space, cannot be grasped fully without this pivotal religious dimension. Rather than merely signifying an ethnic group, Amhara reveals, similar to *Islaama,* the complex intertwined intersection of religion and ethnicity – as two tightly woven and mutually reinforcing dimensions in the making of a particular peoplehood. Being embodied in the *beteseb* and in the hierarchy of local clergy, as well as emplaced in homes, hamlets, and in parish churches dotting the landscape, ethnicity and religion were merged in a way that produced a sense of belonging that was locally anchored and simultaneously – through genealogies as well as religious narratives – opened up for belonging that transcended immediacy, time, and space.

---

[9] For more details about kinship, social structures, and land tenure among the Amhara, see Hoben (1973). The issue of Amhara individualism is discussed in depth by Levine (1965: 238f.).

However, while the transcendence of such immediacy in the case of *Islaama* entailed an attachment to the wider world of Islam, the situation for the Amhara was crucially different. On the one hand, rather than being inclusively oriented to the world of Christendom, it was circumscribed by the particularities of Ethiopian Orthodox Christianity and the isolationism of the church. This demarcated clear boundaries that set the Ethiopian Christian nation apart – and made it unique – from the rest of the Christian world, thus forging strong self-protective and xenophobic notions. On the other hand, as the religious dimension of Amhara was firmly attached to a Christian kingdom and a territorial state, manifest through a monarchy and a church, it took on a political dimension. This generated the perception of Amhara peoplehood as distinctly superior and as having a divine destiny – in turn being decisive for the production of a particular form of expansionism.

Religious-imperial Expansionism

The supra-local dimension of Amhara peoplehood had clear implications for their spatial embeddedness and their notions of being-in-the-world – paving the way for the imagination of territory at a scale beyond immediate locality.[10] A hegemonic political system centered on the monarch and based upon the Solomonic myth, an omnipresent church, a hierarchical and tribute-based feudal system, and the notion of being a superior Christian civilization were all significant components in creating a particular national space, a territorial kingdom. While this national space to a certain extent entailed demarcated boundaries, the same boundaries also generated the imaging of other territories beyond them – territories that could be conquered. Territoriality became particularly pronounced after Menelik's conquests, when the establishment of internationally recognized borders enabled the idea of Ethiopia to "became anchored for the first time in a fixed geographic space" (Marzagora 2015: 77).

The pivotal point here is that Amhara exceptionalism was underpinned by an expansionist or imperialist ideology that meant that the kingdom's "violent expansion was just and righteous [and] a form of holy war" (Reid 2011: 27). This religious aspect is illustrated by the

---

[10] See van Heur (2004: 24) for a discussion about space and scale.

fact that the *tabot*[11] followed the emperor during his military campaigns; believed to protect the forces and secure victory. Even more so, wars and conquest were depicted as "struggles between good and evil, light and darkness, attributing victories to the might of God while describing the enemy as being guided by Satan" (Markakis 1974: 32). Areas like those in the south were thus depicted as home to non-nations, inferior and evil – at the same time containing rich resources.

With the so-called restoration of the Solomonic dynasty in the thirteenth century, the political center of gravity gradually moved to Shoa in the southern parts of the Ethiopian highlands – followed by a shift in the expansionist policy further to the south – particularly aimed at the Muslim sultanates in the southeast where the Amhara jostled with them for control over the lucrative trade routes. The northern Christian kingdom's encounters with these areas became increasingly violent from the thirteenth century, primarily during the reigns of Yekunno Amlak (1270–1285) and Amda Siyon (1314–1344). As the Christian kingdom expansions in the southeast reduced the Muslim sultanates to tributaries, the Muslims gradually responded with armed resistance, and the better parts of the thirteenth and fourteenth centuries were characterized by a general state of unrest. As briefly noted in Chapter 2, the Sultanate of Adal, which succeeded Ifat (defeated in 1415), eventually emerged as the focal point for opposition against the Christian kingdom, led by Ahmed Gragn. Initiating his military campaigns in 1529, Ahmed Gragn quickly penetrated deep into the core northern highlands and nearly defeated the emperor. The tide turned, however, when the Amhara forces, with the help of the Portuguese, killed Ahmed Gragn in a battle by Lake Tana in 1542.

The victory sealed Islam's fate as a political and military power and left the Christian kingdom as the politically unchallenged hegemon in the Horn. It also laid the ground for a particular religious fault line, which shaped the Amhara's image of the Muslim "other" and forged interreligious relations of a distinct asymmetric character. The rulers' attitudes, relations, and policies toward the Muslim population in the Horn were complex and followed an uneven trajectory in the course of time. Such variations greatly depended on the political situation in the broader region and on fluctuating balances of power, as well as being shaped by the nature of interreligious encounters (Abir 1980). Crucial,

---

[11] The *tabot* is the replica of the Ark of the Covenant found in Orthodox churches.

however, was that the Amhara's apprehension of the Muslims was very much related to the experience of the Ahmed Gragn. A Russian military attaché reported as late as in 1890 that Ahmed Gragn "still lives in the memory of the people, who ascribe him supernatural qualities" (quoted in Reid 2011: 64). Such memories generated a view of Islam as a potential external threat to the survival of the kingdom and made the Amhara distrustful toward the Muslim population and fearful of how they could align themselves with outside Muslim forces. Islam was in other words, "the enemy within, as well as the enemy beyond" (Reid 2011: 62).[12]

These attitudes were translated into concrete policies aimed at keeping the Muslims at bay. This was already evident during the reign of Lebna Dengel (1508–1540), who issued an edict prohibiting Muslims "from carrying arms and riding horses" and banning marriages between Christians and Muslims (Abir 1980: 84f.). Emperor Yohannes I (1667–1682) followed the same lines, forcing Gondar's Muslims to live in separate quarters and prohibiting them from owning land. Muslims were also subject to a range of other discriminatory practices, seen, for example, in the way Christians – as a sign of contempt – would greet the Muslims using the left hand (Abir 1978: 130). Religious policies became even more pronounced during the nineteenth century when Emperor Tewodros II (1855–1868) attempted to counterweigh centrifugal regional forces. Reinvigorating the traditional religiously underpinned national narrative and displaying a distinct Christian zeal, he issued decrees ordering all subjects to convert to Christianity or face expulsion from the kingdom. While such conversions never were enforced during his reign, Emperor Yohannes IV (1872–1889) went a step further when, through the edict of Boru Meda, he required all Muslims to accept Christianity. Such a religiously militant attitude can partly be explained by Emperor Yohannes IV's own personal religious zeal and his determination to create a religiously homogeneous society, but it was also connected to how the legacy of the "Muslim threat" was made manifest through the conflict with the Muslim Mahdist forces from Sudan.

---

[12] Muslim communities within the kingdom had grown significantly as a result of Ahmad Gragn's conquest, and it was said that about the Christians that "[h]ardly one in ten retained his religion." While this is clearly an exaggeration, an observer in the seventeenth century estimated that a third of Ethiopia's population were Muslim (Markakis 1974: 62f.).

It has commonly been assumed that the main motive for the Amhara expansion southeast was economic, whereas the religious dimension became strengthened through the campaigns of Ahmad Gragn. Mordechai Abir (1980) has argued that the role of religion was exaggerated due to the particular style of Ahmed Gragn's chronicle, which was penned by a religious scholar (Shibab ad-Din 2003 [1559]) and claims that the rulers' religious sentiments remained separate from politics. However, Abir's attempt to dissociate the "purely politico-economic motivated wars" from the "deep religious sentiments of the rulers" (1980: 73) not only reflects an unwarranted dichotomy between material and religious motives but also reduces the latter as less "real." Patrick Gilkes provides a more balanced view, arguing that religion was "a major pre-occupation of the Emperors" (1975: 16), and Taddesse Tamrat (1972: 185, 231f.), through his discussion of Emperor Zara Yaqob (1434–1468), has demonstrated how the emperor not only sought to extend his economic influence but also that he simultaneously was driven by a motive to spread Christianity, to expand the realm of the Christian state, and to build a homogeneous Christian nation. This is supported by the actual policies he implemented: active efforts to convert the Muslims, harsh measures seeking to end non-Christian rituals, and punitive actions toward those who left the Christian faith.

Evangelism efforts followed, however, an uneven trajectory, and paradoxically, the Orthodox Church, which would reasonably be expected to be the main agent of religious change, did not initially display much interest in missionary activities. Often riven by internal doctrinal conflicts, its clergy lived a rather sheltered life within the confines of the northern heartland. When new areas were conquered, representatives of the church were dispatched to render basic service to the Christian soldiers and settlers, but they largely left non-Christian groups alone. It was not until the formation and growth of monasticism and the reforms of *Abuna* Yaqob (1337–1344) that evangelization efforts increased (Taddesse Tamrat 1972: 158f.). The establishment of numerous monasteries, education of the clergy, and internal restructuring of the church were important factors for intensified evangelization among groups both within and beyond the confines of the kingdom. This also came to affect the Muslims in the southeast. While being forced to pay tribute to the Christian kingdom, Muslims had previously been omitted from proselytization activities. However, as the kingdom secured political control over the southeast, the church intensified its efforts seeking to convert the Muslim inhabitants, leading to the gradual decline of Islam in the southeastern fringes of the Christian kingdom (Abir 1980: 27; Taddesse Tamrat 1972: 186, 231). What is important is how Amhara expansionism became an imperial-religious project, involving both state and church, where evangelization "followed very closely the expansion of the Christian state" (Taddesse Tamrat 1972: 156). Different from Protestant missionary activities, it was not a purely spiritual project aimed at producing new individual believers but was intrinsically linked to the display of political power and subjugation of enemies, as well as to building a Christian nation. The state and the church worked in tandem with the aim "of turning converts into nationals" (Messay Kebede 1999: 99). Local leaders in newly conquered areas were commanded to accept Christianity, making conversion a sign of submission. For example, when the leader of one of the Gurage sub-groups fighting Menelik's forces surrendered, it was said that "he was baptized on the spot with Menelik acting as his godfather" (Markakis 2011: 96).

Notions of exceptionalism became increasingly pronounced through the Christian kingdom's expansions, which strengthened both Amhara self-consciousness and the pejorative attitudes they harbored toward the opposite "other." While the Amhara viewed themselves as being part of a history that had produced the kingdom of Ethiopia – with elaborate political structures, a written language, an outstanding military force, and not the least with the Christian faith – other groups were dichotomized as being backward, primitive, barbarian, and heathen. This is something expressed in the Amharic saying – *Amhara yazzal inji atazzezim* ("The Amhara is to rule, and not to be ruled") (Levine 1974: 149). A story told by the British traveler and officer Chauncey H. Stigand visiting Addis Ababa in the early twentieth century further illustrates this. Narrating a conversation he had with an Amhara about his time in Zanzibar, the latter asked Stigand if he knew a certain famous Amhara who also had lived in Zanzibar. Stigand responded that Zanzibar was a large island, and that it was impossible to know everyone there. To underscore his point, Stigand rhetorically said that he had known a Somali who had lived in Addis Ababa and asked the Amhara if he knew him. The Amhara then answered condescendingly: "A Somali is only a dog; how should I know him?" (Stigand 1910: 317).

Again, I argue, it was the religious dimension that remained particularly important in such processes of "othering." A relevant case in point is the use of the word *Galla* – a laden pejorative expression commonly associated with the Oromo. The reality, however, is that this term often had a religious connotation, referring to being pagan, Muslim, and non-Christian in general. Shiferaw Bekele has, in a study of nineteenth century Ethiopia, produced convincing evidence for this. He demonstrates that both Oromo and other non-Christian groups were referred to as Galla, but when a member of such groups converted to Christianity he or she was called an Amhara (1990: 166).

Inclusion, Exclusion, and Islam

Even if Ethiopian exceptionalism and accompanying processes of "othering" clearly defined the status of non-Amhara groups, assimilation represented, at the same time, opportunities for inclusion and social mobility. Hierarchical structures in the Ethiopian context were at the outset rigid, yet not impervious. Social mobility and access to the elite *was* a possibility, even for the people from the south. Teshale Tibebu (1995) offers an interesting comparison between chauvinistic attitudes among the Amhara and European colonizers, convincingly arguing that while colonized Africans never could be included in a European universe and fully recognized, in Ethiopia, ascension to the Amhara cultural and political core was a possibility. The process of transforming people from other ethnicities into Amhara points to the plasticity of Amhara, and although the Solomonic myth was based on a primordialist, and thus exclusive, notion of "pureblood," it was also flexible enough to allow for intermarriages across existing boundaries. Negotiations of lineages were possible and gave individuals of "mixed origin" access to the elite and even to the throne.[13]

The questions of assimilation, integration, and nation building became increasingly complex as Ethiopia entered the twentieth century. Becoming increasingly heterogeneous demographically, it was difficult to maintain the earlier rigid religious policies, forcing the rulers to apply a "policy of guarded tolerance" (Hussein Ahmed 2006). Nation building in the form of "integration" also became more urgent, and a pivotal aspect of this was how Amhara gained a new meaning –

[13] For additional perspectives on this, see Clapham (1975).

becoming equated with being Ethiopian. What this entailed was a re-imagination of Amhara, from being tied to a particular geography and associated with a distinct people to something that constituted a national peoplehood. Becoming Amhara in this manner was about identifying oneself with the national ethos, being loyal to the emperor, and embodying a particular set of – redefined – cultural traits. Amhara thus became, according to Marzagora, "an ethnicity, but the true face of the nation, the bearer of national unity. Amharic and Geez are pan-national languages, able to accommodate and represent everyone. *Habasha* heritage is compared to a mother, welcoming in its protective arms all the small children living with her" (2015: 92).

Becoming Amhara/Ethiopian, therefore, represented something attractive. It was, as noted, the gateway for inclusion; it opened up possibilities for social mobility and promised access to resources. This was clearly seen in relation to Haile Selassie's modernization process, which included the emergence and expansion of educated and salaried officials, gradually replacing the feudal lords. These officials were appointed as administrators, bureaucrats, and teachers across the country and came to embody what has been called the "new Amhara" (Chernetsov 1996: 31). Many of them could originally hail from different ethnic groups; however, as they assimilated into the fold of the Ethiopian national narrative, they represented the expanding state and constituted a new cultural elite. While Amharization and the production of the new Amhara illustrate how the ethnic dimension of Amhara peoplehood could be negotiated, it still contained a religious dimension that continued to sustain the complexity inherent in Amhara as a category.

This is not to say that the process of Amharization was enforced equally in all cases; sometimes it took place in rather explicit ways, but often it happened in a subtler manner. There is, however, nothing unique about this form of nation building, as enforced assimilation of minorities has been a common practice across the world. The particular form of nation building in Ethiopia resembles what Anderson called "official nationalisms," which were the "means for combining natur-alization with retention of dynastic power ... or for stretching the short, tight, skin of the nation over the gigantic body of the empire" (1983: 86). From the perspective of the nation builders, it was the natural and necessary process for the creation of a manageable nation-state:

Those who share the Abyssinian identity belong, psychologically at least, to the dominant nationality, and live relatively secure in the embrace of a culture defended by the state. It is this culture that the mass in the periphery is expected to embrace, willingly or not, in order for the nation-state project to be completed. (Markakis 2011: 8)

The narrative of the ancient and sophisticated Ethiopian Christian Kingdom remained foundational for the imagination of the new nation, wherein the notion of Amhara as superior and the non-Amhara as inferior was very much alive. This was succinctly expressed by one of Emperor Haile Selassie's officials as "[i]t is for the Galla to become Amhara [not the other way around]; for the latter possess a written language, a superior religion and superior customs and mores" (Bahru Zewde 2002: 132). An official statement published in the Amharic newspaper *Berhane Selam* (Light of Peace) made this even clearer: "The plans of the Ethiopian Government are plain. It likes to have all the people of the country speak Amharic. With language unity there is also a unity of ideas" (cited in Marzagora 2015: 197).

While becoming fluent in Amharic, taking an Amhara name, and adopting "Amhara culture" were crucial factors for assimilation, for access to the elite, and for being recognized as belonging to the nation, Markakis correctly points out that "[a]cceptance of Christianity has been the cardinal criterion and crucial catalyst" for the successful integration to the Amhara peoplehood, for access to political positions and to a new cultural community – thus constituting the determining criterion for inclusion in the Christian nation (Markakis 1974: 32; cf. Markakis 2011: 95; Taddesse Tamrat 1972: 233). Conversion was far more than a change of creed; it was "a naturalization, an admittance to citizenship" (Messay Kebede 1999: 99) and, as such, the defining marker for integration, belonging, and acceptance (Teshale Tibebu 1995: 17). Among the Oromo in Wollega (western Ethiopia), for example, conversion to Christianity enabled the local elite to maintain its position, and four of Emperor Haile Selassie's descendants married Wollega Oromo (Clapham 1975: 77). Refusal to convert, on the other hand, made it impossible for non-Christians to be included in the elite, to ascend to power, and to be counted as "true members" of the nation. In other words, the fact that Amharization meant ultimately becoming a Christian clearly illustrates the limits of the plasticity of Amhara as a category.

Unsurprisingly, the group most reluctant to convert were the Muslims. For them, conversion was both the loss of religious and social identity and submission to a "foreign" force. As Christianity constituted the main component in Ethiopian nationalism, Muslims' refusal to convert implied "a rejection of assimilation into the dominant [Christian] culture of the core" (Clapham 1975: 77). This not only made the Muslims the religious other; they were consequently considered the antithesis to Ethiopianess – never granted full equality and barely recognized as citizens. The presence of the Muslims as the other also inadvertently contributed to maintaining religious plurality and to keeping the historic religious fault line intact. Religious plurality, however, was perceived as imbued with a certain danger, in turn making it necessary to underscore the Christian nature of Ethiopia – a notion that was articulated in the phrase of Ethiopia as "a Christian island in a sea of Muslims and pagans." While this notion became popularized by the end of the nineteenth century (Caulk 2002; Markakis 1989; Rubenson 2009), the idea of the Christian island can be traced back to Emperor Zar'a Yaqob (1434–1468), who declared that "Ethiopia [is surrounded by] pagans and Muslims in the east as well as in the west" (Taddesse Tamrat 1972: 231). The expression was continuously used in the twentieth century, seen, for example, in Emperor Haile Selassie's address to the US Congress in 1954, when he referred to Ethiopia as a Christian island as well as the "largest Christian state in the Middle East" (Markakis 1974: 338, 1989: 119).

The geography of this sea of Muslims and pagans was never specified, and one can only assume that it referred to non-Christian areas found beyond Ethiopia's borders. The dilemma, however, was that the expansion of the kingdom and the incorporation of a large non-Christian population in the late nineteenth century meant that a significant portion of Ethiopian Muslims were now found within Ethiopia's borders. The notion of the "Christian island" reflected the continued pejorative attitudes toward the Muslims and points, moreover, to the contradictory nature of the emerging modern Ethiopian state – and its ambiguous relationship to the Muslim community. While the state, at least theoretically, granted full citizenship and equal rights to all groups, religion continued to be a core component of Ethiopia's national narrative. A story that linked Ethiopianess to King Solomon and to the Ark of the Covenant left little room for any Muslims or other non-Christians. This was so entrenched in the

Christian Ethiopian psyche that it was basically inconceivable to recognize Muslims as part of the nation. They were there, but they did not really belong.

These perceptions have implications for how we understand Christian-Muslim relations in Ethiopia, which somewhat simplistically have been celebrated as peaceful and harmonious. There is, on the one hand, no doubt that interreligious interactions have been common on the grassroots level, and that relations between the two communities in general have been cordial. Christians and Muslims have shared the same localities, have spoken the same languages, and have cooperated in a practical manner. Boundaries are, at the same time, clearly demarcated, which in Ethiopia has a particular embodied aspect – revolving around the consumption of meat. Animals slaughtered by a Muslim are labeled "Muslim meat," and those slaughtered by a Christian are called "Christian meat," and neither a Muslim nor a Christian will eat the meat of the other. While the slaughtering ritual is nearly identical, there is the notion that the invocation of God (either as the Trinity or as Allah) consecrates the meat into a consumable substance, and animals slaughtered without invoking the name of God is seen as impure by both Muslims and Christians.[14] In addition, there are a number of stereotyped perceptions of the other's food as unhygienic and not properly prepared. Eating meat is therefore important as a profession of faith and as a marker of religious boundaries, which consequently means that the consumption of the other's meat is an expression of conversion.[15]

Peaceful relations, on the other hand, are not the same as religious parity, and important for Christian-Muslim relations in Ethiopia is that the two groups' positions and statuses have been clearly defined and demarcated, which has contributed to the production of a particular form of asymmetric relationship. As I have argued elsewhere, peaceful coexistence was in fact made possible because of the asymmetric nature of Christian-Muslim relations – defining the Muslims as inferior and as second-class citizens (Østebø 2008, 2012: 188). Such an asymmetric

---

[14] Both communities kill the animal by cutting the jugular vein and emptying its blood. The difference is that Muslims say *bismillah* (in the name of God), while the Christians say *b'sim ab, b'sim wold, b'sim menfes qidddus* (in the name of the Father, the Son, and the Holy Spirit).

[15] For more details on the role of meat in Ethiopia's interreligious relations, see Ficquet (2006).

relationship had implications for Muslims' identity: the Christian dominance and the positioning of Muslims as the peripheral other resulted in a certain degree of internalization of the dominant ideology's external ascriptions. My argument is that the totality and multidimensional nature of the Christian Kingdom's hegemony effectively placed the Muslims at such a subaltern level that clearly affected their confidence and deprived them of the needed capital to explicitly challenge the status quo. We do not know much of how this was practically played out, and the centrist perspective of Ethiopian historiography has left significant gaps in our knowledge of how Muslims negotiated this asymmetric relationship.

Withdrawal and Resistance

The way the Muslims negotiated their status in relation to the Christian hegemony can best be captured through what I call the *politics of withdrawal*. This entailed the withdrawal from broader public life and from engagement in affairs beyond their own constituencies, consequently producing Muslim communities that were secluded and self-protective of their limited space. Such sentiments can, according to Hussein Ahmad, be traced back to the early history of Islam in Ethiopia, when the Sufis "kept a low profile" in fear of the Christian rulers – who could suspect them of having political aspirations (2001: 36). Self-protective attitudes were moreover evident in nineteenth-century Wollo, where Emperor Yohannes IV's campaigns forcing Muslims to convert created a strategy of acquiescence and pretense (of adhering to Christianity) – expressed in the phrase "Christians by day and Muslim by night" (Hussein Ahmed 2001: 182). Strategies of self-seclusion consequently produced a community with "a very low sense of community involvement outside their own group" and to a situation where Muslims were seeing "themselves and are seen by others as a community apart" (Markakis 1974: 168). Hector Blackhurst has, with reference to the Muslim Arsi Oromo, argued that they "retreated behind a social and cultural barrier" with little or no contact with any of the Amhara (1980: 57). The politics of withdrawal consequently "deprived Islam of the potential for political action and ... enabled the Ethiopian government essentially to ignore its existence" (Markakis 1974: 69).

This politics of withdrawal should not, however, be understood in a way that excludes any form of Muslim political activism or acts of resistance. In fact, there are those who argue that Islam enhanced its relevance as an "ideology of resistance" in the course of Menelik's conquest. Different from a Gramscian counter-hegemonic discourse, this was expressed through conversion to Islam as a means for voicing opposition to the Christian dominance. This has been most explicitly argued by Mohammed Hassan (1992), but also Ulrich Braukämper (2002: 163) and Trimingham (1952: 101) have alluded to this as a major reason for the expansion of Islam starting in the late nineteenth century. Conversion as an act of resistance has also been noted elsewhere in Africa during colonial rule, and there is substantial evidence that Islam expanded during this period (Kaba 1974; Soares and Launay 1999). While conversion to Islam may have been an expression of resistance in certain parts of Ethiopia, thus contributing to the expansion of Islam, the lack of empirical proof from different localities can easily lead to an oversimplified understanding of the resistance thesis. In Bale, for example, the available evidence tells us that the expansion of Islam was interconnected with an ongoing and broader Islamization process that preceded the arrival of the Amhara.

Rather than applying the resistance thesis mainly in relation to conversion to Islam, it would be more fruitful to investigate the role of Islam in more explicit acts of resistance. Particularly important here is the short reign of Lij Iyasu (1913–1916) – a period that has been considered an anomaly and dubbed an "interlude" in Ethiopian political history (Bahru Zewde 1991: 120). Lij Iyasu was the grandson of Emperor Menelik and the son of *Ras* Mikael (*Ras* Ali) of Wollo, a convert from Islam to Christianity. Designated as the heir of the throne by Emperor Menelik, Lij Iyasu became the de facto ruler of Ethiopia when Menelik died in 1913. Young and inexperienced, his rapid reforms and disregard for the older generation of the nobility gradually placed him at odds with the dominating Shoan elite, forcing him to turn to both Wollo as well as to the Muslim communities in Hararge to find alternative alliances. This brought him into contact with the Ottomans, who courted him to secure Ethiopia's support in their war against the Allies during World War I. Lij Iyasu saw, on his side, the Ottomans as an important tool in defying the colonial powers' interest in the region (Smidt 2014: 200). While such actions exacerbated tensions between him and the Shoan nobility, Lij Iyasu's flirting with Islam was the straw that broke the camel's back. His issuing of grants for the construction of mosques and marrying daughters of prominent Muslim leaders led the Christian establishment to believe that he had left the true faith, that he was undermining Orthodox Christianity, and turning Ethiopia into an Islamic country. According to the clergy, the proof was that "[h]e claims that he eats flesh of cattle slain by Muslims in order to extend frontiers and to win their hearts" (Bahru Zewde 1991: 127). The church consequently excommunicated him in 1916, while the Shoan elite organized a military campaign, led by *Ras* Teferri (later Emperor Haile Selassie), to remove him from power. Faced with *Ras* Teferri's forces, Lij Iyasu subsequently fled to Jijiga, where he tried to organize an army (Erlich 1994a: 83f.; Touval 1963: 74).

The conflict around Lij Iyasu also produced an alliance between the Muslim Somalis and Oromo in the southeast in support of him. Encouraged by Lij Iyasu's attitudes toward Islam, and fearing that the nobility's and the church's actions against him would reinforce Christian dominance, the Muslims eagerly rallied around him. Particularly relevant for our story was the surfacing of a spirit of resistance among Muslim Oromo in Bale and Arsi. In Arsi, news of an impending conflict with the Christians enhanced the people's image of Lij Iyasu as their savior from Amhara domination and led in 1916 to the formation of a movement called Allahu Da'imu (Arabic; God forever) at Sakina, a shrine dedicated to Sheikh Hussein. A delegation of prominent elders traveled from Arsi to meet with Lij Iyasu in Hararge, where they received arms to be brought back. The movement also solicited volunteers to fight with him. Unrest soon erupted in Arsi, where the Muslim Arsi Oromo burned down Amhara villages and churches (Abbas H. Gnamo 1992: 252f.; Temam Haji 2002: 36). Armed resistance also spread to Raytu and Dello in Bale, where, as already discussed, the fighting in Raytu was led by Dhadhi Terre (Abbas H. Gnamo 1992: 253; Shiferaw Bekele 2014: 161). The unrest was quickly quelled by the state, and the rebellions had no lasting political impact. The Allahu Da'imu movement, as a rather spontaneous phenomenon never gained popular support and was consequently rather marginal.[16] Lij Iyasu was defeated on September 27, 1916, and kept in house arrest until he died in 1935.[17]

---

[16] This is the view of informants in the Arsi region, who moreover link the movement with Sheikh Nasrallah Abba Tayba, a native of Wollo (email correspondence with Hassan Muhammad Kawo, April 10, 2018).
[17] More recent research on Lij Iyasu has questioned the claim that he aimed to turn Ethiopia to Islam, and Bahru Zewde has argued that he rather sought to redress

It needs to be added that Ethiopian history also contains an instance of Muslims playing a relatively important role in political life. This occurred during the so-called *zamana masafent* (the era of the princes) from 1750 to 1855, a period characterized by political disintegration and regionalism. The lack of a strong center enabled an Oromo Muslim dynasty from Wollo – the Warra Sheh – to gain significant political power in the northern highlands. This represented a departure from earlier periods and created a peculiar situation where "the national elite was made up of two groups: Christian and Moslem" (Shiferaw Bekele 1990: 165). However, the intrinsic religious dimension of political power made this untenable in the long run. The Muslim rulers were unable to perform duties with a Christian character and fill central institutions related to the church and were moreover constantly resented by other competing Christian lords and by the Christian population in general.[18]

Conclusion

The role of religion in the production of Ethiopia's national narrative, the particular nationalistic attributes of Ethiopian Christianity, and how this underpinned the southern expansions are topics never fully recognized in Ethiopian historiography. A similar deficit is the lack of attention to Muslims in Ethiopia, how they remained unacknowledged as a part of the Ethiopian fabric, and to the continued relevance of a religious fault line. Rather than understanding religion as secondary to ethnic boundaries, or as ancillary to socioeconomic and political developments, my argument is that religion has been – and is – far more fundamental in the production of political narratives, distinctive communities, and experiences of belonging, and for perceptions of "self" and "other." Religion has moreover remained crucial as an integral part of antagonistic relations that recurrently became manifest in open conflict.

The notion of Ethiopia as Christian, the intimate relations between church and state, and the connections between Christianity, Amhara, and nationhood constituted a crucial part of the multidimensional

"injustices of the past, of making the Muslims feel at home in their own country" (Bahru Zewde 1991: 124). For new perspectives on Lij Iyasu, see Ficquet and Smidt (2014) and Marzagora (2015: 192f.).

[18] For more details on this period, see Shiferaw Bekele (1990).

hegemonic nature of Ethiopia as a polity and continued to inform politics during the twentieth century. At the same time, important changes took place. As Menelik's conquest and the demarcation of contemporary Ethiopia produced an increasingly heterogeneous state, the Amhara rulers' urgency in integrating the conquered groups into one single nation intensified. This process of nation building was not a voluntary endeavor but essentially a process of Amharization that entailed enforced deculturation and assimilation – and reaffirmed the state's hegemonic position.

Resentment toward the state, however, was simmering in many areas, being particularly strong among pastoralist Muslims in the southeastern lowlands. Memories of past atrocities and continued political suppression were crucial for the deepening of existing animosity. Religion constituted a powerful aspect of this animosity by the way the Muslims viewed the state as the Christian opposite, and by the way the negative treatment of the Muslims was perceived as religiously based. This led, reciprocally, to the strengthening of the religious dimension of peoplehood among Muslims from different localities, where shared religious affiliation forged a strong sense of unity, and which also became a powerful force for mobilizing action against what was viewed as a common enemy. Alliances between the different groups were made possible by the pastoralists' mobility and by landscapes that enabled movements. All this facilitated links between different communities, the flow of ideas, and access to material resources – particularly in the form of armed support from the Somali government. Eventually, it led to the surfacing of a wave of insurgencies across the southeast during the 1960s – the topic of the next chapter.

9 | *Trans-local Dynamics: The Bale Insurgency in the Context of the Horn*

While the Bale insurgency had its own causes and distinct trajectory, it remained intersected with broader currents of armed resistance emerging across the Horn in the postwar period. These currents cut through both time and space and remain crucial for understanding what happened in Bale. Moreover, situating the insurgency in Bale within a broader context and investigating the links between that insurgency and other movements will contribute to a clearer picture of armed resistance in the Horn, and possibly beyond.

The common trend for insurgency movements in Africa from the 1950s was their fight for self-government from colonial or white minority rule, which soon became the "normal expression of African demands" (Clapham 1998: 2). The Horn of Africa similarly saw a whole range of insurgencies surfacing in the 1960s, particularly along the eastern perimeters of the Ethiopian state – from Eritrea in the north, to the southeastern parts of Ogaden and Bale, as well as in the northeastern corner of Kenya. None of these were directed against foreign colonial powers but were largely about redrawing of postcolonial borders. Several could be characterized as explicitly irredentist, while others are not that easy to categorize. They were in many ways caused or affected by broader regional developments, yet triggered by more local factors – as pointed out by Whittaker in her discussion of the Kenyan *shifta* war (2015: 17). This speaks directly to Paul Williams's suggestions, who by using Arjun Appadurai's notion of *scapes*, argues for the need to duly consider the interconnectedness of global, national, regional, and local "warscapes" when trying to understand African insurgencies (Williams 2016: 45f.). Some of these connections were rather explicit, while others were subtle.

The fact that many of the insurgencies in the Horn were informal and decentered means that they have largely escaped the attention of observers and analysts. Richard Reid's extensive study of conflicts in the

Horn of Africa since 1800 is therefore a valuable contribution. Pointing to a "mosaic of fault lines and frontier zones" in the Horn of Africa, he argues that such zones should not be understood as static in any way but rather as "intertwined and overlapping," and as "flexible and fluid" (2011: 13). Reid also demonstrates how both zones and conflicts have been important in shaping ethnic identities, while also recognizing that these identities "indeed have deep root[s] and defined character-istics" (2011: 13). However, while the Horn undoubtedly contains a number of fault lines and frontier zones, Reid arguably downplays those produced in relation to the dominant Ethiopian state. To say that ethnic groups in response to this polity have merely "sharpened their own ethnic edges" is clearly an understatement (2011: 13, 23). This deficit is evident in his typology of frontier zones, which fails to capture the frontier zone that materializes itself through the asymmetrical encounters between a structured and militarized state and decentra-lized, unstructured, and noncombatant actors.[1]

Although Reid is concerned "with the economic, cultural, and ethnic dimensions of war" and moreover argues that conflicts are "more rooted in the past than might be assumed" (Reid 2011: 19), attention to religion is glaringly absent in his analyses. My discussion of the role of Christianity as part of the national narrative and as important for the formation of Amhara exceptionalism and expansionism in the previous chapter clearly demonstrates the importance of religion. This chapter furthers this discussion by elucidating how the people in the southeast responded to the expansion of the Ethiopian state, arguing that expan-sion heightened the religious dimension. While I believe that acknowl-edging the religious dimension is imperative if we want to understand the conflictual landscapes in the Horn, I also argue for an approach that treats religion as integrated with other dynamics and recognizes reli-gion as one of several dimensions of conflict.

Pastoralist Insurgents and the Highland-Lowland Dichotomy

Common for most insurgencies surfacing in the Horn during the 1960s was that they were fought by pastoralists and that the main theater of

---

[1] The first zone is said to exist between states, the second relates to ethnic or national boundaries (which are highly fluid), and the third is identified as physical frontiers that also contributes to the construction of the two former ones (Reid 2011: 22).

operations was in the lowland areas. This was the case for the early Eritrean uprising launched by Idris Muhammad Awate and the subsequent struggle of the Eritrean Liberation Front (ELF), the insurgency across the Ethiopian Ogaden, and the armed struggle in northeastern Kenya. The role of pastoralists in insurgency movements has generated a rather stereotypical picture of African pastoralists as "warlike and aggressive" (Fukui and Turton 1979), and although this image has been disproved as too simplistic, one could ask whether it is possible to argue for the existence of a particular culture of warfare among pastoralists, for example, among the Somalis, as some have suggested (Prunier 1997: 384). Others have suggested that the lack of continued political stability and the absence of monopolies of violence in pastoral areas were important factors contributing to such a culture (van Walraven and Abbink 2003: 9). Still others have argued that a "cultural fit" existed between pastoralism and warfare, wherein mobility, physical endurance produced by environmental constraints, and warrior socialization are emphasized (Baxter 1977). Among the Arsi Oromo, it is said that a newborn girl would be fed milk, while a male baby would only be given water. The reason was to train the boy – as a future warrior – to endure hardship.

I believe, however, that we should be very careful not to overemphasize such cultural factors in ways that unduly essentialize the culture of pastoralists as inherently violent. I would instead argue for an approach that investigates the issues and aspects that could potentially underpin, lead up to, and trigger conflict in specific localities. Such an approach, however, should not isolate sociopolitical and cultural dynamics as abstract phenomena but analyze them as integrated with the material environment of the given locality, that is, to recognize the relevance of landscapes and topographies. Ana Maria Alonso has pointed to the role of material space in the demarcation of boundaries, and in her discussion of space in relation to ethnicity, she demonstrates how ethnicity is used to mark certain places. This entails a process whereby "ethnic differentiation can be construed according to location within national territory" – meaning that the hegemon group of the nation locates the subordinated at the geographical periphery (Alonso 1994: 394, 395). I believe that such processes are far more complex and argue for a perspective that acknowledges how space *in itself* also dialectically can produce such positionalities and inequalities, and which in relation to the state serves as the basis for inclusion and exclusion of certain groups.

Investigating this in the context of the Horn brings us back to the highland-lowland dichotomy, which succinctly has been labeled as one of Ethiopia's last frontiers (Markakis 2011: 12f.).[2] The complex relationship between the Amhara and *Islaama* in Bale – and in the broader southeast – had a distinct spatial dimension, wherein the highlands and lowlands as opposite geographies "reinforced notions of ethnic uniqueness and difference" (Reid 2011: 10). Such an imagination reflected the selective and hegemonic tradition underpinning the nation and was mirrored in actual environmental, climatic, and topographical particularities. The highland Amhara viewed the lowlands as the very definition of the periphery, in fact, representing nothing short of a geographical "otherness." As agriculturalists, they looked upon these areas with distain as a distinct ecological and cultural zone – hot and arid, inhabitable, ridden with disease, and unstable. With agriculture as the model for an advanced form of living, the Somali and Oromo as pastoralists were imagined as backward, primitive, and lazy. These attitudes toward the lowlanders were further entrenched by the Amhara self-image of belonging to a superior civilization, and where Christianity served as "the highlanders' ideological shield in the perennial confrontation with the Muslim lowlands" (Markakis 1987: 12). Images of the lowlands often took on a nearly mythical character, generating notions of hostile territories, as dominated by lawlessness, and as home to the "Muslim danger." The lowland periphery was thus, from the perspective of the center, not only located at a geographical distance from the center but also peripheral in terms of power, economy, and culture. This made center-periphery relations constituted by distinct power structures, by different socioeconomic systems and modes of production, by a particular political economy, by evaluative perceptions, and by geography. Lowland peripheries were produced by "their level of incorporation into the coercive and economic structures of government, and their degree of association with the legitimizing myths of nationhood" (Clapham 2002: 11).

The lowlands, at the same time, were useful reservoirs for the violent extraction of resources and became, as seen in previous chapters, subject to state-led violent pillaging campaigns. This left people

---

[2] The concept of *frontier* was, as noted, used earlier by Alessandro Triulzi (1994), who without considering the physical and symbolic importance of the highland-lowland dichotomy reduced it to an "Amhara-Oromo dispute."

desolate, and the accumulation of the lowlands' resources at the "center" further exacerbated their disadvantage (Abbink 2002: 157). The violence and plundering also produced very strong senses of fear, subjection, and powerlessness among the pastoralist population. Such sentiments would be traced back to the time of Menelik's conquest and have become part of the people's collective memory: "the Amhara looted and plundered us every time they came here. They would come and stay for a month, and steal our cattle. They knew all the wealth was here, and they came and took it."[3] Such traumatic experiences were undoubtedly crucial for the pastoralist insurgencies as responses to the state's violence against pastoralist communities. This was the case both in Bale and in the southeast more broadly and dovetails with Williams's comments on contemporary insurgencies in Africa, where he notes that while states might have limited influence over "peripheral" pastoralist communities, the state was "a force to be reckoned with when it came to wielding instruments of violence" (Williams 2016: 55).

The physical environment also has direct relevance to the type of insurgency (Clapham 1998: 12), and it is obvious that the lowland landscape was especially conducive for armed struggle. While the lowlanders were subject to suppressive policies, the lowland "frontier" served, at the same time, as a valve for escaping the state's tentacles and for providing opportunities to interact with other actors with similar goals (Oba 2013: 6). As the state largely ignored the lowlands, these areas received very little in terms of government investment. A limited state presence also meant that the pastoralists remained in many ways detached from the government. Pastoralists' marginal position, the facts that they functioned outside the state's framework and that the pastoralist lifestyle was often incompatible with the structures of the state have been suggested as crucial for understanding African pastoralists' involvement in armed struggle in both colonial and postcolonial periods (Bevan 2007: 2).

In contrast to the highlands, where people, as noted, became more tied to the land, the arid, vast, and boundless lowlands produced a lifestyle that allowed for constant movement. I have already discussed how embodiment entails location, in the sense that humans cannot be in more than one place at the time. Location does not mean, however, being static. People's constant movements across space alter their positioning, and such repositioning brings them into contact with

---

[3] Interview, Semir Halkano, Raytu, June 12, 2018.

other places, provides them with new experiences, and affects their perception of place itself. Movement can be permanent, temporal, or, as in this case, recurrent in the form of the pastoralists' constant migrations. Movements result in the externalization of one's primary place, in the sense of redefining and reconstructing space in light of memories and new experiences, and the pastoralists' mobile lifestyle clearly affected their scale of landscapes. Their movements were about constant shifting of locations along numerous paths, thus creating a line of continuum wherein "every position in the total network of trails or life-lines is itself an emplacement" (Ingold 2000: 145). While the mobility among the pastoralist insurgents certainly was conducive for their guerrilla-style tactics, it is also possible to suggest that the Bale insurgency to a certain degree was an extension of a pastoralist lifestyle, and their reliance on livestock as a means of survival meant that they were not tied to any particular place:

The environment mattered and our people were clever; they knew how to live off the nature. We knew to get food from the surroundings. Also, we were not depending on food that was tied to land. Our food – livestock – was moving with us. This doesn't necessarily mean that we as fighters brought the livestock with us, but we could get support from the people wherever we moved. We were already accustomed to a nomad lifestyle, and that helped us in the fighting.[4]

Existing at the "margin" of the state, the lowland pastoralists moved across spaces intimately familiar and oriented themselves to centers that provided ideological inspiration and material support outside the framework of the state. As one informant claimed: "there were more Amhara in the highlands, and they controlled the people. Here, we were free to move – we could move all the way to Mogadishu if we wanted."[5] Thus accustomed to crossing boundaries, the pastoralists' migratory patterns served as an important means for the spread of ideas and news and propaganda, particularly from Somalia's easily crossed international border, reaching the scattered pastoralist communities (Touval 1963: 134).

Muslim Unity and Ethno-Nationalism in the Horn

In addition to being pastoralists, another feature common to the insurgencies in the southeast was that all those involved were Muslims.

[4] Interview, Jowar Kadir, Sewena, June 13, 2018.
[5] Interview, Jowar Kadir, Sewena, June 13, 2018.

Facing a state with an obvious Christian underpinning, wherein religious othering was a part of its policy, clearly accentuated the religious dimension and strengthened the insurgents' Muslim identity. The hegemonic nature of the state's religious ideology also influenced the insurgents by producing the "questions to be asked and the issues to be debated" (Glassman 1995: 17). I believe Jonathon Glassman goes too far, though, when arguing that rebellious ideologies are "usually expressed in the language marked by the hegemonic ideas" (1995: 19). I will in the following point to the existence of independent agency and creativity, and to how trans-local interactions contributed to augment the repertoire of ideas.

The intertwined nature of religion and ethnicity in the southeast meant that while Harari, Somali, and Oromo saw themselves as distinct from one another, as different peoples, the fact that they all adhered to Islam mitigated existing boundaries and laid the ground for a sense of unity.[6] The religious dimension was also augmented by how they viewed the Amhara and the European colonizers through a religious lens. In addition to being illegitimate invading forces, they were also depicted in religious terms, as *Christian* powers and as opposed to the Harari, Oromo, and Somali Islamic identity (Hersi 1977: 271; Touval 1963: 62). This illustrates, as discussed in Chapter 1, how peoplehood generates segmentary forms of belonging and how the religious dimension of peoplehood transcends more immediate and local boundaries. Critical here is how this potentially enables the production of a broader sense of identity and – situational – alliances against a common enemy. It also demonstrates how the religious and the ethnic dimensions can be negotiated in relation to each other – which in this case allowed for a stronger emphasis on the former. While interactions between peoples had a long history in the southeast – as embodied in contacts along well-traversed paths across landscapes of the southeast – improved means of communication in the course of the twentieth century facilitated increased trans-local contacts, which in turn became important for furthering solidarity.

The role of Islam as a dimension of resistance in the southeast was already noticeable in the conflict surrounding Sayyid Muhammad

---

[6] Islam's role as a unifying factor has been important in balancing the centrifugal potential of clannism among Somalis and constitutes something that "permeates all aspect of their [Somali] lives" (Lewis 1958: 358).

Abdile Hassan, dubbed by the British as the "Mad Mullah."[7] He appeared in the early twentieth century at a time when Ethiopia and the European colonial powers had effectively divided the southeastern parts of the Horn among themselves; the British had established its Somaliland Protectorate in 1887, the French had taken control over Djibouti in 1888, the Italians occupied southern Somalia during the 1890s, while Ethiopia had conquered the Ogaden. Sayyid Muhammad was initially an Islamic teacher and came early on to harbor a distinct religious zeal. This was gradually developed during his repeated pilgrimages to Mecca, where he became inspired by Muhammad Salih, the founder of the Sufi order Sahiliyyah. Starting to propagate the Sahiliyyah teaching in the British protectorate of Somaliland, he soon declared himself *Mahdi*,[8] labeled his enemies infidels, and proclaimed a jihad against the colonizers.[9] His first target was Ethiopia; in March 1900, he launched a massive attack on the Ethiopian garrison in Jijiga. The attack ended with a disastrous defeat for Sayyid Muhammad, who then chose to focus on the British protectorate instead. Avoiding engaging the British directly, he raided other Somali clans as well as Sufi orders (Ahmediyya and Qadiriyyah) that refused to acknowledge his authority. He eventually created so much instability that the British decided to take action against him. Coordinating with Ethiopian forces, the British campaign lasted from 1900 to 1904. After becoming significantly weakened, Sayyid Muhammad had no choice but to strike an agreement with the British. The Europeans granted him a defined territory within the Italian colony, in return for his promise to end his incursions. In 1908, however, Sayyid Muhammad again started attacking neighboring clans. The British decided not to intervene, retreated to the coast, and left the interior in a state of violent anarchy. It was not until fighting gradually reached the coast that the British responded. World War I, however, hampered their reactions; but as soon as the war ended, they managed to drive him out of the protectorate. Sayyid

---

[7] For an extensive discussion of Sayyid Muhammad Abdile Hassan, see Samatar (1982) and Jardine (1923).
[8] The *Madhi* in Islam is understood to be an eschatological "Messianic" figure expected to appear before the day of judgment.
[9] He was denounced, however, by Muhammed Salih in 1909 because of his violent acts (Touval 1963: 56).

Muhammad fled into Ethiopia, where he died of influenza in Imi (in the Ogaden) in 1920.

While Sayyid Muhammad appeared as a religious leader who used an explicit religious language during the struggle, his goal was, at the same time, independence from foreign rule. It would be mistaken, however, to see the religious dimension as something separate from his anti-colonial sentiment and similarly difficult to construe religion as an isolated variable in the production of political action. To be a Somali was equated with being Muslim, and being a non-Muslim Somali was simply unthinkable. Islam was thus an obvious reference expressing nationalist/ethnic sentiments. In other words, the religious and natio-nalistic/ethnic dimensions of peoplehood overlapped and were mutually reinforcing – in turn cementing boundaries vis-à-vis the racially, ethnically, and religiously different other.

Developments in Somalia continued to be important for anti-Ethiopian sentiments across the southeast throughout the twentieth century, as the Somalis portrayed themselves as liberators of the var-ious Muslim groups. Connections to Somalia came to play an increas-ingly important role in the postwar period, where a nascent Somali nationalist movement provided both symbolic and material support for movements of resistance in the broader southeastern parts of Ethiopia. It would be wrong, however, to reduce the conflictual landscape to a product of Somali propaganda and aggressive expansionism. Rather, we need to pay due attention to the motives and agendas of a wide spectrum of actors across the region and carefully analyze the complex nature of trans-local interactions, how broader impetuses for resistance were appropriated locally, and how these were negotiated in relation to local grievances. All these intersected processes created composite land-scapes where ideas traveled along multiple paths, and where impetuses could be both complementary and contradictory.

Somali nationalism emerged in direct opposition to the European colonial powers' presence and partition of Somalia.[10] The first modern Somali nationalist movement emerged in the 1920s in the British Protectorate as the Somali Islamic Association, and in the years that followed, several small nationalist clubs appeared in the north (Touval

---

[10] This fits with Crummey's (1986c: 15) argument that it was not until the late 1940s that popular rebellions displaying nationalist ideologies surfaced in Africa.

1963: 65). It was not until after World War II, however, that Somali nationalism started to gain traction. As in other parts of Africa, the war itself stimulated heightened awareness of the colonial situation, and the thousands of Somalis who served as soldiers were influenced by emerging nationalist currents.

The most prominent organization was the Somali Youth Club (SYC), established in Mogadishu on May 5, 1943 – changing its name to the Somali Youth League (SYL) on April 1, 1947 (Pankhurst 1951: 175). SYL was, as the name indicates, dominated by youth who viewed themselves as different from "reactionary elders who did not understand modern requirements" (Carmichael 2001: 194). Its leaders were the few Somalis who had received education beyond the elementary level, and its members were recruited from urban areas, particularly Mogadishu, where a young and entrepreneurial middle class had emerged (Barnes 2007: 280; Lewis 2002: 113; Markakis 1987: 52). It developed relatively elaborate structures and came in this way to represent something new within Somali society. With an emphasis on education, SYL sought to teach "the youth in modern ideas and civilization by schools and cultural circles" (Pankhurst 1951: 176). While "anti-imperialist" rhetoric was common among the Somali nationalists, they did not, as was common in other parts of Africa, espouse much affinity for socialist or Marxist ideas. Only a few figures and parties could be characterized as having a leftist leaning and attempting to establish connections with the Soviet Union and China. SYL itself had a certain pro-Western bias, but this never played a central part in its program (Touval 1963: 91, 99). While SYL explicitly embraced modernity – and sought to transcend restrictive Somali traditional customs – it was, at the same time, actively referring to Islam as a source of inspiration.

Islam remained an important and an integral part of all the emerging nationalist currents in Somalia, and all the key figures within SYL descended from prominent leaders of Somalia's Sufi orders (Carmichael 2001: 197). The commitment to Islam was made explicit in the SYL constitution, which stated its aim to "found a government based on Islamic principles, with all laws and judgements being based in the religion" (Carmichael 2001: 199). However, the fact that SYL, after coming to power, stripped the *qadi* courts (Islamic courts) of criminal jurisdiction demonstrates how it sought to reduce the role of religion and make it subject to a secular political framework (Markakis

1987: 87). SYL also viewed Islam as integral to its nationalist program, seen by how it made references to earlier instances of resistance, presenting Sayyid Muhammad Abdile Hassan as an important archetype for anti-colonial activism (Lewis 2002: 114). It also referred to the sixteenth-century war between the Christian kingdom and the sultanates in the east and celebrated Ahmed Gragn as the champion for Muslim rights against the oppressive Christian state (Greenfield 1965: 290; Rahji Abdella 1994: 37).

Particularly important were SYL's emphasis on Somali unity, and its efforts to instill new political attitudes among the Somalis. It viewed itself as a political party transcending clan divisions and displaying a pan-Somali ideology. This ideology was expressed through the notion of "Greater Somalia," which proved to have enduring relevance even up to the present. Originally launched by the British Foreign Secretary Ernest Bevin during the period of the British Military Administration (1941–1949), the Greater Somalia idea entailed the unification of all Somalis in the Horn – irrespective of international boundaries – under a future independent Somalia. The SYL readily adopted this idea, and together with other Somali parties, it argued that Somalis across the Horn had been subject to colonization by both European powers and Ethiopia, and that reunification was a legitimate goal. Ethiopia was vehemently opposed to this, and Emperor Menelik had in 1891 created his own idea of a "Greater Ethiopia," claiming that his territories "extended to Khartoum and Lake Victoria in the west, and to the sea in the east and southeast" (Touval 1963: 141). Emperor Haile Selassie later reiterated this claim in 1945, as did Foreign Minister Aklilu Habte-Wold in 1947 (Pankhurst 1951: 217, 221). The Western powers in charge of Somalia's future immediately after World War II were similarly opposed to the idea of Greater Somalia but struggled to agree on what to do with Somalia. SYL obviously wanted independence instantly, but when the Four Power Commission of Investigation for the Former Italian Colonies (Britain, France, the United States, and the Soviet Union) decided to place Somalia under Italian trusteeship in 1948, that door was effectively closed. It was only the promise of Somali independence within a ten-year period that enabled SYL to accept the Four Power Commission's decision.

Ethno-nationalism in Somalia was also stimulated by the broader anti-colonial movement traveling across the Global South, and the young nationalists heard about Indonesia, Burma, India, and

Pakistan gaining independence (Touval 1963). More important, however, were impulses stemming from the Arab world. Haggai Erlich (2007: 80f.) has claimed that Islamic reformism in the form of Salafism arriving from Saudi Arabia was directly connected to the political and ethno-national currents that impacted the Horn during the twentieth century, arguing that the objective of the Salafi movement was the establishment of an Islamic political order in Ethiopia's southeast. I believe that this is far too simplistic. It is true that Salafism made inroads from the 1930s, facilitated, somewhat ironically, by the Italians. As part of their colonial divide-and-rule policy favoring the Muslims, the Italians provided Ethiopians going on *hajj* (pilgrimage to Mecca) with means of transportation to Saudi Arabia and subsidized their travels. Exposed to Salafism while in Saudi Arabia, some of these pilgrims started to disseminate the new ideas when they returned. Important figures here were Hajji Hassan Ibrahim and Hajji Umar Muhammed Abd al-Rahman, who were instrumental in the founding of the Jamiyya School in Harar in 1933 (Erlich 2007: 26, 81f.). There was, however, considerable resistance to the new ideas, and Salafism never managed to gain widespread support among the Hararis. There are no indications that the Salafis dominated the nationalist movement in Harar, and no evidence that they even tried to influence it. Neither was the idea of establishing an Islamic state based on *shari'a* prominent in the Harari opposition to the state (Rahji Abdella 1994: 42).

Rather than Salafism, the insurgencies across the southeast were influenced more by secular Arab nationalism and pan-Arabism stemming from Egypt during the time of Gamal Abdel Nasser. The Egyptians had historically played an active role in the Horn, yet the postwar period saw more direct Egyptian involvement in Somalia. This was embodied in religious teachers touring Somalia and offering youth scholarships to study in Cairo, and teachings channeled through Radio Cairo became an effective propaganda tool for Egypt (Lewis 1958: 360f., 2002: 141; Tibebe Eshete 1991: 23). Nasser, who rose to power in 1952, followed a policy of encouraging anti-colonial sentiments in Africa in general, and Egypt's references to European imperialism – as well as Ethiopian imperialism – resonated well with the Somali nationalists. Somali support for Egypt was evidenced by the Somali nationalists' position during the Suez crisis in 1957 and strong pro-Egyptian attitudes were evident until the early 1960s (Lewis 1958: 359f.; Morone 2017).

While Nasser's Africa policy was based on the notion of pan-Arabism, shared religious affiliation between Egypt and the Muslims in southeastern Ethiopia was a contributing factor for the Somali sympathy toward Egypt. The Egyptian regime also deliberately referred to the value of Muslim solidarity and depicted the colonizing powers, especially Ethiopia, as Christian powers suppressing Muslim rights (Lewis 1958: 360). It is important to underscore here that Islam as a source of inspiration along with "secular" ideologies, such as Nasser's pan-Arabism were appropriated in rather idiosyncratic ways. The Somali urban intelligentsia was more ready to differentiate between the two, but this was not always the case as the ideas traveled into the rural areas. Gamel Abdel Nasser consequently became both the liberator from colonial rule and the guarantor for Muslim rights.

Egypt's attitudes toward Ethiopia were of a mixed character.[11] Some Egyptians criticized Ethiopia for its unfair treatment of its Muslim population. Others hailed Ethiopia for its protection of the Prophet's followers during the Axumite Hijra, and who, with reference to the Egyptian Coptic Church and the Ethiopian Orthodox Church as well as the Nile, underscored Egypt's close historical ties with Ethiopia. These praised Ethiopia for its resistance against the Italian colonizers, and the period leading up to World War II saw a strengthening of pro-Ethiopian sentiments in Egypt. Nationalist and anti-fascist Egyptians also sought to provide active support for Ethiopia, seen for example by the Society of Young Muslims (Jamiyyat al-Subban al-Muslimin) establishing a Committee for the Defense of Ethiopia (Erlich 2002: 105). There are some indications of contacts between Ethiopian Muslims and Islamist movements (see "SYL in Ethiopia" later in this chapter), but such ideas had little impact:

The Muslim Brotherhood was not strong at that time, and few became influenced by them. There was a thinking among the Muslim Brotherhood to support the Muslims in Ethiopia – who they saw as suppressed, but the Muslim Brotherhood was not dominant among the Ethiopians in Somalia. The strongest political idea at that time was Nasserism.[12]

The popularity of Nasser was evident by the fact that pictures of him were commonly found in Ethiopian Muslim homes.[13] Muslim

---

[11] See Abir (1980) for more details on Ethiopian-Egyptian relations.
[12] Interview, Feisal Ali, Addis Ababa, July 10, 2011.
[13] Interview, Getnet Waqayyo, Addis Ababa, August 4, 2011.

enthusiasm for Nasser was moreover demonstrated when more than 100,000 Muslims greeted him at Addis Ababa airport when he came to participate in the inauguration of the Organization of Africa Unity (OAU) in 1963 (Erlich 1994b: 134; Hussein Ahmed 1994). Such sentiments rejuvenated the ancient Ethiopian fear of "foreign Islam," and although Nasser sought to give an impression of having cordial relations with Ethiopia, his pan-Arab and anti-colonial rhetoric about the plight of imperialism, which also included Ethiopian imperialism, caused alarm from the side of the Ethiopian government (Touval 1963: 82). Emperor Haile Selassie claimed that Nasser was "trying to stir up the large Muslim minority [in Ethiopia] with the aim of dismembering this Christian kingdom,"[14] causing him to curtail Ethiopian Muslims' contact with Egypt. This worked to some degree; yet, it is estimated that around 100 Ethiopian Muslims were receiving religious education at the al-Azhar University during the 1960s (Mohammed Ali 2005: 14).

Baathist ideas also made some inroads into the Horn during the 1960s and 1970s, but few details about this are known (Hagmann and Khalif 2008: 40). Such influence came mainly through Somalis studying in the Arab world and, to a lesser degree, through Ethiopians enrolled in universities in the Middle East. It is unclear how many they were, but I have seen records that show that Ethiopian student associations existed in Iraq, Syria, and Lebanon. While many of the students left Ethiopia legally, some traveled illegally via Somalia. These were individuals involved in different forms of anti-government activities, and their transit in Somalia obviously impacted the political discourse there. Sheikh Hussein Sura, as mentioned in Chapter 5, was instrumental in connecting with the Arabs, and by the end of the 1960s, Syrian Baathists offered military training both within Somalia and in Syria. The Palestine Liberation Organization (PLO) offered similar training, and some insurgents were even sent to North Korea. Those traveling to North Korea were both Oromo and Somalis; going in groups of 50 or 100, they often stayed for six months, receiving both military and political training.[15] Many of them discovered with surprise that the North Korean Marxists had little tolerance for their Muslim identity: "They wouldn't let us fast or pray there: 'Why do

---

[14] The *Daily Telegraph,* February 16, 1957 – cited by Erlich (1994b: 134).
[15] Interview, Hajji Semir Idris, Addis Ababa, August 3, 2011.

you need to fast and pray', they asked. But we got the permission to pray in secrecy."[16] My conversations with this informant were quite amusing – particularly when he started singing songs praising Kim Il-Sung – in Korean.

SYL in Ethiopia

The nationalist sentiments of SYL were already in the 1940s reaching the broader southeastern parts of Ethiopia, becoming a source of inspiration for both Somalis and non-Somalis voicing their resistance to Ethiopian rule. The political situation in this part of the country was, at the time, precarious. According to the Anglo-Ethiopian Agreements of 1942 and 1944, Ogaden and the "Reserved Areas" of Haud (an area adjacent to British Somaliland) were placed under British Military Administration and not returned to Ethiopia before 1948 and 1954, respectively (Markakis 1974: 368). While under British control, the undecided fate of these areas brought them to the center of SYL's attention, which saw this as an opportunity to realize its goal of a "Greater Somalia." It also created favorable conditions for the expansion of SYL into Ethiopia, where it quickly managed to recruit thousands of followers (Barnes 2007). In this process, SYL made explicit references to Islam as a unifying force of solidarity, seen, for example, by SYL posters placed on government offices in Dirre Dawa calling for the unification of all Muslims against their enemies (Barnes 2007: 286). While SYL and other nationalist groups readily merged their aspirations on this basis, it would be inaccurate to say that the non-Somali groups subsumed their own aspirations under the Somali objectives. While the Somali nationalist sentiment was an important source of inspiration, the deep-seated animosity toward Ethiopia harbored by other groups in the southeast was real enough, and it predated the arrival of SYL.

By 1947, SYL had established offices in Somaliland, Djibouti, Ogaden, and Kenya, and it managed also to extend its presence beyond Somali areas in Ethiopia, reportedly creating 172 branches in Arsi, Hararge, and Bale (Carmichael 2001: 201; Markakis 1987: 174; Rahji Abdella 1994: 32; Turton 1972: 136). A key figure here was Makhtal Tahir, briefly mentioned in Chapter 4, from the Isa sub-clan of

[16] Interview, Hafiz Hassan, Addis Ababa, June 16, 2011.

the Ogaden, who had a reputation of getting into trouble with both Ethiopian and European colonial authorities. He had been a member of the local Ethiopian administration in Ogaden before the Italian invasion and fought on the Ethiopian side against the Italians. He initially vehemently opposed the British presence in the Ogaden and turned similarly resistant to the plans of restoring Ethiopian rule in the region (Barnes 2007: 284f.; Carmichael 2001: 218; Markakis 1983: 301; Rahji Abdella 1994: 40). While part of Makhtal Tahir's growing anti-Ethiopian attitudes were based on his perception of not being sufficiently rewarded for his loyalty to the emperor during the Italian occupation, an important part of his grievances concerned religion. He accused the Ethiopian state of harboring ethnic and religious prejudices, claiming that these were especially directed against Muslims in general and Somalis in particular. In a written statement from 1948, Makhtal Tahir pointed to how the Amhara in the southeast were given preferential treatment at the expense of Somalis, how the jurisdiction of the *qadi* courts was not respected, and how Christian missionaries were allowed to proselytize among the Arsi Oromo (Carmichael 2001: 214f.). Makhtal Tahir, however, would soon temporarily disappear from the scene. In 1949, he was sentenced to death in Jijiga, a sentence that was changed to life in prison due to appeals by local elders. He then languished in the infamous Alem Baqegn (Farewell to the World) prison in Addis Ababa until 1958 and was barred from returning to Ogaden until 1962 (Markakis 1983: 301).

Makhtal Tahir managed, before he was removed, to open a SYL office in Harar in 1946. The Harari themselves had up to this point not shown much interest in SYL's activities and had after the Italian period established their own group called Jamiyya al-Wataniyya (The Nationalist Society, or the Society for Harari Freedom; popularly referred to as Watani) in the mid-1940s.[17] This group had no secessionist program and was instead focused on strengthening Harar's self-administration and on restoring the rights of Muslim Harari according

---

[17] The organization was sometimes referred to as Jamiyya Hurriyya al-Harariyya, and Erlich (2007: 82) uses the name al-Jamiyya al-Wataniyya al-Islamiyya (the National Islamic Association). An organization with the same name had been formed in Mogadishu in the early 1940s, but there are no indications of any links between the two (Carmichael 2001: 196).

to the treaty made with Menelik in the late nineteenth century (Rahji Abdella 1994: 44).[18] However, when the SYL office was established in Harar, many Harari joined the movement. SYL's position was further boosted through its merger with *Watani* in 1947; a merger that was centered on notions of shared religion as a unifying factor and around the historical relations between the Harari and the Somalis. The Harari also believed that the Somalis, with the support of the British, would help them in their quest for increased self-administration (Rahji Abdella 1994: 40f.).[19] The Harari did not use the name SYL but referred to it as the Kulub-Hanalatto movement. The word *kulub* became, as noted, the label for anti-government resistance in postwar Ethiopia in general and for the Bale insurgency in particular, while *hanalatto* was a Somali slogan literally meaning "long live," used in demonstrations against the political authorities (Rahji Abdella 1994: 2).

The Harari gradually developed more secessionist attitudes, seeking unification with a Greater Somalia. This became apparent by the inclusion of thirteen Harari in the delegation sent from Ethiopia to meet with the Four Power Commission in Mogadishu in 1948, where they argued for the unification of Harar with Somalia (Barnes 2007: 286; Rahji Abdella 1994: 46f.). The commission dismissed their call. Meanwhile in Ethiopia, the government ransacked SYL's offices in Harar, conducted mass arrests, and confiscated individual and community property. The latter included the Jamiyya School established in 1933, which was converted into a government-run school (Carmichael 2001: 223). The majority of the arrested were soon released, yet eighty-one of the main prominent leaders remained imprisoned. Because of the situation in Harar, the Harari delegation in Mogadishu opted not to return home and embarked instead on a tour of the Middle East – which is a further testimony of how local nationalist aspirations intersected with broader discourses. First, they traveled to Saudi Arabia where they met with the minister of foreign affairs (and later king)

---

[18] The quest for self-determination dates back to the year 1887 when Emperor Menelik conquered the town. Through an agreement with the town's dignitaries, Harar was granted a certain degree of autonomy. However, the gradual expansion of Amhara provincial rule led to a political and cultural alienation of the local population – in turn enhancing the enmity toward the new rulers (Caulk 1973; Rahji Abdella 1994: 4f.).

[19] Interview, Hajji Saleh Kamal, Addis Ababa, August 5, 2011.

Feisal Abdulaziz, and then to Egypt where they met with the leaders of the Wafd Party, the Arab League, and Hassan al-Banna, the leader of the Muslim Brotherhood (Carmichael 2001: 224; Rahji Abdella 1994: 49). We do not know anything about the content of these meetings, but it is safe to assume that they revolved around the unfair treatment of Muslims under Ethiopian rule. It is moreover interesting to note how the Harari delegation approached groups with very different ideological positions. In Harar, meanwhile, negotiations between the local leaders and the Ethiopian government continued, and the authorities promised that if the Harari agreed to return from Egypt, the eighty-one prisoners would be released. The exiles agreed, and when they arrived in Addis Ababa in the middle of 1949, the prisoners were pardoned by Emperor Haile Selassie (Carmichael 2001: 225; Rahji Abdella 1994: 52).

While this marked the end of organized Harari resistance, and although SYL subsequently was banned, Somali nationalism continued to have an impact on developments in the southeastern parts of Ethiopia, including Bale. The ideological discourses served as an important source of inspiration, and there was active communication between the different movements. SYL had, as already noted, managed to establish branches in Bale in the latter part of the 1940s, attracting quite a number of followers.[20] The main site for SYL activism was, however, the shrine of Sheikh Hussein, a place renowned for exchanging anti-government ideas. Already in the early 1930s, Qadi Ahmed Imama, introduced in Chapter 5, reportedly met with several prominent Muslim leaders at the shrine – making plans for more coordinated armed resistance against the Ethiopian regime. These Muslim leaders included Sheikh Ali Abd al-Rahman ("Ali al-Sufi"), Hajji Isaq Dhadhi of Raytu, and a certain Hajji Siraj. Sheikh Ali Abd al-Rahman was the first director of the already mentioned Jamiyya School in Harar and would become part of the leadership of the Nasrallah (God's Grace) organization (see next section). Hajji Siraj was a well-known scholar from Wollo. The plans never materialized, however, and Qadi Ahmed Imama was arrested for conspiring against the state and placed under house arrest in Addis Ababa in 1942.[21] SYL's presence at the shrine is

[20] Bale Province's High Court: Verdict against *Grazmach* Umar Hussein, Goba, June 13, 1967.
[21] Interview, Kadir Abdu, Addis Ababa, September 25, 2006; Bale Province's High Court: Verdict against *Fitawrari* Ahmed Imama, Goba, June 13, 1967.

evidenced by the fact that the movement's badge made of ivory – with SYL's name, a crescent, and a tree carved out – was worn by people at the shrine (Gebru Tareke 1977: 290; Rahji Abdella 1994: 43).[22] Such badges were widely used by SYL members throughout the southeast and constituted an important marker of oppositional identity. Somali officials continued to visit the shrine during the 1960s, and one particular report narrates how one such official participated during the pilgrimage in September 1966. Underscoring the unity of Muslims from Mogadishu to Bale, he promised that the Somali government was ready to provide arms to anyone willing to fight the Ethiopian state.[23]

Insurgents in the Ogaden and Kenya

As the emperor gradually became aware of the growing anti-Ethiopian sentiments among the Somalis, he attempted soothe the situation by making a few policy changes. On the one hand, he sought to extend the state's influences into the lowlands by increasing the presence of the police and the military, a move that was aimed at controlling the pastoralists. On the other hand, the emperor did make some concessions by appointing traditional Somali leaders as *worreda* administrators. However, the speech he made in Ogaden in 1956 clearly demonstrates how poorly the emperor read the situation. Talking about integrating the Somalis, he told them that the changes would "foster understanding and cooperation among the military, the police and the civilian population" (Touval 1963: 144). The long history of Ethiopian looting of Somali livestock and raiding of villages and pastoralist settlements effectively invalidated any attempt of reform. The emperor's aim of co-opting local Somali leaders was a complete failure, as the appointed officials actively participated in activities against the state (Markakis 1987: 175).

Escalation of tensions seemed unavoidable and discontent gradually gave birth to unorganized resistance across the Ogaden and in Bale's El

---

[22] Interviews, Kadir Abdu, Addis Ababa, September 25, 2006; Hajji Semir Idris, Addis Ababa, December 9, 2017. There are some disagreements about the badge: some saying it had only a tree, with others claiming that the tree was actually a clover (Carmichael 2001: 206).

[23] Bale Province's High Court: Verdict against *Fitawrari* Ahmed Imama, Goba, June 13, 1967.

Kere *awraja.* One uprising took place in 1947, led by Jegihart, and another occurred in 1958, led by Abdul Selam Harsi (Gebru Tareke 1977: 288). While the provincial authorities easily quelled these instances, they signaled a convergence of movements, a more actively defiant population, and increasingly articulated resistance.

There is no doubt that the independence of Somalia in 1960 became particularly important in boosting anti-government activism across the southeast. Its SYL-dominated post-independent government remained guided by the notion of Greater Somalia and continued to advocate for the unification of all Somali clans. It actively used radio broadcasting that reached deep into southeastern Ethiopia, distributed propaganda pamphlets, and infiltrated local communities with its political message. The scope of these activities demonstrates that the new Somali government not only had the Somalis in mind but also aimed at "liberating" other oppressed peoples in the south. The religious dimension remained intrinsic, and Somali propaganda vigorously referred to Islam as a common denominator and to Muslim unity. Religion thus gradually became an integral part of the armed resistance, being appropriated and formulated by the different movements.

The early 1950s saw the increase of more resolute resistance in the Ogaden – represented by a few important organizations. The initial one was the Tawfiq Trading Company established in Qalafo in the Ogaden in 1953. It rapidly expanded with branches in Dhagahbour, Warder, and Kebre Dehar, and in 1958 it merged with the Ogaden Company for Trade and Industry (OCTI) (Hagmann 2014: 729). Although it engaged in business and trading, its covert objectives were to recruit Somalis for the struggle to liberate the Ogaden from Ethiopian rule and to generate revenues for this struggle (Barnes and Abdullahi n.d.: 2). Parallel to this, more explicit Muslim organizations also emerged, including the Hizbi Illahi (God's Party), founded by Hajji Yasin Handuleh in 1956, and Haqu Illahi (God's Truth). The most important one was, however, the Nasrallah (God's Grace) organization established in the late 1950s by Osman Hassan "Gab," Abdi Nasser, Siad Hajji Muhammad, Ahmed Nur Hussein, and Sherif Muhammad (Markakis 1983: 296f.; Tibebe Eshete 1991: 23). In June 1960, it held its first congress in Mogadishu, where Dr. Ibrahim Hashi, a religious scholar educated in Egypt was elected president. Sheikh Ali Abd al-Rahman ("Ali al-Sufi") was, as noted, part of the leadership

(Barnes and Abdullahi n.d.: 3). Nasrallah was also linked with the OCTI, and, as the latter operated as a legal entity, it could provide the needed cover for Nasrallah's clandestine activities.

In the early 1960s, Nasrallah had managed to establish itself in Mogadishu and created branches in different districts of the Ogaden. It also sent representatives to various Arab capitals, advocating for its cause and seeking support. We do not know much about Nasrallah's ideological underpinnings; yet, there is a vague mention of it being inspired by the Muslim Brotherhood (Barnes and Abdullahi n.d.: 5). The struggle for independence was anyhow couched in an explicit religious language, evoking the notion of *jihad* against Christian domination, and promising the fighters martyrdom. While nothing indicates that Nasrallah ever became engaged in any form of armed struggle against the Ethiopian state, it remained important in providing an ideological rationale for the Ethiopian Ogadenis' demands for self-rule. Such demands gained new meaning with the establishment of independent Somalia and birthed calls for unification with the new state. Petitions from Ethiopian Ogadenis for unification with Somalia were – to no surprise – furiously rejected by Emperor Haile Selassie (Barnes and Abdullahi n.d.: 4).

The introduction of the livestock tax in February 1963 was a crucial turning point for Somali resistance. This was, in fact, the first tax imposed on the Somali pastoralists during the entire postwar period (Markakis 1987: 177). It was the main triggering point for the insurgency in the Ogaden and immediately spurred a range of meetings between members of the Nasrallah at different locations and led to dispatches of Ogaden leaders to Mogadishu to seek advice from Somali politicians. The main problem was access to arms, and although the government in Somalia was hesitant to do anything that could provoke Ethiopia, it could not, at the same time, refuse to support the Ogadenis (Markakis 1987: 178). The insurgency itself was launched on June 16, 1963, at a large, yet secret conference in Hodoyo, a village in Danot district. It brought together figures within the OCTI, Mogadishu exiles, and prominent Ogadeni oppositional leaders, who all agreed to form a broad front for the independence of Ogaden from Ethiopia. There are some disagreements when it comes to what role Nasrallah played in the insurgency. While Markakis argues that it "played no significant part"

(Markakis 1983: 297), others claim that Nasrallah was deeply involved through Al-Jeysh, a militia led by key leaders of Nasrallah. The Al-Jeysh militia rapidly recruited a significant number of fighters and by September, it reportedly had between 3,000 and 3,500 men under arms (Hagmann 2014: 729; Markakis 1983: 304). And it is here that Makhtal Tahir reenters the scene – emerging as the main leader of the insurgency in the Ogaden. After he was released from prison and allowed back to the Ogaden, as part of Emperor Haile Selassie's attempt to win local support, he was appointed as a *worreda* adminis-trator in Dhagahbour in 1962 and granted the title *Dejazmach*. Makhtal Tahir's loyalty to the emperor quickly vanished, and in 1963, he fled to Somalia and resumed his resistance to the Ethiopian state (Markakis 1983: 302).

The nascent insurgency movement's initial focus was on military training, and its activities were limited to isolated hit-and-run attacks on government infrastructure (Barnes and Abdullahi n.d.: 5). Al-Jeysh fighters also moved across the border to Somalia, where they were provided with arms. There were limits, however, to the support the Somali state could provide. Being poorly trained, insufficiently armed, and lacking coordinated leadership, the small bands of insurgents avoided engaging the Ethiopian army directly and focused instead on attacking outlying police posts. Nevertheless, the movement managed to gain control over large parts of the Ogaden, causing the Ethiopians to retreat to the main administrative centers. At several locations in the Ogaden, the local people flew the Somali flag, while burning the Ethiopian one (Touval 1963: 135). Calling for unity with the nascent Somali state, the leadership of the insurgency urged the locals to sever any connection with Ethiopia, to refuse to pay taxes, and to refrain from selling their livestock at local markets. Such rhetoric enhanced the movement's popularity and enabled it to further extend its area of operation (Gebru Tareke 1977: 296; Markakis 1987: 179). While one should be careful not to exaggerate the size and role of the Somali-led insurgency, it would take the Ethiopian army until March 1967 to crush it (Markakis 1987: 196f.).

Parallel to developments in the Ogaden, several other smaller insur-gencies surfaced in Borana and in Guji areas. These initially emerged, as discussed in Chapter 4, in the wake of increased tensions between the Borana, Guji, and Somali groups, tensions that were interlinked with the expansion of Somalis into Borana land. When the Borana, armed by the Ethiopian government, started to sporadically attack Somali clans and other non-Borana, it soon created a general state of insecurity in the whole area. What initially were defensive acts against the Borana soon grew into broader insurgency, organized along clan lines: the Garre led by the famous leader Hajji Hassan Gababa and his brother, the Degodia led by El-Kedir Hussein, and the Marehan led by Warsane Gafarsa.

Armed struggle was not limited only to southeastern Ethiopia and along the Somali border but expanded into northern Kenya with the so-called *Shifta* War (1963–1968). As Kenya was moving toward independence in the beginning of the 1960s, it called for a referendum in the Northern Frontier District (NFD), asking the locals whether they wanted to remain within Kenya or join the newly established Somali state. The latter option clearly corresponded with SYL's dream of Greater Somalia. Prior to the referendum, SYL had played an active role in securing support for this idea. Propaganda material had been smuggled into the NFD since the 1940s, and SYL offices were opened in Wajir and other places in the NFD already in 1946 (Markakis 1987: 57; Touval 1963: 95). The British colonial authorities banned the SYL a few years later, and while this curtailed organized Somali activism, pro-Somali sentiments remained present in the region, particularly among urban educated youth (Touval 1963: 149). When the referendum showed that an overwhelming majority of the Somalis voted for unification with Somalia, both the outgoing British colonial authorities and the incoming Kenyan government immediately rejected the results. This soon caused intermittent clashes between armed Somali groups and the authorities – which rapidly developed into a full-fledged insurgency. While this forged a strong alliance between the nascent Somali government and insurgent groups in the NFD, where the former readily supported the latter with arms, it would be too simplistic to reduce the *Shifta* War and the quest for secession as something orchestrated by Somalia. Rather, it was made up of additional complex layers and would contribute to fuel latent tensions between a range of disparate actors.[24]

---

[24] Much of this was related to competition over scarce resources, rising to the surface in the course of the unrest. As such, the *Shifta* War created opportunities for individuals and communities to settle old scores and to extend their power.

The NFD had not received much attention from the British colonial authorities, which early on placed the region in an economically disadvantaged position. The British, in an attempt to suppress interethnic and inter-clan warfare, had also put restrictions on movements in and out of the region – thus augmenting the NFD's isolation from the rest of Kenya. Such developments fed into the already existing socioeconomic and religious-cultural differences between the population in the NFD and the Kenyan majority population – following lines of lowlanders vs highlanders, pastoralists vs agriculturalists, and Muslims vs Christians. Whereas the majority of those who wanted secession were Somalis, several other pastoralist Muslim groups felt an affinity with the new Somali state – something evidenced by the fact that between 10 percent and 20 percent of the insurgents were Borana and Rendille (Whittaker 2015: 8).[25] Religion constituted the main decisive factor for such engagement – both facilitating a shared sense of belonging among the different Muslims groups in the NFD and marking the boundary toward the non-Muslim Kenyans. The latter were indiscriminately viewed as Christians, and it was commonly believed that remaining part of Kenya would in the end undermine Islam. The crucial point here is that existing socioeconomic and religious-cultural differences gained new relevance as tensions increased and which moreover facilitated the emergence of two competing nationalisms – one oriented toward Somalia and the other toward Kenya. The fluid political situation and growing tensions also fueled existing tensions between the different groups in the NFD.

Conclusion

The Horn of Africa saw a wave of insurgencies along the eastern perimeters of the Ethiopian state during the 1960s. Some of them could be characterized as explicitly irredentist, while others are more difficult to categorize. Many of them were products of local dynamics; yet, it is clear that they were influenced by broader developments across the region. It is similarly clear that the different peoples across this landscape shared the same underlying sentiments of alienation and discontent – sentiments that had roots in largely shared experiences

---

[25] The Borana was the second-largest ethnic group in NFD. The Rendille is a Cushitic-speaking group found in northeastern Kenya.

of violent encounters with the Ethiopian state and eventually caused the people to rise. This means that while the Bale insurgency had its own causes and separate trajectory, it is impossible to fully understand it without considering the way it was intersected with the broader currents of resistance traveling across the Horn.

Some of these currents were rather explicit, while others were of a subtler character – reflecting underlying developments going back to earlier decades. Particularly important, however, was the role of Islam in providing a common point of orientation and a force for political mobilization. Religion should not, as noted, be construed as a separate isolated factor but as an integrated dimension of peoplehood. The crucial point is that religion served to transcend locality, thus enabling an imagination of a shared peoplehood beyond local embeddedness. This notion of commonality was intensified by both the Ethiopian state's own Christian underpinning and its othering of religious difference, which reciprocally meant that the insurgents – and the broader population – came to view the state as a Christian power. In addition to strengthening the religious (Muslim) dimension of peoplehood, the nature of the state moreover accentuated the religious dimension of the conflicts. Yet, the integrated nature of religion and ethnicity – as well as other factors – makes it impossible to dissect such conflicts as either religious or ethnic.

While trans-local interactions and broader currents remain crucial for understanding the Bale insurgency, and while Somalia was essential in providing arms, training, and refuge for the insurgents, local dynamics and developments remain critically important. The next chapter will circle in on the locality of Bale and further explore how the Amhara presence contributed to accentuate the religious and ethnic dimension of peoplehood, how this intensified animosity along these dimensions, and how it eventually led to the eruption of conflict.

10 | Islaama *vs Amhara and the Making of Local Antagonism*

Anafi si, akka Islaama fi Amhara

(I and you are like a Muslim and an Amhara)

This proverb, used by the Arsi Oromo and others, is a common, explicit, and forceful expression of deep enmity.[1] Although it refers to religious difference, it is not merely or necessarily about religion but refers to enmity in its broadest sense. However, the fact that religion is the metaphor of seemingly unbridgeable division is interesting and points to the importance of religion and the salience of religious divisions within Ethiopia. More than that, the proverb also reveals the difficulty in the construction of identity in this region – juxtaposing a term with an obvious religious connotation (*Islaama*) with a term that commonly is understood as an ethnic one (Amhara). This brings us back to the inherent complexity between ethnicity and religion and illustrates how inseparable these dimensions were for the development of antagonism in Bale.

This chapter explores this further by bringing us back to the locality of Bale and to the role of local actors. Seeking to elucidate the many aspects of the local conflictual dynamics, I will start by revisiting the question of class and in particular explore the relevance of class in relation to religion and ethnicity, where I argue that interpretations that favor and isolate one of these categories at the expense of the other inevitably bring forth a one-sided and incomplete picture. Only an integrated approach and nuanced analyses can unpack the many layers of complexity surrounding these issues. I believe the notion of peoplehood helps us unpack this, and I will moreover connect the concept with a discussion of how the insurgents themselves formulated and articulated the movement's objectives. Trying to understand the

---

[1] The expression is also common among the Amhara: *ene'na ante lik'ende Islem'na Amharanen.*

insurgency's ideological underpinning, I continue with an analysis of the role of the highland activists, where my argument is that they were instrumental for further elaborating the movement's ideological thinking and, moreover, that religion and ethnicity remained foundational in this regard. Their status as religious leaders and traditional authorities was important for this emphasis and contributed to giving the insurgency direction. While the highland activists could be characterized as ethnic/religious entrepreneurs mobilizing the broader population, it does not mean that they deliberately and purposely sought to utilize ethnicity and religion.

The questions of religion and ethnicity are fleshed out in the chapter's second part, where I devote significant space to discussing how deeply affective and embodied the religious and ethnic dimensions were in the broader population and demonstrate how both the insurgents' and the highland activists' acts and ideas were expressions of deeply felt popular sentiments. I will discuss how Amhara exceptionalism was expressed and experienced in Bale, focusing on the roles of religion and ethnicity as integral to politics of domination. I will especially demonstrate how this strengthened the notion of *Islaama* peoplehood in Bale, positioned the locals in opposition to their ethnically and religiously other, as well as cementing their antagonistic attitudes – eventually becoming manifest in the insurgency.

In line with this study's overall framework of emphasizing the embodied and emplaced nature of religion and ethnicity, I again argue for a perspective that moves beyond the assumption of the economic as an objective reality (Laclau and Mouffe 1985) that views religious and ethnic domination as less "real" than class, economic exploitation, and political subjugation. Glassman has along the same lines argued that "'cultural' and 'religious' issues could exert considerable material force," and rather than favoring the *homo economicus* in conflicts, he points to how conflicts in African contexts usually "took the form of multivalent struggles" (1995: 20). James Scott is even more explicit as he points to the limits of "structuralist variants of neo-Marxism" that assume the a priori existence of class relations in any society:

In place of simply assuming a one-to-one correspondence between "objective" class structure and consciousness, is it not far preferable to understand how those structures are apprehended by flesh-and-blood human actors? Class, after all, does not exhaust the total explanatory space of social actions.

Nowhere is this more true than within the peasant village, where class may compete with kinship, neighborhood, faction, and ritual links as foci of human identity and solidarity. Beyond the village level, it may also compete with ethnicity, language group, religion, and region as a focus of loyalty. (Scott 1985: 43)

While I regard all these dynamics as intimately intertwined, I also suggest that religion and ethnicity underpinned the economic and political domination: whereas domination in the north occurred in a situation with ethnic and religious homogeneity, in the south it was based upon notions of religious and ethnic superiority.[2] A key part of my argument, however, is that there is an overlooked side of the asymmetric relations between the ruling Amhara and their southern subjects: all southerners were inferior, but there were those who were more inferior than others. The Muslims remained the antithesis to Christian Ethiopia, and this religious otherness added a particular dimension exacerbating the Amhara's distain for the Muslim Arsi Oromo.

What Makes a Class?

On several occasions, I have argued against Gebru Tareke's claim that the insurgency "quintessentially [was] a peasant question," and I disagree with his statement that the "simple presentation of the problem as a contest between Christian Amhara and Muslim Oromo/ Somali – critically [has] undermined the class aspect and the transformative potential of the revolt" (1991: 159). However, while arguing that interpreting the insurgency solely from the perspective of class conflict is insufficient is not the same as saying that class is irrelevant. There is no doubt that changing land-tenure systems, taxation, and processes of privatization of land caused the erosion of traditional forms of belonging and the creation of new social categories. The critical point, however, is that the nature, content, and results of these changes should not be deterministically presumed but rather analyzed within the particular context.

---

[2] Markakis reduces this to social distance, thus overlooking that the northerners' pejorative attitudes were underpinned by a fundamental ethno-religious sense of superiority (Markakis 1974: 299).

What makes a class? What is class conflict, and, in particular, how do we understand class in relation to religion and ethnicity? This latter question has, according to Hall, "proven to be the most complex and difficult theoretical problems to address" (1986: 24).[3] While it has been common to view religion and ethnicity as dependent on class, it is also possible to understand religion and ethnicity as producing a certain social positioning – or to view religion and ethnicity as manifested in class differences. Before continuing my discussion, a few clarifications are needed. To the extent that Marxist analyses reduce complex social phenomena to a single determining variable in the quest for a "scientific" theory of history and society that gives primacy to the economic, it easily risks an essentialization of class and class conflict, consequently blinding us for how this is socially contingent and thus an area for analytical enquiry (Anthias 2001: 380; Laclau and Mouffe 1985). Similarly difficult is the Marxist assumption of class as dialectically objective and subjective. While human realities obviously are made up of people with unequal access to material (and other) resources, the question remains whether this necessarily means that we therefore can talk about social groups identifiable as classes. It is moreover erroneous to assume that unequal distribution of resources in itself generates distinct class consciousness – in the sense of politically unified groups sharing the same interest.

Similar to my earlier stated objections of talking about distinct ethnic or religious groups, I argue that perceiving class as a separate group is the wrong way to go. Instead, applying the concept of peoplehood provides us with the needed flexibility to deal with the complexity of social life while grounded in primary embodied and emplaced experiences. I moreover suggest that class can best be understood as a dimension of peoplehood. Important, however, is that unequal access to resources among members of a people should not merely be understood vis-à-vis the means of production but also as a result of emplacement in the totality of their social, cultural, and ecological environment. While the class dimension certainly has the potential to create strong notions of unity and belonging, my argument remains that the ethnic and religious dimensions, as *primary* dimensions of peoplehood, cut deeper in the production of internal cohesion and

---

[3] Hall largely restricts his discussions to the issue of race (as ethnicity), but I believe it is possible to include religion alongside ethnicity.

belonging, in the demarcation of boundaries and in processes of other-ing. Being a member of a labor union is not the same as being member of a nation.

Although I differ with Hall's argument that "ethnic and racial difference can be constructed as a set of economic, political or ideological antagonisms *within* a class" (1986: 25, italics in original), he makes the important point that a too narrow focus on economic modes of production overlooks simultaneous modes of exploitation. Hall moreover argues for an approach that is historically and contextually specific. One of his main points is that ethnicity not only has retained relevance in the development of global capitalism but also that ethnicity has indeed been "*developed* and *refined*" and further "provided the means for differentiated forms of exploitation" (Hall 1986: 24, italics in original). What is important is that religion and ethnicity may be the bases for "the allocation of hierarchies of value, inferiorization as well as unequal resource allocation" – irrespective of and separate from production relations (Anthias 2001: 380).

Relating this to the question of so-called class conflict, my argument is that it is difficult to talk about religious, ethnic, or class conflicts as separate events. The relevance of these dimensions in conflict is situational, in the sense that one dimension in one situation may play a stronger role than the others or alternatively serve to reinforce the others. Allowing for an integrated approach enables us to see conflict as occurring along multiple dimensions and allows us to see ethnicity and religion as more than merely class in disguise or as "false consciousness." Such an approach is different from a perspective that sees class and inequality as "axiomatic" and which reduces ethnic inequality to be "largely in the eyes of the beholder" (Young 1982: 93). I would argue that notions of material or economic inequality can also very much be in the eyes of the beholder, and as I will illustrate, material inequality is often interpreted by the actors involved as determined by religious and ethnic differences.

Questions of class and class conflict bring us back to the (refined) Gramscian notion of hegemony, which, as already discussed in Chapter 8, is best understood as multidimensional and as alliances between different sectors. Important here is that hegemony transcends the purely economic field and brings different subordinate groups together and creates different forms of unity (Laclau and Mouffe 1985) and has the effect of "creating the hegemony of a fundamental social group over

a series of subordinate groups" – wherein the state often is a crucial actor
(Gramsci 1971: 182). This way of understanding the nature of hegemony
also has consequences for the dimensions that conflicts revolve around,
and for articulating "the questions around which the struggle rages" (Hall
1986: 14). The nature of this hegemony will be different according to
context, and as we will see in this particular case, it had particular
relevance for how Amhara peoplehood in itself entailed hegemony and
for how Amhara–Arsi Oromo antagonisms surpassed the purely economic. What we have is a far messier picture where conflict is not merely
class vs class but rather along other and "deeper" boundaries and involving far more encompassing antagonism – beyond the strict economic
domain.

Class, Ethnicity, and Religion in Bale

These outlined perspectives are highly relevant when seeking to understand the question of class in relation to religion and ethnicity in Bale –
as well as in Ethiopia more broadly. Whereas I want to focus on the
southern parts, the fact that the political and economic structures
imposed in these areas to a certain extent mirrored those of the north
makes it important to say something about the situation in that area.
Class and social differences in the north have been a topic of much
investigation, and the generally accepted idea is that while defined
social groups clearly existed – largely based upon land rights – there
was a general lack of class consciousness and that this "rarely expressed
itself openly; and certainly never in spectacular uprisings" (Crummey
1980: 127). The key factor here is that there was a lack of sharp
differentiation between the different groups – tenants, landowning
peasants, and nobles – in the sense of significant material inequality,
and moreover, that one did not see the development of distinct elite and
commoner cultures (Hoben 1975; Levine 1965: 156; Merid Wolde
Aregay 1984). Although there were those who accumulated resources,
reflected in large houses, sizeable entourages, and other extravaganza,
they were not "endowed with a symbolic or cultural value for them to
be seen as socially meaningful" (Anthias 2001: 379). They remained
insufficient for the crystallization of an "elite stratum with its own high
culture" (Donham 1986: 10).[4]

---

[4] This is also something observed by Young (1982) in other parts of Africa.

In addition, the fact that social structures, even if hierarchical, allowed for social mobility between the peasantry was important in mitigating the development of demarcated class categories (Donham 1986: 5; Fernyhough 2010: 253). More significant, however, was how the image of society itself and the idea that peasants and nobles within a locality belonged to the same descent system, and that they shared the myth of provenance – consequently placing the peasant at the same level as the nobleman (Donham 1986: 5f.). Particularly important for such notion of commonality, however, was the shared religious affiliation as an important aspect of unified Amhara people-hood. The very content of Orthodox Christianity moreover served to both legitimize social inequalities and assuage class conflict. Intrinsic to this, and which has not gained the attention it deserves, was the emphasis on submission to authority – integral to all sectors of society – wherein divine authority constituted the ultimate source for submission at the different levels. The juxtaposition of divine and earthly authority was expressed in appeals to various rebellious forces during the twentieth century – evident during the rebellion in Tigray in the 1940s, when representatives of the Orthodox Church excommunicated the rebels and compared them to "Judas who sold his Master" (Gebru Tareke 1977: 481).

The Amhara living in Bale were not any homogenous socioeconomic group but included Amhara political officials, wealthy Amhara land-owners, many of whom lived in Addis Ababa, urban merchants, and Amhara peasants and tenants. The provincial Amhara political elite was a tight-knit urban group that worked closely together with the Amhara landowners in maintaining power and extracting as many resources as possible, and the defined hierarchical structures distanced them from the rural Amhara settlers. However, no obvious class con-sciousness existed among the Amhara, who remained, irrespective of material inequality, a united, cohesive group set apart from the local Arsi Oromo population. Linguistic affinity was one important integra-tive factor, the notion of belonging to the Ethiopian core was another, and vertical structures, marked by dependency and respect for author-ity, tied the Amhara peasants to the elite. Again, shared religion was particularly critical in producing a strong sense of belonging to the same peoplehood, and as orthodox Christians, the Amhara encoun-tered one another in the churches, fasted on the same days, and shared the same narrative of national provenance.

Addressing the question of economic changes, Fernyhough has argued – *pace* Hobsbawm – that the emerging insurgencies in the south were caused by changing modes of production, triggered by internal invasion, which brought about a society based upon class (Fernyhough 2010: 261). I have throughout this study argued that this is inaccurate and will here further elaborate on the role and relevance of class – as interrelated with religion and ethnicity among the Arsi Oromo. Even if changes in land tenure paved the way for privatization of land and led to increased social stratification, there are no indications that this produced a society based on explicit social classes. It would be relevant, however, to examine how the *balabat* institution might have affected socioeconomic relations.

It has been argued that the *balabat* institution, both in southern Ethiopia in general and in Bale in particular, came to constitute a local gentry, or an "auxiliary elite" aligned more with the Amhara than with the local population (Gebru Tareke 1977: 245; Markakis 2011: 8). This might have been the case in certain areas; I argue that the situation was different in Bale. While it is true that the *balabats* came to constitute a group set apart from the rest of the population, it is incorrect that a "cultural fusion" emerged between the *balabats* and the Amhara, that the Arsi Oromo *balabats* in Bale gradually became Amharasized, by adopting Amharic, and that they started to intermarry with Amhara (Gebru Tareke 1977: 245). This is in stark contrast to my findings, and all my informants agreed that there was a clear demarcated boundary between the *balabats* and the Amhara. The situation for the *balabats* (and the *burqas*) was undoubtedly complicated – serving both as agents of the state and as representatives of the people. This did create a dilemma for the *balabats*, and while they at the outset were respected as embodying traditional inherited authority, the reconfiguration of authority affected their relations to the people. Being responsible for collecting taxes provided opportunities for accumulating resources and opened the door for corruption. Being part of the state's hierarchical structures left them, at the same time, at the mercy of the state and required total obedience to the authorities.

The fact that the *balabats* benefited economically from their position would, from a classical class-conflict perspective, mean that they would be those least interested in the armed struggle. The general consensus among my informants, however, is that the *balabats* shared the same antagonistic attitudes toward the Amhara as the rest of the population and that they played a decisive role in the insurgency. The *balabats* in the lowlands actively participated in the fighting, and many in the highlands worked together with the highland activists collecting support for the fighters. In Wabe *awraja,* for example, it is reported that eleven out of eighteen *balabats* were actively involved in the struggle.[5] Furthermore, the *balabats'* liminal position circumscribed their authority in the eyes of the people but did not abolish it. The fact that many of them came from *abbaa boku* lineages meant that they already had considerable respect among the clans. As the *balabats'* authority remained connected to clan affiliation, the people still viewed them – and depended upon them – as their leaders. Moreover, their role as being responsible for the well-being of the clans made them obvious leaders, and gave them a certain degree of leverage that enabled them to mobilize their kinsfolk into action.

The insurgency was not dominated by any assumed lower class, or by those who had suffered the most due to "feudal oppression," but drew people from all walks of life. This serves to further demonstrate that a unilateral focus on the class dimension remains insufficient to fully understand the insurgency or explain the multifaceted nature of hegemony and domination. Even if the Arsi Oromo were wealthier than many of the Amhara, the latter always considered the former as subordinate and inferior as a people. Among the Arsi Oromo, the land-clan connection – in spite of increased social stratification – prevailed as the primary principle for social organization, internal cohesion, and the foundation for resistance. And it was religion and ethnicity as shared dimensions and bases for Amhara domination that produced and sustained the Arsi Oromo's antagonism and united them in the struggle against the Amhara.

Insurgent Ideology

Although insurgencies in Ethiopia commonly have been viewed from a class-conflict perspective, interpretations of ideologies have been rather dismissive. In his discussion of peasant uprisings in northern Ethiopia, Fernyhough has applied Hobsbawm's notions of the "primitive rebellion" and "revolutionary traditionalists" and concluded that they lacked class ideology and class coconsciousness, thus reducing

---

[5] Interrogation Report, Sayyid Mustafa, August 29, 1967.

them to "primitive proponents of class struggle" (2010: 242, 251). The dominating interpretation of the Bale insurgency as a class-based peasant rebellion has birthed similar views, where it is said that the "rebels of Bale were simple peasants without any revolutionary ideology" (Gebru Tareke 1977: 350). Gilkes has claimed that it was a peasant rebellion that grew to become "a nationalist revolutionary movement" (1975: 226). I believe Gebru Tareke is right in arguing that the movement did not have a revolutionary ideology in any strict Marxist sense, but I believe that we also should be careful labeling it a nationalist movement. My point is that the insurgency does not that easily fall into any neat categories, which in turn reflects the need for far more accuracy when we talk about insurgent ideology in modern African history.

Scholarship on African insurgencies has increasingly moved away from a classical understanding of insurgency ideologies as comprehensive and coherent systems of thought to rather thinking of ideology as a discourse "encompassing any views, ideas or thoughts purporting to provide meaning to cultural reality, political systems or social existence, at whatever level of abstraction and complexity" (van Walraven and Abbink 2003: 26; cf. Clapham 1998). This dovetails very much with my own empirical findings, and I have found Glassman's Gramscian suggestions fruitful when seeking to understand the ideological underpinnings of the Bale insurgency. Glassman argues for viewing the ideology of the oppressed in the direction of continuous discourse – and importantly – that which "create[s] the terrain in which men move, acquire consciousness of their position, struggle, etc." (Glassman 1995: 17; cf. Gramsci 1971: 377). It is this discursive process that forms actors' popular consciousness as well as creating the realities they live in. It is what produces consciousness about their conditions and their subjugated state and contributes to shaping their struggle. Popular consciousness is inherently fragmented, much of it emanating from daily experiences gathered over time and across space. Following Gramsci's postulate that "hegemonic ideologies" remain a powerful force shaping popular consciousness, the subjugated subjects inevitably absorb parts of the hegemon's ideas, which then clash with daily experiences of domination. Popular consciousness is thus not completely revolutionary, and it is this absorption of the hegemon's ideas contrasted with daily experiences that creates a frustration that in turn results in contradictory consciousness, or a *contradictory rebellious consciousness*. This then forms the basis for rebellious action that is continuously "crafted in the course of the struggle, in which individuals espousing many different agendas could find justification" (Glassman 1995: 19). Ideology as a discursive process means, in other words, that ideology does not exist as any pre-text. It is not necessarily a fixed set of coherent ideas or a program ready to be adopted, providing a ready-made blueprint for political action. Goals and objectives may, in the same manner, be somewhat articulated but are often vague and ambiguous and may, rather than being fixed, change over time (Glassman 1995: 16f.).

When it comes to the particular case of the Bale insurgency, there is unfortunately very little explicit documentation of ideological underpinnings and political goals. All of my informants – both those actively involved in the struggle and those closely connected to the movement – underscore that it was about *bliisumaa* – freedom. However, when asked to elaborate on the meaning and content of freedom, they added few details. *Bliisumaa* was about ending the suppression, getting rid of the Amhara, and establishing freedom. The only written document talking about the goals of the insurgency is a pamphlet Waqo Gutu issued on the eve of the struggled, which is included in Gebru Tareke dissertation:

It is essential that you first and foremost remember that since the enemy occupied your country in 1885–1891 you have been robbed of your land and property, your history has been destroyed and your dignity violated. You have been crushed for 80 years now. Since the Amharas occupied our country with the help of European imperialists our people have been massacred en masse, our possessions confiscated for various reasons, our land has been divided amongst the Amhara invaders and consequently we have been made and remain to this day gebbars. Those who survived the massacre had been allocated like slaves to the melkengnas who abused and violated their human dignity and crushed their manhood by imprisoning then in mule barns. They have distorted and plundered our legacy that is widely known and have called us filthy Galla. Remember how many times you have been denied justice in the courts of law; and you Muslims, remember that your religion has been abused and that you have no equality [with the Christians] at all. Innumerable crimes that have not been committed by the European colonialists on the African peoples have been perpetrated upon you. (Gebru Tareke 1977: 482)

Before going into details about the content of the pamphlet, it is necessary to include a couple of critical remarks. First of all, the fact that Waqo Gutu was from the remote rural areas without any formal education and that the statement was published in Somalia leads one to ask whether the writing actually came from Waqo Gutu's own hand or whether it was a product of the Somali government. To opt for the latter would be both reductionist and too simplistic, as it belittles and outrightly dismisses the role of local agency. The point to be made is that the discursive process that created the motivations for the insurgency entailed the involvement of multiple actors. Waqo Gutu was himself an important part of this discourse, who, in turn, did not act or think in a vacuum. There is no doubt that his stays in Somalia exposed him to anti-colonial and ethno-national sentiments that influenced him, and it is similarly reasonable to assume that the Somalis helped him articulate them.[6]

Secondly, Clapham (1998: 13) has, among others, argued that to gain local support, insurgency leaders had to exaggerate the distinction – and disjunction – between indigenous ethnicity and that of the other. Crucial here was both to make the enemy explicit and to garnish internal cohesion and solidarity. It would thus be relevant to ask whether the pamphlet was a deliberate propaganda tool to stir hatred and a means to gather support for the insurgency. This again, I argue, becomes simplistic. Nothing points in the direction that the sentiments expressed were deliberately used as an instrument by entrepreneurial leaders to coax an agentless population. Rather, and as I alluded to earlier, the notions of loss and humiliation and animosity toward the Amhara that Waqo Gutu articulated were widely shared sentiments among the Arsi Oromo in Bale.

Returning to the pamphlet, the message it conveys is interesting in many ways. To begin with, it makes unequivocal and direct references to the illegitimate invasion by a different and alien group and to the sufferings the people have endured since Menelik's conquest. Pointing in particular to massacres carried out during the violent campaigns, especially in the lowlands, it moreover laments the loss of property and confiscations of land experienced as a result of new political realities, and how the new feudal system deprived the local people of their rights and reduced them to "slaves of the *melkenyas.*" Moreover, the

[6]   It has been claimed that he had the role as the movement's main political officer, being responsible for formulating the movement's political program (interview, Hajji Semir Idris, Addis Ababa, June 22, 2017). However, it is doubtful that the insurgency ever had such a position.

statement is explicitly anti-colonial in its rhetoric, seen by the way the Amhara invasion is said to have been both aided by and made possible by European imperialism. Interesting to note, however, is that Amhara colonization is portrayed as far worse than that by the Europeans. In the same pamphlet, Waqo Gutu compared the Bale insurgency with the struggle of the North Vietnamese, espousing in that way certain "third-worldism" views (Gebru Tareke 1991: 154). Anti-colonial sentiments were also expressed by my informants, and there is, as I will return to, no doubt of news about African liberation reaching Bale during the 1960s:

The reason [for the insurgency] was not only tax. We lost our authority, we lost our culture. It was also a time when other [African] people started to liberate themselves, we saw others get their freedom. And we started to wonder how long we would have to live under the Amhara. We thought of the white as oppressing the people when they slept, but when people woke up they would get their freedom. But the Amhara didn't leave us.[7]

A certain caveat is needed here. My conversation with this informant occurred decades after the insurgency, and his words would possibly be colored by a more recent and elaborate Oromo ethno-nationalism and by the current politicization of ethnicity in contemporary Ethiopia. I remember talking to other informants who, while speaking in Oromo (language) used the English word "colonization" rather than the Oromo word *cunqursaa* when talking about their reason for armed struggle.[8] While there are good reasons to think of the use of the word "colonization" as a projection of current discourses to a different past, siting face to face with these and other informants, I came to realize that this was how they in essence felt about their past condition.

What is particularly important in Waqo Gutu's statement is how colonization and subjugation had destroyed the people's history and, in particular, the underscoring of the religious and ethnic dimensions – in the sense that ill treatment was based upon ethnic and religious belonging, as being Oromo and Muslim. Indirect references were made to the already discussed notion of Amhara exceptionalism, making it clear that this was manifested in their pejorative attitudes toward the local population, through processes of othering, and integrated into the

---

[7] Interview, Muhammad Tahir, Raytu, June 12, 2017.
[8] Interviews, Hajji Abdurazak Hussein, Lais Hafiz, Ahmed Hussein, and Tahir Malik, Dello-Menna, June 15, 2017.

system of religious and ethnic suppression and inequality. The fact that this is expressed through tropes like the violation of "human dignity" and crushing of "manhood" is noticeable. These are not abstract or ineffable feelings but generated by embodied and emplaced experiences. The reference to manhood is particularly revealing, wherein the damage done to bodied masculinity reveals the depth and extent of loss.[9]

The intersection of these sentiments with concrete issues such as land is noticeable and points back to my discussion of how new socioeconomic realities and the introduction of a new land-tenure system affected the land-clan connection, how this created discontinuity and thus impacted notions of belonging. The underscoring of religion and ethnicity in relation to loss and humiliation brings us to the core of this. The role of religion and ethnicity as primary dimensions of peoplehood reveals both how deeply the treatment by Amhara affected the notion of *Islaamaa* peoplehood and, at the same time, how pivotal these two dimensions were for the crystallization of this notion, for the demarcation of boundaries, and for the production of antagonistic relations.

Insurgency, Resistance, and Islam

Religion was, to begin with, an explicit point of reference for why people joined the movement. Hussein Indhessa has claimed that a particular passage from the Qur'an was used for this recruitment purpose: "O ye who believe! fight the unbelievers who gird you about, and let them find firmness in you: and know that Allah is with those who fear Him" (Sura 9: 123). He also says that Islam remained an important source of inspiration for the fighters, and that religious references were commonly invoked throughout the struggle (Hussein Indhessa 2016: 132). There is also a report that claims that when the insurgents received arms in Somalia, they had to take an oath swearing on the Qur'an before returning to Bale.[10] Islam was similarly invoked in relation to leaving the insurgency, seen, for example, by how one of the main leaders at the Dello front, Kadir Waqo, argued that

---

[9] Although Waqo Gutu does not explore this further, it seems to correspond to Fanon's (1967) notion of masculinity.

[10] Interrogation Report, Ahmed Mahmoud, Muhammad Yunus, Oda Gutama, Hassan Jobir, February 11, 1967.

surrendering to the authorities was equal to betraying Islam.[11] The religious component can also be found in references talking about the aim of the struggle. One source recounts a speech Hajji Isaq Dhadhi made to fighters arriving in Somalia in search of weapons, encouraging them to be strong, and to continue the fight to chase out the Amhara. If they did that, he said, "they would, God willing, be able to establish their own government."[12]

The invocation of Islam in relation to politics and the establishment of a new government makes it relevant to ask whether one could characterize the insurgency as a form of jihad. This was surely how the local authorities interpreted the insurgency, and they constantly sought to present it in strictly religious terms. While some have suggested that they did this tactically to deliberately stigmatize the movement and discourage the local population from joining it (Hussein Indhessa 2016: 132), there is, at the same time, no doubt that the government truly interpreted the insurgency as exclusively driven by religious motives. The authorities' underscoring of religion must arguably be seen in relation to the history of interreligious conflict and the government's long-standing notion of the "foreign Islamic threat." The state thus sought to create a narrative of the insurgency "as a Somali plot to trigger the balkanization of Ethiopia along religious and tribal lines" (Gebru Tareke 1977: 345). The highland activists were also viewed as seeking to unite the Muslims of Bale with the regime in Somalia – to create one single powerful force in the fight against the Amhara government.[13] They were, along the same lines, accused for cooperating with other Muslim states, and Hajji Adam Saddo, as noted in Chapter 5, was said to have sent youth to "Arab countries" to study. The fact that one of Qadi Ahmed Imama's daughter was married to an Egyptian national and lived in Cairo was proof of his militant Islamic ideas.[14]

The term *jihad* has gained a multifaceted meaning in recent decades, and we should be careful to uncritically extrapolate contemporary

[11] Interrogation Report, Hassan Hussein, July 10, 1968.
[12] Interrogation Report, Kadir Yunus, September 17, 1967; Interrogation Report, Ibrahim Kadir, September 12, 1967.
[13] Bale Province's High Court: Verdict against Hajji Adam Saddo, Goba, June 13, 1967.
[14] Bale Province's High Court: Verdict against *Fitawrari* Ahmed Imama, Goba, June 13, 1967.

understandings of the term to the Bale context. What we need to recognize is that jihad was a natural part of the Muslim Arsi Oromo's religious vocabulary. The term, however, was not necessarily understood in accordance with the commonly accepted Islamic doctrines but rather interpreted in a manner that fitted their immediate context and situation. One informant expressed it as follows: "Jihad is Arabic for struggle, like *qawso* [struggle] in the Oromo language. The Oromo were colonised, and this was an ethnic jihad. It was not to fight for Islam, it was to fight for ethnic freedom."[15] The word *jihad* was also tactically used for recruiting fighters and for motivating them to fight, because, according to another informant: "there is no surrender, no going back in jihad."[16] Hussein Indhessa, on his part, claimed that the local *ulama* (Islamic scholars) promised that those killed in battle would become martyrs, and that those who did not support the jihad would face eternal damnation (2016: 132). This does not correspond with my general findings, and such views were arguably not prevalent within the movement. The use of the word *jihad* was contested, and the local *ulama* argued that the insurgents did not properly understand the word:

There was a mix of jihad and national struggle. As *ulama* we didn't agree to that. For the *Sowra*, jihad meant freedom. But when you go to jihad, all the soldiers need to pray, but among the *Sowra*, very few were praying ... . According to Islam, jihad is defense, and you shouldn't fight against Christians. But the *Sowra* were fighting against both Christians and Muslims. Jihad is not that simple, it has its own steps, its own process.[17]

The word *Sowra* is interesting here and was, in addition to *Kuluba*, another term for the Bale insurgency.[18] *Sowra* is an Oromification of the Arabic *thawra,* which means revolution, revolt, or rebellion. At the outset, the word does not have a particular religious connotation; as it became gradually more common in Arab political thought during the nineteenth century, it was largely construed in a negative sense as producing anarchy and instability. From the early twentieth century, *thawra* was increasingly used by Arab nationalists and later by Arab

---

[15] Interview, Hajji Ibrahim Mustafa, Robe, March 14, 2006.
[16] Interview, Sheikh Ahmed Aliye, Robe, October 6, 2005.
[17] Interview, Sheikh Ahmed Aliye, Robe, October 6, 2005.
[18] The word *Sowra* would become more common during the continued insurgency in the Derg period.

socialists as denoting positive change (Dupont 2008: 131). Making references to European revolutions, Arab nationalists also connected the term to the anti-colonial struggle, wherein the goal of *thawra* was freedom from alien oppression. *Thawra* continued to be used with reference to nationalist struggles in the postcolonial period, most prominently by the Palestinian movements, and it gradually became the favorite term among revolutionaries of different shades in areas such as Egypt, Yemen, Syria, and Iraq (Ayalon 1987; Bengio 1998: 19f.). Few, if any, in Bale had much knowledge of these ideological overtones, but it is interesting to note that the insurgents – and their supporters – referred to themselves as *Sowra* – as "secular" revolutionaries – and not as *mujahideen*, those fighting the jihad.

The highland activists were similar to the insurgents in viewing Islam as an important source of inspiration, and a careful reading of available sources reveals consistent religious references. For example, they encouraged the Muslim Arsi Oromo to revolt against the government, promising them the establishment of an "Islamic government."[19] Hajji Adam Saddo, moreover, urged the insurgents to continue "to fight for Islam and for your freedom," to overthrow the "Amhara government," and to establish an independent government.[20] *Grazmach* Umar Hussein is said to have called the people to "disrespect the Amhara flag and to respect the Islamic one" as part of the struggle.[21] Qadi Ahmed Imama had encouraged the people to distance themselves from the Amhara and had allegedly used a rather colorful expression – comparing the Amhara to "meat stuck between the teeth which had to be cleared out with a toothpick."[22]

---

[19] Letter to the Ethiopian Imperial Government's High Court, Goba, May 19, 1967; Bale Province's High Court: Verdict against Hajji Adam Saddo, Goba, May 31, 1967.

[20] Charges against *Grazmach* Adam Saddo – from Seyoum Haile-Michael, Prosecutor to the General Prosecutor, Bale Province's High Court, Goba, January 16, 1967. No. 84/59; charges against *Fitawrari* Ahmed Imama – from Seyoum Haile-Michael, Prosecutor to the General Prosecutor, Bale Province's High Court, Goba, October 4, 1966. No. 45/59; letter from Hajji Adam Saddo to the Ethiopian Imperial Government's High Court, Goba, January 24, 1967; letter to the Ethiopian Imperial Government's High Court, Goba, May 19, 1967.

[21] Bale Province's High Court: Verdict against *Grazmach* Umar Hussein, Goba, June 13, 1967.

[22] Bale Province's High Court: Verdict against *Fitawrari* Ahmed Imama, Goba, June 13, 1967.

One key point illuminating the central role of religion for the highland activists was how they labeled their adversaries. None of my informants ever referred to the Ethiopian state when depicting their enemy but consistently used the word *Amhara* (sometimes combined with Christian). During the trials against Hajji Adam Saddo and the other highland activists, the accusation was that they wanted to rid Bale of the *Amhara* and overthrow the *Amhara* government.[23] The word *Amhara* was also what the population at large used – depicting everyone and everything associated with the state apparatus as Amhara. There is no doubt that they placed much weight on the religious dimension of Amhara peoplehood, something confirmed by the fact that people still today talk about *foon Amhara* when referring to "Christian meat."[24] Amhara was the religious opposite and was moreover synonymous with the alien invaders, the violent conquerors, and the hegemonic power to which they had to succumb.

Hajji Adam Saddo was in particular concerned with what he viewed as religious oppression, and this was one of the main reasons for his opposition to the government. For him, adherence to Islam would be the means to unite the Arsi Oromo, and he was constantly urging people to remain faithful Muslims (Muusaa Haaji Aadam Saaddoo 2014: 37). He was deeply worried that people would gradually convert to Christianity and argued that accepting *amantii warri Minilik* (the religion of Menelik's people) was the ultimate form of succumbing to Amhara domination. Conversion to Christianity would mean that the Arsi Oromo would lose their identity, and he was similarly concerned that the Amhara presence would eradicate Islam – predicting that Islam would disappear within a five-year period.[25] Both he and Qadi Ahmed Imama claimed that Muslim youth were converting to Christianity as they were given jobs within the government administration.[26] The connection made between conversion and official structures is interesting and points to how religion was perceived as being closely associated

---

[23] Letter from Hajji Adam Saddo to the Ethiopian Imperial Government's High Court, Goba, January 24, 1967.

[24] Similar perceptions were found among other Muslim communities in the south, equating Amhara with Christian (Greenfield 1965: 57).

[25] Testimony by *Grazmach* Hassan Mesfin, November 24, 1966.

[26] Bale Province's High Court: Verdict against Hajji Adam Saddo, Goba, June 13, 1967; Bale Province's High Court: Verdict against *Fitawrari* Ahmed Imama, Goba, June 13, 1967.

with state structures, and that affiliation with those structures would have religious implications.

The highland activists were also much occupied with the lack of religious freedom. They believed that the Amhara presence curbed the rights of the Muslims and were constantly pointing to how this produced religious inequality. Hajji Adam Saddo was again the one who most explicitly voiced such concerns, arguing that schools and health facilities were created to benefit only the Christians, or the "children of the Amhara." While he linked conversion with public service, Hajji Adam Saddo complained, somewhat ironically, that it always was the Christians who got access to jobs in public administration, and that they were the ones promoted to higher positions.[27] The highland activists also criticized the government for restricting the construction of mosques, and when General Wolde-Selassie Bereka, the governor of Bale (1967–1970) ordered all the people in and around Goba – both Christians and Muslims – to contribute money for the construction of a new church in the town, Hajji Adam Saddo confronted him. Pointing out that there were four churches already in Goba, and only one mosque (constructed by the Italians), he argued that the collected money should be divided in two – and also used for the construction of a mosque. The general, who was eager to strengthen his relations with the Muslims, unprecedentedly agreed to Hajji Adam Saddo's demand (Muusaa Haaji Aadam Saaddoo 2014: 28). Hajji Adam Saddo, moreover, lamented that the priests of the Orthodox Church were paid regular salaries, while Muslims sheikhs received nothing.[28] Different from the church-schools that benefited from land-grant and tax exemptions, sheikhs teaching the Qur'an instead lived off support from the local community, which in the case of Bale placed them in a precarious situation. The Amhara governors and landlords feared that the support for the religious students would reduce what they could extract from the people and were rather hostile to the Islamic teaching. This clearly impinged on the people's ability to aid the sheikhs and resulted in a situation where the sheikhs and their students often had to move from village to village to survive.

---

[27] Qadi Ahmed Imama, while working as a *worreda* administrator, was said to have promised that he would exclusively hire Muslims to public office and in this way reduce the number of Christians in office.

[28] Bale Province's High Court: Verdict against Hajji Adam Saddo, Goba, June 13, 1959.

The insurgents' and the highlanders' reference to and invocation of Islam seem to indicate that the struggle was all – and only – about religion. This becomes highly inaccurate, and a nuanced understanding of the role of Islam requires fine-tuned analyses. To begin with, the references to Islam should not be equated with those of modern-day Islamists who aim to establish an Islamic political order based on *shari'a* rule. Rather, when the insurgents spoke about an Islamic government as an alternative, it was both about securing religious freedom for Islam and *bliisumaa* – freedom – for them as an *Islaama* peoplehood. Nor should the role of Islam be understood alongside individualistic perceptions of religion, in the sense of being a matter of inner faith, wherein joining the insurgency was a personal religious duty. While Islam was a real factor in the struggle, it did not play an independent, separate, and overshadowing role. Religion remained, rather, integral, which means, generally speaking, that it interacted with ethnicity – as well as other factors – in a highly complex manner. Both religion and ethnicity were primary dimensions for the imagination of a common peoplehood, of being *Islaama*, and similarly important for generating awareness of distinctiveness and boundaries toward the Amhara.

Amhara vs *Islaama*

The causes of the insurgents' struggle and the highland activists' involvement were rooted in their daily experience of domination, which mirrored the broader population's realities. The political and economic aspects of domination were entangled with the religious and ethnic dimensions of peoplehood that contributed to a reciprocal process of heightened consciousness and demarcation of boundaries. References to religion and ethnicity were both explicit and subtle, yet decisive for the Muslim Arsi Oromo's "contradictory rebellious consciousness." The insurgency thus became the articulation and enactment of the people's willingness to contest domination.

The combination of the Amhara notion of exceptionalism and expansionism had a clear impact on how the Amhara in Bale viewed themselves and the local population. To begin with, they were surely conscious of being different from the native population yet did not see themselves as illegitimate intruders. Rather, understanding themselves as embodying the Ethiopian *nation,* and framing their emplaced

belonging within the territoriality of the Ethiopian state, the Amhara
viewed the conquered areas as legitimate parts of the empire, which
thus could be considered as "homeland" (cf. Levine 1974: 185).
Subscribing to the notion of Ethiopian expansionism as a righteous
destiny, they clearly saw themselves as superior to the Arsi Oromo.
This clearly affected the nature and degree of interactions with the
locals, and although Amharization as a project in principle allowed
for the integration of peoples of the south, the Amhara living in Bale
guarded the boundaries between themselves and what they considered
the inferior Arsi Oromo.

The Amhara's pejorative views were made explicit through labels
applied to the peoples in the south – such as Wolamu, Shankala, and
Geleb, and the word *Galla,* which could, as noted in Chapter 8, have
a religious connotation. However, during the twentieth century, it
gradually became the term applied to the Oromo. This was also how
the word was used in Bale, and rather than Arsi, *Galla* was the most
common word used by the Amhara when referring to the local Oromo
population. Many Amhara argue – even today – that it had no derogatory meaning or that they were unaware of any possible negative
connotation. One of my (Amhara) informants contests this, however,
and although the northern Amhara settlers had little knowledge about
those they settled among, he claimed that Galla undoubtedly was used
it as an insult.[29] Other informants said that the word had a broader
meaning: "It was used for someone who was backward, and it could be
used by those in the towns when talking about the people in the rural
areas, indicating that they were more primitive."[30] Galla was moreover
commonly used in combination with words like "dirty," and "filthy" –
as expressed in Amharic sayings like *Galla-na shinfilla biyatbutim
ayteram* (Galla and intestines will never become clean) and *Galla
qamal ballah* (the Galla eats fleas). Like other derogatory tropes
applied to others on the basis of peoplehood, it had the clear purpose
of dehumanizing the other, and there is no doubt that the Arsi Oromo
themselves understood the word Galla very negatively. For them it was
a term that epitomized Amhara arrogance and their patronizing
attitudes:

[29] Interview, Mekonnen Abebe, Robe, December 16, 2000.
[30] Interview, Abebe Girma, Robe, June 13, 2017.

I and some friends were waiting for the bus in Goba when a man came to buy tickets. This was a known and rich man, and almost considered untouchable. When he got off his mule, and his servant took his mule, he started going toward the office. Behind him came the servant. When he saw that, he turned to the man and said: "What do you want, you Galla, you are not a man but an animal." I and my friends were very much angry about this, and we talked about it on the bus all the way to Robe.[31]

It would have been unthinkable for both the servant and those witnessing to challenge the man's behavior, and the informant's words serve to paint a picture of encompassing domination. Dessalegn Rahmato, applying Eric Wolf's notion of a surrounding field of power, has aptly characterized the total domination of the Amhara in the south as marked by "dependency and powerlessness" (1985: 24). Such domination was first of all embodied in those who filled the official structures of governance, and there were basically no limits to the all-encompassing power of the Amhara officials. This extended beyond the class of officials, however, and was manifest in the Amhara in Bale in general, who, through a sense of shared peoplehood with the ruling elite, felt a particular entitlement. Such interdependency between any Amhara and the authorities created a situation where even the poorest among them would view him- or herself as attached to the ruling political elite. Simply being Amhara was enough for such inclusion, and this belongingness made him or her untouchable. The result was a local Amhara hegemony that effectively enveloped the people and generated a distinct sense of powerlessness – as illustrated by the following poem:

Ka garbarte jabadhuu
ka dheesetu fagadhuu
Amarii bakaka qaba

To you that were made tenants, be strong
To you that ran away, stay far away
The Amhara has lightning

Such a sense of powerlessness was particularly felt among the pastoralists. As an outsider, I was never able to fully comprehend the extent of this. One informant from the lowlands told me that when they brought their cattle to the market in Ginir, "we could risk that the Amhara took

[31] Interview, Obse Ibrahim, Robe, January 9, 2000.

them all. If we went to the court, the court wouldn't help us."[32] Not only were the pastoralists treated in such a capricious manner – there was literally no one they could turn to. The Amhara filled all positions of local administrations, and it was moreover not uncommon that the Amhara government official, the Amhara landlord, the Amhara judge, and the Amhara policeman were embodied in the same person. These were all part of the state's structures of domination that they also industriously utilized for personal enrichment. The one stealing the cattle might as well have been a police officer, who then would pay off the judge with part of the loot. The power of ordinary Amhara and their sense of prerogatives can be illustrated by another informant's story about an Amhara merchant coming to Raytu *worreda*, where a local Arsi Oromo accidentally injured the Amhara's head. The Amhara was reportedly fuming with rage, saying that this "was the same as if someone had hurt the government's head." The people were terrified and pleaded with the man – who only was satisfied when he received a bull as compensation.[33]

While both the religious and ethnic dimensions were critical to such treatments, my claim, however, is that in addition to the ethnic dimension, being Muslim added a particular dimension to the policies of discrimination toward the Arsi Oromo. According to my informants, the Muslim Arsi Oromo were in a separate situation wherein the religious and ethnic dimensions exacerbated their situation: "there was double suppression; the Christian Oromo were only suppressed because of their ethnicity, but the Muslim Oromo were suppressed both because of ethnicity and religion."[34] Another informant said, "the Muslims were the ones worst insulted."[35] Such *double suppression* confirms the particular relevance of religion in the process of othering. Religion was pivotal for the Amhara's sense of exceptionalism, as well as informing the existing historical religious fault line, whereby the Amhara viewed the Muslims with a great deal of suspicion. The religious dimension was in addition reciprocally reinforced by the way the two groups explicitly articulated it – as the basis for pejorative othering, on the one hand, and as the source for resistance, on the other hand.

---

[32] Interview, Nuri Muhammad, Raytu, June 12, 2017.
[33] Interview, Adam Yunus, Raytu, June 10, 2017.
[34] Interview, Mekonnen Abebe, Robe, December 16, 2000.
[35] Interview, Hajji Semir Idris, Addis Ababa, December 9, 2017.

The parameters for Amhara peoplehood and boundaries vis-à-vis *Islamaa* in Bale gradually changed in the latter part of the twentieth century. This transformation was linked to the already discussed processes of nation building, to the emergence of the "new Amhara" as a category, and to Emperor Haile Selassie's modernization efforts. These new Amhara thus became indispensable as civilizing agents for the building of an enlightened nation, which was a project framed within a narrative orienting Ethiopia toward a new linear future of progress (Donham 1999: 2). It consequently meant that the others – pagan or Muslims – were no longer only religiously different; they were also "traditional," "backward," and "uneducated." The process of modernization indirectly entailed a form of secularization, which Emperor Haile Selassie formulated through the famous phrase *hager y'gara new, haymanot y'gil new* (the country is for all, religion is private). While it was meant to be benevolently inclusive, it had an inescapable religious dimension. The aim was to integrate the uneducated non-Christians into the modern Ethiopian nation; yet, this nation was, at the same time, imagined as a modern Christian nation – *one* Ethiopia under God and emperor. The status of the Orthodox Church as the state church and of the emperor as the "Elect of God" effectively secured the position of Christianity as the superior religion and as intimately associated with civilization and enlightenment, which consequently made adherence to other religions an obstacle.

An important dimension of this project of enlightenment was the spread of Amharic as the national language. Amharic, as mentioned in Chapter 8, was intrinsic to the Amhara notion of exceptionalism, and while taking pride in their long literary tradition, the lack of any such tradition among the southerners further confirmed the Amhara perception of these as backward. Emperor Haile Selassie, in a meeting with Somalis in Ogaden, made this explicit by telling them that they could only advance themselves "through the medium of Amharic" (Lewis 2002: 182). The establishment and teaching of Amharic as the only official national language effectively meant that any other Ethiopian language was disqualified. No other language was allowed as a medium of instruction in schools or to be printed or broadcast (Markakis 2011: 133). In fact, writing and printing in another language would often be seen as an anti-government activity. Marzagora even claims that the government's fear of the role of Arabic in potentially unifying the Muslims consequently meant that the "Muslims became primary targets of the policy of Amharisation" (2015: 203). Yet, for the nation builders, the spread of Amharic was not perceived as enforcing one particular ethnic identity but in line with the notion of "official nationalism" and based upon the notion of the Amhara as the historical ruling group; it was the natural point of departure. It was, in other words, the Amhara version of the "white man's burden" – not much different from the colonial states where "[h]egemony was a paternal obligation" (Young 1982: 76).

There were, however, few Arsi Oromo who learned Amharic, mainly due to the lack of interaction between the two groups but also because of their aversion to the Amhara. Want of proficiency in Amharic reciprocally reinforced the Amhara's disdain for the local people and was also a means through which such contempt could be practically expressed in daily lives, and it was actively used to humiliate the local population:

Going to public offices in the old days meant that we would be very much insulted if we couldn't speak Amharic. If you entered there with your business and spoke in *Oromiffa* [the Oromo language], you were insulted and commanded to wait for a long time, while those speaking Amharic did their things. This was of course a very humiliating experience.[36]

The spread of Amharic, nation building, and modernization were intimately intertwined with public education. Although it was recognized that only a quarter of Ethiopia's population actually spoke Amharic, that did not discourage the government from introducing Amharic as the language instruction in public schools. Language, however, was not considered a neutral thing, and what is intriguing was how the Muslim Arsi Oromo viewed Amharic as a language connected to Christianity. It was therefore not only the schools' Christian character and attachment to the Orthodox Church that made them keep the children away; the very use of Amharic created a fear among the Muslims that education and learning the language would drive their children away from Islam. One of my key informants recounted his experiences from the early 1960s as follows:

All the [people] knew was that Christianity came with the Amhara. When I was a child my father sent me to school . . . . I was the first in my area who received modern education. At that time, all the people in our area objected

---

[36] Interview, Obse Ibrahim, Robe, October 23, 2000.

[to] my father. They complained and said that I would be like an Amhara, meaning that I would become a Christian. The main reason for this was because the teaching was conducted in Amharic. When a person, an Oromo, spoke Amharic, he was considered to be an Amhara, a Christian.[37]

This statement illustrates that conversion to Christianity was not primarily about changing one's faith but included the adoption of traits commonly associated with ethnic identity. This clearly highlights how religion and ethnicity remained intimately interwoven in demarcating the boundary between Amhara and *Islaama*. The religious dimension constituted, at the same time, an addition to the antagonistic relationship between the Muslim Oromo and the new rulers. While other non-Christian groups in the south could be assimilated and incorporated into the new notion of the Ethiopian nation more easily – wherein adoption of Christianity was a primary factor – the Muslims unwillingness to convert placed them in a precarious situation. The Christian underpinnings of the Ethiopian national space maintained the existing religious fault line that prevented the full inclusion of the Muslims. They were not only seen as inferior but also treated with suspicion as a potential threat to the imagined cohesiveness of the nation.

While government investments in the area of education were negligible in the first part of the twentieth century, the 1950s saw a significant expansion of schools across the country.[38] Educational investments in Bale remained, in contrast, rather marginal. The governor *Dejazmach* Nasibu Zamanuel (1932–1935) established the first school in Goba in the early 1930s, and a few additional schools – at the primary level – were opened after the Italian period in Ginir, Dodola, Adaba, and Kokosa (Abbas H. Gnamo 1992: 259). However, only eight teachers were available in the whole of Bale in 1945, and until 1959, the total number of schools in Bale was no more than twenty-five, with a student population of only 2,007 ("Education in Bale" 2005; Assefa Teshome 1990: 14). The number of schools increased to seventy-two in 1960 (with a student body of 18,330); yet in 1969, enrollment at primary and secondary levels remained at only at 14.1 percent and 1.9 percent, respectively ("Education in Bale" 2005). All of the schools in Bale were located in the urban areas –

---

[37] Interview, Obse Ibrahim, Robe, September 1, 2002. Markakis has confirmed similar attitudes elsewhere in Ethiopia (1974: 158).

[38] For more on this, see Tekeste Negash (1990, 2006).

meaning that most students were Amhara – and there were very few in
the lowland areas. The total number of students in Dello *awraja* in
1970 was only 378, whereas in the whole of El Kere *awraja,* there were
no more than sixty-four students (Aberra Ketsela 1971).

While public education was supposed to have a secular profile, and
although education was free of any explicit religious subjects or
instruction, religion did play an important yet surreptitious role, with
religious subjects disguised as "civics" or moral education. Moreover,
the schools' attachment to the Orthodox Church meant that all students – regardless of faith – were required to say the "Our Father"
prayer and a Christian blessing for Emperor Haile Selassie every morning. In addition, all students were forced to attend church during
Orthodox Christian holidays:

We marched in line from the school to the church and participated in the
ceremony at the church .... To go to the church was a must for everybody ....
But when we got older, and understood what this was about, we remained in
the back, not participating in the ceremonies .... There were no celebrations
during the Muslim holidays.[39]

This obviously made the Muslims sceptical of the school system, and
similar to colonial Africa, where education was in the hands of
Christian missionaries, Ethiopian Muslims were reluctant to send
their children to the government schools (Aman Seifedin 1987: 35;
Gebru Tareke 1977: 277; Markakis 1974: 156f.). In Bale, Muslims
accounted for only about 9 percent of all the 2,191 students in Goba
during the 1969/1970 academic year. At the high school in Goba, only
86 Muslim students attended – out of a total of 682, and of the 25
students in twelfth grade, only one was Muslim (Aberra Ketsela 1971:
15; Gebru Tareke 1977: 277). The situation was similar across the
country, and educational inequality based on religion is something that
has characterized Ethiopia until recent decades. As schooling was the
key to employment in the growing state apparatus, its lack among the
Muslims augmented their marginal position.

The arrival of Salafism, parallel to the Bale insurgency, contributed
to a more complex religious landscape, and I will end this chapter by
asking if it had any impact on the armed resistance. The Salafi movement, as noted in Chapter 2, was at a rather embryonic stage during the

[39] Interview, Obse Ibrahim, Robe, August 7, 2005.

1960s. An increasing number of Arsi Oromo were seeking further religious education in Saudi Arabia, but they would not have much impact on the religious landscape until the early 1970s. The fact that the shrine of Sheikh Hussein – which the Salafis viewed very negatively – played a key role as a hub for insurgency-related activism did not exactly encourage the participation of any Salafi faithful.

The Salafi reformers were little concerned with politics and played a minimal role in anti-government activism. To my knowledge, only one individual, Sheikh Muhammad Amin Chaffa, actively supported the insurgency. Originally from the Arsi region, he was a merchant by profession, and the leading figure in the small group of reformists in Robe. He was influenced by ethno-nationalist politics while living in Harar, and after arriving in Bale, he was in frequent contact with Hajji Adam Saddo.[40] In contrast, some Salafis were directly opposed to the insurgency, and one leading Salafi scholar and a former imam in Robe described the fighters as untrustworthy and violent.[41]

These different views on the insurgency are important for two reasons. First of all, they contribute to underscore how religion was not a distinct, isolated dimension of the insurgency in the sense of making the struggle "purely religious." It was not based upon or driven by any particular religious doctrines – Salafi or other. Secondly, these diverse views challenge the common (mis)representations of Salafism as a political, extremist, and even jihadi movement. Such a one-sided understanding of Salafism as unilaterally and inescapably having politically objectives reflects a broader tendency of essentializing political Islam. Salafism is not, as argued by Thomas Hegghammer (2009), a political movement but primarily a theological one. The Bale case is thus a clear demonstration of Salafism's inherent complexity and reminds us not to uncritically extrapolate contemporary concepts and phenomena upon a historical context but rather to recognize the situatedness of local representations of Salafism.

Conclusion

This chapter has demonstrated how the dimensions of class, ethnicity, and religion remained so interrelated that it is impossible to isolate any

---

[40] Interview, Hasina Hassan, Robe, August 4, 2005.
[41] Interview, Sheikh Ahmed Aliye, Robe, October 6, 2005.

one of them as the cause of the insurgency. It is incorrect to reduce ethnicity and religion to expressions underlying class as the "real" issue of the conflict. What we have seen is that the conflict did not align itself along neatly defined class categories, thus making it difficult to classify the insurgency as an explicit class conflict. It is also clear that ethnicity and religion proved immensely crucial for the demarcation of a complex set of boundaries. This does not mean that ethnicity and religion simply trumped class in the making of the conflict, but it points back to the inherent complex relations among these dimensions. Religion and ethnicity should, furthermore, not merely be construed as something dislocated and abstract. I have already demonstrated how the changing realities during the twentieth century led to increased economic pressure and to the reconfiguring of sociopolitical organiza-tions in Bale's conquest, but I have also – through my discussion of the land-clan connection – pointed to how socioeconomic changes criti-cally affected notions of identity and belonging.

This all harks back to the overarching argument of this study: of religion and ethnicity as based on visceral experiences, as based on embodied and emplaced experiences, and as intimately connected to primary relations and primary places. The emotional aspect of this is inevitable, and in the particular case of Bale, tangible forms of domina-tion resulted in deep feelings of loss, humiliation, and anger. The derogatory treatment along the religious and ethnic dimensions touched at the core of the notion of peoplehood and became the prism through which the other aspects of subjugation were interpreted. The role of religion and ethnicity as intrinsic dimensions of peoplehood and in demarcating boundaries had, however, additional complicating layers. I will turn to these layers in the next chapter, focusing on how the insurgency contributed to muddying the water by bringing religion to the surface in a manner that complicated the question of ethnicity.

11 | *The Bale Insurgency,* Islaama, *and Oromo Ethno-nationalism*

I will end this story by focusing on how the ethnic and religious dimensions of peoplehood complicated the insurgency movement's interactions with other Oromo groups and movements in Bale and beyond. This relates first of all to the Shoa Oromo community in Bale – a group that at the outset would ostensibly be close to the Arsi Oromo and share similar antagonist sentiments toward the Amhara and assumingly side with the insurgents against the state. The fact that they did not is noticeable and can only, I argue, be explained by examining the religious dimension. Secondly, it relates to the nascent Oromo ethno-nationalist movement surfacing in the 1960s. As a largely urban elitist movement and dominated by Christian Oromo, it was significantly different from the Bale insurgency. The two movements managed to connect, however, and it is interesting how the religious dimension seemingly did not affect their relationship. This does not mean that religion was irrelevant, and I will in my discussion tease out the complex interplay between ethnicity and religion during these interactions.

The relevance of religion in demarcating boundaries and reinforcing conflictual lines would assumingly be strengthened by the arrival of Salafism to Bale in the same period. The Ethiopian government was, as we have seen, highly sensitive to the religious factor, repeatedly accusing the insurgents of being instruments of "foreign Islam" aimed at establishing an Islamic political order in Ethiopia. I will in the latter part of the chapter explore what role the embryonic Salafi movement played in relation to the insurgency, arguing for the need to move beyond established assumptions and teleological perspectives when thinking of Islam and politics and demonstrating that this cannot always be neatly categorized as political Islam or Islamism.

Religion, Ethnicity, and the Shoa Oromo

In July 2018, a violent conflict erupted in Bale's old capital town of Goba. The controversy was related to the local authorities' plans to erect a statue of Hajji Adam Saddo in the town's main square. The arrival of Arsi Oromo youth from the rural areas on July 21 to push for the construction led to protests and clashes between opposing groups, killing six people. News reports presented the violence as being between Muslim Arsi Oromo and the town's Amhara population; the latter allegedly opposing the statue because the square was central to the celebration the Christian Orthodox holiday *timket* (epiphany) (Etenesh Aberra and Mahlet Fasil 2018). My sources contest this, one claiming instead that the conflict was between Muslim Arsi Oromo and Christian Shoa Oromo.[1] This might seem surprising but reveals how the presence of the Shoa Oromo in Bale added a complex and important layer to the local situation. The presence of the Shoa Oromo across the south is not commonly captured in macro-level studies of Amhara domination, yet it is highly relevant when seeking to understand the multifaceted connections between class, religion, and ethnicity. Any attempt to fully understand this requires fine-tuned analyses and the need to move beyond dualistic frameworks exclusively focused on Amhara-Oromo relations of domination and resistance. We need to pay attention to how the existing trilateral configuration of the Arsi Oromo, Amhara, and the Shoa Oromo crosscut one another along a variety of dimensions (Blackhurst 1980).

As landless tenants, the Shoa Oromo constituted a largely homogenous group in terms of socioeconomics and could, as such, be considered a distinct and disadvantaged "class." This would mean, again according to a class-conflict perspective, that they would be the group with the strongest incentive to take up arms against the hegemonic structures of domination and join the insurgency. The fact that except for a very few individuals, they did not but instead found themselves siding with and supporting the government is yet another illustration of how a unilateral focus on class remains insufficient for understanding the insurgency. It also points to the complexity of ethnicity in Bale and to the lack of Oromo unity alongside an isolated ethnic dimension and also speaks to the need to consider other aspects. I will demonstrate

---

[1] Telephone conversation with Yasin Muhammad, July 27, 2018.

how the religious dimension in particular contributed to divide the Arsi and the Shoa Oromo, and to how religion complicated the notion of belonging and peoplehood.

As discussed in Chapter 6, the Shoa Oromo originated from the region of Shoa, in the central parts of the country. They had lived there for centuries in close proximity with the local Amhara population, consequently bringing them culturally close to the latter. While Oromo was their main language, most of the Shoa Oromo were fluent in Amharic. The Shoa Oromo had at an early stage adopted orthodox Christianity, which was a crucial step toward assimilation. This blurred the boundaries, allowing for intermarriages with the Amhara and also enabling the local Shoa Oromo gentry to become part of the political elite, where they also through intermarriages even had become part of the royal family (Blackhurst 1974: 8f.; Tsegaye Zeleke 2002).

Lack of land in Shoa and harsh treatment by the nobility were, as noted, the reasons for migrations to the south starting in the 1920s, and many Shoa Oromo started to arrive in the Arsi and Bale regions from the 1940s. While the Shoa Oromo consisted of a number of different clans, the main clan arriving in Bale was the Salale, originating from the area of Fiche, ca 120 km north of Addis Ababa. As settlers, the Shoa Oromo arrived in a disorganized manner and were initially mainly young married men who – until they found land – left their families behind. Alone and without any kinship networks, they thus often found themselves in a precarious situation as they arrived in Bale, where they were forced to negotiate their position and identity in relation to both the indigenous Arsi Oromo and the Amhara.

As tenants and sharecroppers under mainly Arsi Oromo landowners, a mutual dependency relationship soon developed between the two groups. The Shoa Oromo's cultivation of the land helped the Arsi Oromo pay their taxes, while the Arsi Oromo provided the Shoa Oromo with the protection they needed. However, as the number of Shoa Oromo grew and as some were able to purchase land for themselves, their dependency on the Arsi Oromo diminished. They also gradually established their own communities, separated themselves from the Arsi Oromo, and presented themselves as a homogenous and united vis-à-vis the Arsi Oromo (Blackhurst 1980: 58f.). I do not agree with Blackhurst's (1980: 61) instrumentalist perspective, through which he argues that the Shoa Oromo's attempt to distance themselves from the Arsi Oromo was mainly an economic question being disguised and expressed along an ethnic dimension. It is important here to note that this separation was complicated by the spatial proximity between the two groups. In contrast to the urban Amhara, who had very limited day-to-day interactions with the Arsi Oromo, the Shoa Oromo communities were exclusively found in the rural areas, where they were never far from the native population.

Shoa Oromo distinctiveness was clearly seen through the self-descriptive label they applied to themselves. While they used their clan names, they never called themselves "Oromo." Instead they referred to themselves as "Amhara."[2] The term *Amhara* obviously denotes the Shoa Oromo as orthodox Christians, and although Haberland called them "Galla-speaking Amhara" (1963: 776), this does not mean a complete abandonment of being Oromo, or of practices associated with this. It does, however, point to the intimate relevance of religion as part of Shoa Oromo peoplehood. It also demonstrates how religion gained more relevance for them as strangers. According to one of Abbas H. Gnamo's Shoa Oromo informants: "celui qui traversé le fleuve Awash est Amhara" (whoever crosses the Awash River is Amhara) (Abbas H. Gnamo 1992: 268).

My argument is that religion was the most important factor demarcating the boundary the Shoa Oromo and the Arsi Oromo. This boundary was characterized by social distance that was embodied, for example, by the way the two groups were unable to share a meal (meat) or intermarry. While the Shoa Oromo most commonly referred to the Arsi Oromo as *Islaama*, or sometimes as Arsi, what is particularly interesting is that they also used the derogatory word *Galla* – which in this context was synonymous with Muslim (Blackhurst 1974: 8). The Shoa Oromo also came to share many of the prejudices of the Amhara settlers and saw the Muslim Arsi Oromo as backward and primitive and viewed their pastoral lifestyle as a sign of laziness. They also developed a whole range of stereotypes, denoting the Arsi Oromo as unclean and sexually immoral. The fact that they at the same time were economically weaker and reliant on the Arsi Oromo obviously created a rather awkward situation.

The Shoa Oromo's attitudes were based on their view of themselves as culturally superior, and, as expressed by one of my informants, "it was religion that drove us close to the Amhara."[3] The most obvious

---

[2] Interview, Abebe Girma, Robe, June 13, 2017.
[3] Interview, Abebe Girma, Robe, June 13, 2017.

indication of this was that they as Christians could marry Amhara, as well as those from other Christian settler groups (Blackhurst 1980: 60). The Shoa Oromo moreover underscored the religious commonality between themselves and the Amhara in a deliberate attempt to associate themselves even more closely with the Amhara, and in this way, further demarcate the boundary with the Muslim Arsi Oromo. The relationship between the Shoa Oromo and the Amhara, however, was tenuous, and the Shoa Oromo were never considered on par with the Amhara. The Amhara, on their side, had no need for the Shoa Oromo and made a point of distinguishing themselves from them. They never referred to them as Amhara and used instead the word *Galla* for both the Arsi and the Shoa Oromo, calling the latter Shoa Galla.

The Arsi Oromo, on their part, viewed the Shoa Oromo as similar to any other outsiders and engaged in their own processes of boundary making. The Shoa Oromo were at the outset excluded from the Arsi Oromo clan structures and alien to the land-clan connection. This mean that even if the Shoa Oromo gained access to land, there were no means that would allow them to be included. In fact, purchase of land by the Shoa Oromo was part of the privatization and commodification of land that gradually eroded the land-clan connection. However, the main factor distancing the Arsi Oromo from the Shoa Oromo was religion, and the Shoa Oromo's adherence to Christianity caused the Arsi Oromo to demarcate clear boundaries toward them (Blackhurst 1974: 19).[4] Although the Arsi Oromo would refer to the Shoa Oromo as Salale, thus indirectly acknowledging their Oromo character, the majority of the Arsi Oromo did not differentiate between the Shoa Oromo and the Amhara; they were both subsumed under the Amhara category – meaning Christian.[5] The fact that being Christian and being Amhara were so intimately linked with the state and political power clearly affected the Arsi Oromo's attitudes toward the Shoa Oromo; viewing them with suspicion, as intruders and even as enemies (Abbas H. Gnamo 1992: 268).[6] Such sentiments were clearly expressed in the following poem:

---

[4] Interviews, Obse Ibrahim, Robe, April 15, 2005; Hussein Mahmoud, Robe, August 2, 2005.
[5] Interview, Obse Ibrahim, Robe, September 1, 2002.
[6] Interview, Galgalo Dereje, Robe, September 30, 2002.

Salaalee hin amaninaa
Yoo Islaamaa ta'ees
Kirri kutee kiisii kaa'ata
Yoo haaliin hin mija'in
Debisee mormatti godhataa

Don't trust the Salale
Even if he becomes a Muslim
He will cut his thread[7] and put in his pocket
But when it suits him
He will change his mind[8]

The aspect of enmity was also colored and complicated by narratives of conflict, dating back to the time of Menelik's expansions. During the conquest of Arsi, *Ras* Gobena Dache, Menelik's general, commanded a large contingent of Shoa Oromo soldiers who were instrumental in crushing the Arsi Oromo resistance to settle in Arsi. This laid the foundation for a tense relationship between the two groups, which occasionally erupted into open conflict. For example, during the fighting leading up to the Italian occupation (1936–1941), the Arsi Oromo – siding with the Italians – started to attack the outside settlers in the Bale and Arsi regions. Those targeted were both Amhara and Shoa Oromo, a fact that brought the two groups into a close alliance against the Arsi Oromo (Abbas H. Gnamo 1992: 269f.).

As noted, a few Shoa Oromo joined the Bale insurgency, but the overwhelming majority viewed the insurgents with trepidation – as dangerous enemies and a threat to their lives. Hajji Adam Saddo and Qadi Ahmed Imama tried to secure the Shoa Oromo's support, and through contact with a certain Lemma Dinqu, they sought to influence prominent Shoa Oromo elders. These efforts bore little fruit (Muusaa Haaji Aadam Saaddoo 2014: 105f.). Living in the rural areas and being a minority of outsiders, the Shoa Oromo were convinced they would be targeted by the insurgents. When they actively came out supporting the government and thus came to be viewed as collaborators, their fear turned out to be true. In fact, the Shoa Oromo were the ones who suffered the most in the hands of the insurgents, while the Amhara, who were found in the urban centers, largely escaped. Attacks on civilian

---

[7] This refers to the *mateb*, a thread Ethiopian Orthodox Christians wear around their neck as a sign of baptism.

[8] Interview, Hajji Idris Boru, Addis Ababa, June 14, 2011.

Shoa Oromo increased in the course of the insurgency, and as the fighters became increasingly desperate in search of food for survival, the Shoa Oromo were the obvious targets. The combination of politics, religion, and the need to defend themselves caused the Shoa Oromo to become more involved in fighting the insurgents, and the bulk of the *nech lebash* and the volunteers assisting the Ethiopian regular forces was made up of Shoa Oromo.[9] This inevitably contributed to exacerbating a reciprocal spiral of violence between them and the insurgents. As the Shoa Oromo's role in the conflict made them targets by the insurgents, they, in turn, used their position as *nech lebash* to loot civilian Arsi Oromo. In the areas around Goba and Ginir, for example, the Shoa Oromo set fire to private houses and plundered the owners.[10] As the violence increased, the local Arsi Oromo population found themselves in a thorny position:

The Muslims were afraid of the Salale [Shoa Oromo], the government, and the *Sowra* [insurgents]. It was complicated. If you joined the *Sowra*, the government or the Salale could take action on you. If you sided with the government, the *Sowra* could take action on you. Many couldn't decide on who to side with. They didn't know. Also, they didn't know who was who, who to trust ... being a Muslim meant that you could be attacked by the Salale.[11]

Violence between the Shoa and the Arsi Oromo would increase dramatically in the beginning of the Derg period – during the insurgency leading up to the Ogaden war (1977–1978) – which was devastating for both groups. Particularly important incidents took place around Jarra town in Gololcha *worreda*. When the insurgents started to move around in that area, seeking to recruit fighters, the local Shoa Oromo of a village called Gullale became increasingly worried, and in 1975, they asked the authorities for guns to protect themselves. News of this soon reached the insurgents, who then attacked the Shoa Oromo, killing seven individuals. The Shoa Oromo then resolutely decided to throw their lot in with the government, which provided them with arms. A few years later, in the middle of 1977, some Shoa Oromo from a village called Dobi (ca 20 km from Jarra town) killed a few

---

[9] Interviews, Hajji Hussein Awol, Robe, March 7, 2006; Obse Ibrahim, Robe, April 15, 2005.
[10] Interview, Obse Ibrahim, Robe, April 15, 2005.
[11] Interview, Obse Ibrahim, Robe, August 25, 2005.

insurgents, which caused the insurgents to retaliate – stealing the cattle of the Shoa Oromo. The conflict soon spiraled out of control and ended with the insurgents burning down all the houses and looting the cattle of the Shoa Oromo in Dobi village. As a result, "the Muslim villagers came peacefully to the Shoa Oromo, and said that it was better for them to leave the area. This was to keep them safe. The Shoa Oromo agreed to move, and they took their remaining belonging and left."[12]

It is relevant to ask whether the Shoa Oromo's lack of support for the insurgency was due to the government's propaganda, which portrayed the insurgents both as instruments for Somali irredentism and as seeking to establish an Islamic political order. It is inaccurate to think that the authorities used this propaganda in any instrumentalist manner, and it is clear that the Shoa Oromo and the rest of the Christians in Bale – irrespective of the propaganda – viewed the insurgency as mainly a religious movement. The religious dimension thus undoubtedly constituted a crucial underlying factor that positioned the insurgents and by extension the Muslim Arsi Oromo as the antithesis of being Ethiopian. The religious aspect was also intersected with the Christians' common perception of the Muslims as a "foreign" menace, obviously reinforced by the insurgents' links to Somalia.

The triangular relationship between the Arsi Oromo, the Shoa Oromo, and the Amhara clearly demonstrates how categories such as religion, ethnicity, and class do not always create simple and one-dimensional boundaries and, moreover, how the complex crisscrossing of religion and ethnicity complicates notions of peoplehood. While religion and ethnicity may mutually reinforce notions of peoplehood, religion, as discussed earlier, has the potential to transcend the embedded character of peoplehood, producing a sense of shared belonging beyond this embeddedness, which also speaks to the segmentary nature of peoplehood. In the case of the Shoa Oromo and the Arsi Oromo, the religious dimension was so strong that it seriously impacted notions of shared Oromo-ness between the two groups. The insurgency obviously contributed to exacerbate divisions and to further enhance the importance of religion. It may be difficult here to establish simple, one-directional causal connections, but the fact that the Shoa Oromo sided with the government was for the Arsi Oromo a confirmation that they effectively were Amhara, and the composition

[12] Interview, Abebe Girma, Robe, June 13, 2017.

of the insurgency as consisting of only Muslim Arsi Oromo was for the Shoa Oromo a clear indication of the religious nature of the struggle.

Furthermore, this division between the two groups complicates the notion of the Bale insurgency as an early, or first, expression of Oromo ethno-nationalism. The way these two Oromo groups found themselves on opposite sides of the battlefield makes it difficult to uncritically accept this claim and challenges the notion that the "Oromo nationalist spirit cuts across class, religious, and regional differences and fuses the Oromo into a nation" (Mohammed Hassan 2006: 238). Recognizing that things are far more complicated, Georg Haneke (2002) has argued that the idea of a united Oromo ethno-nationalism is not reflected in actual realities, serving the purpose of generating support for the Oromo ethno-nationalist movement's political goals. That activists have such objectives is hardly surprising, but for anyone seeking to understand the complexity on the ground, the case of Bale is an illustration that serves to challenge simplistic explanations.[13]

Oromo Ethno-nationalism

While the Arsi Oromo insurgents were at odds with the Shoa Oromo in Bale, they established links to the Oromo ethno-nationalist movement emerging in the 1960s – a movement that ironically was dominated by Shoa Oromo. This movement was also different from the Bale insurgency in many other ways, and the connections between the two movement is yet another illustration of the intriguing complexity generated by the interplay between religion and ethnicity. This section first introduces the Oromo ethno-nationalist movement before discussing its connections with the Bale insurgency in the next section.

The Oromo ethno-nationalist movement surfacing in the 1960s was primarily embodied in the Macha Tulama Self-help Association (MTSA), which was established on January 24, 1963.[14] The key figures were Colonel Alemu Qitessa and Haile-Mariam Gamada, a lawyer and the formulator of the bylaws of the association. Colonel Alemu Qitessa

---

[13]   For some other nuanced and balanced perspectives on ethnicity and ethnonationalism in Ethiopia, see Merera Gudina (2003), Paulos Chanie (1998), and in particular Schlee (2003).

[14]   *Macha Tulama* refers to two branches of the Oromo, the former located in Wollega, western Ethiopia, while the latter is composed of the Shoa Oromo.

and Haile-Mariam Gamada were MTSA's president and general secretary, respectively, and the first group of leaders included Bekele Nadhi (vice-president) and Colonel Qadida Guremessa.[15] The association also involved high-profile individuals such as General Tadesse Birru, General Jagama Kello, *Dejazmach* Kebede Buzunesh, and even Princess Mahestena Habte-Mariam, the wife of one of the late sons of Emperor Haile Selassie. Other important persons were Lieutenant Mamo Mazamir, Baro Tumsa, and Ibsa Gutama, many of whom would become founding members of the Oromo Liberation Front (OLF) (Mohammed Hassan 1997: 215, 218).

MTSA's main aims were to improve the educational level, health conditions, and the general economic situation for the Oromo. The association soon started to mobilize local Oromo communities through public meetings across the country. The MTSA would gradually move in a more political direction, particularly after General Tadesse Birru, a powerful Oromo officer with significant political influence, joined the association. While initially reluctant to join, saying he did not want to get involved in "tribal politics," he formally became a member on June 23, 1964 (Olana Zoga 1985: 24).[16]

One of the main areas for MTSA activism was the Arsi province, and an important meeting took place in the town of Iteya (ca 50 km south of Adama town) in May 1966. The meeting came to constitute a watershed for MTSA and for Oromo ethno-nationalism, and Mohammed Hassan claims that it served as the "heralding [of] the birth of Oromo nationalism" (Mohammed Hassan 1997: 214). It gathered thousands of Oromo from different regions, which both surprised and alarmed the government. The leaders of MTSA openly advocated for Oromo unity as a political force but were careful not to push the political agenda too far; they framed this within notions of ethnic equality (Olana Zoga 1985: 51).[17] One important objective of the meeting was to bring Christian Oromo and Muslim Oromo together, and particularly interesting in this regard is that during the meeting both Christians and Muslims are said to have shared and eaten meat without considering who had slaughtered it (Olana Zoga 1985: 51, 172). The MTSA leadership obviously recognized the role of

---

[15] Interview, Beyene Nabe, Addis Ababa, June 14, 2011.
[16] Interview, Fayisa Megersa, Addis Ababa, June 18, 2011.
[17] A key speaker here was Hajji Robale Ture, the father of Jamal Robale (aka Gutuma Hawash), a key leader in the OLF.

religion as a divisive factor, and the attempt to have the two groups eat together points to how they deliberately sought to transcend this divide by underscoring the ethnic dimension of shared peoplehood. MTSA expanded steadily after Iteya, and in the course of 1966, it established branches in Arsi, Bale, Hararge, Jimma, Shoa, and Wollega. Another meeting was held in Dhera town in Arsi (ca 30 km south of Adama) on October 16, 1966. This time the authorities were more prepared, cracking down on the meeting and arresting the main organizers. Inevitably, this contributed to the further politicization of the association (Olana: 114).

When the government started laying plans for closing down the association, the MTSA leaders, as faithful military officers and public servants, believed that this was carried out by officials without the emperor's consent. But as he did nothing to prevent this, the MTSA leaders' faith in the emperor eroded and even led General Tadesse Birru to lay plans to overthrow the government through the assassination of the emperor. A planning meeting was held on November 2, 1966, where MTSA leaders from within the armed forces (together with regular soldiers) participated, and where it was decided to kill the emperor on his way to the St. George Church the very next day – on the sixty-third anniversary of his coronation. The plan was to throw a hand grenade at the emperor, and General Tadesse Birru would take power in the ensuing confusion, declaring himself as the leader of a new republic. The plans were hastily and poorly put together, and as the government had planted a spy among the conspirators, the attempted coup was over before it started (Olana Zoga 1985: 122f.). One of my informants who participated in the event gave a vivid account of the chaos that followed:

The night before the coup Tadesse Birru, *Dejazmach* Daniel Abebe, [future] Minister of Foreign Affairs Katama Yefiu ... *Dejazmach* Kebede Buzunesh, Tesfaye Degaga, and I spent the night in Katta outside of Addis Ababa. We were there waiting to hear news about the coup. In the morning *Dejazmach* Daniel and Katama Yefiu returned to Addis Ababa. When we didn't hear anything in the morning, we became unsure .... We moved to Asko [now a suburb of Addis Ababa] and hid ourselves in the forest. That was Tadesse Birru, Tesfaye Degaga, another person, and me. I was told to drive back into Addis Ababa and find out what had happened .... I went home to my house, met my wife and left a note to my relatives about what was going on. I was not sure if I would survive, and I wanted to notify them in case something happened. I then left and returned for Asko ... [when I arrived there] I couldn't find Tadesse Birru, so I left for *Dejazmach* Kebede Buzuneh's house .... At 7pm one priest, Abba Habte Mariam, arrived to negotiate with us. He said that if we surrendered now, we would be pardoned by Haile Selassie .... We discussed with *Dejazmach* Kebede Buzuneh, saying that we shouldn't fight and that we were not prepared. We wanted to negotiate .... I then went in my car with Tadesse's wife and the priest ... [and] came to the queen's palace, behind Yekatit hospital, and Tadesse's wife was escorted into the palace.[18]

General Tadesse Birru and the other main leaders were pardoned and put under house arrest. On November 19, 1966, a bomb exploded in one of the capital's main cinemas – an attack that was blamed on MTSA. Lieutenant and MTSA leader Mamo Mazamir was arrested and accused of the attack, and the incident became the pretext for further action against the MTSA.[19] Security forces moved to arrest General Tadesse Birru and surrounded his house. However, rather than surrendering, the general fought the soldiers and escaped:

Tesfaye [Degaga] came to me in the evening, informing me about what was going on. I took my gun and we went to Tadesse's house. We snuck in from behind, and started firing upon the soldiers. We also gave sign to Tadesse, and he jumped out of the window and joined us. From there, he escaped out of Addis Ababa. I and Tesfaye went home, and Tadesse was on his own .... In the countryside he met a *qallicha*[20] called Abba Jifar [Waqayo] and stayed with him. Abba Jifar [Waqayo] soon informed the government about his whereabouts, and shortly after Tadesse was captured in Jibat.[21]

The MTSA was banned in 1967, and that was effectively the end of the association. General Tadesse Birru and the other leaders were put on trial, and both he and Mamo Mazamir were sentenced to death. Haile-Mariam Gamada died in prison as a result of torture, and the rest of the leadership received long prison sentences. General Tadesse Birru's sentence was later changed to life imprisonment, while Mamo

---

[18] Interview, Fayisa Megersa, Addis Ababa, July 9, 2011.
[19] My informant confirms that Mamo Mazamir placed the bomb in the cinema (interview, Fayisa Megersa, Addis Ababa, July 9, 2011), while others claim that the government fabricated the incident (Mohammed Hassan 1997: 222; Olana Zoga 1985: 138f.).
[20] Traditional healer, religious figure.
[21] Interview, Fayisa Megersa, Addis Ababa, July 9, 2011.

Mazamir was hanged in 1969 (Mohammed Hassan 1997: 227; Olana Zoga 1985).

The MTSA never became a mass movement, and the composition of the leadership clearly points to the association's elitist profile. These individuals were also clearly Amharized, which meant "they had much more in common with the Amhara ruling class ... than with the ordinary Oromo." Many could only communicate in Amharic and had to use an interpreter when speaking to the rural Oromo (Mohammed Hassan 2006: 248, 252). While they perceived themselves as being the vanguard for the Oromo masses, speaking on behalf of the subaltern, they were, at the same time, situated at the margins of the society they wanted to represent. Although they all hailed from rural local communities that embodied Oromo peoplehood, they had crossed a boundary – through education and social mobility – that allowed them access to the elite. This meant, according to Bas van Heur, that they had managed to "escape *their* people" – finding themselves positioned "at a site of privilege" (2004: 40, 43; italics in original). Such movement and their subsequent repositioning through involvement in MTSA clearly colored the process of identity negotiating and their "becoming Oromo," as well as enabling both a particular spatial imagination of the Oromo-inhabited areas and the political meaning of being Oromo. It also generated imaginations that to a certain extent were distant from the Oromo localities, and even sometimes at odds with them.

The Bale Insurgency and Oromo Ethno-nationalism

Although the MTSA gradually moved in a more radical direction, the leaders did not think of the MTSA as a tool for armed struggle. In contrast to the Bale insurgency, the MTSA's leadership and followers were dominated by orthodox Christian Oromo and were largely from highland agriculturalist areas. The association strove to surpass existing intra-Oromo boundaries, seen, for example, in the Iteya meeting discussed earlier, but regional, socioeconomic, and religious differences proved enduring – and has arguably haunted the Oromo ethno-nationalist movement until today.[22]

---

[22] It is interesting to see that most of those involved in the clandestine MTSA group in the Arsi region mostly were Shoa Oromo (Olana Zoga 1985: 52).

In spite of these differences, lines of communication existed between the MTSA and the Bale insurgency. Contact intensified in 1966, when the MTSA leadership actively sought to embrace the Bale *arbenyas* (Amharic; patriots) and to make use of shiftas in other areas (Olana Zoga 1985: 118). Important in facilitating the contacts were a group of Arsi Oromo from Bale living in Addis Ababa, including Muhammad Hussein Fako, Hajji Korme Kimo, and *Qenazmach* Abdulkadir Ahmed Imama (the son of Qadi Ahmed Imama and a member of parliament), Hajji Ibrahim Bakaro, Ahmed Buna (from Arsi), and Sheikh Hussein Sura.[23] Some of these were merchants providing goods to the embryonic group of local traders in Robe. They were, however, instrumental in offering goods of a different nature:

I was a trader at that time, and I was purchasing guns from the bomb terra [the bomb section] at Mercato. We were buying Uzi, Tshitshi (short guns), and Albini. This was illegal at that time, but we brought the guns to Bale and distributed them among the insurgents. Eventually the soldiers of Haile Selassie burned down the bomb terra.[24]

A key individual among these traders was the already mentioned Sheikh Hussein Sura (see Figure 11.1). His real name was Hussein Muhammad Sheikh Aliye, and he was born around 1920 in Sura, in Ginir *worreda*. He started studying Islam at an early age in his home area and continued his studies at Dirre Sheikh Hussein (most likely under Sheikh Aburahman Ismail "Adere"), before leaving for Harar where he taught at the already mentioned Jamiyya School and under Sheikh Ali Abd al-Rahman ("Ali al-Sufi") – and where he also got involved in the SYL (see Chapter 9). His career as a religious scholar was short, however, and soon he established himself as a tailor, while also investing in commercial farming around Shasmane, a town 200 km south of Addis Ababa.[25] In 1962, he arrived in Addis Ababa and established contact with other Arsi Oromo from Bale (Jalata 1994). He

---

[23] Interviews, Ibrahim Hussein, Addis Ababa, December 10, 2017; Hajji Semir Idris, Addis Ababa, March 8, 2011 and December 9, 2017.
[24] Interview, Ibrahim Hussein, Addis Ababa, December 10, 2017.
[25] Interviews, Feisal Ali, Addis Ababa, June 24, 2011; Hajji Isaq Ismail, Skype, September 30, 2019.

Figure 11.1 Sheikh Hussein Sura

was particularly close to Hajji Isaq Dhadhi: their wives were sisters and they lived in close proximity.[26]

Sheikh Hussein Sura was exposed to broader ideological currents at an early stage. He was a passionate reader and subscribed to newspapers and magazines coming from the Arab world, including *Rose al-Yusuf* and *al-Ahram* from Egypt, both nationalized by President Gamal Abdel-Nasser in 1960. In Addis Ababa, he regularly frequented the Egyptian and Somali embassies, where he was provided with literature. While this exposed him to various forms of Islamic reformist currents, informants claimed that he was mainly influenced by Nasserist

[26] Interview, Hajji Semir Idris, Addis Ababa, December 9, 2017.

ideas.[27] Sheikh Hussein Sura became active in Salaam Y'Muslim Mahaber, an early Muslim association founded in Addis Ababa in 1962 (Østebø 2012: 187).[28] He also soon got involved in the Oromo ethno-nationalist movement, and in 1963 he joined the MTSA. This brought him into contact with Colonel Alemu Qitessa and General Tadesse Birru, and he played an important role linking the MTSA with the Muslim Oromo in the southeast and with the Bale insurgency. For example, he was instrumental in organizing the previously mentioned meeting in Dhera in 1966. When the MTSA was banned and the leadership arrested in 1967, Sheikh Hussein Sura himself became a wanted man. Dressed up as an orthodox priest, he fled Addis Ababa for Bale, where he made contact with Hussein Bune at Mt. Gona. Shortly after he escaped to Somalia, where he continued his political activism.[29]

Informants disagree on how many Arsi Oromo from Bale were members of MTSA. One source claims that these included highland activists such as Hajji Adam Saddo, Qadi Ahmed Imama, Hajji Umar Hajji Adam Labano, *Qenazmach* Abubakr Darga, *Grazmach* Umar Hussein, and Adam Jima, while another source argues that it was only Hajji Adam Saddo and *Qenazmach* Abubakr Darga.[30] An important figure in facilitating contacts was the previously mentioned Ahmed Buna from Arsi, who had already connected with Waqo Gutu in 1965. He reportedly disguised himself as a *geriba* (devotee to Sheikh Hussein or pilgrim traveling far distances) and traveled to Bale with a letter addressed to Waqo Gutu hidden in his shoe.[31] This resulted in the first meeting between representatives of the Bale insurgency and General Tadesse Birru and other MTSA leaders in Addis Ababa (Mohammed Hassan 2000: 136; Muusaa Haaji Aadam Saaddoo 2014: 137).[32] One informant who participated in the meeting recounted it as follows:

---

[27] Interview, Ibrahim Hussein, Addis Ababa, December 10, 2017.
[28] The government closed down the association in 1967.
[29] Interrogation Report, Aliye Ahmed, January 17, 1967; interviews, Feisal Ali, Addis Ababa, June 24, 2011; Ibrahim Hussein, Addis Ababa, July 30, 2011; Hajji Isaq Ismail, Skype, September 30, 2019.
[30] Interviews, Ibrahim Hussein, Addis Ababa, December 10, 2017; Amina Hajji Yusuf, Robe, July 2, 2011.
[31] Interview, Hajji Idris Boru, Addis Ababa, June 14, 2011.
[32] Interview, Ibrahim Hussein, Addis Ababa, June 12, 2011. Sheikh Hussein Sura and Ahmed Buna facilitated the meeting.

In 1965, Mamo Mazamir, Tadesse Birru, Tesfaye Dagage, and I had a meeting with Waqo Gutu and Hajji Adam Saddo here in Addis Ababa. We said to them that we were ready to come and join their struggle ... . General Jagama Kello was also involved. The meeting was held in Tadesse Birru's house ... [also] present were Hajji Robale Ture, and Wolde-Emanuel [Dubale] from Sidama.[33]

The link between the Bale insurgency and the MTSA was first and foremost embodied in Hajji Adam Saddo, who acted as the leader of MTSA in Bale (Asafa Jalata 1993: 182). Hajji Adam Saddo traveled extensively and was consequently well informed about broader political developments in Ethiopia. He reportedly knew about the conditions of the Oromo in other parts of the country, information he would disperse among his compatriots in Bale. He also spent three years in Harar (dates unknown) (Muusaa Haaji Aadam Saaddoo 2014: 40). In addition, he traveled to Mecca for *hajj* several times, and the *hajj* in 1962 proved to be decisive for his political views. Interacting with pilgrims from different African countries, he was struck by their anti-colonial and nationalist sentiments. He also noticed the relatively high levels of education among his fellow African pilgrims – compared with those in Bale, and when he returned to Ethiopia, he purportedly made a pledge to work to enlighten the people, to strengthen their unity, and to fight against the Amhara (Muusaa Haaji Aadam Saaddoo 2014: 44). The government realized, in the meantime, that the *hajj* to Saudi Arabia was becoming an important occasion for communication between the people and the insurgents, and sought consequently to ban pilgrims from Bale.[34]

Shortly after the meeting between Hajji Adam Saddo, Waqo Gutu, and the leaders to MTSA, Mamo Mazamir wrote a letter to the insurgents in Bale on September 10, 1965, where he pledged support for the insurgency:

The life and death struggle of the oppressed masses in the Ethiopian Empire against the hegemony of the Amhara and their allies headed by American imperialism is a sacred liberation struggle of millions of oppressed and humiliated people ... . That struggle will surely intensify in the course of time as the oppressed people's organizational means and consciousness

---

[33] Interviews, Fayisa Megersa, Addis Ababa, June 18 ?&? 26, 2011. Wolde-Emanuel Dubale would later become the founder of the Sidama Liberation Front (SLM).

[34] Letter to General Worqu Metaferia, Governor of Bale, June 13, 1967, No. 118.

become deeply rooted .... As you learnt in our discussions, the Macha and Tulama democratic movement, which was created to raise the consciousness of the Oromo people, in the present concrete situation is working day and night to put in hand coordination activities that are within our reach .... In fact, the militant members are working now on the means of organizing a nationwide people's movement which is based on realizing the aspirations of Oromo people as a whole .... Please, keep up your heroic armed struggle, defending every inch of the Oromo Nation to the last drop of your blood. The decisive war of resistance you are conducting in Bale will, despite the maneuvers of imperialism, zionism and local reaction, be victorious. We shall continue doing everything we can to keep in touch with you. (Cited in Mohammed Hassan 1997: 228f.)

The letter reached Waqo Gutu in Dello and was shared among the leaders at the Dello front, who were eager to establish a link with the MTSA. It would, however, take nearly a year before the leaders of the Dello front responded to Mamo Mazamir's letter – presumably around May–June 1966. The response was penned by Sheikh Hussein Sura, and signed – among others – by those in the accompanying table.

Waqo Gutu	Sheikh Hussein Sura
Dubro Waqo	Waqo Lugu
Adam Jilo	Hajji Gobena Yubo
Aliye Chirri	Kadir Waqo
Chirri Jarra	Sadiq Roba

Although the letter itself is lost today, its main content has been made known by Aliye Chirri, one of its signatories.[35] In the letter, the insurgency leaders appealed for the help and support from the MTSA on a variety of issues. Firstly, they argued that the majority of the government's soldiers fighting the insurgents were Oromo from different parts of the country, and they asked the MTSA leadership to urge these Oromo not to fight with the enemy. Secondly, they appealed to the MTSA to make the struggle in Bale known internationally, and thirdly, they requested the MTSA to send them educated youth who could support the insurgency by building its organizational capacity. Lastly, they urged the MTSA to inform other Oromo not to believe the government propaganda that

---

[35] Muusaa Haaji Aadam Saaddoo (2014: 118) interviewed Aliyeh Chire.

accused the insurgents of being simple thieves and tools for the Somali regime. Particularly important was the letter's underscoring of Oromo unity in spite of religious difference. Acknowledging that the insurgents shared the same religious affiliation with the Somalis, they emphasized their Oromo identity, and that their struggle was an Oromo struggle (Muusaa Haaji Aadam Saaddoo 2014: 118f.).

Hajji Adam Saddo was tasked with bringing the letter to the MTSA leadership in Addis Ababa, and the events that unfolded are among those that have given him such a legendary status. Arriving by plane one morning in late November 1966, he immediately phoned General Tadesse Birru.[36] This was after the general had managed to escape arrest, and the authorities were busy cracking down on the MTSA (Olana Zoga 1985: 176). Unaware of these developments, Hajji Adam Saddo did not know that the person answering General Tadesse Birru's phone was a military officer impersonating the general. The officer offered to send a car to escort Hajji Adam Saddo to the general's house. Hajji Adam Saddo described what he looked like and the type of clothes he was wearing, and they agreed that he would be picked up at the Ministry of the Interior.[37] When the car arrived, an officer came out saying General Taddesse Birru sent him, and Hajji Adam Saddo entered the car without any suspicion. However, as the car took them to a police station, he gradually realized that something was wrong. When he entered the police station, he asked to be taken to the bathroom. While the police stood guard outside, he tore up the letter he was carrying and started swallowing the pieces. One of the officers sensed that something was wrong and ordered the others to break in the door. But before they could wrestle him to the floor, he had managed to swallow most of the letter (Muusaa Haaji Aadam Saaddoo 2014: 125f.).

Hajji Adam Saddo was then imprisoned in Addis Ababa while the authorities investigated his connections to the MTSA. Unable to find any evidence, they were forced to release him. When news about this reached the local authorities in Bale, they asked that he be transferred to Goba. He arrived in Bale and was imprisoned in Goba on January 8,

---

[36] One source claims that Hajji Adam Saddo traveled to Addis Ababa with the letter in June 1966 (Muusaa Haaji Aadam Saaddoo 2014: 128), but this does not fit with the broader timeline.

[37] This is today the Ministry of Immigration, located along Churchill Road.

1967.[38] That was the start of the lengthy trial he and other highland activists went through – discussed in the previous chapter.

While this points to a sense of unanimity between the Bale insurgency and the broader Oromo ethno-nationalist movement – and between the Arsi Oromo and Shoa Oromo beyond the locality of Bale – one could easily get the impression that religious boundaries did not really matter. I argue that things were not that simple, and that religious difference remained an issue for the ethno-nationalist movement. This is clearly reflected in the letter Hajji Adam Saddo brought to the MTSA leaders, and the fact that the letter underscored unity in spite of religious difference confirms its continued relevance. It could, of course, be argued that such references reflected the particular situation in Bale, that is, the division between the Arsi Oromo and the Shoa Oromo, but the way the insurgents emphasized that they – even if they were Muslims – also were Oromo is noteworthy. The same is true for their references to the Somalis and how the letter emphasized that they were not merely instruments for Somali expansionism. There are, however, those who argued that the insurgents and their supporters deliberately stressed either the religious or the ethnic dimension according to the context. One informant claimed, for example, that Hajji Adam Saddo (during the Derg period) was most concerned with the Muslims' conditions:

He was emphasizing the religious aspect, being negative to the Christians. He didn't want the Christians to rule the Muslims; he wanted independence. For him it was better to be under Siad Barre than under the Derg – at least the Somalis were Muslims. Yet he was a nationalist, and it remained a dilemma for him.[39]

It is also clear that notions of solidarity beyond religious boundaries were unevenly felt among the insurgents. The communications that took place between the two movements, via Hajji Adam Saddo and other highland activists, remained restricted to the main leadership of the insurgency and were only to a very limited degree affecting the rank and file. The lack of organizational structures made it difficult to disseminate what was going on and prevented awareness and penetration of the type of Oromo ethno-nationalist sentiments advocated by the MTSA. The vast majority of the insurgents referred to themselves as

---

[38] Letter from the Prison Office of Bale Province to the Ethiopian Imperial Government's High Court, Goba, January 18, 1967. No 821/59.
[39] Interview, Getnet Waqayyo, Addis Ababa, August 4, 2011.

Islaama, whereby religion remained firmly integrated as part of their identity and their struggle. Moreover, the fact that the local Shoa Oromo sided with the state contributed to the continued relevance of religious difference.

My argument, however, is that religious boundaries remained relevant at a deeper level, that they reinforced other differences and thus contributed to complicating notions of shared peoplehood. I also believe that this has continued to be an issue for Oromo ethno-nationalism. To begin with, the idea of an ancient and primordial pan-Oromo harmonious unity devoid of any conflict is fictitious. There existed, as I have pointed out on several occasions, conflictual relations both within and between the different Oromo branches where a well-established culture of war impinged on notions of unity. Furthermore, the religious boundaries that existed also corresponded with socioeconomic differences between pastoralists and agriculturalists alongside the already discussed highland-lowland dichotomy – wherein the Shoa Oromo saw themselves as more advanced and the pastoralist Arsi Oromo as lazy and backward. The MTSA leaders made an effort to reign in such attitudes, but they also harbored a subtle undercurrent of ascendancy. This was confirmed by many of my informants, and as they were reminiscing about the insurgency and reflecting on their experiences with the broader Oromo ethno-nationalist movement, they often talked about a lingering sense of inferiority.

Notions of ascendancy reflected broader regional-cultural and social differences, which also need to be seen in light of ongoing processes of modernization. The MTSA leadership's urban and elitist character was in stark contrast to the pastoralist insurgents from the rural lowlands, who "didn't have the culture of education."[40] The fact that many of the insurgents had gone through religious training also added an evaluative aspect to education, wherein religious schooling was never considered on par with a formal secular education. Highlander vs lowlander, educated vs uneducated, and modern vs traditional all interacted with religious difference and contributed in this way to reinforce feelings of superiority vs inferiority among the Oromo:

---

[40] Interview, Ibrahim Hussein, Addis Ababa, June 24, 2011.

The main reason why the Oromo movement was not successful was religion. The Christians and the Muslims opposed each other; this was the main case. The Muslim Oromo from the lowlands didn't understand that there were other non-Muslim Oromo .... There was [the] strongest hate from the Christian side towards the Muslims. The Christian Oromo were affiliated with the government. They saw the Muslim Oromo as only Muslims; they didn't regard them as Oromo. They had no experience with a Muslim government but [were] fearing that. The Muslims then hated the Christians in return. This was all exacerbated by politics; the Somali supported the Muslims and Haile Selassie supported the Christians.[41]

Conclusion

The dynamic character of the ethnic and religious dimensions and the segmentary nature of belonging illuminate the complexity of peoplehood. While the tensions between the embeddedness of ethnicity – its location in terms of space and time (as in provenance) – and religion's potential to transcend boundaries obviously problematize notions of peoplehood, it points, at the same time, to how the flexibility inherent in the concept makes it analytically fruitful in grasping such fluid complexities. The ambivalent relations between the Shoa Oromo and the Arsi Oromo and the links between the Bale insurgency and the broader Oromo ethno-nationalist movement are all cases in point illustrating the complexity in the interplay among ethnicity, religion, and class.

Here, it is crucial to understand that these dynamics always will be situational. They played out and expressed themselves in a particular way in Bale during the 1960s, where both a range of local factors and the flow of influences traveling across the larger southeast produced the content of the conflict, the alignment of different groups, and the language through which it was articulated. My argument, however, is that the particular has the potential to shed light on the general, and I believe that the close examination of the dynamics pertaining to the Bale insurgency can serve as an analytical tool for understanding similar situations

---

[41] Interview, Ibrahim Hussein, Addis Ababa, July 30, 2011.

within and beyond the Horn of Africa. As I will demonstrate in the study's conclusion, this is directly relevant for the understanding of Oromo protests in recent years. I will also suggest that the lessons learned about the embodied and emplaced nature of the insurgency can be very useful in the study of how religion and ethnicity interact, particularly in conflict situations.

12 | Conclusions

The objectives of this study have been to untangle the intricate relations between ethnicity and religion and to point to the relevance of religion for understanding Ethiopian dynamics. With the Bale insurgency as the case in point, I provided new insights to crucial and integrated roles of ethnicity and religion for deep-seated antagonistic relationships between people, the ruling elite, and the state. While recognizing the distinctiveness of this particular locality, I also believe that my findings and perspectives have relevance for other parts of southern Ethiopia. The study has discussed the trajectory of the insurgency, the main actors involved, and how the clan structure affected its organizational structures. Revisiting established perspectives that largely have interpreted the insurgency alongside class conflict, I have demonstrated that land is more than an economic commodity and have through the land-clan connection pointed to how the clan system had a spatial dimension crucial for notions of identity and belonging – and to how changes in land tenure leading to privatization and commodification of land severely disrupted these notions. Moreover, seeking to balance the class perspective with ethnicity and religion, I have situated my case within a broader context, focusing on the importance of orthodox Christianity as part of Ethiopia's national narrative, the notion of Amhara peoplehood, and how "Ethiopian exceptionalism" contributed to lasting conflictual relations with the region's non-Christians. I subsequently demonstrated how this spurred several movements of resistance across the southeast and how these diverse movements drew inspiration from one another. Lastly, circling back to the locality of Bale, I analyzed how the ethnic and religious dimensions of peoplehood generated antagonism and exacerbated hostile relations between the local Arsi Oromo and the Amhara – eventually causing armed conflict.

A similarly important aim of this study has been to offer a new theoretical framework for a broader understanding of how ethnicity and religion are connected. Attempting to reign in a too excessive semiotic constructivism that dislocates the mind from the body, culture from nature, and the symbolic from the material, I have applied the notion of imagined peoplehood as the analytical point of departure and have argued that ethnicity and religion constitute the two foundational dimensions of peoplehood, both formed through primary embodied relations and emplaced realities. I will return to this at the end of this chapter, where I also will discuss the broader relevance of my thesis. Yet, before doing this, I will point to the continued salience of ethnicity and religion in the context of Ethiopia.

Ethnicity and Religion: Change and Continuity

The instability created by the revolution in 1974 and the arrival of the new military Derg regime created opportunities for the Bale insurgents to again take up arms. Waqo Gutu and his followers soon found their way to Somalia, and together with individuals like Hussein Bune and Hajji Siraj Hajji Isaq (the son of Hajji Isaq Dhadhi) – and armed by the Siad Barre government – they eagerly returned to Ethiopia to fight the new government. While the continued struggle was referred to as the *Sowra* locally, it was formally organized under the Somali Abbo Liberation Front (SALF), which together with the Western Somali Liberation Front (WSLF) spearheaded the Somali invasion in 1977.[1] The invasion quickly turned into a disaster for Mogadishu, as the Ethiopian military, heavily supported by the Soviet Union and Cuba, effectively pushed out the Somalis and crushed both the SALF and the WSLF, forcing the insurgents to flee to Somalia.[2]

This round of fighting again illustrates how ethnicity, religion, and class were activated as forces for mobilization. While Islam remained relevant as a unifying dimension for the insurgents, Oromo ethno-nationalism became a more articulated motivator among the Arsi Oromo. Important, however, is also the fact that the movement recruited disgruntled Muslim Oromo landowners from the highlands

---

[1] Based on estimates made by Ethiopian military officials, the manpower of SALF and WSLF combined was said to be around 34,000 in July 1977, increasing to around 63,000 in the course of the war (Gebru Tareke 2000: 640).

[2] The number of Ethiopian refugees in Somalia was estimated to be more than 800,000 by the end of 1980. Although the larger proportion was from Ogaden, as many as 200,000 were Oromo, mainly from Hararge and Bale. See Clay (1988: 137) and Human Rights Watch ("Evil Days: Thirty Years of War and Famine in Ethiopia" 1991: 84).

who had lost their property as a result of the Derg regime's sweeping land reform in 1975. Although the reform's main target was the largely Amhara feudal lords, the ones losing land in Bale were the landowning Arsi Oromo. They were now labeled feudalists, contra-revolutionaries, and enemies.[3] Religion contributed to complicating the *Sowra*'s relations with other groups engaged in armed struggle during the 1970s and 1980s – particularly with the Oromo Liberation Front (OLF).[4] Although several Muslim Oromo from the southeast were among the founding members, the leadership came gradually to be dominated by individuals from the central and western parts of Ethiopia.[5] The OLF was critical to the "Somali Abbo" name and viewed the *Sowra* as a tool for Somali irredentism. Although one should be careful not to over-emphasize the religious dimension as a potential divisive factor, there is no doubt that it in a subtle way impacted the cooperation between the two movements.

Ethnicity and religion certainly continued to play important roles in post-Derg Ethiopia. With the political takeover by the Tigray People's Liberation Front (TPLF) in 1991 and the establishment of the Ethiopian People's Revolutionary Front (EPRDF), Ethiopia saw a significant change toward institutionalization and politicization of ethnicity. The former was materialized through the introduction of a system of ethnic federalism in 1995 that entailed the division of the country into nine regional states on the basis of ethno-linguistic criteria. The politicization of ethnicity took the form of the establishment of ethnic-based parties and a political discourse that made ethnicity the only possible basis for political engagement. All this led to complex processes of boundary demarcations, which meant that ethnic belonging became inescapable.[6] The 1990s also saw a general resurgence of religion and the arrival of various Islamic reform movements –

---

[3] Interview, Obse Ibrahim, Robe, August 25, 2005. For a more general discussion about the situation for local landowners in the south, see Lefort (1983: 108f.).

[4] The OLF was founded around 1973–1974 and would soon grow to the most important Oromo ethno-nationalist movement.

[5] This included figures such as Megersa Bari, Gada Gamada, Lencho Lata, Baro Tumsa, and Dima Nego.

[6] An interesting aspect of this is the establishment of "ethnic" banks: the Oromia Cooperative Bank and Awash Bank for the Oromo, Buna Bank for the Amhara, Wegagen Bank for the Tigray, NIB Bank for the Gurage, Debub Global Bank for the southerners, and Abyssinia Bank for people from Gojam. There is also a new bank, Berhan Bank, said to be for Pentecostal Christians.

complicating the relations between religion and ethnicity. Contemporary Islamic reformism is said to be accompanied by what has been characterized as a *process of objectification*, where "basic questions come to the fore in the consciousness" and where reasons for believing have to be articulated and objectified (Eickelman and Piscatori 1996: 38f.). Generating questions such as "what is my religion?" and "what does this mean for me?" objectification represents a certain "individualization of religion." Reformism also caused a stronger demarcation of religious boundaries and a situation where religious belonging became rather inescapable.

While objectification has been limited to processes of religious reform, I also believe it is possible to extend the concept further to what can be called *ethnic objectification*. In this particular context, it entails an articulation of the ethnic dimension and the reconstruction of "being Oromo," wherein ethnicity became something made explicit, articulated, and underscored. These processes of objectification also contributed to the making of ethnicity and religion as self-contained systems, and to the demarcation of a distinct Muslim identity separate from ethnicity. Such distinction between religious and ethnic affiliation became evident by the way the term *Islaama* was supplanted gradually by *Oromo* as denoting communal belonging. This is not to say that *Islaama* became irrelevant but rather that it related more explicitly to being Muslim; transcending the boundary of locality and denoting shared belonging with individuals adhering to the same religious tradition. Being Muslim became an individual matter by which human beings identified themselves in relation to God:

Islam is my religion . . . . Being Oromo and Muslim means that Islam is my private religion, and being Oromo is for anyone, I am proud of that. Private religion means that religion is a right; it is a choice. But my nation is Oromo, that is what I am born to be, I cannot change that.[7]

While the EPRDF believed that Ethiopia's ethnic and religious questions had been solved by its new policies and the 1995 Ethiopian Constitution, ethnic- and religious-based tensions continued to simmer, reaching new highs as the country entered the twenty-first century. This was noticeable first through widespread Muslim protests taking place in Addis Ababa and other major cities from January 2012. The

---

[7] Interview, Abdi Muktar, Robe, June 13, 2005.

protesters reacted against what they saw as the government's unlawful interference in religious affairs and were triggered by the so-called al-Ahbash campaign.[8] The al-Ahbash, or the Lebanese Association of Islamic Charitable Projects (AICP), launched extensive and mandatory training campaigns in the fall of 2011 aimed at admonishing the Muslims against the perils of "Islamic extremism." The training was conducted in close cooperation with the government, which the protesters saw as a breach of Ethiopia's secular framework (Østebø 2013a). The authorities' reactions were initially careful, but in July 2012 they arrested the leaders and through a massive armed intervention during the Id al-Fitr celebration in Addis Ababa in August 2013, the protests were violently crushed.[9]

Unrest again flared up in April 2014, this time among Oromo students protesting the proposed Addis Ababa Master Plan and plans to expand the boundaries of the capital into the surrounding Oromia region. The protests were suppressed by Ethiopian security forces within a few months, before the second round erupted in November 2014. This time the protests spread like wildfire across Oromia, soon becoming a serious challenge to EPRDF's hegemonic position. In July 2016, the unrest spread to the Amhara region, where it quickly turned more violent. The authorities responded with the use of force, leaving (estimated) hundreds killed, thousands injured, and tens of thousands arrested (Human Rights Watch 2016: 21). The government, however, was unable to create order, and the tense situation led to the resignation of Prime Minister Haile Mariam Desalegn in February 2018, and to the appointment of Abiy Ahmed as his successor in April. The new prime minister initiated widespread and unprecedented democratic reforms brought an end to the protests. Widespread unrest continued, however, across the country where numerous armed conflicts occurred between different groups. This has, at the time of writing, resulted in an unknown number of causalities, nearly 3 million internally displaced, and a highly fragile political situation.

The Oromo and Amhara protests were, as the names indicate, presented and conceived in ethnic terms. The ethnic factor was, at the same

---

[8] For more detailed discussions of this, see Østebø (2013a) and Østebø and Wallelign Shemsedin (2017).

[9] The committee members were charged with terrorist activities and sentenced to prison terms up to twenty-two years. They were gradually released – with the last one freed in the spring of 2018.

time, intersected with deep-seated socioeconomic grievances, particularly related to a high level of unemployment and lack of opportunities for economic progress among the youth.[10] Lack of land was another serious issue, caused mainly by population growth but also by increased commercial farming. This reminds us to not think of ethnicity as impalpable and separated from assumed "real" socioeconomic factors. Adding to this was the political context wherein ethnicity had become the only available language through which grievances could be interpreted and expressed.

Important to note, however, is that while ethnicity has overshadowed the picture in recent years, religion has far from become irrelevant. Since 1991, there has been a general increase in clashes between Muslims and Christians across the country, often related to the construction of churches and mosques and in connection with public performance of religious rituals (Abbink 2011; Hussein Ahmed 2006; Østebø 2008). An important reason why the religious dimension has remained rather subtle relates to how the regime's underscoring of Ethiopia's secular framework effectively has contributed to keeping religion out of public discourse. Although religion flies in one's face everywhere one goes in Ethiopia – from elaborate religious structures, public performance of religious rituals, and to an increasingly vociferous religious soundscape – it is carefully kept out of public discourses. Reiterating the initial objective of this study of bringing religion back in as an integrated and forceful variable of Ethiopian studies, future developments in Ethiopia cannot be fully understood without keeping a close eye on the religious dimension.

Peoplehood and the Salience of Ethnicity and Religion

Beyond Ethiopia, the increase of ethnic conflicts in the 1990s and the resurgence of so-called religious extremism demonstrate how continuously powerful ethnicity and religion are. This harks back to the main

---

[10] More than 70 percent of Ethiopia's population is younger than thirty, and urban youth employment is estimated to be around 27 percent. Average wages remain very low (ca $70 per month), and real wages have declined (United Nations Economic Commission for Africa 2018).

thesis of this study – that these dimensions are foundational for people-hood, that they are intimately connected, and that the enduring salience of these dimensions is based on primary embodied and emplaced experiences.

While constructed, ethnicity is not, as noted, emanating out of "thin air." Viewing both ethnicity and religion from a too detached constructivist viewpoint is unfruitful and problematic, wherein a Cartesian perspective thwarts us from more integrative entry points. One of these entry points is to recognize the material underpinning of ethnicity and religion – how they are based upon primary embodied relations (of family) and emplaced realities (of home). Important here is that these relational and material realities of being-with-others and being-in-the-world serve as the bases for imagination of peoplehood, which, in its flexible manner, allows for notions of belonging that are both segmentary and multifaceted. Similarly important is how the content, scope, and contours of peoplehood are produced, elaborated, and sustained by transmissions of collective memories and narratives that transgress time and space.

Moreover, I believe the notion of peoplehood allows us to comprehend the intimate connections between ethnicity and religion. Whereas most agree that a connection exists, very few attempts have been made to explain the actual nature of it. This study has avoided a too Western and too Protestant perception of religion as individualized faith and amply demonstrated how religion more often appears as marking collective identity, as something one is "born" into, as associated with tropes of family and home, and as pivotal for notions of groupness. Again, we need to recognize the embodied and emplaced underpinning of religion – the ways primary relations of family and emplaced realities of home are instrumental for creating and maintaining the religious dimension of peoplehood. Peoplehood, in other words, allows us to think more holistically in ways where human existence is not marked by any either-or, or of separately belonging to an ethnic group, to a nation, or to a religious community.

While, as noted, peoplehood is clearly segmentary in nature, and hence potentially fluid, the embodied and emplaced bases for the ethnic and religious dimensions are what give ethnicity and religion their salience and their emotional force. It is this that produces durable attachments and loyalties – as well as potentially persistent external animosity and enmity. This emotional force is not ineffable but gains its meaning only when recognizing its concrete material underpinning. Fighting – and dying – for the fatherland are thus not hollow and abstract, but inevitably real.

This theoretical framework has proven fruitful for this particular case, allowing me to go beyond simplistic and reductive analyses based on a single explanatory variable, and offers a richer account of the complex dynamics behind the Bale insurrection. Beyond that, I do believe that my theorization around the notion of peoplehood may serve as a robust framework that could be relevant for other cases as well. Well-known conflicts, such as in Northern Ireland and the Balkans, have alternatively been labeled ethnic and religious, and although both dimensions have been recognized, preference for one or the other has produced incomplete interpretations. There are those who have tried to forward more integrative perspectives on these conflicts, like Xavier Bougarel (2018) and Jennifer Todd (n.s., 2010), but which, arguably, remain deficient by not being grounded enough. Using the concept of *peoplehood* as the analytic tool, recognizing ethnicity and religion as primary dimensions of peoplehood, paying attention to the embodied and emplaced bases for ethnicity and religion, and carefully and empirically analyze this constitute the fruitful way to fully understand the complexity of these cases.

I do recognize, as noted in the first chapter, that my emphasis on primary embodied and emplaced realities through the usage of tropes of family and home can be judged as being too essentialistic. I am willing to take that risk, and I seriously believe that after decades of deconstructing, the time is ripe for constructing. I moreover believe that the so-called material turn, in all its vagueness, provides opportunities to move beyond excessive constructivist perspectives and to realize that human realities are constituted by, integrated with, and bound by the materiality of our bodies and natural environments. It is not everything that "melts into the air."

Glossary

Aanaa (Oromo) Family, smallest kinship unit

Abbaa boku (Oromo) Literally, father of the sceptre – a leader in the *gadaa* system. In Bale; a leader of a clan

Abbaa lafa (Oromo) Father of the land, landowner

Abbaa muuda (Oromo) A religious office within the *gadaa* system, or the shaman-like figure in Dello venerated by the Oromo

Abuna (Amharic) Bishop, patriarch

Angafa (Oromo) Oldest son

Asrat (Amharic), Tax, one-tenth

Ateetee (Oromo) Ritual restricted for females

Awaama (Oromo) Polytheist

Awraja (Amharic) Administrative unit within a province during the period of Haile Selassie and the Derg

Ayaanaa (Oromo) Spirit

Baaro (Oromo) Prayer poem dedicated to Sheikh Hussein

Bahira (Oromo) An office in the *gadaa* system; the second-in-command after the *abbaa boku*

Balbalaa (Oromo) Literally, door, gate. Refers to a sub-clan

Balabat (Amharic) Local (indigenous) chiefs appointed by the Amhara

Beteseb (Amharic) Family

Bliisumaa (Oromo) Freedom

Burqa (Oromo) The next-in-rank to the *balabat*

Darga (Oromo) The guardians of the shrine of Sheikh Hussein

Dejazmach (Amharic) Feudal title, commander of the provincial headquarter

Dhadacha (Oromo) Confederacy of clans according to the *gadaa* system

Dhanqe (Oromo) Y-forked stick used by the pilgrims to the shrine of Sheikh Hussein

Dhombir (Oromo) The Carcano rifle

Emir (Arabic) Commander, a political leader

Fiqh (Arabic) Islamic jurisprudence

Fitawrari (Amharic) Feudal title, commander of the vanguard

Fuqra (Oromo) Sufi ascetic, wandering mystic

Gabbar (Amharic) Tribute-paying peasant, tenant

Gadaa (Oromo) Generation-set system and a key concept for the structure of the traditional Oromo society. The concept has both political and religious connotations

Galla (Amharic) Pejorative word used for the Oromo up until the 1980s

Gammojii (Oromo) Lowlands

Geriba (Oromo) Devotee to Sheikh Hussein or pilgrim traveling far distances

Gossa (Oromo) Clan

Grazmach (Amharic) Feudal title, commander of the left flank

Guma (Oromo) Blood money

Habasha (Amharic) Abyssinian, Ethiopian

Jinn (Arabic) Sprit, demon

Karaama (Arabic) A miracle done by the Prophet or other saintly persons. In Bale, the word is commonly used as the very ability or power to perform miracles

Kebele (Amharic) Urban association, neighbourhood

Kuluba (Oromo) Local term for the Bale insurgency

Madeira (Amharic) Land given as grant

Mamaksa (Oromo) Proverb

Mawlid al-Nabi (Arabic) The birthday of Prophet Muhammad

Melkenya (Amharic) Landlord, and sometimes local governor

Mogaasuu (Oromo) Adoption of an individual or a group by the Oromo and name giving

Murtii (Oromo) Decision, regulation according to the *seera* – Oromo law

Nagaa (Oromo) Peace

Nech lebash (Amharic) "Those who wear white"; local militia

Neftenya (Amharic) "Man with a gun"; soldier-settler from the north

Odaa (Oromo) Sycamore tree, venerated in the Oromo religion

Oda Roba (Oromo) A traditional site for veneration and pilgrimage located in the eastern lowlands of Bale

Otubaa (Oromo) Land as common property

Qadi (Arabic) The judge of a *shari'a*-court

Qalad (Amharic) Type of land measurement

Qallu (Oromo) A Shaman-like ritual expert in the Oromo religion

Qenazmach (Amharic) Feudal title, commander of the right flank

Ras (Amharic) Prince

Rist (Amharic) Inheritable land, inherence right (to land)

Saddeeta (Oromo) *Gadaa council of eight*

Sakina (Oromo) Community at Dirre Sheikh Hussein

Shannoo (Oromo) Gadaa council of five

Shifta (Amharic) Bandit, outlaw

Sowra (Oromo/Arabic) From *thawra;* struggle, also name for the Bale insurgency

Tabot (Amharic) The replica of the Ark of the Covenant found in Orthodox churches

Teklay Gezat (Amharic) Province

Ulama (sg. alim) (Arabic) Islamic scholar

Umma (Arabic) Global Muslim community

Umra (Arabic) The lesser pilgrimage to Mecca

Wali (pl., *awliah*) (Arabic) Signifies a person that is near to, or loved by God. In the Sufi tradition it has often constituted a certain holy person, and usually translated into English as "saint"

Waaqa (Oromo) God

Waqeffana/waqeffata (Oromo) Oromo religion/adherent to the Oromo religion

Wayyuu (Oromo) Sacred, respected, and set apart

Worreda (Amharic) Administrative district

References

Abbas H. Gnamo. "L'ethiopie Va-T-Elle ÉClater? Conflits Politiques, ÉConomie Et SociéTé En Pays Arssi (1900–1935)." *Cahiers d'Études africaines* 32, no. 126 (1992): 239–284.

Conquest and Resistance in the Ethiopian Empire, 1880–1974: The Case of the Arsi Oromo. Leiden: Brill, 2014.

Abbink, Jon. "Paradoxes of Power and Culture in an Old Periphery: Surma, 1974–1998." In *Remapping Ethiopia: Socialism and After,* edited by Wendy James, Donald Donham, Eisei Kurimoto, and Alessandro Triulzi, 155–172. London: James Currey, 2002.

"Religion in Public Spaces: Emerging Muslim–Christian Polemics in Ethiopia." *African Affairs* 110, no. 439 (2011): 253–274.

Abdullatif Dire. "Aayoo Makka Remembers the Battle of Dhombir." *Opride .com,* www.opride.com/2013/08/30/aayyoo-makka-remembers-the-battle-of-dhombir/ (accessed March 1, 2018).

Aberra Ketsela. "The Rebellion in Bale." BA thesis in History, Addis Ababa: Addis Ababa University, 1971.

Abir, Mordechai. "Trade and Christian-Muslim Relations in Post-Medieval Ethiopia." Paper presented at the Fifth International Conference on Ethiopian Studies, Chicago, 1978.

Ethiopia and the Red Sea: The Rise and Decline of the Solomonic Dynasty and Muslim-European Rivalry in the Region. London: Frank Cass, 1980.

Agnew, John. "Nationalism." In *A Companion to Cultural Geography,* edited by James S. Duncan, Nuala C. Johnson, and Richard H. Schein, 223–237. Oxford: Blackwell Publishing, 2004.

Ahmed Zekaria. "Some Notes on the Account Books of Amir Abd Al-Shakur B, Yusuf (1783–1794) of Harar." *Sudanic Africa* 8 (1997): 17–36.

Ahned Abdalla, and Abdukariim Hasan. *Qorannoo Seenaa Obboo Huseen Kadiir (Huseen Teleegiraama) [in Afan Oromo: A Study of the History of Hussein Kadir].* Micha, Sewena: Sewena Culture and Tourism Office, 2010.

Akenson, Donald H. *God's People: Covenant and Land in South Africa, Israel, and Ulster.* Ithaca: Cornell University Press, 1992.

Alonso, Ana Maria. "The Politics of Space, Time and Substance: State Formation, Nationalism, and Ethnicity." *Annual Review of Anthropology* 23 (1994): 379–405.

Aman Seifedin. "The Muslim Community of Gobba: 1890–1960." BA thesis in History, Addis Ababa: Addis Ababa University, 1987.

Ammerman, Nancy T. "Studying Everyday Religion: Challenges for the Future." In *Everyday Religion: Observing Modern Religious Lives*, edited by Nancy T. Ammerman, 219–238. Oxford: Oxford University Press, 2007.

Andargachew Tiruneh. *The Ethiopian Revolution 1974–1987: A Transformation from an Aristocratic to a Totalitarian Autocracy.* Cambridge: Cambridge University Press, 1993.

Anderson, Benedict. *Imagined Communities: Reflections on the Origin and Spread of Nationalism.* London & New York: Verso, 1983.

Andrzejewski, Bogumil W. "Sheikh Hussein of Bali in Galla Oral Traditions." In *IV Congresso Internationale Di Studi Etiopici*, edited by Enrico Cerulli, 463–480. Roma: Accademia Nazionale dei Lincei, 1974.

Anonymous. "African Hero." Unknown publisher, 2006.

Anthias, Fiona. "The Material and Symbolic in Theorizing Social Stratification: Issues of Gender, Ethnicity and Class." *British Journal of Sociology* 50, no. 3 (2001): 367–390.

Aregawi Berhe. "Revisiting Resistance in Italian-Occupied Ethiopia: The Patriots' Movement (1936–1941) and the Redefinition of Post-War Ethiopia." In *Rethinking Resistance: Revolt and Violence in African History*, edited by Jon Abbink, Mirjam de Bruin, and Klaes van Walraven, 87–113. Leiden: Brill, 2003.

Asad, Talal. *Genealogies of Religion: Discipline and Reasons of Power in Christianity and Islam.* Baltimore: Johns Hopkins University Press, 1993.

Asafa Jalata. "Sheikh Hussein Suura and the Oromo Struggle." *The Oromo Commentary* 4, no. 1 (1994): 5–7.

Oromia & Ethiopia: State Formation and Ethnonational Conflicts 1868–1992. Trenton, NJ: Red Sea Press, 2005.

Ashmore, Richard, Kay Deaux, and Tracy McLaughlin-Volpe. "An Organizing Framework for Collective Identity: Articulation and Significance of Multidimensionality." *Psychological Bulletin* 130, no. 1 (2004): 80–114.

Asmaron Legesse. *Gada: Three Approaches to the Study of African Societies.* New York: The Free Press, 1973.

Assefa Addissu. "Peasant Uprising in Southern Ethiopia: The Case of Gedeo and Bale." BA thesis in Anthropology, Addis Ababa: Addis Ababa University, 1980.

Assefa Dula. "Land Tenure in Chercher Province." *Ethiopia Observer* 12, no. 2 (1969): 137–139.

Assefa Teshome. "The History of the Azmach Deglehan School in Goba (1950–1974)." BA thesis in History, Addis Ababa: Addis Ababa University, 1990.

Austen, Ralph A. "Social Bandits and Other Heroic Criminals: Western Models of Resistance and Their Relevance for Africa." In *Banditry, Rebellion and Social Protest in Africa*, edited by Donald Crummey, 89–108. London: Heineman, 1986.

Ayalew Gebre. *Pastoralism under Pressure: Land Alienation and Pastoral Transformation among the Karrayu of Eastern Ethiopia, 1941 to the Present*. Maastricht: Shaker Publishing, 2001.

Ayalon, Ami. "From Fitna to Thawra." *Studia Islamica* no. 66 (1987): 145–174.

Ayele Gebre Mariam. "Bale Sub-Highlands Socio-Economic Study." n.d.: Unpublished Report to the Southern Highlands Livestock Development Project, 1976.

Aynalem Adugna. "The Spatial Pattern of the Ethiopian Population." MA thesis in Geography, Durham: Durham University, 1984.

Azarya, Victor. *Nomads and the State in Africa*. Aldershot: Avebury, 1996.

Bahrey, Almeida, G. W. B. Huntingford, and C. F. Beckingham. *History of the Galla (Oromo) of Ethiopia: With Ethnology and History of South West Ethiopia*. Oakland: African Sun Publishing, 1993.

Bahru Zewde. *A History of Modern Ethiopia, 1855–1974*. London: James Currey, 1991.

Pioneers of Change in Ethiopia: The Reformist Intellectuals of the Early Twentieth Century. Oxford: James Currey, 2002.

Bairu Tafla. "Ras Dargé Sahlä-Sellasé, c. 1827–1900." *Journal of Ethiopian Studies* 13, no. 2 (1975): 17–37.

Bale Zone Department of Finance & Economic Development. *Atlas of Bale Zone*. Asella: Regional State of Oromia, 2004.

Banks, Marcus. *Ethnicity: Anthropological Constructions*. New York: Routledge, 1996.

Banton, Michael. "Ethnic Conflict." *Sociology* 34, no. 3 (2000): 481–498.

Barnes, Cedric. "The Ethiopian State and Its Somali Periphery Circa 1888–1948." PhD dissertation in History, Cambridge: Cambridge University, 2000.

"*U Dhashay – Ku Dhashay*: Genealogical and Territorial Discourse in Somali History." *Social Identities* 12, no. 4 (2006): 487–498.

"The Somali Youth League, Ethiopian Somalis and the Greater Somalia Idea, c. 1946–48." *journal of Eastern African Studies* 1, no. 2 (2007): 277–291.

Barnes, Cedric, and Abdi Abdullahi. "Genealogies of Somali Islamic Politics: The Contribution of 'Ethiopian' Somalis." Unpublished paper, n.d. Copy in possession of authors.

Barrett, Justin L., and Frank C. Keil. "Conceptualizing a Nonnatural Entity: Anthropomorphism in God Concepts." *Cognitive Psychology* 31, no. 3 (1996): 219–247.

Bartels, Lambert. "Birth Customs and Birth Songs of the Macca Galla." *Ethnology* 8, no. 4 (1969): 406–22.

Oromo Religion. Berlin: Dietrich Reimer Verlag, 1983.

Barth, Fredrik. "Introduction." In *Ethnic Groups and Boundaries*, edited by Fredrik Barth, 9–38. Oslo: Universitetsforlaget, 1969.

"A General Perspective on Nomad-Sedentary Relations in the Middle East." In *The Desert and the Sown: Nomads in the Wider Society*, edited by Cynthia Nelson, 11–21. Berkeley: University of California Press, 1973.

Basso, Keith. *Wisdom Sits in Places: Landscape and Language among Western Apache*. Albuquerque: University of New Mexico Press, 1996.

Baxter, Paul. "Some Consequences of Sedentarization for Social Relationships." In *Pastoralism in Tropical Africa*, edited by Theodore Monod, 206–229. Oxford: Oxford University Press, 1975.

"Boran Age-Sets and Warfare." In *Warfare among East African Herders*, edited by Katsuyoshi Fukui and David Turton, 69–95. Osaka: Senri Ethnological Studies, 1977.

"Atete in a Highland Arssi Neighborhood." *Northeast African Studies* 1, no. 2 (1979): 1–22.

"'Big Men' and Cattle Licks in Oromoland." In *When the Grass Is Gone*, edited by Paul Baxter, 192–212. Uppsala: The Scandinavian Institute of African Studies, 1991.

Beckingham, Charles F., and Bernard Hamilton (eds.). *Prester John, the Mongols and the Ten Lost Tribes*. Aldershot: Variorum, 1996.

Benjamin, David N. "Introduction." In *The Home: Words, Interpretations, Meanings, and Environments*, edited by David N Benjamin, David Stea, and David Saile, 1–14. London: Avebury, 1995.

Berezin, Mabel. "Secure States: Towards a Political Sociology of Emotions." *The Sociological Review* 50, no. 2 (2002): 33–52.

Bevan, James. "Between a Rock and a Hard Place: Armed Violence in African Pastoral Communities." Geneva: UNDP Report, 2007.

Billig, Michael. *Banal Nationalism*. London: Sage, 1995.

Birch-Iensen, Charles. *Ett Okant Mecka: Forskning Och Aventyr I Etiopien [an Unknown Mecca: Research and Adventure in Ethiopia]*. Stockholm: Natur och Kultur, 1960.

Blackhurst, Hector. "A Community of Shoa Galla in Southern Ethiopia." PhD thesis in Social Anthropology, Manchester: University of Manchester, 1974.

"Ethnicity in Southern Ethiopia: The General and the Particular." *Africa* 50, no. 1 (1980): 55–65.

"Adopting an Ambiguous Position: Oromo Relationship with Strangers." In *Being and Becoming Oromo*, edited by P. T. W. Baxter, Jan Hultin, and Alessandro Triulzi, 239–250. Lawrenceville: Red Sea Press, 1996.

Bøås, Morten, and Kevin C. Dunn. "Introduction." In *African Guerillas: Raging against the Machine*, edited by Morten Bøås and Kevin C. Dunn, 1–8. Boulder: Lynne Rienner, 2007.

Bougarel, Xavier. *Islam and Nationhood in Bosnia-Herzegovina: Surviving Empires*. London: Routledge, 2018.

Bourdieu, Pierre. *Outline of a Theory of Practice*. Cambridge: Cambridge University Press, 1977.

Boylston, Tom. *The Stranger and the Feast: Prohibition and Mediation in an Ethiopian Orthodox Christian Community*. California: California University Press, 2018.

Braukämper, Ulrich. *Geschichte Der Hadyia Süd-Äthiopiens*. Wiesbaden: Franz Steiner Verlag, 1980a.

"Oromo Country of Origin: A Reconsideration of Hypothesis." Paper presented at the 6th International Conference of Ethiopian Studies, Tel Aviv, April 14–17, 1980b.

Islamic History and Culture in Southern Ethiopia: Collected Essays. Hamburg: Lit Verlag, 2002.

Brooks, Miguel F. *Kebra Negast – English Translation*. Lawrenceville: Red Sea Press, 1996.

Brow, James. "Community, Hegemony, and the Uses of the Past." *Anthropological Quarterly* 63, no. 1 (1990): 1–6.

Brown, Michael. "The Causes and Regional Dimensions of Internal Conflicts." In *The International Dimensions of Internal Conflicts*, edited by Michael Brown, 571–602. Cambridge, MA: MIT Press, 1996.

Brubaker, Roger. "Ethnicity without Groups." *Archives européenes de sociologie* 43 (2002): 163–189.

Ethnicity without Groups. Cambridge, MA: Harvard University Press, 2004.

Burkitt, Ian. *Bodies of Thought*. London: SAGE Publications, 1987.

"The Shifting Concept of the Self." *History of the Human Sciences* 7, no. 2 (1994): 7–28.

Butler, Judith. *Gender Trouble: Feminsim and the Subversion of Identity*. New York: Routledge, 1990.

Carmichael, Tim. "Approaching Ethiopian History: Addis Ababa and Local Governance in Harar, C. 1900–1950." PhD dissertation in History, Lansing: Michigan State University, 2001.

Caulk, Richard. "Harar Town in the 19th Century and Its Neighbours." Paper presented at the International Congress of Africanists, Addis Ababa, 1973.

"Menelik's Conquest and Local Leaders in Harar." Paper presented at the History and Culture of the People of Harar Province, Addis Ababa, 1975.

"Bad Men of the Borders: Shum and *Shefta* in Northern Ethiopia in the Nineteenth Century." *International Journal of African Historical Studies* 17, no. 2 (1984): 201–227.

Between the Jaws of the Hyenas: A Diplomatic History of Ethiopia, 1876–1896. Wiesbaden: Otto Harrassowitz, 2002.

Cavendish, H. S. H. "Through Somaliland and around South of Lake Rudolf." *The Geographical Journal* 11, no. 4 (1898): 372–396.

Central Statistical Office. "Statistical Abstract: 1971." Addis Ababa, 1971.

"The 1984 Population and Housing Census of Ethiopia: Analytical Report at National Level." Addis Abeba: Issued by the Office of the Population and Housing Census Commission, Addis Ababa, 1985.

"The 1994 Population and Housing Census of Ethiopia: Results for Oromiya Region." Issued by Office of Population and Housing Census Commission: Addis Ababa, 1994.

"The 2007 Census: Preliminary Report." Issued by the Office of the Population and Housing Census Commission, Addis Ababa, 2008.

Cerulli, Enrico. "The Folk Literature of the Galla in Southern Ethiopia." *Harvard African studies* 3, no. 13 (1922).

Somalia-Scritti Vari Editi Ed Inediti. 3 vols. Roma: Ist. Poligrafico dello Stato, 1957–64.

Chanie, Paulos. "The Rise of Politicized Ethnicity among the Oromo in Ethiopia." In *Ethnicity and the State in Eastern Africa*, edited by M. A. Mohammed Salih and John Markakis, 95–107. Uppsala: Nordic Africa Institute, 1998.

Chernetsov, Sevir. "On the Problem of Ethnogenesis of the Amhara." In *Der Sudan in Vergangenheit Und Gegenwart*, edited by Rolf Gundlach, Manfred Kropp, and Analis Leibundgut, 17–35. Frankfurt am Main: Peter Land, 1996.

Clapham, Christopher. *Haile Sellassie's Government*. New York: Praeger, 1969.

"Centralization and Local Response in Southern Ethiopia." *African Affairs* 74, no. 294 (1975): 72–81.

Transformation and Continuity in Revolutionary Ethiopia. Cambridge: Cambridge University Press, 1988.

"Introduction: Analysing African Insurgencies." In *African Guerillas*, edited by Christopher Clapham, 1–18. Oxford: James Currey, 1998.

"Controlling Space in Ethiopia." In *Remapping Ethiopia: Socialism &
After*, edited by Wendy James, Donald Donham, and
Alessandro Triulzi, 9–32. Oxford: James Currey, 2002.

"African Guerrillas Revisited." In *African Guerrillas: Raging against the
Machine*, edited by Morten Bøås and Kevin C. Dunn, 221–233. Boulder:
Lynne Rienner, 2007.

Clay, Jason W. "The Case of Bale." In *The Spoils of Famine: Ethiopian
Famine Policy and Peasant Agriculture*, edited by Jason W. Clay,
Sandra Steingraber, and Peter Niggli, 136–156. Cambridge, MA:
Cultural Survival Inc., 1988.

Cohen, Adam B., and Peter C. Hill. "Religion as Culture: Religious
Individualism and Collectivism among American Catholics, Jews,
and Protestants." *Journal of Personality* 75, no. 4 (2007):
709–742.

Cohen, Anthony P. *The Symbolic Construction of Community*. London:
Tavistock, 1985.

Cohen, John M., Arthur A. Goldsmith, and John W. Mellor. *Revolution and
Land Reform in Ethiopia: Peasant Associations, Local Government,
and Rural Development*. Ithaca: Cornell University Center for
International Studies, 1976.

and Dov Weintraub. *Land and Peasants in Imperial Ethiopia*. Assen:
Koninklijke Van Gorcum, 1975.

Cohen, Ronald. "Ethnicity: Problem and Focus in Anthropology." *Annual
Review of Anthropology* 7 (1978): 379–403.

Comaroff, Jean. *Body of Power, Spirit of Resistance: The Culture and
History of a South African People*. Chicago: University of Chicago
Press, 1985.

Connor, Walter. "The Politics of Ethno-Nationalism." *Journal of
International Affairs* 27, no. 1 (1972): 1–21.

Ethnonationalism: A Quest for Understanding. Princeton: Princeton
University Press, 1994.

Cornell, Stephen. "The Variable Ties That Bind: Content and Circumstance
in Ethnic Processes." *Ethnic and Racial Studies* 19, no. 2 (1996):
265–289.

Croucher, Sheila. "The Politics and Perils of Peoplehood." *International
Studies Review* 8, no. 1 (2006): 77–89.

Crummey, Donald. "Abyssinian Feudalism." *Past and Present* no. 89
(1980): 115–138.

"Banditry and Resistance: Noble and Peasant in Nineteenth-Century
Ethiopia." In *Banditry, Rebellion and Social Protest in Africa*, edited
by Donald Crummey, 133–150. London: Heineman, 1986a.

(ed.). *Banditry, Rebellion and Social Protest in Africa*. London: Heineman, 1986b.

"Introduction: The Great Beast." In *Banditry, Rebellion and Social Protest in Africa*. edited by Donald Crummey, 1–29. London: Heineman, 1986c.

Csordas, Thomas J. "Introduction: The Body as Representation and Being-in-the-World." In *Embodiment and Experience: The Existential Ground of Culture and Self*, edited by Thomas J. Csordas, 1–24. Cambridge: Cambrdge University Press, 1994.

"Embodiment and Cultural Phenomenology." In *Perspectives on Embodiment: The Intersections of Nature and Culture*, edited by Gail Weiss and Honi F. Haber, 143–162. New York: Routledge, 1999.

Currens, Gerald, and Oscar Nydal. *Unevangelized Areas Project Survey IV: Awash Valley, Shoa, Arusi, Bale*. Addis Ababa: Evangelical Church Mekane Yesus, 1974.

Dahl, Gudrun. "Ecology and Equality: The Boran Case." In *Pastoral Production and Society*, edited by Equipe Ecologie, 261–281. Cambridge: Cambridge University Press, 1979.

Day, Abby. *Believing in Belonging: Belief and Social Identity in the Modern World*. Oxford: Oxford University Press, 2011.

de Waal, Alex. "Contemporary Warfare in Africa: Changing Context, Changing Strategies." *IDS Bulletin* 27, no. 3 (1997): 6–16.

Demerath, Jay N. "The Rise of Cultural Religion in European Christianity: Learning from Poland, Northern Ireland, and Sweden." *Social Compass* 47, no. 1 (2000): 127–139.

Dereje Tadesse Wakjira. "Governance of Social-Ecological Systems in an Afromontane Forest of Southeast Ethiopia: Exploring Interactions between Systems." PhD dissertation in Ecology, Aberdeen: University of Aberdeen, 2013.

Desplat, Patrick. *Heilige Stadt – Stadt Der Heiligen. Kontroversen Und Ambivalenzen Islamischer Heiligkeit in Harar/Äthiopien*. Köln: Rüdiger Köppe Verlag, 2010.

Dessalegn Rahmato. *Agrarian Reform in Ethiopia*. Trenton, NJ: Red Sea Press, 1985.

Dion, Delphine, Lionel Sitz, and Eric Rémy. "Embodied Ethnicity: The Ethnic Affiliation Grounded in the Body." *Consumption Markets & Culture* 14, no. 3 (2011): 311–331.

"Do You Know Hajj Adam Sado." *Seif Nabalbal (Amharic)*, 5 August 2005.

Doja, Albert. "The Politics of Religion in the Construction of Identities: The Albanian Situation." *Critique of Anthropology* 20, no. 4 (2000): 421–438.

Donaldson Smith, Arthur. *Through Unknown African Countries; the First Expedition from Somaliland to Lake Lamu.* London: E. Arnold, 1897.

Donham, Donald. "Old Abyssinia and the New Ethiopian Empire: Themes in Social History." In *The Southern Marches of Imperial Ethiopia*, edited by Donald Donham and Wendy James, 3–48. London: James Currey, 1986.

Marxist Modern. Berkeley: University of California Press, 1999.

Douglas, Mary. *Natural Symbols.* London: Barry and Rockliff, 1970.

Duncan, James S., and David Lambert. "Landscapes of Home." In *A Companian to Cultural Geography*, edited by James S. Duncan, Nuala C. Johnson, and Richard H. Schein, 382–403. Oxford: Blackwell Publishing, 2004.

Dupont, Anne-Laure. "The Ottoman Revolution of 1908 as Seen by *Al-Hilal* and *Al-Manar*: The Triumph and Diversification of the Reformist Spirit." In *Liberal Thought in the Eastern Mediterrenean: Late 19th Century until the 1960s*, edited by Christopher Schuman, 123–146. Leiden: Brill, 2008.

"Education in Bale." Issued by the Bale Education and Capacity Office, Robe, 2005.

Eickelman, Dale F., and James Piscatori. *Muslim Politics.* Princeton: Princeton University Press, 1996.

Eide, Øyvind. *Revolution & Religion in Ethiopia, 1974–85.* Oxford: James Currey, 2000.

Eliade, Mircea. *The Sacred and the Profane.* New York: Harcourt Brace Jovanovich, 1959.

Engelke, Matthew. *A Problem of Presence: Beyond Scripture in an African Church.* Berkeley: University of California Press, 2007.

Enloe, Cynthia. "Religion and Ethnicity." In *Ethnic Diversity and Conflict in Eastern Europe*, edited by Peter F. Sugar, 350–360. Santa Barbara: ABC-Clio, 1980.

Erlich, Haggai. *Ethiopia and the Middle East.* Boulder & London: Lynne Rienner, 1994a.

"Ethiopia and the Middle East: Rethinking History." In *New Trends in Ethiopian Studies. Papers of the 12th International Conference of Ethiopian Studies*, edited by Harold G. Marcus and Grover Hudson, 631–642. Lawrenceville, NJ: The Red Sea Press, 1994b.

The Cross and the River: Ethiopia, Egypt and the Nile. Boulder & London: Lynne Rienner Publishers, 2002.

Saudi Arabia and Ethiopia: Islam, Christianity, and Politics Entwined. Boulder & London: Lynne Rienner, 2007.

Etenesh Aberra, and Mahlet Fasil. "At Least Six People Killed in Goba, after Controversy over Monument Led to Inter-Communal Tensions." *Addis Standard*, July 23, 2018. https://addisstandard.com/news-at-least-six-people-killed-in-goba-bale-after-controversy-over-monument-led-to-inter-communal-tensions/ (accessed August 19, 2018).

Falmataa Oromo. "Evidence: Menelik's Genocide against Oromo and Other Nations." *Oromia Times*, January 4, 2014. https://oromiatimes.org/20 14/01/04/evidence-meneliks-genocide-against-oromo-and-other-nations/ (accessed March 13, 2018).

Fanon, Frantz. *Black Skin, White Masks*. New York: Grove Press, 1967.

Fearon, James D., and David D. Laitin. "Violence and the Social Construction of Ethnic Identity." *International Organization* 54, no. 4 (2000): 845–877.

Fernyhough, Timothy D. *Serfs, Slaves and Shifta: Modes of Production and Resistance in Pre-Revolutionary Ethiopia*. Addis Ababa: Shama Books, 2010.

Ficquet, Eloi. "Flesh Soaked in Faith: Meat as a Marker of the Boundary between Christians and Muslims in Ethiopia." In *Muslim-Christian Encounters in Africa*, edited by Benjamin F. Soares, 39–56. Leiden: Brill, 2006.

Ficquet, Eloi, and Wolbert G. C. Smidt (eds.). *The Life and Times of Lij Iyasu of Ethiopia*. Berlin: Lit Verlag, 2014.

Flintan, Fiona, Worku Chibsa, Dida Wako, and Andrew Ridgewell. "Livestock and Livestock Systems in the Bale Mountains Ecoregion." Addis Ababa: SOS Sahel Ethiopia and FARM Africa, 2008.

Foucault, Michel. *Discipline and Punish: The Birth of the Prison*. New York: Vintage, 1979.

  The History of Sexuality. Volume I: Introduction. New York: Vintage, 1980.

Fukui, Katsouyoshi, and David Turton. "Introduction." In *Warfare among East African Herders*, edited by Katsouyoshi Fukui and David Turton, 1–13. Osaka: Senri Ethnological Studies, 1979.

Gadaa Melbaa. *Oromia*. Khartoum: No publisher stated, 1988a.

  Oromiya; an Introduction. Khartoum: No publisher stated, 1988b.

Galtung, Johan. "Religion: Hard and Soft." *Cross Currents* Winter, 1997–98 (1997).

Gans, Herbert J. "Symbolic Ethnicity and Symbolic Religiosity: Towards a Comparison of Ethnic and Religious Generation." *Ethnic and Racial Studies* 17, no. 4 (1994): 577–692.

Garretson, Peter. "Ethiopian Expansion into the Ogaadeen and Its Relations with the Somali (1887 to 1906)." Unpublished paper, 2001.

Gates, Scott. "Recruitment and Allegiance: The Microfoundations of Rebellion." *Journal of Conflict Resolution* 46, no. 1 (2002): 111–130.

Gebre-Wold Ingida Worq. "Ethiopia's Traditional System of Land Tenure and Taxation." *Ethiopia Observer* 4, no. 4 (1962): 302–339.

Gebru Tareke. "Rural Protest in Ethiopia, 1941–1970: A Study of Three Rebellions." PhD dissertation in History, Syracuse: Syracuse University, 1977.

  Power and Protest: Peasant Revolts in the Twentieth Century. Cambridge: Cambridge University Press, 1991.

  "The Ethiopia-Somalia War of 1977 Revisited." *International Journal of African Historical Studies* 33, no. 3 (2000): 635–667.

Geertz, Clifford. "The Integrative Revolution: Primordial Sentiments and Civil Politics in the New States." In *Old Societies and New States*, edited by Clifford Geertz, 105–157. Glencoe: The Free Press, 1963.

  The Interpretation of Cultures: Selected Essays. New York: Basic Books, 1973.

Gemechu Megersa. *The Oromo Worldview.* Nazareth: No publisher stated, 1998.

Geschiere, Peter. *The Perils of Belonging: Autochthont, Citizenship, and Exclusion in Africa and Europe.* Chicago: University of Chicago Press, 2009.

Geshekter, Charles L. "Anti-Colonialism and Class Formation: The Eastern Horn of Africa before 1950." *The International Journal of African Historical Studies* 18, no. 1 (1985): 1–32.

Getnet Bekele. *Ploughing New Ground: Food, Farming & Environmental Change in Ethiopia.* Suffolk: James Currey, 2017.

Geurts, Kathryn. *Culture and the Senses: Bodily Ways of Knowing in an African Community.* Berkeley: University of California Press, 2002.

Gilkes, Patrick. *The Dying Lion: Feudalism and Modernization in Ethiopia.* New York: Palgrave Macmillan, 1975.

Glassman, Jonathon. *Feasts and Riots: Revelry, Rebellion, and Popular Consciousness on the Swahili Coast, 1856–1888.* London: James Currey, 1995.

Goody, Jack. "Bitter Icons." *New Left Review* 7 (2001): 5–15.

Graham, Jesse, and Jonathan Haidt. "Beyond Beliefs: Religions Bind Individuals into Moral Communities." *Personality and Social Psychology Review* 14, no. 1 (2010): 140–150.

Gramsci, Antonio. *Selections from the Prison Notebooks of Antonio Gramsci.* Translated by Quintin Hoare and Geoffrey N. Smith. New York: International Publishers, 1971.

Graw, Knut. "Culture of Hope in West Africa." *ISIM Review* Autumn, no. 16 (2005): 28–29.

Greenfield, Richard. *Ethiopia: A New Political History.* London: Pall Mall Press, 1965.

Grosby, Steven. "The Verdict of History: The Inexpungeable Tie of Primordiality – a Response to Eller and Coughlan." *Ethnic and Racial Studies* 17, no. 1 (1994): 164–171.

Gurr, Ted Roberts. *Peoples Versus States.* Washington, DC: United States Institute of Peace, 2000.

Gwynn, Charles William. "A Journey in Southern Abyssinia." *Geographical Journal* 38, no. 2 (1911): 113–139.

Haberland, Eike. *Galla Süd-Äthiopiens.* Stuttgart: Kohlhammer, 1963.

Habermas, Jürgen. *Theory of Communicative Action.* Cambridge: Polity Press, 1984.

Hagmann, Tobias. "Punishing the Periphery: Legacies of State Repression in the Ethiopian Ogaden." *Journal of Eastern African Studies* 8, no. 4 (2014): 725–739.

Hagmann, Tobias, and Mohamud K. Khalif. "State and Politics in Ethiopia's Somali Region since 1991." *Bildhaan* 6 (2008): 25–49.

Hall, Stuart. "Gramsci's Relevance for the Study of Race and Ethnicity." *Journal of Communication Inquiry* 10, no. 2 (1986): 5–27.

"Introduction: Who Needs 'Identity'?" In *Questions of Cultural Identity*, edited by Stuart Hall and Paul Du Gay, 1–17. London: SAGE Publications, 1996.

Handelman, Don. "The Organization of Ethnicity." *Ethnic Groups* 1, (1977): 187–200.

Haneke, Georg. "The Multidimensionality of Oromo Identity." In *Imagined Differences: Hatred and the Construction of Identity*, edited by Günther Schlee, 131–153. Hamburg: Lit Verlag, 2002.

Hannig, Anita. *Beyond Surgery: Injury, Healing, and Religion at an Ethiopian Hospital.* Chicago: University of Chicago Press, 2017.

Haraway, Donna J. *Simians, Cyborgs and Women: The Reinvention of Nature.* New York: Routledge, 1991.

Haustein, Jürg. *Writing Religious History: The Historiography of Ethiopian Pentecostalism.* Wiesbaden: Harrassowitz Verlag, 2011.

Haykel, Bernard. "On the Nature of Salafi Thought and Action." In *Global Salafism: Islam's New Religious Movement*, edited by Roel Meijer, 33–56. London: Hurst & Company, 2009.

Heald, Suzette. "Joking and Avoidance, Hostility and Incest: An Essay on Gisu Moral Categories." *Man* 25, no. 1 (1990): 377–392.

Hegghammer, Thomas. "Jihadi-Salafis or Revolutionaries? On Religion and Politics in the Study of Militant Islamism." In *Global Salafism: Islam's*

New Religious Movement, edited by Roel Meijer, 244–266. London: Hurst & Company, 2009.

Helland, Johan. "Pastoral Land Tenure in Ethiopia." Paper presented at the Colloque international "Les frontières de la question foncière – At the frontier of land issues," Montpellier, 2006.

Henze, Paul B. *Rebels and Separatists in Ethiopia: Regional Resistance to a Marxist Regime*. Santa Monica, CA: RAND Cooperation 1985.

Layers of Time: A History of Ethiopia. Addis Ababa: Shama Books, 2000.

Heran, Sereke. "Ethiopia: A Historical Consideration of Amhara Identity." In *New Trends in Ethiopian Studies. Papers of the 12th International Conference of Ethiopian Studies*, edited by Harold G. Marcus and Grover Hudson, 742–774. Lawrenceville, NJ: The Red Sea Press, 1994.

Hersi, Abdirahman Ali. "The Arab Factor in Somali History: The Origins and Development of Arab Enterprise and Cultural Influence in the Somali Peninsula." PhD dissertation in History, Los Angeles: University of California, 1977.

Higgens, Rosalyn. *Problems and Process: International Law and How We Use It*. Oxford: Oxford University Press, 1994.

Hoben, Allan. "The Role of Ambilineal Descent Groups in Gojjam Amhara Social Organization." Berkeley: University of California Press, 1963.

Land Tenure among the Amhara of Ethiopia. Chicago: University of Chicago Press, 1973.

"Family, Land, and Class in Northwest Europe and Northern Highland Ethiopia." Paper presented at the First United States Conference on Ethiopian Studies, East Lansing, 1975.

Hobsbawm, Eric. *Primitive Rebels: Studies in Archaic Forms of Social Movement in the 19th and 20th Centuries*. Manchester: W. W. Norton, 1959.

Bandits. London: The New Press, 1969.

Hochchild, Arlie. *The Managed Heart: Commercialization of Human Feeling*. Berkeley: University of California Press, 1983.

Hodgson, Dorothy. *Once Intrepid Warriors: Gender, Ethnicity, and the Cultural Politics of Maasai Development*. Bloomington: Indiana University Press, 1999.

Hodson, Arnold W. *Seven Years in Southern Abyssinia*. Westport: Negro Universities Press, 1927.

Holcomb, Bonnie K., and Sisai Ibssa. *The Invention of Ethiopia: The Making of Dependent Colonial State in the North East Africa*. Trenton, NJ: Red Sea Press, 1990.

Holm, Tom J. Diana Pearson, and Ben Chavis. "Peoplehood: A Model for the Extension of Sovereignty in American Indian Studies." *Wicazo Sa Review* 18, no. 1 (2003): 7–24.

Honneth, Alex. *Reification: A New Look at an Old Idea*. Oxford: Oxford University Press, 2008.

Horowitz, Donald L. *Ethnic Groups in Conflict*. Berkeley: University of California Press, 1985.

Hultin, Jan. "The Land Is Crying: State Intervention and Cultural Resistance among the Macha Oromo." In *A River of Blessings: Essays in Honor of Paul Baxter*, edited by David Brokensha, 68–81. New York: Maxwell School of Citizenship and Public Affairs, Syracuse University, 1994.

Human Rights Watch. "Evil Days: Thirty Years of War and Famine in Ethiopia." *An Africa Watch Report*, New York: Human Rights Watch, 1991.

"Such a Brutal Crackdown: Killings and Arrests in Response to Ethiopia's Oromo Protests." London: Human Rights Watch, 2016.

Huntingford, G. W. B. *The Galla of Ethiopia, the Kingdom of Kafa and Janjero*. London: International African Institute, 1975.

Huntington, Samuel. *The Clash of Civilizations and the Remaking of World Order*. New York: Simon & Schuster, 1996.

Hussein Ahmed. "The Historiography of Islam in Ethiopia." *Journal of Islamic Studies* 3, no. 1 (1992): 15–46.

"Islam and Islamic Discourse in Ethiopia (1973–1993)." In *New Trends in Ethiopian Studies. Papers of the 12th International Conference of Ethiopian Studies*, edited by Harold G. Marcus and Grover Hudson, 775–801. Lawrenceville, NJ: The Red Sea Press, 1994.

Islam in Nineteenth-Century Wallo, Ethiopia. Leiden: Brill, 2001.

"Coexistence and/or Confrontation: Towards a Reappraisal of Christian-Muslim Encounters in Contemporary Ethiopia." *Journal of Religion in Africa* 36, no. 1 (2006): 4–22.

Hussein Badhaasoo. *Haxiiti Balabaatota Arsii Baalee-Diida'a [Haxi and Balabats of Arsi Bale-Dida]*. Addis Ababa: No publisher stated, 2017.

Hussein Indhessa. *Seenaa Qabsoo Ummata Oromoo Baalee Fi Ollaa Isaa*. Addis Ababa: No publisher stated, 2016.

Hussein Jemma. "Politics and Property Rights Regimes in Land in Arsi Negele and Hetossa, South-Central Oromia, Ethiopia: Late 1880s–2006." PhD dissertation in Political Science, Aas: Norwegian University of Life Sciences, 2010.

Hylander, Fride. *Ett År I Telt [a Year in Tent]*. Stockholm: Evangeliska Fosterlands-stiftelsens Bokforlag, 1936.

"Afrika-Upplevelser for 40 År Sedan Aktualiserade I Dag." *Missionsblad för E. F. S i Södermanland-Östergötland* (1972): 1–8.

Iannaccone, Laurence, and Eli Berman. "Religious Extremism: The Good, the Bad, and the Deadly." *Public Choice* 128, no. 1–2 (2006): 109–129.

Ibsa Gutamaa. "Odaa Nabee in Oromo Oral Tradition." *Oromo Commentary* 7, no. 2 (1997): 14–15.

Ingold, Tim. *The Perception of the Environment: Essays on Livelihood, Dwelling and Skill*. London: Routledge, 2000.

Ishihara, Minako. "Textual Analysis of a Poetic Verse in a Muslim Oromo Society in Jimma Area, Southwestern Ethiopia." *Senri Ethnological Studies* 43, (1996): 207–232.

Issa-Salwe, Abdisalam M. *Cold War Fallout: Boundary Politics and Conflict in the Horn of Africa*. London: HAAN, 2000.

Jardine, Douglas. *The Mad Mullah of Somaliland*. London: Hodder and Stoughton, 1923.

Jenkins, Richard. *Social Identity*. London: Routledge, 1996.

Rethinking Ethnicity: Arguments and Explorations. London: SAGE Publications, 2008.

Jensen, Adolf E. "Neuere Notizen Über Das *Gada* System." *Paideuma* 2 (1942): 84–94.

Jeylan W. Hussein. "The Functions of African Oral Arts: The Arsi-Oromo Oral Arts in Focus." *African Study Monographs* 26, no. 1 (2005): 15–58.

Johnson, Mark L. *The Body in the Mind: The Bodily Basis of Meaning, Imagination, and Reason*. Chicago: University of Chicago Press, 1987.

"Embodied Reason." In *Perspectives on Embodiment: The Intersections of Nature and Culture*, edited by Gail Weiss and Honi F. Haber, 81–102. New York: Routledge, 1999.

Kaba, Lansine. *The Wahhabiyya: Islamic Reform and Politics in French West Africa*. Evanston: Northwestern University Press, 1974.

Kaplan, Mordecai. *Judaism as Civilization: Towards a Reconstruction of American Jewish Life*. Philadelphia: The Jewish Publication Center, 1934.

Kaufman, Stuart. "Symbolic Politics or Rational Choice? Testing Theories of Extreme Ethnic Violence." *International Security* 30, no. 4 (2006): 45–86.

Keller, Edmond J. *Revolutionary Ethiopia*. Bloomington & Indianapolis: Indiana University Press, 1988.

Ketebo Abdiyo. "The Political Economy of Land and Agrarian Development in Arssi: 1941–1991." PhD dissertation in History, Addis, Ababa: Addis Ababa University, 2010.

Ketema Meskela. "The Evolution of Land-Ownership in High-Land Bale, a Case Study of Goba, Sinana and Dodola to 1974." MA thesis in History, Addis Ababa University, 2001.

King, Richard. *Orientalism and Religion: Postcolonial Theory, India and "the Mystic East."* London: Routledge, 1999.

Knutsson, Karl Eric. *Authority and Change: The Study of the Kallu Institution among the Macha Galla of Ethiopia.* Göteborg: Etnografiska Museet, 1967.

"Dichotomization and Integration: Aspects of Inter-Ethnic Relations in Southern Ethiopia." In *Ethnic Groups and Boundaries: The Social Organization of Cultural Difference,* edited by Fredrik Barth, 86–100. Oslo: Universitetsforlaget, 1969.

Laclau, Ernesto, and Chantal Mouffe. *Hegemony and Socialist Strategy Towards a Radical Democratic Politics.* London: Verso, 1985.

Lake, David A., and Donald Rothchild (eds.). *The International Spread of Ethnic Conflict: Fear, Diffusion, and Escalation.* Princeton: Princeton University Press, 1998.

Lakoff, George, and Mark L. Johnson. *Metaphors We Live By.* Chicago: University of Chicago Press, 1980.

Latour, Bruno. "Thou Shall Not Freeze-Frame – or How Not to Misunderstand the Science and Religion Debate." In *Science, Religion, and the Human Experience,* edited by James D. Proctor, 27–48. Oxford: Oxford University Press, 2005.

Lefort, René. *Ethiopia: An Heretical Revolution?* London: Zed Press, 1983.

Lemmings, David, and Ann Brooks. "The Emotional Turn in the Humanities and Social Sciences." In *Emotions and Social Change: Historical and Sociological Perspectives,* edited by David Lemmings and Ann Brooks, 3–18. New York: Routledge, 2014.

Leus, Tom, and Cynthia Salvadori. *Aadaa Boraanaa: A Dictionary of Borana Culture.* Addis Ababa: Shama Books, 2006.

Levine, Donald. *Wax & Gold: Tradition and Innovation in Ethiopian Culture.* Chicago: University of Chicago Press, 1965.

Greater Ethiopia; the Evolution of a Multiethnic Society. Chicago: University of Chicago Press, 1974.

Levtzion, Nehemia. "Toward a Comparative Study of Islamization." In *Conversion to Islam,* edited by Nehemia Levtzion, 1–23. London & New York: Holmes & Meier Publishers, 1979.

Lewis, Herbert S. "The Origins of Galla and Somali." *Journal of African History* 7, no. 1 (1966a): 27–46.

Lewis, Ioan M. "Modern Political Movements in Somaliland. II". *Africa* 28, no. 4 (1958): 344–363.

Pastoralist Democracy: A Study of Pastoralism and Politics among the Northern Somali of the Horn of Africa. Oxford: Oxford University Press, 1961.

"Introduction." In *Islam in Tropical Africa,* edited by Ioan. M. Lewis, 1–97. London: Hutchinson, 1966b.

"The Western Somali Liberation Front (WSLF) and the Legacy of Sheikh Hussein of Bale." In *Modern Ethiopia,* edited by Joseph Tubiana, 409–415. 1980.

The Modern History of Somaliland: From Nation to State. Oxford: James Currey, 2002.

Lie, John. *Midern Peoplehood.* Cambridge, MA: Harvard University Press, 2004.

Little, David. "Belief, Ethnicity, and Nationalism." *Nationalism and Ethnic Politics* 1, no. 2 (1995): 284–301.

Lukács, Georg. *History and Class Consciousness: Studies in Marxist Dialectics.* Cambridge, MA: MIT Press, 1968 [1923].

Lyon, Margot L., and Jack M. Barbalet. "Society's Body: Emotions and the 'Somatization' of Social Theory." In *Embodiment and Experience: The Essential Ground for Culture and Self,* edited by Thomas J. Csordas, 48–66. Cambridge: Cambridge University Press, 1994.

Mackonen Michael. "Who Is Amhara?" *African Identities* 6, no. 4 (2008): 393–404.

Makinda, Samuel M. "Superpower Involvement in the Horn of Africa, 1974–1982." PhD dissertation in Political Science, Canberra: Australian National University, 1985.

Malara, Diego Maria, and Tom Boylston. "Vertical Love: Forms of Submission and Top-Down Power in Orthodox Ethiopia." *Social Analyis* 61, no. 4 (2016): 40–57.

Mamo Hebo. "Land, Local Customs & State 'Laws': A Study of Land Tenure Systems and Land Disputes Settlements among the Arsii Oromo, Southern Ethiopia." PhD dissertation in African Studies, Kyoto: Kyoto University, 2004.

"Disguised Land Sale Practices among the Arsii Oromo of Kokossa District, Southern Ethiopia." *Asian and African Area Studies* 6, no. 2 (2007): 352–372.

Markakis, John. *Ethiopia: Anatomy of a Traditional Polity.* London: Oxford University Press, 1974.

"The 1963 Rebellion in the Ogaden." Paper presented at the Second International Congress of Somali Studies, Hamburg, 1983.

National and Class Conflict in the Horn of Africa. Cambridge: Cambridge University Press, 1987.

"Nationalities and the State in Ethiopia." *Third World Quarterly* 11, no. 4 (1989): 118–130.

Ethiopia: The Last Two Frontiers. New York: James Currey, 2011.

Martin, Bradford G. *Muslim Brotherhoods in Nineteenth-Century Africa* Cambridge: Cambridge University Press, 1976.

Marzagora, Sara. "Alterity, Coloniality and Modernity in Ethiopian Political Thought: The First Three Generations of 20th Century Amharic-Language Intellectuals." PhD dissertation in Literature, London: School of Oriental and African Studies, 2015.

Maskal H. Fisseha. "Atete." *Bulletin of the University College of Addis Ababa*, no. 9 (1959): 45–51.

McCann, James. "The Political Economy of Rural Rebellion in Ethiopia: Northern Resistance to Imperial Expansion, 1928–1935." *The International Journal of African Historical Studies* 18, no. 4 (1985): 601–623.

McCutcheon, Russel. *The Discipline of Religion: Structure, Meaning, Rhetoric*. London: Routledge, 2003.

Meijer, Roel. "Introduction." In *Global Salafism: Islam's New Religious Movement*, edited by Roel Meijer, 1–32. London: Hurst & Company, 2009.

Merera Gudina. *Ethiopia: Competing Ethnic Nationalism and the Quest for Democracy, 1960–2000*. Addis Ababa: No publisher stated, 2003.

"Ethnicity, Democratisation and Decentralization in Ethiopia: The Case of Oromia." *Eastern Africa Social Science Research Review* 23, no. 1 (2007): 81–106.

Merid Wolde Aregay. "Political Geography of Ethiopia at the Beginning of the Sixteenth Century." Paper presented at the IV Congresso Internationale di Studi Etiopici, Rome, April 10–15, 1974a.

"Population Movements as a Possible Factor in the Christian-Muslim Conflict of Medieval Ethiopia." Paper presented at the Symposium Leo Frobenius, Pullach bei Munchen, 1974b.

"Society and Technology in Ethiopia, 1500–1800." Paper presented at the Second Annual Seminar of the Department of History, Addis Ababa, 1984.

Merleau-Ponty, Marice. *The Phenomenology of Perception: An Introduction*. London: Routledge & Kegan Paul, 1962.

Mesfin Wolde Mariam. "An Estimate of the Population in Ethiopia." *Ethiopia Observer* 5, no. 2 (1961): 135–142.

Suffering under God's Environment: A Vertical Study of the Predicament of Peasants in North-Central Ethiopia. Berne: African Mountain Association and Geographica Bernensia, 1991.

Messay Kebede. *Survival and Modernisation – Ethiopia's Enigmatic Present: A Philosophic Discourse*. Lawrenceville, NJ: Red Sea Press, 1999.

Michael Weldeghiorghis Tedla. "The Eritrean Liberation Front: Social and Political Factors Shaping Its Emergence, Development and Demise,

1960–1981." MA thesis in African Studies, Leiden: University of Leiden, 2014.

Mindaye Abebe. "The Oromo of Bale: A Historical Survey to 1974." MA thesis in History, Addis Ababa: Addis Ababa University, 2005.

Ministry of Land Reform and Administration. "Report on Land Tenure Survey of Bale Province." Addis Ababa: Imperial Ethiopian Government, 1969.

"Bale Governorate General: A Short Geographical Account." Addis Ababa: Imperial Ethiopian Government, 1971.

Mitchell, Claire. "The Religious Content of Ethnic Identities." *Sociology* 40, no. 6 (2006): 1135–1152.

"The Push and Pull between Religion and Ethnicity: The Case of Loyalists in Northern Ireland." *Ethnopolitics* 91, no. 1 (2010): 53–69.

Mohammed Ali. "The Lives and Times of Sheikh Umar Hussein Abdul Wahid and Sheikh Hussein Awol." BA thesis in History, Addis Ababa: Addis Ababa University, 2005.

Mohammed Hassan. "Islam as a Resistance Ideology among the Oromo of Ethiopia: The Wallo Case, 1700–1900." In *In the Shadow of Conquest: Islam in Colonial Northeast Africa*, edited by Said Samatar, 75–101. Trenton, NJ: Red Sea Press, 1992.

The Oromo of Ethiopia: A History 1570–1860. Trenton, NJ: Red Sea Press, 1994.

"Review Essay: Gezetena Gezot, Macha Tulama Self-Help Association, by Olana Zoga." *Journal of Oromo Studies* 4, no. 1–2 (1997): 203–238.

"A Short History of Oromo Colonial Experience: Part Two, Colonial Consolidation and Resistance 1935–2000." *Journal of Oromo Studies* 7, no. 1–2 (2000): 109–198.

"Elemo Qilituu." In *Encyclopaedia Aethiopica*, 252–253. Leiden: Brill, 2005a.

"Pilgrimage to the *Abba Muudaa*." *Journal of Oromo Studies* 12, no. 1–2 (2005b): 142–157.

"The History of Oromo Nationalism: 1960s–1990s." In *Arrested Development in Ethiopia: Essays on Underdevelopment, Democracy and Self-Determination*, edited by Seyoum Hameso and Mohammed Hassan, 237–278. Lawrenceville, NJ: Red Sea Press, 2006.

The Oromo and the Christian Kingdom of Ethiopia 1300–1700. Suffolk: James Currey, 2015.

Morone, Antonio M. "Somali Independence and Its Political Connections with Nasser's Egypt." In *The Horn of Africa since the 1960s: Local and International Politics Intertwined*, edited by Aleksi Ylönen and Aleksi Záhořík, 109–120. London: Routledge, 2017.

Muusaa Haaji Aadam Saaddoo. *Waan Garaa Nu Baate: Seenaa Diddaa Gabrummaa Haaji Aadam Saaddoo, Bara 1877–1981*. Addis Ababa: No publisher stated, 2014.

Nash, Manning. *The Cauldron of Ethnicity in the Modern World*. Chicago: University of Chicago Press, 1988.

"Natural and Cultural Properties to Be Inscribed in the World Heritage List from Bale Zone." Issued by the Bale Zone Cultural and Information Department, Robe, 1998.

Neisser, Ulrich. "Five Kinds of Self-Knowledge." *Philosophical Psychology* 1, no. 1 (1988): 35–59.

Nydal, Oscar. "Unevangelized Areas Project Survey I: Bale." Addis Ababa: Evangelical Church Mekane Yesus, 1972.

Oba, Gufu. *Nomads in the Shadows of Empires: Contests, Conflicts, and Legacies on the Southern Ethiopian-Northern Kenyan Frontier*. Leiden: Brill, 2013.

Olana Zoga. *Gezetena Gezot: Macha Tulama Merdadja Mahaber [in Amharic: Restraint and Suppression: The Macha Tulama Self-Help Association]*. Addis Ababa: No publisher stated, 1985.

Orsi, Robert A. *Between Heaven and Earth: The Religious Worlds People Make and the Scholars Who Study Them*. Princeton: Princeton University Press, 2005.

Østebø, Terje. *A History of Islam and Inter-Religious Relations in Bale, Ethiopia*. Stockholm: Almquist & Wiksell International, 2005.

"Christian-Muslim Relations in Ethiopia." In *Striving in Faith: Christians and Muslims in Africa*, edited by Anne N. Kubai and Tarakegn Adebo, 71–89. Uppsala: Life & Peace Institute, 2008.

Localising Salafism: Religious Change among Oromo Muslims in Bale, Ethiopia. Leiden: Brill, 2012.

"Islam and State Relations in Ethiopia: From Containment to the Production of a 'Governmental Islam'." *Journal of American Academy of Religion* 81, no. 4 (2013a): 1029–1060.

"The Revenge of the Jinns: Spirits, Salafi Reform, and the Continuity in Change in Contemporary Ethiopia." *Contemporary Islam* 8, no. 1 (2013b): 17–36.

Østebø, Terje, and Wallelign Shemsedin. "Ethiopian Muslims and the Discourse About Moderation." *Journal of Modern African Studies* 55, no. 2 (2017): 225–249.

Østebø, Marit Tolo. "Respected Women: A Study of *Wayyuu* and Its Implications for Women's Sexual Rights among the Arsi Oromo of Ethiopia." MA thesis in International Health, Bergen: University of Bergen, Centre for International Health, 2007.

"Can Respect Be Key to Gender Justice?" *Journal of Royal Anthropological Institute* 24, no. 1 (2018): 71–89.

Ottaway, Marina, and David Ottaway. *Ethiopia: Empire in Revolution.* New York: Africana, 1978.

Otto, Rudolf. *The Idea of the Holy.* Oxford: Oxford University Press, 1958.

Pallasma, Juhani. "Identity, Intimacy, and Domicile." In *The Home: Words, Interpretations, Meanings, and Environments* edited by David N. Benjamin, David Stea, and Edward Saile, 33–40. London: Avebury, 1995.

Pankhurst, Richard. "Nineteenth and Early Twentieth Century Population Guesses." *Ethiopia Observer* 5, no. 2 (1961): 147–151.

State and Land in Ethiopian History. Addis Ababa: The Institute of Ethiopian Studies, 1966.

Economic History of Ethiopia: 1800–1935. Addis Ababa: Haile Selassie I University Press, 1968.

The Ethiopian Borderlands. Lawrenceville, NJ: Red Sea Press, 1997.

Pankhurst, Sylvia E. *Ex-Italian Somaliland.* London: Watts & Co., 1951.

Paulitschke, Philip. "Die Wanderungen Der Oromo Order Gallas Ost-Afrikas." *Mittheilungen der Anthropologischen Gessellschaaft zu Wien* 19, (1889): 165–177.

Pausewang, Siegfried. *Methods and Concepts of Social Research in a Rural Developing Society: A Critical Appraisal Based on Experience in Ethiopia.* München: Weltforum Verlag, 1973.

Perham, Margery. *The Government of Ethiopia.* London: Faber, 1969.

Peters, Krijn, and Paul Richards. "Why We Fight: Voices of Youth Combatants in Sierra Leone." *Africa* 68, no. 2 (1998): 183–210.

Pianko, Noam. *Jewish Peoplehood.* New Brunswick: Rutgers University Press, 2015.

Prunier, Gérard. "Segmentarité Et Violence Dans L'espace Somali, 1840–1992." *Cahiers d'Études africaines* 37, no. 146 (1997): 379–401.

Rahji Abdella. "The Kulub-Hannolatto Movement by the Harari, 1946–1948." BA thesis in History, Addis Ababa: Addis Ababa University, 1994.

Ranger, Terence. "Concluding Summary: Religion, Development and Identity." In *Religion, Development and African Identity*, edited by Kristin Holst Petersen, 145–162. Uppsala: Scandinavian Institute of African Studies, 1987.

"The Invention of Tradition Revisited: The Case of Colonial Africa." In *Legitimacy and the State in Twentieth-Century Africa*, edited by Terence Ranger and Olufemi Vaughan, 62–111. London: Macmillan, 1993.

Rapoport, Amos. "A Critical Look at the Concept of 'Home.' In *The Home: Words, Interpretations, Meanings, and Environments*, edited by David N. Benjamin, David Stea, and David Saile, 25–52. London: Avebury, 1995.

Reid, Richard J. *Frontiers of Violence in North-East Africa*. Oxford: Oxford University Press, 2011.

Reinharz, Shulamit. "The 'Jewish Peoplehood' Concept: Complications and Suggestions." In *Reconsidering Israel-Diaspora Relations*, edited by Eliezer Ben-Rafael, Judit Bokser Liverant, and Yosef Gorny, 66–85. Leiden: Brill, 2014.

Retsikas, Konstantinos. "The Power of the Senses: Ethnicity, History and Embodiment in East Java, Indonesia." *Indonesia and the Malay World* 35, no. 102 (2007): 183–210.

Revolutionary Vigor in Somali Abo through History. Mogadishu: No publisher stated, 1979.

Rodaway, Paul. *Senseuous Geographies: Body, Sense, and Place*. London: Routledge, 1994.

Rønning Balsvik, Randi. *Haile Sellasie's Students: The Intellectual and Social Background to Revolution, 1952–1977*. Addis Ababa: Addis Ababa University Press, 2005.

Ruane, Joseph. "Ethnicity, Religion and Peoplehood: Protestants in France and in Ireland." *Ethnopolitics* 9, no. 1 (2010): 121–135.

The Roots of Intense Ethnic Conflicts May Not in Fact Be Ethnic: Categories, Communities and Path Dependence, ISSC Discussion Papers Series: Institute for the Study of Social Change, 2003.

"Ethnicity and Religion: Redefining the Research Agenda." *Ethnopolitics* 9, no. 1 (2009): 1–8.

Rubenson, Samuel. "A Christian Island? The Impact of Colonialism on the Perceptions of Islam and Christianity in Nineteenth Century Ethiopia." In *The Fuzzy Logic of Encounter: New Perspectives on Cultural Contact*, edited by Sunne Juterczenka and Gesa Mackenthun, 117–126. Munster: Waxman, 2009.

Salviac, Martial de. *An Ancient People in the State of Menelik: The Oromo*. Translated by Ayalew Kanno. Addis Ababa: Oromia Culture and Tourism Bureau, 2005 [1901].

Salzman, Philip. "Introduction: Processes of Sedentarization as Adaption and Response." In *When Nomads Settle*, edited by Philip Salzman, 1–19. New York: Praeger, 1980.

Samatar, Said. *Oral Poetry and Somali Nationalism*. Cambridge: Cambridge University Press, 1982.

Sanderson, G. N. "The Nile Basin and the Eastern Horn, 1870–1879." In *Cambridge History of Africa*, edited by Roland Oliver and

G. N. Sanderson, 592–679. Cambridge: Cambridge University Press, 1985.

Sbacchi, Alberto. *Ethiopia under Mussolini: Fascism and Colonial Experience*. London: Zed Press, 1985.

Schaefer, Donovan. *Religious Affect: Animality, Evolution, and Power*. Durham: Duke University Press, 2015.

Schielke, Samuli, and Georg Stauth. "Introduction." In *Dimensions of Locality: Muslim Saints, Their Place and Space*, edited by Samuli Schielke and Georg Stauth, 7–24. Bielefeld: Transcript Verlag, 2008.

Schlee, Günther. "Interethnic Clan Identities among Cushitic-Speaking Pastoralists of Northern Kenya." *Africa* 55, no. 1 (1985): 17–38.

Identities on the Move: Clanship and Pastoralism in Northern Kenya. Manchester: Manchester University Press, 1989.

Competition and Exclusion in Islamic and Non-Islamic Societies: An Essay on Purity and Power, Working Papers No. 52. Halle: Max Planck Institute for Social Anthropology, 2003.

How Enemies Are Made: Towards a Theory of Ethnic and Religious Conflicts. New York: Berghahn Books, 2010.

"Introduction." In *Pastoralism & Politics in Northern Kenya & Southern Ethiopia*, edited by Günther Schlee and Abdullahi A. Shongolo, 1–34. Suffolk: James Currey, 2012.

Schlee, Günther, and Abdullahi A. Shongolo. "Local War and Its Impact on Ethnic and Religious Identification in Southern Ethiopia." *Geojournal* 36, no. 1 (1995): 7–17.

Schneider, Harold K. *Livestock and Equality in East Africa: The Economic Basis for Social Structures*. Bloomington: Indiana University Press, 1979.

Schutz, Alfred. *The Phenomenology of the Social World*. Evanston: Northwestern University Press, 1967.

Scott, James. *Weapons of the Weak: Everyday Forms of Peasant Resistance*. New Haven: Yale University Press, 1985.

Seul, Jeffrey R. "'Ours Is the Way of God': Religion, Identity, and Intergroup Conflict." *Journal of Peace Research* 36, no. 5 (1999): 553–569.

Shack, William. *The Central Ethiopians: Amhara, Tigrina and Related People*. London: International African Institute, 1974.

Shetler, Jan Bender. *Imagining Serengeti: A History of Landscape Memory in Tanzania from Earliest Times to the Present*. Athens: Ohio University Press, 2007.

Shibab ad-Din. *Futuh Al-Habasha*. Translated by Paul Lester Stenhouse. Hollywood: Tshehai, 2003[1559].

Shiferaw Bekele. "Reflections on the Power Elite of the Wara Seh Masfenate (1786–1853)." *Annales d'Ethiopie* 15 (1990): 157–179.

"The Evolution of Land Tenure in Imperial Ethiopia." In *An Economic History of Modern Ethiopia*, edited by Shiferaw Bekele, 72–142. Oxford: CODESRIA, 1995.

"The Railway, Dirre Dawa and Harar During the Coup d'Etat of 1916." In *The Life and Times of Lij Iyasu of Ethiopia*, edited by Eloi Ficquet and Wolbert G. C. Smidt, 151–163. Berlin: Lit Verlag, 2014.

Sintayehu Kassaye. "Goba: Foundation, Growth and Development to 1974." BA thesis in History, Addis Ababa: Addis Ababa University, 1985.

Smidt, Wolbert G. C. "Glossary of Terms and Events of the *Lij* Iyasu Period: Controversial and Non-Controversial Facts and Interpretations." In *The Life and Times of Lij Iyasu of Ethiopia*, edited by Eloi Ficquet and Wolbert G. C. Smidt, 181–205. Berlin: Lit Verlag, 2014.

Smith, Anthony. "Ethnic Election and National Destiny: Some Religious Origins of Nationalist Ideals." *Nations and Nationalism* 5, no. 3 (1999): 331–355.

Smith, Rogers. *Stories of Peoplehood*. Cambridge: Cambridge University Press, 2003.

Soares, Benjamin, and Robert Launay. "The Formation of an 'Islamic Sphere' in French Colonial West Africa." *Economy and Society* 28, no. 4 (1999): 497–519.

Sobek, David. *The Causes of War*. Cambridge: Polity, 2008.

Sorensen, John. *Imagining Ethiopia: Struggles for History and Identity in the Horn of Africa*. New Brunswick: Rutgers University Press, 1993.

Stahl, Michael. *Ethiopia: Political Contradictions in Agricultural Development*. Stockholm: Raben & Sjogren, 1974.

Stea, David. "House and Home: Identity, Dichotomy, or Dialectics." In *The Home: Words, Interpretations, Meanings, and Environments*, edited by David N. Benjamin, David Stea, and David Saile, 181–201. London: Avebury, 1995.

Stewart, Francis. *Religion Versus Ethnicity as a Source of Mobilisation: Are There Differences?* Microcon Research Working Paper 18. Brighton: University of Sussex, 2009.

Stigand, Chauncey H. *To Abyssinia through an Unknown Land*. London: J.B. Lippincot, 1910.

The Story of Hussein Bune. Micha, Sewena: Sewena Culture and Tourism Office, 2008.

Suganami, Hidemi. "Stories of War Origins: A Narrativist Theory of the Causes of War." *Review of International Studies* 23, no. 4 (1997): 401–418.

Sultan Usman, and Adamu Zeleke. "Characterization of Malt Barley Based Farming Systems in Bale Highlands and West Arsi Zone of Oromia, South Eastern Ethiopia." *Journal of Agricultural Economics and Rural Development* 3, no. 2 (2017): 215–222.

T. Abate, A. Ebro, and L. Nigatu. "Traditional Rangeland Resource Utilisation Practices and Pastoralists' Perceptions on Land Degradation in South-East Ethiopia." *Tropical Grasslands* 4, (2010): 202–212.

Taddesse Tamrat. *Church and State 1270–1527*. Oxford: Oxford University Press, 1972.

"Ethiopia, the Red Sea and the Horn." In *Cambridge History of Africa*, edited by Roland Oliver and John D. Fage, 98–182. Cambridge: Cambridge University Press, 1977.

Talle, Aud. "A Child Is a Child: Disability and Equality among the Kenya Maasai." In *Disability and Culture*, edited by Benedicte Ingstad and Susan R. Whyte, 56–72. Berkeley: University of California Press, 1995.

Tamir, Yael. "Theoretical Difficulties in the Study of Nationalism." In *Theorizing Nationalism*, edited by Ronald Beiner, 67–90. Albany: State University of New York Press, 1999.

Tarekegn Adebo. "Ethnicity vs. Class: Concepts in the Analysis of the Ethiopian Revolution." In *Proceedings of the Seventh International Conference of Ethiopian Studies*, edited by Sven Rubenson, 541–550. Addis Ababa: Institute of Ethiopian Studies, 1984.

Teferra Haile Selassie. *The Ethiopian Revolution*. London: Keegan Paul, 1997.

Tekeste Negash. *The Crisis of Ethiopian Education: Some Implications for Nation-Building*. Uppsala: Department of Education, Uppsala University, 1990.

Education in Ethiopia: From Crisis to the Brink of Collapse. Uppsala: Nordic Africa Institute, 2006.

Temam Haji. "Islam in Arsi, Southeast Ethiopia (ca. 1840–1974)." MA thesis in History, Addis Ababa: Addis Ababa University, 2002.

Teshale Tibebu. *The Making of Modern Ethiopia 1896–1974*. Lawrenceville, NJ: Red Sea Press, 1995.

Teshome Abate, Alule Ebro, and Lisanework Nigatu. "Traditional Utilization Practices and Condition Assessment of the Rangelands in Rayitu District of Bale Zone, Ethiopia." Haramaya: Haramaya University, 2006.

Thesiger, Wilfred. *The Danakil Diary, Journeys through Abyssinia 1930–34*. London: Flamingo, 2002.

Thomas, Robert K. "The Tap-Roots of Peoplehood." In *Getting to the Heart of Matter: Collected Letters and Papers*, edited by Daphne J. Anderson, 25–32. Vancouver: Native Ministries Consortium, 1990.

Thrift, Nigel. *Non-Representational Theory: Space, Politics, Affect*. London: Routledge, 2007.

Tibebe Eshete. "The Root Causes of the Political Problems in the Ogaden, 1942–1960." *Northeast African Studies* 13, no. 1 (1991): 9–28.

The Evangelical Movement in Ethiopia: Resistance and Resilience. Waco: Baylor University Press, 2009.

Todd, Jennifer. "Symbolic Complexity and Political Divisions: The Changing Role of Religion in Northern Ireland." *Ethnopolitics* 9, no. 1 (2010): 85–102.

"Religion and the Patterns of Conflict in Northern Ireland." Unpublished paper, n.d.

Touval, Saadia. *Somalia Nationalism: The Drive for Unity in the Horn of Africa*. Cambridge, MA: Harvard University Press, 1963.

Trimingham, Spencer J. *Islam in Ethiopia*. London: Frank Cass, 1952.

Triulzi, Alessandro. "Ethiopia: The Making of a Frontier Society." In *Inventions and Boundaries: Historical and Anthropological Approaches to the Study of Ethnicity and Nationalism*, edited by Preben Kaarsholm and Jan Hultin, 235–245. Roskilde: International Development Studies, Roskilde University, 1994.

"Battling with the Past: New Frameworks for Ethiopian Historiography." In *Remapping Ethiopia: Aocialism and After*, edited by Wendy James and Donald Donham, 276–288. Athens: Ohio University Press, 2002.

Tsegaye Zeleke. "The Oromo of Salale: A History (1840–1936)." MA thesis in History, Addis Ababa: Addis Ababa University, 2002.

Tuan, Yi-Fu. *Topophilia: A Study of Environmental Perception, Attitudes, and Values*. Englewood Cliffs, NJ: Prentice-Hall, 1974.

Space and Place: The Perspective of Experience. Minneapolis: University of Minnesota Press, 1977.

"Language and the Making of Place: A Narrative-Descriptive Approach." *Annals of the Association of American Geographers* 81, no. 4 (1991): 684–696.

Turton, David. "Mursi Political Identity & Warfare: The Survival of an Idea." In *Ethnicity and Conflict in the Horn of Africa*, edited by Katsuyoshi Fukui and John Markakis, 15–32. London: James Currey, 1994.

Turton, E. R. "Somali Resistance to Colonial Rule and the Development of Somali Political Activity in Kenya, 1893–1960." *Journal of African History* 13, no. 1 (1972): 117–143.

Tweed, Thomas A. *Crossing and Dwelling: A Theory of Religion.* Cambridge, MA: Harvard University Press, 2006.

Ullendorff, Edward. *The Ethiopians, an Introduction to Country and People.* London: Oxford University Press, 1960.

Umer Nure. "The Pilgrimage to Dirre Sheikh Hussein: Its Social Organization and Overall Roles." MA thesis in Social Anthropology, Addis Ababa: Addis Ababa University, 2006.

United Nations Economic Commission for Africa. "Structural Transformation, Employment, Production and Society (Steps) Profile: Ethiopia." Addis Ababa: United Nations Economic Commission for Africa, 2018.

Van den Berghe, Pierre L. *The Ethnic Phenomenon.* New York: Elsevier, 1981.

van Heur, Bas. "The Spatial Imagination of Oromia: The Ethiopian State and Oromo Transnational Politics." MA thesis in History, Utrecht: Utrecht University, 2004.

van Walraven, Klaes, and Jon Abbink. "Rethinking Resistance in African History: An Introduction." In *Rethinking Resistance: Revolt and Violence in African History*, edited by Jon Abbink, Mirjam de Bruin, and Klaes van Walraven, 1–40. Leiden: Brill, 2003.

Varshney, Ashutosh. "Ethnicity and Ethnic Conflict." In *The Oxford Handbook of Comparative Politics*, edited by Charles Boix and Susan C. Stokes, 274–294. Oxford: Oxford University Press, 2009.

Vasquez, Manuel. *More Than Belief: A Materialist Theory of Religion.* Oxford: Oxford University Press, 2011.

Volkan, Vamik. *Killing in the Name of Identity.* Chicago: Pitchstone Publishing, 2006.

Waldron, Sidney R. "The Political Economy of Harari-Oromo Relationships, 1559–1874." *Northeast African Studies* 6, no. 1–2 (1984): 23–39.

Wallerstein, Immanuel. "The Construction of Peoplehood: Racism, Nationalism, Ethnicity." *Sociological Forum* 2, no. 2 (1987): 373–388.

Weber, Max. *Economy and Society.* Berkeley: University of California Press, 1978.

Weinstein, Jeremy. *Inside Rebellions.* Cambridge: Cambridge University Press, 2007.

Whittaker, Hannah. *Insurgency and Counterinsurgency in Kenya.* Leiden: Brill, 2015.

Williams, Paul. *War & Conflict in Africa.* Cambridge: Polity, 2016.

Woldemariam, Michael. "Why Rebels Collide: Factionalism and Fragmentation in African Insurgencies." PhD dissertation in Political Science, Princeton: Princeton University, 2011.

Yaassiin Mohammad Roobaa and Mohammad Ismaa'il Anbassaa. *Qaanqee Qabsoo Oromoo (the Spark of the Oromo Struggle)*. Addis Ababa: No publisher stated, 2014.

Yitbarek Muluneh. "Modern and Traditional Schools of Wabe Awraja." BA thesis in Education, Haile Sellassie I University, 1970.

Young, Crawford. "Patterns of Social Conflict: State, Class, and Ethnicity." *Daedalus* 111, no. 2 (1982): 71–98.

Index

350

African Studies Series

CPSIA information can be obtained
at www.ICGtesting.com
Printed in the USA
LVHW012154201220
674694LV00004B/76

9 781108 839686